LIGHT FROM LIGHT

An Anthology of
Christian Mysticism

LIGHT FROM LIGHT

An Anthology of Christian Mysticism

Second Edition
Completely Revised and Updated

Edited by
Louis Dupré and
James A. Wiseman, O.S.B.

PAULIST PRESS
New York/Mahwah, N.J.

Book design by Theresa M. Sparacio

Cover design by Cynthia Dunne

Library of Congress Cataloging-in-Publication Data

Light from light : an anthology of Christian mysticism / edited by Louis Dupré and James A. Wiseman.—2nd ed., completely rev. and updated.
   p. cm.
   Includes bibliographical references.
   ISBN 0-8091-4013-6 (alk. paper)
   1. Mysticism. I. Dupré, Louis K., 1925–   II. Wiseman, James A., 1942–

BV5072 .L54 2001b
248.2'2—dc21

                          00-068462

Published by Paulist Press
997 Macarthur Boulevard
Mahwah, New Jersey 07430

www.paulistpress.com

Printed and bound in the
United States of America

Contents

Contents

Preface

Light from Light has been in print for well over a decade, and its editors remain grateful for the friendly reception of a project that grew out of a practical need. But as the years have passed, readers, the publisher, and indeed the editors themselves felt that it could be improved. The bulky format of the original edition, with its wide pages and long lines, made reading uncomfortable. A quick poll taken among some of its readers revealed what the original preface had predicted, that satisfaction with the choice of the selections was not universal. Recommendations from the poll were sufficiently specific, though by no means unanimous, to allow us to make some changes. Spiritual writers of late seventeenth- and early eighteenth-century France found little response from contemporary Americans, so we omitted Fénelon, Jeanne Guyon, and Marie of the Incarnation, though not without pain and in anticipation of future protests. Some authors failed to invite readers because readers hardly recognized their names. Such was regrettably the case with William Law and, in our time, Henri Le Saux—surprisingly also with Maximus the Confessor.

On the opposite side, some readers expressed dissatisfaction with the absence of Francis and Clare of Assisi, while others missed the saintly fellowship of Francis de Sales and Jeanne de Chantal. They were right, and we hasten to remedy the omissions. Having made the changes, however, we realize that they may displease some readers. No one will be *entirely* satisfied with a limited choice, but all may take comfort in the fact that the absence of any anthology of this sort—which originally motivated our work—is no longer a problem. Since the anthologies now available differ in their choice of subjects as well as of excerpts, others may complement what ours does not offer.

The inclusion of such writers as Francis de Sales, Jeanne de Chantal, and Evelyn Underhill in the present edition raises again, and more urgently, the question of the principle of selection. These authors may never have enjoyed the kind of extraordinary experiences that we have come to associate with the term *mysticism*. As we pointed out in the original General Introduction and do so again in the present one, such experiences were never the norm for inclusion, since this would have excluded most spiritual writers of the patristic and medieval epochs. An intense spiritual concern expressed in mostly non-confessional writings determined the past use of the term. Today the term *spirituality* might render the ancient meaning more accurately, but we have preferred to retain the original subtitle of our anthology for the sake of continuity. We have likewise retained the general format of the first edition, with chapter introductions placing each selection in context within the Christian mystical tradition and selected bibliographies, now updated, pointing the reader to further resources.

Finally, we express our sincere thanks to all who made recommendations for improving the first edition of this anthology, and to Donald Brophy, Theresa Sparacio, and their associates at Paulist Press for their assistance in our work of revision.

General Introduction

I. Mysticism and Christian Mysticism

Reading mystical writers—even if they are mediocre stylists, poorly educated, and separated from us by antiquated theologies and questionable methods of exegesis—may be an illuminating experience. It allows a rare glimpse of that mystery that surrounds our entire existence. For a Christian, the translation of doctrine into experience or even into theory about experience may also mean a homecoming into his or her faith. But what counts as a mystical text? The answers have varied from being almost indefinably comprehensive to being almost inapplicably restrictive. No definitive answer has presided over our choice. The history of the term itself has proven to be too slippery to provide hard and fast answers. The adjective *mystikos,* derived from Greek mystery cults, through the Alexandrian writers Clement and Origen, hesitantly found its way into the Christian vocabulary.[1] The objective quality of the original concept, so different from our own emphasis upon private experience, persists through the sixth century. *Mystical* applies to the hidden (Christian) meaning of the Old Testament, to the hidden presence of Christ in the Eucharist, and eventually to the universal Christian experience of God's presence in scripture and in the world around us. All these meanings convey the idea of a reality concealed by surface appearances but accessible to all Christians. Indeed, I doubt whether before the late

---

[1] We may refer the interested reader to Louis Bouyer, *The Spirituality of the New Testament and the Fathers,* vol. 1 of *A History of Christian Spirituality* (New York: Seabury, 1963).

3

Middle Ages the word ever referred to a purely private, inner experience. The meaning continues to shift through the Middle Ages so much that few authors here presented would have agreed on a common definition before the end of the Middle Ages, and none would have used the one common today of a secret knowledge communicated in an extraordinary, personal experience.

Only toward the end of the Middle Ages, when spiritual life itself became marginal to (a still publicly religious) society, did the term move toward the highly individual, subjective meaning we tend to regard as its very essence. Thus Chancellor Gerson, somewhat ahead of his time, defined it as *cognitio experimentalis de Deo*. The last two centuries (at least in Western Christendom) have narrowed that meaning further to an *extraordinary* grace granted to those who directly experience the divine presence. However questionable one may find those restrictions, we editors writing for a modern public have to take them into account. This decision, in turn, creates further complications. For who, by the subjective norms now prevailing, deserves to be included? Clearly, compromises are inevitable, and we had to include much, indeed most, of what was written according to very different definitions of the term *mystical*—and yet with some relation to the modern, private, contemplative conception. This strategy forced us to forgo any judgment concerning a writer's private experience and, even more, concerning the "natural" or "supernatural" quality of what he or she describes. Few of the writers here presented ever appeal to personal experience. Instead, they articulate various theories of God's presence to the soul that we have come to describe as mystical, but which in most cases they themselves never even considered in the light of the private, subjective, or extraordinary experience we attach to the meaning of the term. It remains generally true that mystical texts place a greater emphasis upon the communally or individually *experienced* presence of God than related systematic or pastoral ones do. This provides the reader with no pretext for discarding the theoretical husk in favor of some alleged core of pure experience. We can refer to experience only as it is reflected *in the text,* that is, as the hidden factor to which in some manner (not necessarily private!) the expression itself appeals and which grants it its specific character.

But a text carries a second intentionality by which it refers to the reader's experience. Through the centuries we have come to consider certain texts as mystical more for the unique insight—at once cognitive and affective—in the spiritual nature of reality they convey to the reader than for the assumed (but totally hidden) experience that led to their writing. Ideally, they evoke a response related to the one described by the disciples of Emmaus after their mysterious encounter with the risen Lord: "Did we not feel our hearts on fire at his words?" In this respect the study of a mystical text may be compared to Luther's reading of scripture. Not so much the words as what the Spirit awakens in the hearer or reader through these words—*was Christum treibt*—leads him or her to consider a text inspired. To consider a text mystical, then, often amounts to regarding it as conducive to that special religious perception of reality in which the various functions of the mind, the affective as well as the cognitive, become united in a uniquely harmonious and often intensively experienced manner.

How essential is the mystical element to the Christian faith? One need not share the fierce opposition of extreme "transcendentists" (Catholics as well as Protestants) to any kind of experiential partaking of the divine to question the oft-heard statement that mysticism is the essence of religion. Unqualifiedly thus to describe religion is seriously to distort its nature. Nevertheless, we believe that the mystical *belongs* to the very essence of religion, even though that essence usually contains other elements as well. Not only does it occasionally take a complete hold of some but, more important, it shapes and informs, inspires and renews all religious activity, whether ritual, moral, or theoretical. Without some share of spiritual experience religion withers away in sterile ritualism, arid moralism, or theological intellectualism. Nor is that experience entirely reserved to the few. The same power that overwhelms some exerts an active though often barely conscious momentum on all genuine religious endeavor.

To evaluate the mystical quality of the Christian faith would require a full spiritual history of it. Over the centuries the significance of the mystical has varied, without ever having dominated the entire faith or having lost its impact on that faith altogether. Already the gospels strongly stress the continuous, intimate presence of God to Jesus. The mystical quality of a life so thoroughly penetrated by God's own life receives a unique emphasis in the Fourth Gospel. The presence of Jesus' Spirit turns that quality into a promise to all true believers. It entitles his followers to the very love with which God loves his own Son.

The specific quality of Christian mysticism renders it, of course, distinct from other mystical forms of religion. But it does not separate it from them. Indeed, some mystics have been known to maintain a dialogue with one another across confessional boundaries which exceeded that of officially accepted theoretical exchange. Muslim mystics have been influenced by Christians, and some medieval Jewish mystics betray the impact of Muslim doctrines, while Christians have persistently derived mystical inspiration from pagan writings of the classical age and their religious interpretations by Jews and Muslims. Today, more than ever, spiritual men and women of different faiths tend to form an invisible kinship that often allows them to communicate as easily with mystics of another faith as with believers in their own confession—nor surprisingly, for mystical texts, however distinct in quality, tend to have a universal appeal. This fact has led some to conclude that, from a mystical point of view, all religions are alike, or even that there is only one, universal mystical religion, which subsequent interpretations distinguish according to theologies or schools. This position is, of course, erroneously simplistic and, as our awareness of the specific quality of each religion has increased, the number of advocates of a universal mystical religion is rapidly dwindling. Today most students of the subject would, indeed, deny the existence of any mysticism-in-general. What remains true, however, is that the various mystical traditions show a certain independence vis-à-vis the doctrinal bodies within which they originated. Also, they often display surprising family resemblances with similar trends in other traditions.

II. Types of Christian Mysticism

Incontrovertible as the existence of different characteristics in different mystics or "schools" of mysticism may appear, any attempt to capture a number of them under a single heading results in highly contestable emphases of some traits at the expense of others. To speak of "image mysticism," "apophatic mysticism," "trinitarian mysticism," and "love mysticism" is to conceal more than one reveals. Indeed, only one or two of the writers here presented would fall entirely under one or another of these headings, and then mostly for the simple reason that their writings were the ones to give rise to the concept. Even in their case problems remain. If we rank Gregory of Nyssa among the image mystics, of whom some consider him the prototype, we must still remember that he was also one of the first apophatic theologians as well as one of the earliest writers on mystical love.

The Christian theology of the Image, implicit in the New Testament and first speculatively developed by Origen, survived uninterruptedly in the East. It was based on the following principle: In the same way in which the Word as divine Image holds God's presence in itself, the soul holds the Word's presence by being its image. The mystical ascent then consists in being converted *entirely* to that image with which its inner core already coincides. Hence the soul becomes deified by becoming what, in its innermost nature, it is. Having largely vanished from Western spirituality, it reemerged in twelfth-century Cistercian writers and dominated the mystical schools of the Rhineland and Flanders. It faded away in the fifteenth century, only to reappear with renewed vigor in the twentieth century (Merton, Teilhard de Chardin). The movement toward its image may be described as *ecstatic* insofar as the soul surpasses its given nature, but it consists more in an inward turn than in an "ascent."

There is no doubt, however, that the ecstatic quality defines a mystical trend born in the same Neoplatonic school of thought and frequently combined with that of the image, namely, apophatic or negative theology. We mentioned the pioneering role that Gregory of Nyssa played in the development of both. Yet the definitive model comes from a mysterious sixth-century writer, probably a Syrian monk, who, by presenting his work as the creation of the Dionysius whom Paul converted on the Areopagus, added the weight of apostolic authority to words that already carried a powerful message of their own. He incorporated the entire Neoplatonic theology of descent and ascent into the Christian idea of the soul's spiritual journey. In his *Mystical Theology* he daringly declared God to be beyond all names, even beyond Being. Spiritual life consists in moving beyond all attachments and attributions toward the dark abyss of the Godhead—the nameless One. Few followed Dionysius's radical denying—"beyond the Trinity"—to the end, but the later Greek fathers and a number of Latin writers, either directly or indirectly, underwent his influence.

Augustine also had been schooled in the Neoplatonic tradition and advocated a theology of ascent. But with him there is no question of moving *beyond* the God revealed in his eternal Word. His theology remains "within the light," so to speak. Whether Augustine ever read Gregory of Nyssa, with whom he had a great deal in common, has not been proven. But with him the image consists in an external analogy rather than in an immanent presence, a similarity of the effect to the Cause. His greatest theological work, *De Trinitate,* seeks the "vestiges" of the divine Trinity, most of all in the soul. At first sight these traces appear to be nothing more than external resemblances, though they also possess a deeper spiritual meaning, for they enable the mind to turn to its archetype and thus to become united with God.

In a sense all Christian mysticism has been trinitarian. Even a negative theologian like Eckhart views the spiritual life of the soul with God as a birth of the Word in the soul. Yet while for negative theologians the image, even the divine Image, belongs to the level of manifestation, for trinitarian mystics that manifestation reveals God's very Being. To grow toward the Image, then, for the creature, means to return to its uncreated presence in the divine Word. In early Western theology treatises on the Trinity abound, but the trinitarian mystery played no major role in spiritual doctrine. God's operation in the soul does not reflect the distinctions of God's manifestation. Augustine changed that. If the trinitarian God created the world, there must remain traces of God's internal life in that world and, even more so, in the soul. God's presence to the soul must in some way manifest God's own nature. Characteristic for Augustine (and his followers), however, is that he conceives that manifestation in psychological terms, thus apparently restricting it to the order of creation. There the matter rested for centuries. But underneath Augustine's arbitrary and often shifting analogies lay a deeper insight that initially escaped his readers. Beyond being an external analogy, the trinitarian quality of the soul referred, in a much higher degree, to the soul's relation to its divine origin. In the act of directing its powers to God, then, the mind transforms its external image of the Trinity into an internal one.

For Jan van Ruusbroec, a Flemish priest, the Trinity became the very essence of spiritual life. He fully shared the insight of the negative theologians that God resides beyond light and beyond words. But darkness and silence are no more the *ultimate* goal of the spiritual quest than they are definitive of God's own life. It is precisely the mystery of the Trinity that transforms negative theology into a mysticism of light and charitable communication. Instead of considering the divine darkness as a final point of rest beyond the Trinity, as Eckhart had done, Ruusbroec identified it with the fertile hypostasis of the Father. The Father is darkness ready to break out in Light, silence about to speak the Word. Having reunited itself with the Word, the soul returns with that Word in the Spirit to the divine darkness. But it does not remain there. For in that point of origin the dynamic cycle recommences: "For in this darkness an incomprehensible light is born and shines forth—this is the Son of God in whom a person becomes able to see and to contemplate eternal life" (*Spiritual Espousals* III/1). Ruusbroec's vision not only leads out of the impasse of a consistently negative theology; it also initiates a spiritual theology of action. The human person is called to partake in the *outgoing* movement of the Trinity itself and, while sharing the common life of the triune God, to move outward into creation.

Once this doctrine of God's descent into creation had fully entered the West, it profoundly affected most spiritual writing of the later ages. In a very real sense all Christian mysticism has been love mysticism. The role of love already distinguishes Origen and Gregory of Nyssa from their Platonic sources. Love is what links Eckhart to Bernard, and love is the moving power of Ruusbroec's dynamic theology. Love relates twelfth-century French Cistercian mysticism to that of Francis of Assisi and his thirteenth- and four-teenth-century followers, to that of sixteenth-century Spanish Carmelites and Jesuits, to that of seventeenth-century "devout humanism," and to eighteenth-century French Quietism. Despite this universal presence, there came a moment when love became equated with the very essence of spiritual life in the West, when *contemplatio* came to be defined as *amor.* If we had to assign the beginning of that movement to one man, it would have to be Bernard of Clairvaux. With him the words of Gregory, *amor ipse notitia est,* became the guiding principle of the contemplative life. What Bernard taught in his treatise *De diligendo Deo* and what he preached in his *Sermons on the Song of Songs* must have impressed his contemporaries as a powerful new sound. Ever since Origen, the Song of Songs had served as the favorite biblical vehi-cle for mystical commentary. But what the Greeks had cautiously spiritualized, Bernard applied in its full erotic power to the rela-tion between God and the soul: "No sweeter names can be found to embody that sweet interflow of affections between the Word and the soul than bridegroom and bride."

The religious dawn of twelfth-century humanism was to reshape the civilization of Western Europe. Love suddenly appeared everywhere: it was the subject of Provençal poetry, and it became the topic of monastic treatises such as Aelred's letter on friendship. Forms of spiritual life more and more came to concen-trate on the humanity of Christ. The Crusades functioned proba-bly no less as cause than as effect of the new devotion: in liberating the Holy Land, Christians would be able to see the places and earthly circumstances of Jesus' life and death. The new devotion came to rest in Francis of Assisi. With him the humanity of Christ stands in the very center of mystical love. In that humanity the entire world, in which the incarnation took place, has become sanctified. Francis looked upon nature with eyes different from those of his spiritual predecessors. All of creation came to partake of the incarnational union of the divine and the human. More than before, God's presence came to be sought within nature, rather than beyond it. This, of course, is not to say that a sense of God's immanence within the creature had been absent from earlier mysticism. Still, an unmistakable change in attitude obviously had taken place. Love for the infinite in the finite had constantly characterized Christian mysticism. Yet now the creature more and more appears divinely lovable not only in its core, where, as Eckhart would say, it touches God's own nature, but also in its finitude, even in its weakness. Owing its existence to a divine act of creation, that very finitude has become endowed with a sacred equality. The mystic is now allowed to love the creature *for its own sake*—since that is the mode in which it exists for God. Saying that he or she loves the creature *for God's sake* undervalues the mystical divinization of the finite *as such*.

What Francis initiated, others completed. Being a man of little theological learning, Francis never attempted to unite his spiritual humanism with traditional Christian theology. The task of synthesizing the new with the old fell upon his followers, in the first place upon Bonaventure. In the *Itinerarium Mentis in Deum* he assigned to the new spirituality of creation its place in a traditional mystical theology. Henceforth in all modern schools of spirituality—among them those of the Carmelites, the Capuchins, the Jesuits, and the Quietists—love occupies a central position. Yet there remain a number of differences. John of the Cross, Teresa of Avila, and their followers in the Carmel emphasize the need for total detachment from all creatures except the humanity of Christ. Ignatius of Loyola and the masters of the Society of Jesus set as their ideal the love of God in *all* things and all things in God. The two may appear opposites. But the Jesuits, no less than the

Carmelites, stress the necessity of total abnegation, while the Carmelites down to Thérèse of Lisieux display remarkably human, even erotic, qualities in their love of Christ.

III. Psychological and Cultural Questions

Spiritual movements create a lore of their own, which then in a remarkable way determines their future development. One of the most basic ideas in Western mysticism is that spiritual life moves through stages in an ascending order. The classical division into a purgative, illuminative, and unitive stage, established since the Greek fathers, survived all transitional differences and school polemics. Variations and subdivisions multiplied, but the core of the doctrine remained the same. Even those who deviated from the common division felt obliged to relate their own conception to the canonical one, however much confusion this might cause. The cases of John of the Cross and of Teresa of Avila may serve as examples. John presents the entire mystical ascent as a night. The image conveys the idea both of ever deeper purification (both "active" and "passive") and of "dark" illumination. In neither one of his systematic treatises, *The Ascent of Mount Carmel* and *The Dark Night of the Soul,* does he explicitly discuss the *via unitiva.* Yet the entire spiritual process for him consists in a growing union of the soul with God. The love poem that introduces both works leaves no doubt about the ultimate goal of the night experience. In her description of the stages of spiritual life in *The Interior Castle,* Teresa uses a language of bridal mysticism concluding in spiritual betrothal and marriage, with scant discussion of illumination *as such.* Yet few works provide more classical examples of the "visions" commonly assigned to the *via illuminativa* than Teresa's writings.

Such a desire to conform one's system to the theological or social customs and rules raises the question to what extent descriptions of the mystical life, perhaps even the experience itself, may be conditioned by psychic, social, or generally cultural factors. Could it mean that mystical states are *nothing more than* projections of psychic dispositions? The great psychologist William James knew better and, instead of reducing the unknown to the known, assumed that a full knowledge of the self would demand the inclusion of those states we are unable to explain by common categories of knowledge. A true psychology of the mystical experience should not "apply" what we know about ordinary states of consciousness, but rather expand the field of experience so as to include states of extraordinary spiritual intensity. In this deeper layer of the mind the laws ruling ordinary consciousness appear to be suspended. Space and time recede or are transformed into rhythms and successions of an inner reality. The ordinary consciousness, James wrote, is only one kind of consciousness that is separated from, and surrounded by, completely different forms. Of these the mystical must certainly rank as the most extraordinary. Why, then, does what appears so remote appeal so much to the ordinary? Does this paradoxical fact itself not support the principle that transcendence belongs to the very essence of human existence? Is the concept of the soul at its core still religious, as it was at its origin?

For the mystics, at least, the soul in its innermost self is near to that ultimate mystery which totally transcends it. In John of the Cross's words, "His majesty dwells *substantially* in the soul" and makes his presence felt through "substantial touches of a divine union between the soul and God" (*Dark Night* 2, 23, 11). Many have objected to Eckhart's bold assertion: "There is something in the soul that is so near akin to God that it is one with Him and need never be united to Him....If a man were wholly this, he would be wholly uncreated and uncreatable" (Sermon 13, "Qui Audit Me"). The language may need qualification, but the meaning converges with the older tradition more conventionally referred to as the soul as image of God in which the divine Archetype dwells, or with Ruusbroec's *super-essence* through which the soul abides within the Godhead. Few have sounded the depths of the soul more thoroughly than the mystics. Through often theoretically inadequate and unscientific language, they have succeeded in showing an otherwise unknown dimension in the life of the psyche.

Finally, a word must be said about the relation between culture and mystical movements. In this area most difficulties arise for assessing the meaning and import of mystical writings not only for their own time, but even more for future generations. What in a mystic's message derives from the theology of the time and what is original? The spiritual mutation that our culture underwent between the sixteenth and the eighteenth century and that has since changed our entire way of thinking and feeling poses an unprecedented difficulty to our very capacity for properly *understanding* the mystical literature of an earlier epoch. While we assume that the primary source of meaning and value lies in the mind, our ancestors before the modern age traced it back to a deeper ground that *transcended* the thinking, conscious subject. Everything in the intellectual climate of our age leads us to abandon this view with as much resolution as we have abandoned the theory of a geocentric universe. Most of our educated contemporaries have done so by now. But this causes them to read mystical texts from a perspective alien to the one from which they were written. They focus entirely on the experience, whereas the mystic is exclusively interested in the *God* experienced. If meaning is thought to originate exclusively in the mind, a relation to God comes to mean an experience of the mind. No mental attitude could remove us farther from the ability to understand the message than that one.

This is written not to discourage modern readers but to caution them that, while reading the mystics, they should remain aware of the inadequacy of their intellectual categories for fully understanding the message. Indeed, to understand, in this case, would require nothing less than some sort of mental "conversion" that would render the readers clearly conscious of their own loss and poverty. To approach the mystics on an equal footing, so to speak, as if they were teachers of spiritual "techniques" that any educated person is able to master, merely extends the secular, self-centered attitude of modern culture to religion itself. If there is anything this book does not want to be, it is a manual of technical instructions.

LOUIS DUPRÉ

Origen
(c.185–c.253)

Christianity's first systematic theologian, its first practitioner of the textual criticism of the Bible, and the first to give an orderly description of the principal stages of the Christian's journey toward union with God—such was the man with whom we begin our anthology. Born in Egypt toward the end of the second century, Origen grew up in its major city, Alexandria, at a time when the Roman persecutions of Christianity were at their height. His own father was martyred when Origen was still in his teens, and the early church historian Eusebius writes that Origen would at that time have joined his father in suffering a martyr's death if his mother had not constrained him to remain at home.

Suddenly entrusted with the responsibility of supporting his mother and six younger brothers, Origen first became a teacher of grammar, but since all the Christian catechists had left Alexandria because of the persecution, he, aged only eighteen, was named head of the catechetical school there. He thereby became entrusted with the duty of instructing those who wished to became Christians and of preparing *them* for the possibility of martyrdom. Those coming to him for instruction soon became so numerous that, in Eusebius's words, "they left him no time even to breathe," so he appointed another man to give beginners their first instruction while he retained the more advanced students for himself. These early years of catechetical instruction coincided

15

with Origen's adoption of a severely ascetical way of life, marked by regular fasting, the possession of only one cloak, and a literalistic interpretation of Matthew 19:12 ("and there are eunuchs who have made themselves such for the sake of the kingdom of heaven") that, according to Eusebius, led Origen to emasculate himself—an act his later enemies would hold against him.

As Origen's reputation as a teacher grew, he was at times called abroad by important personages such as the governor of the Roman province of Arabia or the mother of the emperor Alexander Severus to share his learning with them. He also began writing and publishing his works, principally commentaries on various books of scripture. A decisive turning point in his life occurred in the year 230, when, during a visit to Palestine, he allowed himself to be ordained a priest by local bishops without the permission of his own bishop at Alexandria. A synod convened by the latter declared Origen unfit for catechizing and expelled him from the Church of Alexandria. He thereupon settled at Caesarea in Palestine, where he founded another school, continued his writing, and gave homilies almost daily, many of which have been preserved.

In 249–50, while Origen was living in Caesarea, the newly enthroned emperor Decius began a persecution of Christians throughout the empire. Origen was arrested and underwent severe torture upon the rack but did not die before the persecution ceased with the death of the emperor in battle in 251. There is nothing further written about Origen after his release from prison, but it is commonly thought that he died several years later, at least in part because of the torture he had endured.

Within two centuries of his death Origen's work had become the focus of several controversies. Shortly after the Council of Constantinople in 381, the Cypriot bishop Epiphanius scathingly denounced Origen as the principal source of the recently defeated Arian heresy. Two decades later Egyptian monks whose anthropomorphic concepts of God ran directly counter to Origen's understanding of God as spirit prevailed upon the patriarch of Alexandria to expel from their midst those monks who championed the Origenist position. Finally, at the Second Council of Constantinople in

553, Emperor Justinian I secured the condemnation of Origen as a heretic together with Arius, Nestorius, Eutyches, and others. It was not until the Renaissance that there arose a lasting revival of interest in his writings, a revival that has been carried forward in our own time by the work of major theologians such as Henri de Lubac, Jean Daniélou, and Hans Urs von Balthasar.

Our selections from Origen come from two of his most important spiritual works, his *Commentary on the Song of Songs* and his twenty-seventh homily on the Book of Numbers. Hippolytus of Rome had previously given a Christian interpretation to the Song of Songs by depicting it as a dialogue between Christ and the Church. Origen, while retaining this interpretation, became the first Christian writer to see the text as referring also to the love between Christ and the individual soul. As he writes in the prologue to his commentary, "The present book of scripture, then, speaks of this love with which the blessed soul burns and is on fire in regard to the Word of God." With this, Origen became the first in a long line of Christian mystical writers to approach the Song of Songs in this way; others were Gregory of Nyssa, Bernard of Clairvaux, Teresa of Avila, and John of the Cross, to name only some of the best known.

Another important part of Origen's prologue to the *Commentary on the Song of Songs* is his treatment of the way this book of scripture deals with what he calls contemplation. Origen's frequently noted intellectualism is at times evident here, as when he defines the contemplative discipline as that by which we "contemplate something of divine and heavenly things and gaze at them with the mind alone." Other parts of the prologue, however, make it abundantly clear that, for Origen, contemplation was not simply a matter of intellectual insight but also of love, as when he writes that Solomon, in passing on to us the contemplative discipline in the Song of Songs, was "teaching us that we must attain fellowship with God by the paths of loving affection and of love." What Origen means by this is spelled out in greater detail in his commentary on the verse "I have been wounded by love" (Sg 2:5), where he writes:

If there is ever anyone who at any time has burned with this faithful love for the Word of God; if there is anyone who, as the Prophet says, has received the sweet wound of him who is the "chosen dart"; if there is anyone who has been pierced with the lovable spear of his knowledge, so that he sighs and longs for him day and night, is able to speak of nothing else, wishes to hear of nothing else, can think of nothing else, and is not disposed to desire, seek, or hope for anything other than him; then such a soul truly says, "I have been wounded by love."

In the light of such a passage, it is easy to understand how Jean Daniélou could conclude his long study of Origen's thought with the claim that his "mystical theology centered around the Incarnate Word" and that the source of unity in his entire theological enterprise lay not in logical coherence but, "deeper than that, in Origen's intimate knowledge and eager love of the Lord Jesus."[1]

Our second selection, from the twenty-seventh homily on Numbers, embodies several other distinctive aspects of Origen's spiritual doctrine. His interpretation of the Hebrew names of the various stopping places of the Israelites in their exodus from Egypt to the Promised Land may strike many readers today as fanciful, but they were an integral part of his overall understanding of scripture, according to which a hidden or "mystical" sense was to be found beneath or alongside the "narrative" sense. Equally significant is the fact that in the forty-two stages by which one's journey to God is here traced, the overcoming of temptation is not confined simply to the earlier stages. As late as the thirty-ninth, the traveler comes upon "a beehive of temptations," an indication of the realism with which Origen viewed the spiritual journey and a warning to those who might be ignorant of the truth that the way to full union with God is beset with dangers of one kind or another all along the route. Perseverance is needed at all times, not just at the beginning. That Origen did not succumb to apostasy under torture near the end of his life is an indication that he himself lived the doctrine that he taught.

---

[1] Jean Daniélou, *Origen,* trans. Walter Mitchell (London and New York: Sheed and Ward, 1955), 314.

THE PROLOGUE TO THE COMMENTARY ON THE SONG OF SONGS

This book seems to me an epithalamium, that is, a wedding song, written by Solomon in the form of a play, which he recited in the character of a bride who was being married and burned with a heavenly love for her bridegroom, who is the Word of God. For whether she is the soul made after His image or the Church, she has fallen deeply in love with Him. Moreover, this book of Scripture instructs us in the words this marvelous and perfect bridegroom uses toward the soul or the Church that has been united with Him. As well, from the same book, which is entitled Song of Songs, we come to know what the young girls appointed as the bride's companions said, and also what the friends and companions of the bridegroom said. And the friends of the bridegroom were given the ability of saying some things, so far as they could, that they had heard from the bridegroom Himself, since they were rejoicing at His union with the bride. Moreover, the bride addresses not only the bridegroom but also the young girls, and further the bridegroom not only addresses the bride but also turns to the friends of the bridegroom. And this is what we meant a moment ago by saying that it is a wedding song written in the

All selections in this chapter are taken from *Origen: An Exhortation to Martyrdom, Prayer and Selected Works*, trans. Rowan A. Greer, The Classics of Western Spirituality (New York: Paulist, 1979), 217–20, 223–24, 230–32, 235–36, 245–49, 257–58, 267–69. Reprinted with permission of the publisher.

form of a play. For a play is defined as a story, usually acted on the stage, where different characters are introduced, and where with some characters entering and others making their exits the structure of the narrative is completed by different speeches addressed to different characters. Each of these elements the book of Scripture includes by its own order, and its whole body is fashioned together through fine and mysterious words.

But first we must understand that just as children are not moved to the passion of love, so neither is the age of the inner man, if it is that of a little one and an infant, allowed to grasp these words. I am referring to those who are nourished in Christ by milk and not by solid food (cf. Heb 5:12) and who now for the first time long for the milk that is spiritual and without deceit (cf. 1 Pet 2:2). Indeed, in the words of Song of Songs may be found that food of which the Apostle says, "But solid food is for the perfect" and requires such people as listeners who "have their faculties trained by practice to distinguish good from evil" (Heb 5:14). Thus, if those we have called "little ones" come to these places in Scripture, it can happen that they receive no profit at all from this book or even that they are badly injured either by reading what has been written or by examining what has been said to interpret it. But if any one approaches who is a grown man according to the flesh, no little risk and danger arises for such a person from this book of Scripture. For if he does not know how to listen to the names of love purely and with chaste ears, he may twist everything he has heard from the inner man to the outer and fleshly man and be turned away from the Spirit to the flesh. Then he will nourish in himself fleshly desires, and it will seem because of the divine Scriptures that he is impelled and moved to the lusts of the flesh. For this reason I give warning and advice to everyone who is not yet free of the vexations of flesh and blood and who has not withdrawn from the desire for corporeal nature that he completely abstain from reading this book and what is said about it. Indeed, they say that the Hebrews observe the rule that unless some one has attained a perfect and mature age, he is not even permitted to hold this book in his hands. Moreover, we also accept the observance of the following rule from them—it is their custom that all the Scriptures should be given to children by the teachers and the wise, and that at the same time those passages which they call *deuteroseis* should be held back to the last. There are four of them: the beginning of Genesis in which the creation of the world is described, the first chapters of Ezekiel the prophet in which mention is made of the cherubim, the end of Ezekiel, which includes the building of the Temple, and this book, the Song of Songs.

With all this in mind it seems necessary before we begin our discussion of what is written in this book to discuss briefly, first, love itself, which is the chief subject of the book and, next, the order of Solomon's books, among which this book is apparently put in third place. Then we shall also discuss the title of the book itself and why it is called "Song of Songs."...

Among the Greeks a good many learned men, wishing to inquire into the investigation of truth, have published many different books about the nature of love, some of them even written in dialogue style. They have tried to show that the power of love is no other than the power that leads the soul from earth to the lofty heights of heaven and that we cannot arrive at the highest blessedness unless the ardent desire of love impels us. Moreover, questions about love are brought up for discussion, as it were, in banquets among those, I think, who were holding a banquet not of food but of words. Others, as well, have left us certain books or "arts" by which this love is apparently capable of being born or increased in the soul. But fleshly people have carried off these arts to vicious desires and to the mysteries of a faulty love. It is, therefore, no wonder if also with us, where the simple and, consequently, the ignorant seem to be in the majority, we have called the consideration of the nature of love difficult and dangerous. For among the Greeks who were reputed wise and learned there were nevertheless some who did not take these books in the sense in which they were written; but pleading the authority of what had been written about love, they fell headlong into the sins of the flesh and the precipitous paths of lewdness, either by taking suggestions and inducements from the writings we have already mentioned or by presenting the writings of those of old as a veil for their incontinence.

Therefore, lest we also should in any way offend against what was written well and spiritually by those of old through twisting it in a vicious or fleshly sense, let us stretch forth the hands of our soul as of our body to God, that the Lord, who gave His Word to the preachers with great power (Ps 67:12 LXX–Ps 68:11), may also give us the Word with His power, by whom we may be enabled to make clear from our treatise a sound understanding of the name and nature of love and one suitable for building up chastity.

At the beginning of Moses' words, where he describes the creation of the world we find reference to two men that were created, the first made after the image and likeness of God (cf. Gen 1:26) and the second formed from the dust of the ground (cf. Gen 2:7). Paul the Apostle well knew this and possessed a clear understanding of these matters. In his letters he wrote more openly and clearly that every person is two different men. This is what he said, "Though our outer man is wasting away, our inner man is being renewed every day" (2 Cor 4:16) and further, "For I delight in the law of God in my inner man" (Rom 7:22). And he wrote a good many passages like these. On this basis I think that no one ought now to doubt that Moses at the beginning of Genesis wrote about the making or forming of two men, when he sees Paul, who understood better than we do what was written by Moses, saying that every person is two different men. He mentions that one of them, that is, the inner man, is renewed every day; but he asserts that the other, the outer man, in the saints and in people like Paul, is wasting away and growing weak. But if there will appear to be any doubt in the matter, it will be better explained in the proper places. Now, however, that we have made mention of the inner and the outer man, we shall go on....

...Just as there is said to be a fleshly love, which the poets also call Love, according to which the person who loves sows in the flesh, so also there is a spiritual love according to which the inner man when he loves sows in the Spirit (cf. Gal 6:8). And to speak more plainly, if there is someone who still bears the image of the earthly according to the outer man, he is led by an earthly desire and love. But the person who bears the image of the heavenly according to the inner man is led by a heavenly desire and love (cf. 1 Cor 15:49). Indeed, the soul is led by a heavenly love and desire when once the beauty and glory of the Word of God has been perceived, he falls in love with His splendor and by this receives from Him some dart and wound of love. For this Word is the image and brightness of the invisible God, the First Born of all creation, in whom all things were created, in heaven and on earth, visible and invisible (cf. Col 1:1 5f.; Heb 1:3). Therefore, if anyone has been able to hold in the breadth of his mind and to consider the glory and splendor of all those things created in Him, he will be struck by their very beauty and transfixed by the magnificence of their brilliance or, as the prophet says, "by the chosen arrow" (Is 49:2). And he will receive from Him the saving wound and will burn with the blessed fire of His love.

We should also realize that just as illicit and unlawful love can come upon the outer man, for example, that he should love not his bride or wife but a harlot or adulteress, so also there can come upon the inner man, that is, the soul, a love not for its legitimate bridegroom, who we have said is the Word of God, but for some adulterer and seducer. Ezekiel the prophet makes this quite clear, using the same figure, when he brings forward "Oholah" and "Oholibah" to appear for Samaria and Jerusalem depraved by adulterous love (cf. Ezek 23:4ff.). The Scriptural passage in the prophet clearly shows this to those who wish to know more about it. And so the spiritual love of the soul blazes up, as we have taught, sometimes toward certain spirits of wickedness, but sometimes toward the Holy Spirit and the Word of God, who is called the faithful bridegroom and husband of the well-trained soul. And the soul, especially in this book of Scripture we have in hand, is called the Word's bride, as we shall show more fully with the Lord's help when we begin to explain the words of the book itself....

The present book of Scripture, then, speaks of this love with which the blessed soul burns and is on fire in regard to the Word of God. And she sings this wedding song through the Spirit, by which the Church is joined and united with its heavenly bridegroom Christ, desiring to be mingled with Him through the Word so that she may conceive from Him and be enabled to be saved through this chaste bearing of children (cf. 1 Tim 2:15). And this will happen when the children continue in faith and holiness with modesty as they were conceived of the seed of the Word of God and brought forth and born either by the spotless Church or by the soul that seeks nothing corporeal, nothing material, but is on fire with love only for the Word of God.

For the time being these are the thoughts that have been able to come our way concerning love or loving affection, which is the theme of this epithalamium, the Song of Songs....Now let us turn to the other subjects for discussion.

First, let us examine why it is, since the churches of God acknowledge three books written by Solomon, that of them the book of Proverbs is put first, the one called Ecclesiastes second, and the book Song of Songs has third place. The following ideas have been able to come our way about this subject. There are three general disciplines by which one attains knowledge of the universe. The Greeks call them ethics, physics, and enoptics; and we can give them the terms moral, natural, and contemplative....The moral discipline is defined as the one by which an honorable manner of life is equipped and habits conducive to virtue are prepared. The natural discipline is defined as the consideration of the nature of each individual thing, according to which nothing in life happens contrary to nature, but each individual thing is assigned those uses for which it has been brought forth by the Creator. The contemplative discipline is defined as that by which we transcend visible things and contemplate something of divine and heavenly things and gaze at them with the mind alone, since they transcend corporeal appearance.

Now it seems to me that certain wise men of the Greeks took these ideas from Solomon, since it was long before them in age and time that he first gave these teachings through the Spirit of God. The Greeks have brought them forth as their own discoveries, and they have also included them in their books of instructions and left them to be handed down to their successors. But, as we have said, Solomon discovered them before all the rest and taught them through the wisdom he received from God, as it is written, "And God gave Solomon understanding and wisdom beyond measure, and largeness of heart like the sand on the seashore. And his wisdom was made greater than that of all the ancient sons of men and all the wise men of Egypt" (1 Kings 4:29–30). Thus, Solomon, since he wished to distinguish from one another and to separate what we have called earlier the three general disciplines, that is, moral, natural, and contemplative, set them forth in three books, each one in its own logical order.

Thus, he first taught in Proverbs the subject of morals, setting regulations for life together, as was fitting, in concise and brief maxims. And he included the second subject, which is called the natural discipline, in Ecclesiastes, in which he discusses many natural things. And by distinguishing them as empty and vain from what is useful and necessary, he warns that vanity must be abandoned and what is useful and right must be pursued. He also handed down the subject of contemplation in the book we have in hand, that is, Song of Songs, in which he urges upon the soul the love of the heavenly and the divine under the figure of the bride and the bridegroom, teaching us that we must attain fellowship with God by the paths of loving affection and of love....

Therefore, if a person completes the first subject by freeing his habits from faults and keeping the commandments—which is indicated by Proverbs—and if after this, when the vanity of the world has been discovered and the weakness of its perishable things seen clearly, he comes to the point of renouncing the world and everything in the world, then he will come quite suitably also to contemplate and to long for the things that are unseen and are eternal (2 Cor 4:18). But in order to be able to attain them we shall need the divine mercy, if we are indeed to be strong enough, when we have gazed upon the beauty of the Word of God, to be kindled with a saving love for Him, so that He too may think it right to love affectionately a soul that He has seen longing for Him.

Next, the order of our discussion obliges us to speak also about the title of Song of Songs. Indeed, it resembles what is called in the tent of testimony the "Holy of Holies" (cf. Ex 30:29), what is mentioned in the book of Numbers as the "works of works" (cf. Num 4:47), and what in Paul is called the "ages of ages" (cf., e.g., Rom 16:27). But we have discussed, so far as we were able, in our commentaries what the difference is between holies and holy of holies in Exodus and between works and works of works in the book of Numbers (cf. *Hom. Num.* 5:2). Moreover, we have not passed over ages of ages in the places where it occurs; and lest we say the same thing again, let this be enough (cf. *In Ep. ad Rom. comm.* 10:23). But now let us ask first what the songs are of which this is said to be the Song of Songs. I think, then, that they are those that were sung of old by the prophets or by the angels. For the Law is said to have been "ordained by angels by the hand of an intermediary" (Gal 3:19). Thus, all the proclamations made by them were songs that went before, sung by the friends of the bridegroom; but this is the one song that was to be sung in the form of an epithalamium to the bridegroom when He is about to take His bride. In it the bride does not want the song sung to her by the friends of the bridegroom right away, but she longs to hear the words of the bridegroom now present. She says, "Let Him kiss me with the kisses of His mouth" (Sg 1:2). This is why it deserves to be placed before all the other songs. For apparently the other songs, which the Law and the prophets sang, were recited for the bride when she was still a little girl and had not yet crossed the threshold of a mature age; but this song is recited for her when she is grown up, quite strong, and now able to receive manly power and perfect mystery. In accord with this it is said of her that "one is perfect, the dove" (cf. Sg 6:8). Thus, as the perfect bride of the perfect husband she received the words of the perfect teaching.

HOMILY TWENTY-SEVEN ON THE BOOK OF NUMBERS

1. When God established the world, He created numberless different kinds of foods in accordance, of course, with the differences of human desire or of the nature of animals. That is why when a person sees the food of animals, he knows it was created not for him but for the animals. Not only is this the case, but even the animals themselves know their own food; and, for example, the lion uses some; the deer, others; the cow, others; birds, others. Moreover, among men there are some differences in the food that is sought. One person who is quite healthy and has strong bodily constitution needs strong food and has the conviction and confidence he can eat everything, like the strongest of athletes (cf. Rom 14:2). But if someone perceives he is weaker and feeble, he is pleased with vegetables and does not accept strong food because of the weakness of his body. And if someone is a child, although he cannot put what he wants into words, still he seeks no other nourishment than that of milk. So it is that each individual, whether in accordance with his age or his strength or the health of his body, looks for food suitable for himself and fit for his strength.

If you have considered sufficiently this illustration from corporeal things, let us now turn from them to an understanding of spiritual things. Every rational nature needs to be nourished by foods of its own and suitable for it. Now the true food of a rational nature is the Word of God. But just as in the nourishment of the body we have a moment ago granted many differences, so also in the case of a rational nature, which feeds, as we have said, on reason and the

27

Word of God, not every one is nourished by one and the same Word. That is why, as in the corporeal example, the food some have in the Word of God is milk, that is, the more obvious and simpler teachings, as may usually be found in moral instructions and which is customarily given to those who are taking their first steps in divine studies and receiving the abc's of rational instruction. Thus, when they are read some passage from the divine books in which there is nothing apparently obscure, they gladly receive it, for example, the book of Esther or of Judith, or even of Tobit, or the precepts of Wisdom. But if they are read the book of Leviticus, their mind is constantly offended and refuses it as not its own food. For since such a mind comes to learn how to worship God and to accept His commandments of righteousness and true religion, if he hears instead orders given about sacrifices and rites of immolation taught, how could he avoid constantly being inattentive and refusing the food as not suitable for him?

Moreover, when the Gospels or the Apostle or the Psalms are read, another person joyfully receives them, gladly embraces them, and rejoices in assembling from them, as it were, remedies for his weakness. But if the book of Numbers is read to him, and especially those passages we have now in hand, he will judge that there is nothing helpful, nothing as a remedy for his weakness or a benefit for the salvation of his soul. He will constantly reject and spit them out as heavy and burdensome food, because they do not agree with his sick and weak soul. But, for example—to come back to examples from corporeal things—if understanding were given to a lion, he would not constantly blame the abundance of grasses that has been created simply because he feeds himself on raw meat, nor would he say that they have been produced by the Creator unnecessarily because he does not use them as food. Neither should a human being, because he uses bread and other food suitable for him as nourishment, blame God for making snakes, which apparently supply food for deer. Nor should the sheep or the cow, for example, find fault with the fact it has been given to other animals to feed on meat, while grasses alone are enough for them to eat. Now it is just the same way in the case of rational food, I mean the divine books. You should not constantly either blame or reject Scripture when it appears too difficult or too obscure to understand or when it contains what either the beginner and child or the weaker and feebler in his general understanding cannot use and does not think will bring him anything useful or saving. Rather, you should bear in mind that the snake and the sheep, the cow and the human being, and straw are all creatures of God; and their very diversity points to the praise and glory of their Creator, because they either supply or take food suitably and timely for each of those for whom they were created. In just the same way each individual insofar as he perceives himself healthy or weak takes all the passages that are words of God and in which there is different food according to the capacity of the souls.

Moreover, if we examine as carefully as possible, for example, the reading of the Gospel or the apostolic teaching in which you apparently delight and in which you reckon to find the food most suitable and agreeable to you, how many are the points that have escaped your notice, if you investigate and inquire carefully into the commandments of the Lord? But if what seems obscure and difficult is constantly shunned and avoided, you will find even in the passages about which you are confident so many obscure and difficult points that if you persist in your opinion, you will be forced to give it up. Nevertheless, there are a great many passages in them that are spoken openly and simply enough to edify the hearer of limited understanding.

Now we have made all these points first by way of a preface so as to stir up your minds, since the passage we have in hand is one that is hard to understand and seems unnecessary to read. But we cannot say of the Holy Spirit's writings that there is anything useless or unnecessary in them, however much they appear obscure to some. What we ought rather to do is to turn the eyes of our mind toward Him who ordered this to be written and to ask of Him their meaning. We must do this so that if there is weakness in our soul, He who heals all its infirmities (Ps 103:3) may heal us, or so that if we are children in understanding, the Lord may be with us guarding His children and may nourish us and add to the measure of our age (cf. Eph 4:13). For it is in our power to be able to attain both health from weakness and manhood from childhood. It is, then, our part to ask this of God. And it is God's to give to those who ask and to open to those who knock (cf. Mt 7:7). Let this be enough by way of introduction.

2. Now let us turn to the beginning of the passage that has been read so that with God's help we may be able to summarize the main points and explain their meaning, even though we may not expect total clarity. This is what it says, "These are the stages of the children of Israel, when they went forth out of the land of Egypt with their power by the hand of Moses and Aaron. And Moses wrote down their starting places and stages by the Word of the Lord, and so forth" (Num 33:1–2). You have heard that Moses wrote this down by the Word of the Lord. Why did the Lord want him to write it down? Was it so that this passage in Scripture about the stages the children of Israel made might benefit us in some way or that it should bring us no benefit? Who would dare to say that what is written "by the Word of God" is of no use and makes no contribution to salvation, but is merely a narrative of what happened and was over and done a long time ago, but pertains in no way to us when it is told? These opinions are irreligious and foreign to the Catholic faith; they belong only to those who deny that the God and Father of our Lord Jesus Christ (cf. Rom 15:6) is the one and only wise God of the Law and the Gospels. We shall try, then, in a summary fashion so far as time allows, to investigate what a faithful understanding ought to think about these stages.

Now the previous homily gave us the opportunity of speaking about the departure of the children of Israel from Egypt, and we said that in a spiritual sense there can be seen a double exodus from Egypt, either when we leave our life as Gentiles and come to the knowledge of the divine Law or when the soul leaves its dwelling place in the body. Therefore, these stages, which Moses now writes down "by the Word of the Lord," point toward both. Indeed, it is concerning those stages in which souls divested of their bodies or again clothed with bodies will dwell that the Lord made His proclamation in the Gospel by saying, "With my Father are many stages; if it were not so, would I have told you that I go to prepare a stage for you?" (Jn 14:2). Thus, there are many stages that lead to the Father. And in the case of each of them what purpose, what sojourn of use to the soul, or what instruction or enlightenment a person may receive is something only the Father of the age to come knows (cf. Is 9:6). He says of Himself, "I am the door...no one comes to the Father but by me" (Jn 10:9, 14:6). He will probably become in each of the different stages the door for each soul, so that it may go in through Him and go out through Him and find pasture (cf. Jn 10:9), and again so that it may go into another and from there to another stage until it attains to the Father Himself.

But we have nearly forgotten our preface and have suddenly raised your hearing to lofty heights. Let us then, by all means, return to what happens among us and in us. When the children of Israel were in Egypt, they were afflicted with mortar and brick (Ex 1:14) for the works of Pharaoh the king until they cried out in their groaning to the Lord (cf. Ex 2:23). And He heard their cry and sent His Word to them by Moses and led them out of Egypt....

9. So, the children of Israel went forth from Egypt, and setting out from Ramesse, they came to Sochoth. The order of setting out and the distinction of the stages are quite necessary and must be observed by those who follow God and set their minds on progress in the virtues. With respect to this order I remember that already in other places where we have spoken for edification we have pursued the points that the Lord thought right to give us. But we shall now remind you of them again briefly, since you ask it.

Now the first starting place was from Ramesse; and whether the soul starts out from this world and comes to the future age or is converted from the errors of life to the way of virtue and knowledge, it starts out from Ramesse. For in our language Ramesse means "confused agitation" or "agitation of the worm." By this it is made clear that everything in this world is set in agitation and disorder, and also in corruption; for this is what the worm means. The soul should not remain in them, but should set out and come to Sochoth.

31

Sochoth is interpreted "tents." Thus, the first progress of the soul is to be taken away from earthly agitation and to learn that it must dwell in tents like a wanderer, so that it can be, as it were, ready for battle and meet those who lie in wait for it unhindered and free.

Then when the soul thinks it is ready, it sets out from Sochoth and camps at Buthan (Num 33:6, Etham). Buthan means "valley." Now we have said that the stages refer to progress in the virtues. And a virtue is not acquired without training and hard work, nor is it tested as much in prosperity as in adversity. So the soul comes to a valley. For in valleys and in low places the struggle against the devil and the opposing powers takes place. Thus, in the valley the battle must be fought. Then, too, Abraham fought against the barbarian kings in the Valley of Siddim (Gen 14:8), and there he gained the victory. Therefore, this wanderer of ours descends to those who are in deep and low places, not to linger there, but to gain the victory there....

12. ...From there [Gai, the thirty-eighth stage], they come in turn to Dibongad, which bears the meaning "beehive of temptations" (Num 33:45). How marvelous is the caution of divine providence! For look, this wanderer on his heavenly journey comes right up to the highest perfection by a succession of virtues; and nevertheless, temptations do not leave him, though I hear temptations of a new kind. It means "beehive of temptations." Scripture considers the bee a praiseworthy insect, and kings and commoners use what it produces for their health. This may rightly be taken of the words of the prophets and the apostles and all who wrote the sacred books. And I think this can be understood most appropriately as the beehive, that is the entire body of divine Scriptures. Thus, for those who strive for perfection, even in this beehive, that is in the prophetic and apostolic words, there is some temptation. Do you wish to see that the temptation in them is no small one? I find written in the beehive, "Beware lest...when you see the sun and the moon...you worship...things which the Lord your God has allotted to the Gentiles" (Deut 4:19). Do you see what a temptation comes from that beehive? And again when it says, "You shall not revile God" (Ex 22:28). And again in the

beehive of the New Testament, where we read, "Why do you wish to kill me, a man who has told you the truth?" (Jn 8:40). And again the Lord Himself says in another place, "This is why I speak to them in parables so that seeing they may not see and hearing they may not understand, lest they should turn and I heal them" (cf. Mt 13:13, 15). Moreover, when the Apostle says, "In their case the god of this world has blinded the minds of the unbelievers" (2 Cor 4:4). And you will find many temptations of this kind in this divine beehive. Each of the saints must come to them, so that also by them it may be known how perfect and religious his beliefs about God are.

Next, then, they come to Gelmon Deblathaim, which means "scorn of figs," that is, where earthly things are completely scorned and despised (Num 33:46; Almon-diblathaim). For unless what seems to delight us on earth is rejected and scorned, we cannot pass through to heavenly things.

There follows next the stage at Abarim opposite Nabau, which is "passage" (Num 33:47; Abarim, Nebo). But Nabau means "separation." For when the soul has made its journey through all these virtues and has climbed to the height of perfection, it then "passes" from the world and "separates" from it, as it is written of Enoch, "And he was not found, because God had taken him across" (Gen 5:24). Someone like this, even if he seems to be still in the world and to dwell in flesh, nonetheless will not "be found." Where will he not be found? In no worldly deed, in no fleshly thing, in no vain conversation is he found. For God has taken him across from these pursuits and placed him in the realm of the virtues.

The last stage is east of Moab by the Jordan (Num 33:48). For the whole journey takes place, the whole course is run for the purpose of arriving at the river of God, so that we may be made neighbors of the flowing Wisdom and may be watered by the waves of divine knowledge, and so that purified by them all we may be made worthy to enter the promised land. And so, this is what we have been able to touch upon in passing and to expound in public concerning the Israelites' stages according to one method of interpretation.

13. But lest an interpretation of this kind, which depends upon the Hebrews' language and the meaning of their words, should seem to those who do not know the conventions of that language contrived and forced, we shall give a comparison in our language by which the meaning of this logic may be clarified. In the literary game by which children receive elementary instruction, some children are called "abcd's"; others, "syllabarians"; others, "namers"; and others, "counters." And when we hear these names, we know from them how far the children have progressed. Likewise in the liberal arts, when we hear a passage recited or a consolation or an encomium or any other topics in order, we notice by the name of the topic how much progress the youth has made. Why, then, should we not believe that by these names of places as by the names of topics there can be indicated points of progress for those who are learning by divine instructions? In our analogy the students appear to linger in each different topic for public speaking and to make, as it were, stages in them; and they set out from one to the next, and again from it to another. In the same way why should not the names of the stages and the setting out from one to the next and from it to another be believed to indicate the progress of the mind and to signify the acquisition of virtues?

But I leave the rest of the interpretation to be discussed and contemplated on this basis by any who are wise. For it is enough for the wise to give them the opportunity (cf. Prov 9:9 LXX), because it does not help to let the understanding of the hearers remain completely idle and lazy. Therefore, on the basis of this discussion let him meditate upon the rest; indeed, let him contemplate something more perceptive and more divine. "For it is not by measure that God gives the Spirit" (Jn 3:34). But because the Lord is Spirit (2 Cor 3:17), He blows where He wills (cf. Jn 3:8). And we pray that He may blow upon you, so that you may perceive better and higher things than these in the words of the Lord. May you make your journey through the places we have described in our weakness, so that in that better and higher life we may be able, as well, to walk with you. Our Lord Jesus Christ, who is the way and the truth and the life (Jn 14:6), will lead us until we attain to the Father, when Christ hands over the kingdom to God the Father (cf. 1 Cor 15:24) and subjects every principality and power to Him. To Him be glory and power forever and ever. Amen (cf. 1 Pet 5:11).

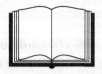

Selected Bibliography

TEXTS

Edition used:
Origen: An Exhortation to Martyrdom, Prayer and Selected Works. Translated by Rowan A. Greer. The Classics of Western Spirituality. New York: Paulist Press; London, SPCK, 1979.

Other sources:
Commentary on the Song of Songs. Translated by R. P. Lawson. Ancient Christian Writers. Westminster, Md.: Newman, 1957. Reprint: New York: Paulist Press, n.d.

Origen—Spirit and Fire: A Thematic Anthology of His Writings. Edited by Hans Urs von Balthasar. Translated by Robert J. Daly. Washington, D.C.: The Catholic University of America Press, 1982.

STUDIES

Anatolios, Khaled. "Christ, Scripture, and the Christian Story of Meaning in Origen." *Gregorianum* 78 (1997): 55–77.

Crouzel, Henri. *Origen.* Translated by A. S. Worrall. San Francisco: Harper & Row, 1989.

———. *Origène et la "connaissance mystique."* Bruges and Paris: Desclée, 1961.

———. "Le thème du mariage mystique chez Origène et ses sources." *Studia Missionalia* 26 (1977): 37–57.

Daniélou, Jean. *Origen.* Translated by Walter Mitchell. London and New York: Sheed and Ward, 1955.

Gregory of Nyssa
(c.335–c.395)

If the holiness of a family could be determined by the number of its members officially recognized as saints, then Gregory of Nyssa could perhaps be said to have belonged to the holiest family in the history of the church: his paternal grandmother, both parents, two brothers, a sister, and Gregory himself all bear the title "Saint"! More important for our purposes is the fact that he was one of the most creative and influential spiritual thinkers of the patristic era; some patrologists have even called him the founder of mystical theology.

Gregory was born in Cappadocia about the year 335. Unlike his elder brother, Basil the Great, he did not pursue higher studies at the great centers of learning, Constantinople and Athens. He was nevertheless very well educated: he had Basil himself as his teacher and gives clear evidence in his writings of a penetrating grasp of scripture, the Platonic corpus, and the works of such theologians as Origen and Clement of Alexandria. After marrying and earning his living for some years as a professional rhetorician, he was persuaded to become a priest by Basil and by their mutual friend Gregory Nazianzen (the three of whom were later to become known as the Cappadocian fathers). In the autumn of 371, Basil, by then archbishop of Caesarea, had Gregory made bishop of the town of Nyssa in the same metropolitan district so that Gregory might be of greater assistance to Basil in the struggle against the Arian heresy. As a bishop, Gregory was several times reproached by his brother for lack of firmness in dealing with people and lack of prudence in matters of church politics and finance. As a theologian, Gregory's efforts were overshadowed by those of Basil during the latter's lifetime. But upon his brother's death in 379, Gregory came into his own as one of the leading theologians of the Christian East. He played a prominent role in defending the orthodox faith at the Council of Constantinople in 381, and from then until his death around the year 395 he remained very active as a preacher and as the author of important doctrinal treatises (especially his *Catechetical Oration,* the first attempt after Origen's *On First Principles* to create a systematic theology) as well as works of spiritual theology (such as the *Life of Moses,* the *Commentary on the Song of Songs,* and *De instituto Christiano,* his final statement on Christian asceticism).

As a mystical theologian, Gregory is perhaps most significant for being one of the first major proponents of the apophatic way, and our selections from his works—from his sixth sermon on the Beatitudes and from the *Life of Moses*—have been chosen primarily to illustrate this aspect of his thought. Whereas for Origen the soul pursues a path of increasing light on its way to God (notwithstanding the presence of temptations all along the way), for Gregory the journey is described instead as one from light to darkness. This is treated most explicitly in the *Life of Moses,* where Moses' entrance into the cloud on Mount Sinai is seen as symbolizing the truth that God is so utterly incomprehensible that true knowledge of God is in fact a "seeing that consists in not seeing" (*Life of Moses,* n. 163). Gregory makes essentially the same point in the sermon on the sixth Beatitude ("Blessed are the clean of heart, for they shall see God") when he writes that this promised sight is not a direct vision of God but rather a matter of having God present within oneself. Moreover, the way to attain this "vision" is not through intellectual abstraction from all sensible reality (as in the extreme Origenism of Evagrius of Pontus) but rather through living in accordance with Christ's teaching that we must refrain not merely from certain outward acts ("Thou shalt not kill") but even from the interior attitudes that lie at the root of such acts. This way of life, says Gregory, will restore in us those divine attributes that were imprinted on our nature at the beginning but were then covered with the evil of sin. In words taken from that same sermon, "If you but return to the grace of the Image with which you were informed from the beginning, you will have all you seek in yourselves. For the Godhead is purity, freedom from passion, and separation from all evil. If therefore these things be in you, God is indeed in you.... You are able to perceive what is invisible to those who are not purified."

For this reason, it could scarcely be emphasized too heavily that for Gregory the utter incomprehensibility of God's nature does not mean that God is absent or inaccessible. Not only is God present to a faithful soul, but this presence can be experienced. If at times this experience is described as one of vision, the "spiritual senses" in which Gregory seems even more interested are those of taste, touch, and smell, ones that more clearly imply that God's presence in the divine darkness can in some way be felt even if not directly seen. As he writes in his *Commentary on the Song of Songs:* "How can that which is invisible reveal itself in the night? By the fact that He gives the soul some sense of His presence *(aisthēsin tina...tēs parousias),* even while he eludes her clear apprehension, concealed as He is by the invisibility of His nature" (*In Cant.,* XI). This mysticism of knowing God beyond knowing, of experiencing God's presence in the darkness of the cloud, was something new in the history of Christian spirituality. Through Pseudo-Dionysius in the early sixth century it would later pass to the West and there lie at the basis of the apophatic formulations of Meister Eckhart, the author of *The Cloud of Unknowing,* John of the Cross, and countless lesser figures.

The final point to be made here concerns a corollary of Gregory's emphasis on God's ultimate incomprehensibility, namely, the fact that the soul's experience of the divine presence can never be fully satisfying and its desire for God never fully satisfied. This—Gregory's doctrine of *epektasis,* of always striving for those things that still lie ahead—is symbolized by Moses' never ceasing to rise higher, but always finding "a step higher than the one he had attained." According to Gregory, "such an experience seems to me to belong to the soul that loves *(erotikē)* what is beautiful. Hope always draws the soul from the beauty that is seen to what is beyond" (*Life of Moses*, n. 231). The reference to *eros* in this passage is significant, for Gregory holds that *eros* is the ecstatic form of *agapē*, as he writes in his *Commentary on the Song of Songs*: The bride "is wounded by a spiritual and fiery dart of *eros*, for *agapē* that is strained to intensity is called *eros*. And no one should be ashamed of this whenever the arrow comes from God and not from the flesh" (*In Cant.*, XIII). If, as we have seen, contemplation for Origen was not exclusively a matter of intellectual insight but also of love, for Gregory this is much more emphatically the case, so much so that for this Cappadocian father the highest level of the spiritual life is not primarily one of knowledge or contemplation *(theoria)*, but rather the way of union through love.[1]

---

[1]On this point, see Jean Daniélou, *Platonisme et théologie mystique: Essai sur la doctrine spirituelle de Saint Grégoire de Nysse*, 2d ed. (Paris, 1954), 199–208.

SERMON SIX ON THE BEATITUDES

When from the sublime words of the Lord resembling the summit of a mountain I looked down into the ineffable depths of His thoughts, my mind had the experience of a man who gazes from a high ridge into the immense sea below him. On the coast one can often see some mountain whose front, facing the sea, is cut off straight from top to bottom, while its projecting upper part forms a peak overhanging the depth. Now if a man looked down from such a high peak into the sea below, he would feel giddy. So also my soul does now, as it is raised from the ground by this great word of the Lord, "Blessed are the clean of heart, for they shall see God" (Mt 5:8). God is promised to the vision of those whose heart has been purified. But "No one has seen God at any time" (Jn 1:18), as says the great John. And the sublime mind of Paul confirms this verdict when he says, "Whom no one has seen or can see" (1 Tim 6:16).

This is the slippery, steep rock that affords no basis for our thoughts, which the teaching of Moses, too, declared to be so inaccessible that our mind can nowhere approach Him. For all possibility of apprehension is taken away by this explicit denial, "No one can see the Lord and live" (cf. Ex 33:20). Yet to see the Lord is eternal life. On the other hand, those pillars of the faith, John and Paul and Moses, declare it to be impossible. Do you realize the vertigo of the soul that is drawn to the depths contemplated in these words? If

From St. Gregory of Nyssa, *The Lord's Prayer; The Beatitudes,* trans. Hilda C. Graef, Ancient Christian Writers (Westminster, Md.: Newman, 1954), 143–44, 146–53. Reprinted with permission of Newman/Paulist Press.

41

God is life, then the man who does not see Him does not see life. On the other hand, the Divinely inspired prophets and apostles testify that God cannot be seen. Is not the hope of man annihilated? Yet the Lord supports this faltering hope, as He did with Peter whom He put back on the water He had made solid, when he was in danger of sinking. If, therefore, the Hand of the Word is stretched out also to us and confirms in a different view those who have lost their balance in the depths of their speculations, we may be without fear, as we are firmly held by the guiding Hand of the Word. For He says, "Blessed are the clean of heart, for they shall see God."...

...How is it then that the voice of the Lord, which promises that God may be seen if we are pure, should not contradict those who, according to St. Paul, evidently speak the truth if they contend that the contemplation of God is beyond our power?

I think it will be best first to say a few words relevant to this subject by way of digression, so that our consideration of the present question may become more methodical. The Divine Nature, whatever It may be in Itself, surpasses every mental concept. For It is altogether inaccessible to reasoning and conjecture, nor has there been found any human faculty capable of perceiving the incomprehensible; for we cannot devise a means of understanding inconceivable things. Therefore the great Apostle calls His ways "unsearchable" (Rom 11:33), meaning by this that the way that leads to the knowledge of the Divine Essence is inaccessible to thought. That is to say, none of those who have passed through life before us has made known to the intelligence so much as a trace by which might be known what is above knowledge.

Since such is He whose nature is above every nature, the Invisible and Incomprehensible is seen and apprehended in another manner. Many are the modes of such perception. For it is possible to see Him who has "made all things in wisdom" (Ps 103:24) by way of inference through the wisdom that appears in the universe. It is the same as with human works of art where, in a way, the mind can perceive the maker of the product that is before it, because he has left on his work the stamp of his art. In this, however, is seen not the nature of the artist, but only his artistic skill which he has left impressed on his handiwork. Thus also, when we look at the order of creation, we form in our mind an image not of the essence, but of the wisdom of Him who has made all things wisely. And if we consider the cause of our life, that He came to create man not from necessity, but from the free decision of His Goodness, we say that we have contemplated God by this way, that we have apprehended his Goodness—though again not His Essence, but His Goodness. It is the same with all other things that raise the mind to transcendent Goodness, all these we can term apprehensions of God, since each one of these sublime meditations places God within our sight. For power, purity, constancy, freedom from contrariety—all these engrave on the soul the impress of a Divine and transcendent Mind. Hence it is clear through what has just been said that the Lord speaks the truth when He promises that God will be seen by those who have a pure heart; nor does Paul deceive when he asserts in his letters that no one has seen God nor can see Him. For He is invisible by nature, but becomes visible in His energies, for He may be contemplated in the things that are referred to Him.

But the meaning of the Beatitude is not only restricted to this, that He who operates can be known by analogy through His operations; for perhaps the wise of this world, too, might gain some knowledge of the transcendent Wisdom and Power from the harmony of the universe. No; I think this magnificent Beatitude proffers another counsel to those able to receive and contemplate what they desire. I make clear by examples what I have in mind.

Bodily health is one of the desirable things in human life; but it is blessed not only to know the principle of health, but to be healthy. For supposing someone had sung the praises of health, yet took some unwholesome food that generated bad juices—what use is it to him to have praised health, seeing he is afflicted with diseases? In the same way, therefore, we should understand the words we are considering. The Lord does not say it is blessed to know something about God, but to have God present within oneself. "Blessed are the clean of heart, for they shall see God." I do not think that if the eye of one's soul has been purified, he is promised a direct vision of God; but perhaps this marvellous saying may suggest what the Word expresses more clearly when He says to others, "The Kingdom of God is within you" (Lk 17:21). By this we should learn that if a man's heart has been purified from every creature and all unruly affections, he will see the Image of the Divine Nature in his own beauty. I think that in this short saying the Word expresses some such counsel as this: There is in you, human beings, a desire to contemplate the true good. But when you hear that the Divine Majesty is exalted above the heavens, that Its glory is inexpressible, Its beauty ineffable, and Its Nature inaccessible, do not despair of ever beholding what you desire. It is indeed within your reach; you have within yourselves the standard by which to apprehend the Divine. For He who made you did at the same time endow your nature with this wonderful quality. For God imprinted on it the likeness of the glories of His own Nature, as if moulding the form of a carving into wax. But the evil that has been poured all around the nature bearing the Divine Image has rendered useless to you this wonderful thing, that lies hidden under vile coverings. If, therefore, you wash off by a good life the filth that has been stuck on your heart like plaster, the Divine Beauty will again shine forth in you.

It is the same as happens in the case of iron. If freed from rust by a whetstone, that which but a moment ago was black will shine and glisten brightly in the sun. So it is also with the inner man, which the Lord calls the heart. When he has scraped off the rust-like dirt which dank decay has caused to appear on his form, he will once more recover the likeness of the archetype and be good. For what is like to the Good is certainly itself good. Hence, if a man who is pure of heart sees himself, he sees in himself what he desires; and thus he becomes blessed, because when he looks at his own purity, he sees the archetype in the image.

To give an example. Though men who see the sun in a mirror do not gaze at the sky itself, yet they see the sun in the reflexion of the mirror no less than those who look at its very orb. So, He says, it is also with you. Even though you are too weak to perceive the Light Itself, yet, if you but return to the grace of the Image with which you were informed from the beginning, you will have all you seek in yourselves. For the Godhead is purity, freedom from passion, and separation from all evil. If therefore these things be in you, God is indeed in you. Hence, if your thought is without any alloy of evil, free from passion, and alien from all stain, you are blessed because you are clear of sight. You are able to perceive what is invisible to those who are not purified, because you have been cleansed; the darkness caused by material entanglements has been removed from the eyes of your soul, and so you see the blessed vision radiant in the pure heaven of your heart. But what is this vision? It is purity, sanctity, simplicity, and other such luminous reflections of the Divine Nature, in which God is contemplated.

Now after what has been said, we do not doubt that such is the case. Yet our sermon is still left with the same impasse which has disconcerted us in the beginning. It is this, that admittedly if someone is in Heaven he shares in the Heavenly marvels; but that the manner of ascent is impossible; and none of the things upon which we have agreed leads us any further. For no one doubts that a man becomes blessed if his heart is purified; but how anyone should cleanse it from its stains, this is what seems to oppose itself to the ascent to Heaven. What then is this Jacob's ladder? How can we find such a fiery chariot by which the prophet Elias was carried up to Heaven, and by which our heart, too, could be lifted up towards the marvels that are above, and shake off this earthly heaviness?...

Now how you can become pure, you may learn through almost the whole teaching of the Gospel. You need only peruse the precepts one by one to find clearly what it is that purifies the heart. For one can divide wickedness under two headings, the one connected with works, the other with thoughts. The former, that is to say, the iniquity that shows itself in works, He has punished through the Old Law. Now, however, He has given the Law regarding the other form of sin, which punishes not so much the evil deed itself, as guards against even the beginning of it. For to remove evil from the very choice of the will is to free life perfectly from bad works. Since evil has many parts and forms, He has opposed by His precepts its own remedy to each of the forbidden things. The disease of wrath is present everywhere all through life, so He begins the cure from what is most prominent, and first lays down the law to refrain from anger. "You have learned," He says, from the Old Law, "You shall not kill" (Mt 5:21). Learn now to keep your soul from wrath against your neighbor....

He then passes on to the healing of the sins committed for the sake of pleasure, and, by His commandment, frees the heart from the vile desire of adultery. Thus you will find in what follows how the Lord corrects them all one by one, opposing by His Law each one of the forms of evil. He prevents the beginning of unjust violence by not even permitting self-defence. He banishes the passion of avarice by ordering a man who has been robbed and stripped to give up also what is left to him. He heals cowardice by commanding to scorn death. And, in general, you will find that by means of each of these commandments the Word digs up the evil roots from the depths of our hearts as if by a plough, and so through them we are purged from bringing forth thorns....

...Hence, as we have learned what is an evil life and what is a good one—for we have it in the power of our free will to choose either of these—let us flee from the form of the devil, let us lay aside the evil mask and put on again the Divine Image. Let us become clean of heart, so that we may become blessed when the Divine Image is formed in us through purity of life, in Christ Jesus Our Lord, to whom be glory for ever and ever. Amen.

THE LIFE OF MOSES

BOOK TWO
CONTEMPLATION ON THE LIFE OF MOSES

The Burning Bush

19. It is upon us who continue in this quiet and peaceful course of life that the truth will shine, illuminating the eyes of our soul with its own rays. This truth, which was then manifested by the ineffable and mysterious illumination which came to Moses, is God.

20. And if the flame by which the soul of the prophet was illuminated was kindled from a thorny bush, even this fact will not be useless for our inquiry. For if truth is God and truth is light—the Gospel testifies by these sublime and divine names to the God who made himself visible to us in the flesh—such guidance of virtue leads us to know that light which has reached down even to human nature. Lest one think that the radiance did not come from a material substance, this light did not shine from some luminary among the stars but came from an earthly bush and surpassed the heavenly luminaries in brilliance.

21. From this we learn also the mystery of the Virgin: The light of divinity which through birth shone from her into human life did not consume the burning bush, even as the flower of her virginity was not withered by giving birth.

From *Gregory of Nyssa: The Life of Moses,* trans. Abraham J. Malherbe and Everett Ferguson, The Classics of Western Spirituality (New York: Paulist Press, 1978), 59–61, 94–95, 113–16. Reprinted with permission of the publisher.

22. That light teaches us what we must do to stand within the rays of the true light: Sandaled feet cannot ascend that height where the light of truth is seen, but the dead and earthly covering of skins, which was placed around our nature at the beginning when we were found naked because of disobedience to the divine will, must be removed from the feet of the soul. When we do this, the knowledge of the truth will result and manifest itself. The full knowledge of being comes about by purifying our opinion concerning nonbeing.

23. In my view the definition of truth is this: not to have a mistaken apprehension of Being. Falsehood is a kind of impression which arises in the understanding about nonbeing: as though what does not exist does, in fact, exist. But truth is the sure apprehension of real Being. So, whoever applies himself in quietness to higher philosophical matters over a long period of time will barely apprehend what true Being is, that is, what possesses existence in its own nature, and what nonbeing is, that is, what is existence only in appearance, with no self-subsisting nature.

24. It seems to me that at the time the great Moses was instructed in the theophany he came to know that none of those things which are apprehended by sense perception and contemplated by the understanding really subsists, but that the transcendent essence and cause of the universe, on which everything depends, alone subsists.

25. For even if the understanding looks upon any other existing things, reason observes in absolutely none of them the self-sufficiency by which they could exist without participating in true Being. On the other hand, that which is always the same, neither increasing nor diminishing, immutable to all change whether to better or to worse (for it is far removed from the inferior and it has no superior), standing in need of nothing else, alone desirable, participated in by all but not lessened by their participation—this is truly real Being. And the apprehension of it is the knowledge of truth.

26. In the same way that Moses on that occasion attained to this knowledge, so now does everyone who, like him, divests himself of the earthly covering and looks to the light shining from the

bramble bush, that is, to the Radiance which shines upon us through this thorny flesh and which is (as the Gospel says) the true light and the truth itself. A person like this becomes able to help others to salvation, to destroy the tyranny which holds power wickedly, and to deliver to freedom everyone held in evil servitude.

The Darkness

162. What does it mean that Moses entered the darkness and then saw God in it? What is now recounted seems somehow to be contradictory to the first theophany, for then the Divine was beheld in light but now he is seen in darkness. Let us not think that this is at variance with the sequence of things we have contemplated spiritually. Scripture teaches by this that religious knowledge comes at first to those who receive it as light. Therefore what is perceived to be contrary to religion is darkness, and the escape from darkness comes about when one participates in light. But as the mind progresses and, through an ever greater and more perfect diligence, comes to apprehend reality, as it approaches more nearly to contemplation, it sees more clearly what of the divine nature is uncontemplated.

163. For leaving behind everything that is observed, not only what sense comprehends but also what the intelligence thinks it sees, it keeps on penetrating deeper until by the intelligence's yearning for understanding it gains access to the invisible and the incomprehensible, and there it sees God. This is the true knowledge of what is sought; this is the seeing that consists in not seeing, because that which is sought transcends all knowledge, being separated on all sides by incomprehensibility as by a kind of darkness. Wherefore John the sublime, who penetrated into the luminous darkness, says, "No one has ever seen God" (Jn 1:18), thus asserting that knowledge of the divine essence is unattainable not only by men but also by every intelligent creature.

164. When, therefore, Moses grew in knowledge, he declared that he had seen God in the darkness, that is, that he had then come to know that what is divine is beyond all knowledge

and comprehension, for the text says, "Moses approached the dark cloud where God was" (Ex 20:21). What God? He who "made darkness his hiding place" (Ps 17:12), as David says, who also was initiated into the mysteries in the same inner sanctuary.

Eternal Progress

225. If nothing comes from above to hinder its upward thrust (for the nature of the Good attracts to itself those who look to it), the soul rises ever higher and will always make its flight yet higher—by its desire of the heavenly things "straining ahead for what is still to come" (Phil 3:13), as the Apostle says.

226. Made to desire and not to abandon the transcendent height by the things already attained, it makes its way upward without ceasing, ever through its prior accomplishments renewing its intensity for the flight. Activity directed toward virtue causes its capacity to grow through exertion; this kind of activity alone does not slacken its intensity by the effort, but increases it.

227. For this reason we also say that the great Moses, as he was becoming ever greater, at no time stopped in his ascent, nor did he set a limit for himself in his upward course. Once having set foot on the ladder which God set up (as Jacob says), he continually climbed to the step above and never ceased to rise higher, because he always found a step higher than the one he had attained.

228. He denied the specious kinship with the Egyptian queen. He avenged the Hebrew. He chose the desert way of life where there was no human being to disturb him. In himself he shepherded a flock of tame animals. He saw the brilliance of the light. Unencumbered, having taken off his sandals, he made his approach to the light. He brought his kinsmen and countrymen out to freedom. He saw the enemy drowning in the sea.

229. He made camps under the cloud. He quenched thirst with the rock. He produced bread from heaven. By stretching out his hands, he overcame the foreigner. He heard the trumpet. He entered the darkness. He slipped into the inner sanctuary of the

tabernacle not made with hands. He learned the secrets of the divine priesthood. He destroyed the idol. He supplicated the divine Being. He restored the Law destroyed by the evil of the Jews.

230. He shone with glory. And although lifted up through such lofty experiences, he is still unsatisfied in his desire for more. He still thirsts for that with which he constantly filled himself to capacity, and he asks to attain as if he had never partaken, beseeching God to appear to him, not according to his capacity to partake, but according to God's true being.

231. Such an experience seems to me to belong to the soul that loves what is beautiful. Hope always draws the soul from the beauty that is seen to what is beyond, always kindles the desire for the hidden through what is constantly perceived. Therefore, the ardent lover of beauty, although receiving what is always visible as an image of what he desires, yet longs to be filled with the very stamp of the archetype.

232. And the bold request which goes up the mountains of desire asks this: to enjoy the Beauty not in mirrors and reflections, but face to face. The divine voice granted what was requested in what was denied, showing in a few words an immeasurable depth of thought. The munificence of God assented to the fulfillment of his desire, but did not promise any cessation or satiety of the desire.

233. He would not have shown himself to his servant if the sight were such as to bring the desire of the beholder to an end, since the true sight of God consists in this, that the one who looks up to God never ceases in that desire. For he says: "You cannot see my face, for man cannot see me and live" (Ex 33:20).

234. Scripture does not indicate that this causes the death of those who look, for how would the face of life ever be the cause of death to those who approach it? On the contrary, the Divine is by its nature life-giving. Yet the characteristic of the divine nature is to transcend all characteristics. Therefore, he who thinks God is something to be known does not have life, because he has turned from true Being to what he considers by sense perception to have being.

235. True Being is true life. This Being is inaccessible to knowledge. If then the life-giving nature transcends knowledge,

that which is perceived certainly is not life. It is not in the nature of what is not life to be the cause of life. Thus, what Moses yearned for is satisfied by the very things which leave his desire unsatisfied....

239. This truly is the vision of God: never to be satisfied in the desire to see him. But one must always, by looking at what he can see, rekindle his desire to see more. Thus, no limit would interrupt growth in the ascent to God, since no limit to the Good can be found nor is the increasing of desire for the Good brought to an end because it is satisfied.

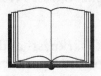

Selected Bibliography

TEXTS

Editions used:
St. Gregory of Nyssa. *The Lord's Prayer; The Beatitudes.* Translated by Hilda C. Graef. Ancient Christian Writers. Westminster, Md.: Newman, 1954. Reprint: New York: Paulist Press, n.d.

Gregory of Nyssa: The Life of Moses. Translated by Abraham J. Malherbe and Everett Ferguson. The Classics of Western Spirituality. New York: Paulist Press; London: SPCK, 1978.

Other sources:
Commentary on the Song of Songs. Translated by Casimir McCambley. Brookline, Mass.: Hellenic College Press, 1987.

From Glory to Glory: Texts from Gregory of Nyssa's Mystical Writings. Translated by Herbert Musurillo, S.J. New York: Charles Scribner's Sons, 1961. Reprint. Crestwood, N.Y.: St. Vladimir's Seminary Press, 1979.

STUDIES

Bebis, George S. "Gregory of Nyssa's 'De Vita Moysis': A Philosophical and Theological Analysis." *Greek Orthodox Theological Review* 12 (1967): 369–93.

Böhm, Thomas. "Die Konzeption der Mystik bei Gregor von Nyssa." *Freiburger Zeitschrift für Philosophie und Theologie* 41 (1994): 45–64.

Crouzel, Henri. "Grégoire de Nysse est-il le fondateur de la théologie mystique?" *Revue d'ascétique et de la mystique* 33 (1957): 189–202.

Daley, Brian E. "'Bright Darkness' and Christian Transformation: Gregory of Nyssa on the Dynamics of Mystical Union." In *Finding God in All Things: Essays in Honor of Michael Buckley,* ed. Michael Himes and Stephen Pope, 215–30. New York: Crossroad, 1996.

Daniélou, Jean. *Platonisme et théologie mystique: Essai sur la doctrine spirituelle de saint Grégoire de Nysse.* 2d ed. Paris, 1954.

Augustine of Hippo
(354–430)

The person who was to become the most influential of all Christian writers after Paul was born in the obscure Numidian town of Thagaste in what is today northeastern Algeria. Although Augustine was enrolled in his infancy as a candidate for baptism, according to the custom of that time the baptism itself was indefinitely postponed to avoid the risk of post-baptismal sin—a postponement that he later sorely regretted. After receiving his early schooling in Thagaste and nearby Madaura, he went on to Carthage for further training and to begin practice as a professional rhetorician. In 383 he left Africa for Rome in the hope of furthering his career, but the following year, in what was to occasion a fundamental reorientation of his life, he moved to Milan to accept a position there.

Throughout these years of youth and early adulthood, Augustine had been avidly seeking the truth about God and the strength to live in accordance with God's will, free from those shackles of selfishness and sensuality he so exhaustively describes in his *Confessions*. For a time he turned to the dualistic religion of the Manichees, and later to the Platonic philosophy of Plotinus and Porphyry; finally, in Milan he came into contact with its great bishop, Ambrose, from whose sermons he learned how one could interpret the Hebrew and Christian scriptures without the sacrifice of one's intelligence. Not long thereafter he underwent his sudden, but long-prepared-for conversion in the garden of his villa. Having earlier dismissed his concubine of many years (not for religious reasons, but because at that time he wished to be free to enter into a lawful marriage with someone of his own standing), he now retired to Cassiciacum, north of Milan, together with his mother Monica, his son, and several friends. There he prepared for baptism and began writing a group of philosophical dialogues, the earliest of his works that have come down to us.

After being baptized by Ambrose at Easter of 387, Augustine set off for his native Africa with his mother and friends. On the way, at the Roman port of Ostia, he and Monica held that religious conversation which, as he later wrote, led them to transcend the realm of matter and even their own minds and so—for a fleeting moment and "with the full impulse of the heart"—touch "the Eternal Wisdom abiding over all." That experience, described in our anthology's first selection from Augustine, was followed by his mother's death at Ostia and Augustine's return to Thagaste, where he lived for several happy and peaceful years in a monastic community that he had founded.

This contemplative way of life changed abruptly when, during a visit to Hippo in 391, he was persuaded by Bishop Valerius to accept ordination to the priesthood. Four years later he was made Valerius's coadjutor and succeeded him as bishop when Valerius died shortly thereafter. During his thirty-five years as bishop of Hippo, Augustine not only showed himself to be thoroughly devoted to the pastoral needs of the people of his diocese but also produced most of the works for which he is best known: the *Confessions, On the Trinity, The City of God,* and his great commentaries on books of the Old and New Testaments. He died on August 28, 430, at the age of 76, while the invading Vandals were besieging his episcopal city.

It is sometimes suggested that the new element in Augustine's spirituality was "the move within." To be sure, interiority is a pervasive theme in his works. God, he tells us, "is in the most secret place of the heart, yet the heart has strayed from him" (*Conf.* 4.12), while in the course of his reflections on memory in book ten of the *Confessions* he breaks forth in the poignant cry: "Late have I loved you, O Beauty, so ancient and so new, late have I loved you! And behold, you were within me and I was outside, and there I sought for you....You were with me, and I was not with you" (*Conf.* 10.27). But this alone did not set Augustine apart from many of his contemporaries, nor is it this alone that makes him so akin to us today. As Augustine's modern biographer Peter Brown observes, it was largely from Plotinus that Augustine inherited a sense of the dynamism of the inner world and a belief that God could be discovered in the memory of this world. But there the similarity ends. For Plotinus, "the inner world was a reassuring continuum. The 'real self' of man lay in its depths; and this real self was divine, it had never lost touch with the world of Ideas....For Augustine, by contrast, the sheer size of the inner world was a source of anxiety quite as much as of strength."[1] In the Neoplatonist, there was accordingly a sense of tranquility that was as foreign to Augustine after his conversion as before:

> Here also is a lamentable darkness in which the capacities within me are hidden from myself, so that when my mind questions itself about its own powers it cannot be assured that its answers are to be believed. For what is in it is often hidden unless manifested by experience, and in this life, described as a continuous trial, no one ought to be overassured that, though he is capable of becoming better instead of worse, he is not actually becoming worse instead of better. Our one hope, our one confidence, our one firm promise is in your mercy. (*Conf.* 10.32)

This sense of the precariousness of our life with God necessarily affected Augustine's mystical theology. In our selection from the fourteenth book of *On the Trinity,* we do indeed see Augustine as a clear representative of what we have called a "mysticism of the image," specifically, the image of the Trinity, which he finds in the mind's power to remember, to understand, and to love its God.

---

[1]Peter Brown, *Augustine of Hippo: A Biography* (Berkeley and Los Angeles: University of California Press, 1967), 178.

In doing this, writes Augustine, the mind attains wisdom and participates in the supreme Light that is God. But he is equally insistent that such participation is never complete in this life, that the possibility of a complete forgetfulness of God must never be presumptuously dismissed, and that "the likeness of God will be perfect in this image only in the perfect vision of God; of which vision the Apostle Paul says: 'Now we see through a glass darkly, but then face-to-face'" (*De Trin.* 14.17).

Our final selection is from *The Literal Meaning of Genesis,* an exhaustive commentary on the first three chapters of Genesis, which Augustine worked on between the years 401–15 (approximately the same period of time as that needed for the composition of *On the Trinity*). The passages we have chosen for this anthology, all from the twelfth and final book of the treatise, were especially influential on later mystical theology in the West, both because of their description of the nature of an "intellectual vision" and because of Augustine's concomitant reflections on the possibility of enjoying a vision of the divine essence in this life. As one would expect, he allows for this possibility only in a very limited sense: such a vision can be granted "only to him who in some way dies to this life," since we are exiled from God "as long as we walk by faith and not by vision, even when we live justly in this world" (*De Gen ad litt.* 12.28). Sixteen years earlier he had made essentially the same point in the famous opening paragraphs of the *Confessions,* addressed to the God whom he had been seeking all his life: "You have made us for yourself, and our hearts are restless until they rest in you."

THE CONFESSIONS

BOOK NINE

The day was now approaching on which she [Augustine's mother Monica] was to depart this life—the day you knew though we did not. It came about, as I believe, by your secret arrangement that she and I stood alone leaning in a window which looked onto the garden inside the house where we were staying, at Ostia on the Tiber where, apart from the group, we were resting for the sea voyage after the weariness of our long journey by land. There we conversed, she and I alone, very sweetly, and "forgetting the things that were behind and straining forward to those ahead" (Phil 3:13), we were discussing in the presence of Truth, which you are, what the eternal life of the saints would be like, "which eye has not seen nor ear heard, nor has it entered into the heart of man" (1 Cor 2:9). But with the mouth of our heart we also panted for the supernal streams from your fountain, the fountain of life which is with you (Ps 35:10), so that if some drops of that fountain, according to our capacity, were to be sprinkled over us, we might somehow be able to think of such high matters.

And our discourse arrived at this point, that the greatest pleasure of the bodily senses, in the brightest corporeal light whatsoever, seemed to us not worthy of comparison with the joy of that eternal life, unworthy of being even mentioned. Then with

The selections from the *Confessions* and *On the Trinity* are from *Augustine of Hippo: Selected Writings*, trans. Mary T. Clark, The Classics of Western Spirituality (New York: Paulist Press, 1984), 114–15, 136–37, 143–44, 342, 346–48, 354, 356–58. Reprinted with permission of the publisher.

our affections burning still more strongly toward the Selfsame we
advanced step by step through the various levels of bodily things,
up to the sky itself from which the sun and moon and stars shine
upon this earth. And higher still we ascended, by thinking
inwardly and speaking and marveling at your works, and we came
to our own minds and transcended them to reach that region of
unfailing abundance where you feed Israel forever on the food of
truth (Ez 34:13). There, life is wisdom by whom all these things
come into being, both those which have been and those which will
be. And wisdom itself is not made; it is as it has ever been and so it
shall be forever. Indeed, "has ever been" and "shall be forever" do
not pertain to it, but it simply is, for it is eternal; whereas "to have
been" and "to be going to be" are not eternal. And while we were
speaking and panting for wisdom we did with the whole impulse
of the heart slightly touch it. We sighed and left behind "the first
fruits of the Spirit" (Rom 8:23) which were bound there, and
returned to the sound of our own tongue where the spoken word
has both beginning and ending. How is it like your word, our
Lord, "remaining ageless in Itself and renewing all things" (Wis
7:27)? We said therefore: If to any man the uproar of the flesh
grew silent, silent the images of earth and sea and air; and if the
heavens also grew silent and the very soul grew silent to itself, and
by not thinking of self ascended beyond self; if all dreams and
imagined revelations grew silent, and every tongue and every sign
and if everything created to pass away were completely silent—
since if one hears them, they all say this: We did not make ourselves, but He who abides made us. Suppose that, having said this
and directed our attention to Him who made them, they also were
to become hushed and He Himself alone were to speak, not by
their voice but in His own, and we were to hear His Word, not
through any tongue of flesh or voice of an angel or sound of thunder or involved allegory, but that we might hear Him whom in all
these things we love, might hear Him in Himself without them,
just as a moment ago we two, as it were, rose beyond ourselves
and in a flash of thought touched the Eternal Wisdom abiding
over all. If this were to continue and other quite different visions

disappear, leaving only this one to ravish and absorb and enclose its beholder in inward joys so that life might forever be such as that one moment of understanding for which we had been sighing, would not this surely be: "Enter into the joy of your Lord" (Mt 25:21)? But when shall it be? Perhaps when "we shall all rise again" and "shall not all be changed" (1 Cor 15)?

BOOK TEN

17. Great is the power of memory! It is something terrifying, my God, a profound and infinite multiplicity; and this is the mind, and I am this myself. What therefore am I, my God? What is my nature? A life various, manifold, and utterly immeasurable.

Behold the plains, caverns and abysses of my memory; they are filled beyond number with innumerable kinds of things, present either in their images as in the case of all bodies or by means of their own presence, as with the arts, or in the form of some kind of notions or impressions, as with the affections of the mind which, even when the mind is not experiencing them, the memory still retains, although whatever is in the memory is also in the mind! Through all this I range in all directions and flit here and there. I dive down as deeply as I can, yet there is no limit. So great is the power of memory, so great is the power of life in man who lives mortally.

What, then, shall I do, my true Life, my God? I shall pass even beyond this power of mine, called memory, I shall pass beyond it that I may draw near to you, sweet Light. What are you saying to me? I am now ascending through my mind to you who dwell above me. I shall pass beyond this power of mine called memory in the desire to touch you at the point where you may be touched, to cleave to you where it is possible to be in contact with you. For even beasts and birds have memory; otherwise, they could never find their lairs and nests, or the many other things to which they become accustomed. In fact, without memory they could not become accustomed to anything. I shall pass beyond memory to find you—oh, where, where shall I find you, my truly good and serene delight? If I find you without memory, I shall not remember you. And how shall I find you if I do not remember you?...

25. But where do you dwell in my memory, O Lord, where do you dwell? What resting place have you fashioned for yourself? What sanctuary have you built for yourself? You have honored my memory by dwelling within it: but in what part of it do you dwell? This I am now considering. For I transcended those parts of it which the beasts also have when I was recalling you (because I did not find you there among the images of material things), and I came to those parts of it where I had stored up the affections of my mind, nor did I find you there. And I entered into the seat of my mind itself (which the mind has in my memory, since the mind remembers itself) and you were not there. For just as you are not a bodily image nor an affection of any living being, such as we feel when we rejoice, sorrow, desire, fear, remember, forget, or whatever else like this we do, no, you are not the mind itself, because you are the Lord God of the mind, and all these things change, but you remain changeless over all things, and you deigned to dwell in my memory ever since I first learned of you, and I find you there when I recall you to mind.

26. Where, then, did I find you so that I might learn of you? For you were not already in my memory before I learned of you. Where, then, did I find you so that I might learn of you, unless in yourself above me? There is no place; we go "backward and forward" (Jb 23:8) yet there is no place. Everywhere, O Truth, you preside over all asking counsel of you and you simultaneously respond to all the diverse requests for counsel. You respond clearly, but not all hear clearly. All ask what they wish, but they do not always hear what they wish. He is your best servant who is not so eager to hear from you what he himself wills as to will what he hears from you.

27. Late have I loved you, O Beauty, so ancient and so new, late have I loved you! And behold, you were within me and I was outside, and there I sought for you, and in my deformity I rushed headlong into the well-formed things that you have made. You were with me, and I was not with you. Those outer beauties held

me far from you, yet if they had not been in you, they would not have existed at all. You called and cried out to me and broke open my deafness; you shone forth upon me and you scattered my blindness; you breathed fragrance, and I drew in my breath and I now pant for you; I tasted and I hunger and thirst; you touched me, and I burned for your peace.

ON THE TRINITY

BOOK FOURTEEN

Chapter Eight

We have now arrived at that point in our discussion where we begin to consider that highest point of the human mind by which it knows or can know God, in order to discover therein an image of God. Although the human mind is not of God's own nature, yet the image of that nature which transcends in excellence every other nature is to be sought and discovered in the most excellent part of our own nature.

But primarily we have to consider the mind in itself, before it participates in God, and there discover His image. We have asserted that it still remains the image of God, although an image obscured and defaced by the loss of its participation in God. This is His image because it has a capacity for God and can participate in God: It has this high destiny only because it is His image.

Here, therefore, is the mind remembering itself, understanding itself, loving itself. Perceiving this, we perceive a trinity—a trinity far less than God, but now finally an image of God. In this trinity the memory has not brought in from outside what it is to retain, nor has the understanding found in the outer world the object for its contemplating, as with the bodily eye. In this case the will has not made outer union of these two, as of the material form and its derivative in the eye of the beholder. An image of the observed external object, taken up, so to speak, and stored in the memory, has not been found by thought directed toward it, with form having been given to the recollecting attention, while the two are linked by an additional activity of will. This was the arrangement manifest in those trinities which we found present in material processes, or somehow passing into our inner experience from the external body through the bodily sense....

Chapter Ten

...But this is not the case with the mind itself. The mind cannot come from outside to itself, as if to a self already in existence there should be added an identical self previously nonexistent, or as if, rather than coming from outside, there should be born in the existing self an identical self which did not previously exist, just as faith arises from nonexistence in the existing mind. Nor does the mind when it knows itself see itself by recollection as constituted in its own memory, as if it had not been there before it became the object of its own knowledge. From the time of its origin the mind has certainly never stopped remembering itself, understanding itself, and loving itself, as already indicated. Consequently, in its act of conversion upon itself in thought, a trinity is manifested in which we can recognize a "word" formed from the act of thinking and united to its origin by will. This is where we may recognize more clearly than before the image we seek....

Chapter Twelve

Now this trinity of the mind is the image of God, not because the mind remembers, understands, and loves itself, but because it also has the power to remember, understand, and love its Maker. And in doing this it attains wisdom. If it does not do this, the memory, understanding, and love of itself is no more than an act of folly. Therefore, let the mind remember its God, to whose image it was made, let it understand and love Him.

In brief, let it worship the uncreated God who created it with the capacity for Himself, and in whom it can be made partaker. Hence it is written: "Behold, the worship of God is wisdom"

(Jb 28:28). By participating in that supreme Light, wisdom will belong to the mind not by its own light, and it will reign in bliss only where the eternal Light is. The wisdom is so called the wisdom of man as to be also that of God. If wisdom were only human it would be vain, for only God's wisdom is true wisdom. Yet when we call it God's wisdom, we do not mean the wisdom by which God is wise: He is not wise by partaking in Himself as the mind is wise by partaking in God. It is more like speaking of the justice of God not only to mean that God is just but to mean the justice He gives to man when He "justifies the ungodly": to which the Apostle alludes when speaking to those who "being ignorant of God's justice, and wanting to establish their own justice, were not subject to the justice of God" (Rom 4:5, 10:3). In this way we might speak of those who, ignorant of the wisdom of God and wanting to establish their own, were not subject to the wisdom of God.

There is an uncreated Being who has made all other beings great and small, certainly more excellent than everything He made, and thus also more excellent than the rational and intellectual being which we have been discussing, namely, the mind of man, made to the image of its Creator. And the Being more excellent than all others is God. Indeed, He is "not far from any one of us," as the Apostle says, adding, "for in him we live and move and have our being" (Acts 17:27f.). Were this said in a material sense we could understand it of our material world: for in it also, in respect to our body, we live and move and are. The text should be taken, however, in a more excellent and also invisible and intelligible way, namely, with respect to the mind that has been made to His image.

In fact, what is there that is not in Him of whom Holy Scripture says: "For from Him and through Him and in Him are all things" (Rom 11:36)? If all things are in Him, in whom except in Him in whom they are can the living live or the moving move? Yet all men are not with Him in the sense in which He says "I am always with you" (Ps 73:23). Nor is He with all things in the sense in which we say, "The Lord be with you." The great misery of man, therefore, is not to be with Him without whom he cannot exist. Unquestionably, man is never without Him in whom man is;

but if a man does not remember Him, does not understand Him or love Him, he is not with Him. But complete forgetfulness makes it impossible even to be reminded of what we have forgotten....

Chapter Sixteen

Those moved by the reminder to convert again to the Lord from that state of deformity wherein worldly desires conformed them to this world have to receive from the Lord their re-formation, as the Apostle says, "Be not conformed to this world, but be reformed in newness of your mind" (Rom 12:2); the beginning of the image's reforming must come from him who first formed it. It cannot of itself reform the self which it could de-form. The Apostle says in another place: "Be renewed in the spirit of your mind, and put on the new man, which has been created according to God in justice and holiness of truth" (Eph 4:23). The words "according to God" agree with what we read elsewhere: "to the image of God" (Gn 1:27). Justice and holiness of truth were lost through sin; hence this image became deformed and discolored. When the image is re-formed and renewed the mind receives what it once had....

Chapter Seventeen

Certainly the renewal we are discussing is not accomplished in one moment of conversion, like the renewal occurring in the moment of baptism by the forgiveness of all sins, none remaining unforgiven. But it is one thing to recover from a fever, and another to regain one's health after weakness resulting from fever. It is one thing to remove the spear from the body, and another to heal the inflicted wound with treatment that follows. So to begin the cure is to remove the cause of sickness: and this occurs through the forgiveness of sins. There is in addition the healing of the sickness itself accomplished gradually by progressive renewal of the image. Both are manifest in one text of the Psalm where we read: "Who shows mercy upon all your iniquities," which occurs in baptism; and then: "Who heals all your sicknesses" (Ps 103:3), which refers to daily advances whereby the image is renewed. The Apostle spoke of this in clear words: "If our outer man decays, yet is our inner man renewed from day to day" (2 Cor 4:16)—but he is "renewed" as he said in the previously quoted texts, "in the knowledge of God," that is, "in justice and holiness of truth." He who is thus renewed by daily progressing in the knowledge of God and holiness of truth, is converting the direction of his love from the temporal to the eternal, from visible to intelligible things, from carnal to spiritual things, trying assiduously to control and reduce all desire for the former and to bind himself by love to the latter. All his success in this depends on divine assistance, for it is God's word that "without me you can do nothing" (Jn 15:5).

When the final day of life reveals a man, in the midst of this progress and growth, holding steadfast to the faith of the Mediator, the holy angels will await him to bring him home to the God whom he has served and by whom he must be perfected; and at the end of the world he will receive an incorruptible body, not for punishment but for glory. For the likeness of God will be perfect in this image only in the perfect vision of God: of which vision the Apostle Paul says: "Now we see through a glass darkly, but then face to face" (1 Cor 13:12). And again: "But we with unveiled face beholding the glory of the Lord are transformed into the same image from glory to glory, as from the spirit of the Lord" (2 Cor 3:18). This describes the daily process in those progressing as they should.

Chapter Eighteen

This statement is from the Apostle John: "Beloved, we are now the children of God, and it has not yet appeared what we shall be: but we know that when He appears we shall be like Him, for we shall see Him as He is" (1 Jn 3:2). This indicates that the full likeness of God is attained in His image only when it has attained the full vision of Him. John's words may indeed be considered as referring to the body's immortality; for also in that we shall be like God, but only like the Son, since He alone in the Trinity took a body in which He died, rose again, and which He bore with Him into heaven. We may also speak here of an image of the Son of God in which we, like Him, shall have an immortal body, conformed in that respect to the image of the Son only, not of the Father nor of the Holy Spirit. For of Him alone do we read and receive with very sound faith that "the Word was made flesh" (Jn 1:14). So the Apostle says: "Whom He foreknew, them He also predestined to be conformed to the image of His Son, that He might be firstborn among many brethren" (Rom 8:29). "Firstborn," in fact, "of the dead," in the words of the same Apostle (Col 1:18)—that death whereby His flesh was sown in dishonor and rose again in glory (1 Cor 15:43). According to this image of the Son, to which we are conformed through immortality in the body, we likewise do that which the same Paul says elsewhere: "As we have borne the image of the earthly, let us also bear the image of Him who is from heaven" (1 Cor 15:49). This means: Let us who were mortal according to Adam believe with true faith and sure and steadfast hope that we shall be immortal according to Christ. For thus we can bear the same image now, not yet in vision but through faith, not yet in reality but in hope. Indeed, in this context the Apostle was speaking of the resurrection of the body.

Chapter Nineteen

But if we consider that image of which it is written: "Let us make man in our image and likeness" (Gn 1:26), not "in my image" or "in your image," we must believe that man was made in the image of the Trinity; and we have devoted our best efforts to discover and understand this. Therefore in respect to this image we may better interpret John's words: "We shall be like Him, for we shall see Him as He is!" Here the Apostle is speaking of Him of whom he has said: "We are the children of God!"

The immortality of the flesh, moreover, will be made perfect in the moment of resurrection which, as Paul says, will be "in the twinkling of an eye, at the last trumpet: and the dead shall be raised uncorrupted, and we shall be changed" (1 Cor 15:52). For in the twinkling of an eye there shall rise again before the judgment that spiritual body in strength, incorruption, and glory, which now as a natural body is being sown in weakness, corruption, and dishonor. But the image that is being renewed day by day in the spirit of the mind, and in the knowledge of God, not outwardly but inwardly, will be perfected by that vision which shall exist after the judgment as face-to-face—the vision which now is only developing, through a glass darkly.

THE LITERAL MEANING OF GENESIS

BOOK TWELVE

15. To see an object not in an image but in itself, yet not through the body, is to see with a vision surpassing all other visions. There are various ways of seeing, and with God's help I shall try to explain them and show how they differ. When we read this one commandment, "You shall love your neighbor as yourself," we experience three kinds of vision: one through the eyes, by which we see the letters; a second through the spirit, by which we think of our neighbor even when he is absent; and a third through an intuition of the mind, by which we see and understand love itself. Of these three kinds of vision the first is clear to everyone: through it we see heaven and earth and in them everything that meets the eye. The second, by which we think of corporeal things that are absent, is not difficult to explain, for we think of heaven and earth and the visible things in them even when we are in the dark. In this case we see nothing with the eyes of the body but in the soul behold corporeal images: whether true images, representing the bodies that we have seen and still hold in memory, or fictitious images, fashioned by the power of thought. My manner of thinking about Carthage, which I know, is different from my manner of thinking about Alexandria, which I do not know. The third kind of vision, by which we see and understand love, embraces those objects which have no images resembling them which are

From Augustine, *The Literal Meaning of Genesis*, trans. John Hammond Taylor, S.J., 2 vols. (New York: Newman, 1982), 2:186–85, 193–94, 216–17, 219, 228–30. Reprinted with permission of the publisher.

not identical with them. A man, a tree, the sun, or any other bodies in heaven or on earth are seen in their own proper form when present, and are thought of, when absent, in images impressed upon the soul. There are two ways of seeing them: one through the bodily senses, the other through the spirit, in which images are contained. But in the case of love, is it seen in one manner when present, in the form in which it exists, and in another manner when absent, in an image resembling it? Certainly not. But in proportion to the clarity of our intellectual vision, love itself is seen by one more clearly, by another less so. If, however, we think of some corporeal image, it is not love that we behold.

16. These are the three kinds of visions about which we had something to say in the preceding books as occasion arose, though we did not there specify their number. Now that we have briefly explained them, since the question under consideration demands a somewhat fuller explanation of them, we must give them definite and appropriate names, in order to avoid the encumbrance of constant circumlocution. Hence let us call the first kind of vision corporeal, because it is perceived through the body and presented to the senses of the body. The second will be spiritual, for whatever is not a body, and yet is something, is rightly called spirit; and certainly the image of an absent body, though it resembles a body, is not itself a body any more than is the act of vision by which it is perceived. The third kind will be intellectual, from the word "intellect." ...

25. ...When, during our waking hours, in full possession of our bodily senses, we experience a corporeal vision, we distinguish between this vision and the spiritual vision by which we think of absent bodies in imagination—whether recalling in memory objects that we know, or somehow forming unknown objects which are in the power of thought possessed by the spirit, or arbitrarily and fancifully fashioning objects which have no real existence. From all such objects we distinguish the bodies which we see and which are present to our senses, so that we have no doubt that these are bodies and that the others are images of bodies. But it may sometimes be that by an excessive application of thought, or by the influence of some disorder (as happens to those who are

delirious with fever), or by the agency of some other spirit, whether good or evil, the images of bodies are produced in the spirit just as if bodies were present to the senses of the body, though the attention of the soul may meanwhile remain alert even in the bodily senses. In this case images of bodies are seen appearing in the spirit, and real bodies are perceived through the eyes. The result is that at the same time one man who is present will be seen with the eyes and another who is absent will be seen in the spirit as if with the eyes. I have known people affected thus, who conversed not only with those truly present but also with others who were absent, addressing them as if they were present. Returning to their normal state, some related what they saw but others were unable to do so. In the same way also some people forget their dreams while others remember theirs.

But when the attention of the mind is completely carried off and turned away from the senses of the body, then there is rather the state called ecstasy. Then any bodies that are present are not seen at all, though the eyes may be wide open; and no sounds at all are heard. The whole soul is intent upon images of bodies present to spiritual vision or upon incorporeal realities present to intellectual vision without benefit of bodily images....

53. There are occasions, then, when the soul is carried off to objects of vision that are similar to corporeal things and are seen by the spirit in such a way that the soul is quite removed from the senses of the body, more than in sleep but less than in death. In such cases it is by virtue of divine guidance and assistance that it realizes it is seeing in a spiritual way not bodies but the likenesses of bodies. Similarly, it sometimes happens that a man in his sleep is aware that he is dreaming even before he awakes. And in spiritual vision it may also be that future events, represented under images present to the soul, are clearly recognized as future because of the fact that divine assistance is given to the human mind or that someone in the vision explains the meaning of it, as happened to John in the Apocalypse. Now the revelation given in such a case must be important, even though it may happen that the man who receives it does not know whether he went out of the body during

the vision or was still in the body but with his spirit withdrawn from the bodily senses. If this information is not revealed to a man who experiences such an ecstasy, it is possible for him to remain in ignorance on this point.

54. Moreover, if a man has not only been carried out of the bodily senses to be among the likenesses of bodies seen by the spirit, but is also carried out of these latter to be conveyed, as it were, to the region of the intellectual or intelligible, here transparent truth is seen without any bodily likenesses, his vision is darkened by no cloud of false opinion, and there the virtues of the soul are not tedious and burdensome. For then there is no restraining of lust by the effort of temperance, no bearing of adversity by fortitude, no punishing of wicked deeds by justice, no avoiding of evil by prudence. The one virtue and the whole of virtue there is to love what you see, and the supreme happiness is to possess what you love. For there beatitude is imbibed at its source, whence some few drops are sprinkled upon this life of ours, that amid the trials of this world we may spend our days with temperance, fortitude, justice, and prudence.

It is surely in pursuit of this end, where there will be secure peace and the unutterable vision of truth, that man undertakes the labor of restraining his desires, of bearing adversities, of relieving the poor, of opposing deceivers. There the brightness of the Lord is seen, not through a symbolic or corporeal vision, as it was seen on Mount Sinai, nor through a spiritual vision such as Isaiah saw and John in the Apocalypse, but through a direct vision and not through a dark image, as far as the human mind elevated by the grace of God can receive it. In such a vision God speaks face to face to him whom he has made worthy of this communion. And here we are speaking not of the face of the body but of that of the mind....

55. ...This vision is granted only to him who in some way dies to this life, whether he quits the body entirely or is turned away and carried out of the bodily sense, so that he really knows not (to use the words of St. Paul) whether he is "in the body or out of the body" (2 Cor 12:2) when he is carried off to this vision.

56. If, then, the Apostle has given the name "third heaven" (2 Cor 12:3) to this third type of vision, which is superior to every corporeal vision by which bodies are perceived through the senses of the body, and superior also to all spiritual vision by which the likenesses of bodies are beheld not by the mind but by the spirit, in this vision the brightness of God is seen by those whose hearts are purified for the vision. Hence it is said, "Blessed are the pure of heart, for they shall see God" (Mt 5:8), not through any symbol fashioned in a corporeal or spiritual manner, as if through a mirror in a riddle, but face to face or "mouth to mouth" (Num 12:8), as it is said of Moses, through a vision, that is, of God's own essence, according to the limited measure that it can be comprehended by a mind distinct from God Himself, even after it has been cleansed from all earthly stain and carried away from all body and likeness of body. From Him we are exiled, laden with a mortal and corruptible burden, as long as we walk by faith and not by vision, even when we live justly in this world....

67. It seems that we are right, then, in understanding the first heaven in general as this whole corporeal heaven (to use a general term), namely, all that is above the waters and the earth, and the second heaven as the object of spiritual vision seen in bodily likenesses (as, for instance, the vision seen by Peter in ecstasy when he saw the dish let down from above full of living creatures), and the third heaven as the objects seen by the mind after it has been so separated and removed and completely carried out of the senses and purified that it is able through the love of the Holy Spirit in mysterious way to see and hear the objects in that heaven, even the essence of God and the Divine Word through whom all things have been made. If all this is true, then I believe that Paul was carried off to that third heaven and that there is a paradise which is more excellent than all others and is, if we may use the term, the paradise of paradises. For if a good soul finds joy in the good that is in every creature, what is more excellent than that joy which is found in the Word of God through whom all things have been made?

68. But why must the spirits of the departed be reunited with their bodies in the resurrection, if they can be admitted to the supreme beatitude without their bodies? This is a problem that may trouble some, but it is too difficult to be answered with complete satisfaction in this essay. There should, however, be no doubt that a man's mind, when it is carried out of the senses of the flesh in ecstasy, or when after death it has departed from the flesh, is unable to see the immutable essence of God just as the holy angels see it, even though it has passed beyond the likenesses of corporeal things. This may be because of some mysterious reason or simply because of the fact that it possesses a kind of natural appetite for managing the body. By reason of this appetite it is somehow hindered from going on with all its force to the highest heaven, so long as it is not joined with the body, for it is in managing the body that this appetite is satisfied.

Moreover, if the body is such that the management of it is difficult and burdensome, as is the case with this corruptible flesh, which is a load upon the soul (coming as it does from a fallen race), the mind is much more readily turned away from the vision of the highest heaven. Hence it must necessarily be carried out of the senses of the flesh in order to be granted this vision as far as it is able. Accordingly, when the soul is made equal to the angels and receives again this body, no longer a natural body but a spiritual one because of the transformation that is to be, it will have the perfect measure of its being, obeying and commanding, vivified and vivifying with such a wonderful ease that what was once its burden will be its glory.

69. ...Finally, although St. Paul was carried out of the senses of the body into the third heaven and Paradise, he was wanting in one point the full and perfect knowledge of things that the angels have: he did not know whether he was in the body or out of the body. But this knowledge will not be wanting to us when we shall be reunited to our bodies at the resurrection of the dead and when this corruptible body will put on incorruption and this mortal body will put on immortality. For everything will be clear without any error and without any ignorance, all things occupying their proper place, the corporeal, the spiritual, and the intellectual, in untainted nature and perfect beatitude.

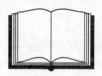

Selected Bibliography

TEXTS

Editions used:
Augustine of Hippo: Selected Writings. Translated by Mary T. Clark. The Classics of Western Spirituality. New York: Paulist Press; London: SPCK, 1984.

The Literal Meaning of Genesis. Translated by John Hammond Taylor, S.J. 2 vols. Ancient Christian Writers. New York: Newman, 1982. Reprint. Paulist Press, n.d.

Other sources:
Confessions. Translated by Henry Chadwick. New York and Oxford: Oxford University Press, 1991.

The Trinity. Translated by Edmund Hill, O.P. New York: New City Press, 1991.

STUDIES

Bonner, Gerald. "The Spirituality of St. Augustine and Its Influence on Western Mysticism." *Sobornost*, n.s. 4 (1982): 143–62.

Brown, Peter. *Augustine of Hippo: A Biography.* Berkeley and Los Angeles: University of California Press; London: Faber, 1967.

Cavadini, John. "The Quest for Truth in Augustine's *De Trinitate*." *Theological Studies* 58 (1997): 429–40.

Chadwick, Henry. *Augustine.* Oxford and New York: Oxford University Press, 1986.

Clark, Mary T. *Augustine*. Washington, D.C.: Georgetown University Press, 1994.

García Alvarez, Jaime. "Saint Augustine and the Experience of God." *Communio* 23 (1996): 252–69.

Pseudo-Dionysius
(early sixth century)

No writer presented in this anthology is likely to have exercised a greater influence upon Christian mysticism—East and West. Yet of none do we know less. Was he a Greek, an Egyptian, or a Syrian? A monk or a lay philosopher? Was he even a Christian? In what century did he live? We are able to answer none of these questions with absolute certainty, though we may safely conjecture that he was a Syrian monk of the sixth century. He himself must bear the main responsibility for the confusion surrounding his identity, since all that he writes about himself has proven to be false. Textual evidence shows that he was not a contemporary of the apostles and not a witness at the crucifixion and at the death of the Virgin. Nor was he the Dionysius whom Paul converted in the Areopagus, nor the third-century martyr believed to have been the first bishop of Paris.

His writings show a clear dependence on Proclus, the Neoplatonic philosopher of the fifth century, who systematized Plotinus's philosophy. Through Dionysius's fake apostolic pedigree, philosophy gained such a firm foothold in the Christian spiritual tradition that it became, together with scripture, its primary source of inspiration. Dionysius's writings once and for all defined the nature of what we now call negative theology. To be sure, negative theology had existed before Dionysius, specifically in Gregory of Nyssa. But it had been a dynamic movement, fully integrated with a theology of the Image. The apophatic extremes attained by Dionysius would probably not have been tolerated had it not been for the respect due to a venerable, apostolic figure. The "Areopagite" applies the ascetic concepts of purification and self-emptying in the most radical way to the discourse about God. The mind must exercise the same continuing self-denial that the desert fathers had applied to the moral order. Beyond all names, even beyond Being itself, lies the dark reality of the divine super-essence. *Super-essential* means that God's "nature" remains beyond definition. Even the character of personhood does not apply. Dionysius calls this Absolute "One," as Plotinus had done. But the unity stands not opposed to plurality or number—God is neither one nor many. It indicates that the Absolute contains in an undifferentiated mode what exists separately in the created world. The Trinity itself, for Dionysius, belongs to the Godhead only insofar as the latter manifests itself. What Western theology calls the Persons of the Trinity are, for Dionysius, super-essential and, hence, super-personal manifestations of the one Godhead.

In creation, God, in an ecstatic move of love, reaches beyond God's own essence. Creation does not lie "outside" God—all that is exists within this one super-essence—yet it belongs neither to the divine super-essence nor to its trinitarian manifestation. In the contemplative life the creature reverses this process, moving beyond all created manifestations and even beyond the internal manifestation of the Trinity, into the darkness of the Godhead. In doing so the human mind surpasses its own created being and, in the ecstatic ascent, loses itself in the divine super-essence. It thereby becomes deified. As one commentator puts it: "As the Super-Essence creates the world and our human souls by a species of divine 'ecstasy,' so the human soul must return by an answering 'ecstasy' to the Super-Essence. On both sides there is the same principle of Self-Transcendence."[1] The deepest mode of "knowing" God, then, consists in a continuous overcoming of all cognitive categories. The ecstatic

---

[1] C. E. Rolt, Introduction to *Dionysius the Areopagite: The Divine Names and Mystical Theology* (London: SPCK, 1940), 29.

movement itself, rather than any cognitive content, directs the mind to its union with God. From the preceding it should appear that this ascent of the mind is primarily an "intellectual" mysticism. Authorities doubt whether Dionysius would deserve the title mystic in the modern sense of extraordinary, private (and strongly affective) experience at all.[2]

Not all of Dionysius's theology, however, is negative, though he reserves the title mystical exclusively to the negative one. Dionysius himself cautions that the mystical theology must be preceded by a theology that affirms the Trinity and all the traditional mysteries of the Catholic faith. *The Outline of Theology,* in which Dionysius claims to have done this, has not been preserved. But *The Divine Names* has. Here he explains the relativity of all attributes predicated of God and thus prepares the way to the final, "dark" theology of negation. This appears clearly in the last chapter (here presented), where Dionysius discusses the ultimate attribute of unity.

Since few medieval scholars in the West could read Greek, it took some time for Dionysius's work to influence the Latin church. The ninth-century Irish theologian John Scottus Eriugena translated him into Latin, but not until the eleventh century did his authority become firmly established. From then on it ever increased in Scholastic theology (Thomas Aquinas wrote a celebrated commentary on *The Divine Names* and constantly invokes the authority of "St. Denys") and, even more, in spiritual writings. Among the mystics featured in this anthology we can clearly trace his impact not only upon the ones we have called negative theologians (such as the author of *The Cloud of Unknowing* and Eckhart), but also upon trinitarian mystics (such as Ruusbroec), and even upon the Carmelites John of the Cross and Teresa of Avila. Even after he lost his arrogated apostolic reputation, his influence did not wane. We still find it effectively present in Merton. The atmosphere of doubt and dogmatic skepticism created by modern secularism has secured for his "divine ignorance" a revived and renewed interest.

---

[2]Jan Vanneste, S.J., *Le mystère de Dieu: Essai sur la structure rationnelle de la doctrine mystique du Pseudo-Denys l'Aréopagite* (Paris, 1959). For the opposite view, see Walther Völker, *Kontemplation und Ekstase bei Pseudo-Dionysius Areopagita* (Wiesbaden, 1958).

THE DIVINE NAMES

CHAPTER THIRTEEN
CONCERNING "PERFECT" AND "ONE"

...Let us proceed now to the most enduring [name] of them all. Theology, attributing every quality to the Cause of everything, calls him "Perfect" and "One." He is perfect not only insofar as he is absolute perfection, defining perfection in himself and from his singular existence and total perfection, but also because he is far beyond being so. He sets a boundary to the boundless and in his total unity he rises above all limitation. He is neither contained nor comprehended by anything. He reaches out to everything and beyond everything and does so with unfailing generosity and unstinted activity.

To speak of perfection is to proclaim that it cannot be increased or diminished, for it is eternally perfect, that it contains all things beforehand in itself, that it overflows in one unceasing, identical, overflowing, and undiminished supply, thereby perfecting the perfect and filling all things with its own perfection.

2. The name "One" means that God is uniquely all things through the transcendence of one unity and that he is the cause of all without ever departing from that oneness. Nothing in the world lacks its share of the One. Just as every number participates in unity—for we refer to one couple, one dozen, one-half, one-third, one-tenth—so everything, and every part of everything, participates

All selections in this chapter are from *Pseudo-Dionysius: The Complete Works*, trans. Colm Luibheid with the collaboration of Paul Rorem, The Classics of Western Spirituality (New York: Paulist Press, 1987), 127–41. Reprinted with permission of the publisher.

in the One. By being the One, it is all things. The One Cause of all things is not one of the many things in the world but actually precedes oneness and multiplicity and indeed defines oneness and multiplicity. For multiplicity cannot exist without some participation in the One. That which is many in its parts is one in its entirety. That which is many in its accidental qualities is one in its subject. That which is many in number or capabilities is one in species. That which is numerous in species is one in genus. That which is numerous in its processions is one in its source. For there is nothing at all lacking a share in that One which in its utterly comprehensive unity uniquely contains all and everything beforehand, even opposites. Without the One there is no multiplicity, but there can still be the One when there is no multiplicity, just as one precedes all multiplied numbers. And, then, if one thinks of all things as united in all things, the totality of things must be presumed to be one.

3. There is something else to remember also. When things are said to be unified, this is in accordance with the preconceived form of the one proper to each. In this way the One may be called the underlying element of all things. And if you take away the One, there will survive neither whole nor part nor anything else in creation. The reality is that all things are contained beforehand in and are embraced by the One in its capacity as an inherent unity. Hence scripture describes the entire thearchy, the Cause of everything, as the One. Furthermore, "there is one God the Father and one Lord Jesus Christ" (1 Cor 8:6) and "one and the same Spirit" (1 Cor 12:11) and this is so in the overwhelming indivisibility of that oneness of God within which all things are banded together as one in the possession of a transcendent unity and in the transcendence of their preexistence. So all things are rightly ascribed to God since it is by him and in him and for him that all things exist, are co-ordered, remain, hold together, are completed, and are returned. You will find nothing in the world which is not in the One, by which the transcendent Godhead is named. Everything owes to the One its individual existence and the process whereby it is perfected and preserved. Given this power of God's unity, we must be returned from the many to the One and our

unique song of praise must be for the single complete deity which is the one cause of all things and which is there before every oneness amid multiplicity, before every part and whole, before the definite and indefinite, before the limited and the unlimited. It is there defining all things that have being, defining Being itself. It is the Cause of things and of the sum total of things. It is simultaneously there with them and before them and beyond them. It is there beyond the one itself, defining this one. Unity among creatures is a unity of number, and number has its own share of being.

But the transcendent unity defines the one itself and every number. For it is the source, and the cause, the number and the order of the one, of number, and of all being. And the fact that the transcendent Godhead is one and triune must not be understood in any of our own typical senses. No. There is the transcendent unity of God and the fruitfulness of God, and as we prepare to sing this truth we use the names Trinity and Unity for that which is in fact beyond every name, calling it the transcendent being above every being. But no unity or trinity, no number or oneness, no fruitfulness, indeed, nothing that is or is known can proclaim that hiddenness beyond every mind and reason of the transcendent Godhead which transcends every being. There is no name for it nor expression. We cannot follow it into its inaccessible dwelling place so far above us and we cannot even call it by the name of goodness. In our urge to find some notion and some language appropriate to that ineffable nature, we reserve for it first the name which is most revered. Here, of course, I am in agreement with the scripture writers. But the real truth of these matters is in fact far beyond us. That is why their preference is for the way up through negations, since this stands the soul outside everything which is correlative with its own finite nature. Such a way guides the soul through all the divine notions, notions which are themselves transcended by that which is far beyond every name, all reason and all knowledge. Beyond the outermost boundaries of the world, the soul is brought into union with God himself to the extent that every one of us is capable of it.

4. These, then, are the divine names. They are conceptual names, and I have explained them as well as I can. But of course I have fallen well short of what they actually mean. Even the angels would have to admit such a failure and I could scarcely speak praises as they do. Even the greatest of our theologians are inferior to the least of the angels. But in this I have fallen wretchedly short not only of the theologians, their hearers and their followers but even of my own peers. So if what I have said is right and if, somehow, I have correctly understood and explicated something of the names of God, the work must be ascribed to the Cause of all good things for having given me the words to speak and the power to use them well. It may be that I have omitted some [name] of similar power, and if so this should be explained using the same methods. And perhaps there is something incorrect or imperfect about what I have done. Perhaps I have completely or partly strayed from the truth. If so I ask you to be charitable, to correct my unwished-for ignorance, to offer an argument to one needing to be taught, to help my faltering strength and to heal my unwanted frailty. I beg that you pass on to me whatever you have discovered by yourself or from others, all received from the Good. Please, let not this kindness to a friend be a burden to you. I have not kept to myself any of the hierarchical words which were handed down to me. I have passed them on unchanged to you and to other sacred men, and I will continue to do so as long as I have the power of words and you have the power to listen. I do an injustice to the tradition only when the strength to conceive and to utter these truths leaves me. May what I do and what I speak be pleasing to God.

So here I finish my treatise on the conceptual names of God, and, with God's guidance, I will move on to *The Symbolic Theology*.

THE MYSTICAL THEOLOGY

CHAPTER ONE
What is the divine darkness?

Trinity!! Higher than any being,
    any divinity, any goodness!
Guide of Christians
Higher in the wisdom of heaven!
Lead us up beyond unknowing and light,
    up to the farthest, highest peak of mystic scripture,
    where the mysteries of God's Word
        lie simple, absolute and unchangeable
        in the brilliant darkness of a hidden silence.
Amid the deepest shadow
    they pour overwhelming light
    on what is most manifest.
Amid the wholly unsensed and unseen
    they completely fill our sightless minds
    with treasures beyond all beauty.

For this I pray; and, Timothy, my friend, my advice to you as you look for a sight of the mysterious things, is to leave behind you everything perceived and understood, everything perceptible and understandable, all that is not and all that is, and, with your understanding laid aside, to strive upward as much as you can toward union with him who is beyond all being and knowledge. By an undivided and absolute abandonment of yourself and everything, shedding all and freed from all, you will be uplifted to the ray of the divine shadow which is above everything that is.

But see to it that none of this comes to the hearing of the uninformed, that is to say, to those caught up with the things of the world, who imagine that there is nothing beyond instances of individual being and who think that by their own intellectual resources they can have a direct knowledge of him who has made the shadows his hiding place. And if initiation into the divine is beyond such people, what is to be said of those others, still more uninformed, who describe the transcendent Cause of all things in terms derived from the lowest orders of being, and who claim that it is in no way superior to the godless, multiformed shapes they themselves have made? What has actually to be said about the Cause of everything is this. Since it is the Cause of all beings, we should posit and ascribe to it all the affirmations we make in regard to beings, and, more appropriately, we should negate all these affirmations, since it surpasses all being. Now we should not conclude that the negations are simply the opposites of the affirmations, but rather that the cause of all is considerably prior to this, beyond privations, beyond every denial, beyond every assertion.

This, at least, is what was taught by the blessed Bartholomew.[1] He says that the Word of God is vast and minuscule, that the Gospel is wide-ranging and yet restricted. To me it seems that in this he is extraordinarily shrewd, for he has grasped that the good cause of all is both eloquent and taciturn, indeed wordless. It has neither word nor act of understanding, since it is on a plane above all this, and it is made manifest only to those who travel through foul and fair, who pass beyond the summit of every holy ascent, who leave behind them every divine light, every voice, every word from heaven, and who plunge into the darkness where, as scripture proclaims, there dwells the One who is beyond all things. It is not for nothing that the blessed Moses is commanded to submit first to purification and then to depart from those who have not undergone this. When every purification is complete, he hears the many-voiced trumpets. He sees the many lights, pure and with rays streaming abundantly. Then, standing

---

[1]Like the other apostles, the Bartholomew of the New Testament was later credited with several apocryphal works.

apart from the crowds and accompanied by chosen priests, he pushes ahead to the summit of the divine ascents. And yet he does not meet God himself, but contemplates not him who is invisible but rather where he dwells. This means, I presume, that the holiest and highest of the things perceived with the eye of the body or the mind are but the rationale which presupposes all that lies below the Transcendent One. Through them, however, his unimaginable presence is shown, walking the heights of those holy places to which the mind at least can rise. But then he [Moses] breaks free of them, away from what sees and is seen, and he plunges into the truly mysterious darkness of unknowing. Here, renouncing all that the mind can conceive, wrapped entirely in the intangible and the invisible, he belongs completely to him who is beyond everything. Here, being neither oneself nor someone else, one is supremely united by a completely unknowing activity of all knowledge, and knows beyond the mind by knowing nothing.

CHAPTER TWO
How one should be united, and attribute praises,
to the Cause of all things who is beyond all things.

I pray we could come to this darkness so far above light! If only we lacked sight and knowledge so as to see, so as to know, unseeing and unknowing, that which lies beyond all vision and knowledge. For this would be really to see and to know: to praise the Transcendent One in a transcending way, namely through the denial of all beings. We would be like sculptors who set out to carve a statue. They remove every obstacle to the pure view of the hidden image, and simply by this act of clearing aside they show up the beauty which is hidden.

Now it seems to me that we should praise the denials quite differently than we do the assertions. When we made assertions we began with the first things, moved down through intermediate terms until we reached the last things. But now as we climb from the last things up to the most primary we deny all things so that we may unhiddenly know that unknowing which itself is hidden from all those possessed of knowing amid all beings, so that we may see above being that darkness concealed from all the light among beings.

CHAPTER THREE
What are the affirmative theologies and what are the negative?

In my *Theological Representations,*[2] I have praised the notions which are most appropriate to affirmative theology. I have shown the sense in which the divine and good nature is said to be one and then triune, how Fatherhood and Sonship are predicated of it, the meaning of the theology of the Spirit, how these core lights of goodness grew from the incorporeal and indivisible good, and how in this sprouting they have remained inseparable from their co-eternal foundation in it, in themselves, and in each other. I have spoken of how Jesus, who is above individual being, became a being with a true human nature. Other revelations of scripture were also praised in *The Theological Representations.*

In *The Divine Names* I have shown the sense in which God is described as good, existent, life, wisdom, power, and whatever other things pertain to the conceptual names for God. In my *Symbolic Theology* I have discussed analogies of God drawn from what we perceive. I have spoken of the images we have of him, of the forms, figures, and instruments proper to him, of the places in which he lives and of the ornaments he wears. I have spoken of his anger, grief, and rage, of how he is said to be drunk and hungover, of his oaths and curses, of his sleeping and waking, and indeed of all those images we have of him, images shaped by the workings of the symbolic representations of God. And I feel sure that you have noticed how these latter come much more abundantly than what went before, since *The Theological Representations* and a discussion of the names appropriate to God are inevitably briefer than what can be said in *The Symbolic Theology.* The fact is that the more we take flight upward, the more our words are confined

---

[2]This lost or fictitious treatise is mentioned and perhaps summarized in the first chapter of *The Divine Names.*

to the ideas we are capable of forming; so that now as we plunge into that darkness which is beyond intellect, we shall find ourselves not simply running short of words but actually speechless and unknowing. In the earlier books my argument traveled downward from the most exalted to the humblest categories, taking in on this downward path an ever-increasing number of ideas which multiplied with every stage of the descent. But my argument now rises from what is below up to the transcendent, and the more it climbs, the more language falters, and when it has passed up and beyond the ascent, it will turn silent completely, since it will finally be at one with him who is indescribable.

Now you may wonder why it is that, after starting out from the highest category when our method involved assertions, we begin now from the lowest category when it involves a denial. The reason is this. When we assert what is beyond every assertion, we must then proceed from what is most akin to it, and as we do so we make the affirmation on which everything else depends. But when we deny that which is beyond every denial, we have to start by denying those qualities which differ most from the goal we hope to attain. Is it not closer to reality to say that God is life and goodness rather than that he is air or stone? Is it not more accurate to deny that drunkenness and rage can be attributed to him than to deny that we can apply to him the terms of speech and thought?[3]

---

[3] "Life," "goodness," "air," etc., are all biblical examples and are discussed elsewhere in the Dionysian corpus. The point here is that not all affirmations concerning God are equally inappropriate; they are arranged in a descending order of descending congruity. Affirmative theology begins with the loftier, more congruous comparisons and then proceeds "down" to the less appropriate ones. Thus, as the author reminds us, *The Theological Representations* began with God's oneness and proceeded down into the multiplicity of affirming the Trinity and the Incarnation. *The Divine Names* then affirmed the more numerous designations for God which come from mental concepts, while *The Symbolic Theology* "descended" into the still more pluralized realm of sense perception and its plethora of symbols for the deity. This pattern of descending affirmations and ascending negations can be interpreted in terms of late Neoplatonism's "procession" from the One down into plurality and the "return" of all back to the One. In this return, not all negations concerning God are equally inappropriate; the attributes to be negated are arranged in an ascending order of decreasing incongruity. Thus the first to be denied are the perceptible attributes, starting with *The Mystical Theology*, chapter 4, which therefore previews the

CHAPTER FOUR
That the supreme Cause of every perceptible thing is not itself perceptible.

So this is what we say. The Cause of all is above all and is not inexistent, lifeless, speechless, mindless. It is not a material body, and hence has neither shape nor form, quality, quantity, or weight. It is not in any place and can neither be seen nor be touched. It is neither perceived nor is it perceptible. It suffers neither disorder nor disturbance and is overwhelmed by no earthly passion. It is not powerless and subject to the disturbances caused by sense perception. It endures no deprivation of light. It passes through no change, decay, division, loss, no ebb and flow, nothing of which the senses may be aware. None of all this can either be identified with it nor attributed to it.

CHAPTER FIVE
That the supreme Cause of every conceptual thing is not itself conceptual.

Again, as we climb higher we say this. It is not soul or mind, nor does it possess imagination, conviction, speech, or understanding. Nor is it speech per se, understanding per se. It cannot be spoken of and it cannot be grasped by understanding. It is not number or order, greatness or smallness, equality or inequality, similarity or dissimilarity. It is not immovable, moving, or at rest. It has no power, it is not power, nor is it light. It does not live nor is it life. It is not a substance, nor is it eternity or time. It cannot be grasped by the understanding since it is neither knowledge nor truth. It is not kingship. It is not wisdom. It is neither one nor one-

---

two subsequent treatises on perceptible symbols, *The Celestial Hierarchy and The Ecclesiastical Hierarchy.* "As we climb higher" in the ascent from the perceptible to the intelligible, chapter 5 of *The Mystical Theology* denies and moves beyond all our concepts or "conceptual" attributes of God and concludes by abandoning all speech and thought, even negations.

On this sequence of treatises, see Paul Rorem, "The Place of *The Mystical Theology* in the Pseudo-Dionysian Corpus," *Dionysius* 4 (1980): 87–98.

ness, divinity nor goodness. Nor is it a spirit, in the sense in which we understand that term. It is not sonship or fatherhood and it is nothing known to us or to any other being. It falls neither within the predicate of nonbeing nor of being. Existing beings do not know it as it actually is and it does not know them as they are. There is no speaking of it, nor name nor knowledge of it. Darkness and light, error and truth—it is none of these. It is beyond assertion and denial. We make assertions and denials of what is next to it, but never of it, for it is both beyond every assertion, being the perfect and unique cause of all things, and, by virtue of its preeminently simple and absolute nature, free of every limitation, beyond every limitation; it is also beyond every denial.

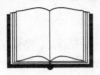

Selected Bibliography

TEXTS

Edition used:
Pseudo-Dionysius: The Complete Works. Translated by Colm Luibheid. The Classics of Western Spirituality. New York: Paulist Press; London: SPCK, 1987.

Other sources:
The Divine Names and Mystical Theology. Translated by C. E. Rolt. London: SPCK, 1940.

The Divine Names and Mystical Theology. Translated by John D. Jones. Milwaukee, Wis.: Marquette University Press, 1980.

STUDIES

Beggiani, Seely. "Theology at the Service of Mysticism: Method in Pseudo-Dionysius." *Theological Studies* 57 (1996): 201–23.

Bernard, Charles André. "La doctrine mystique de Denys l'Aréopagite." *Gregorianum* 68 (1987): 523–66.

Corrigan, Kevin. "'Solitary Mysticism' in Plotinus, Proclus, Gregory of Nyssa, and Pseudo-Dionysius." *Journal of Religion* 76 (1996): 28–42.

Golitzin, Alexander. "The Mysticism of Dionysius Areopagita: Platonist or Christian?" *Mystics Quarterly* 19 (1993): 98–114.

Lossky, Vladimir. "La théologie négative dans la doctrine de Denys l'Aréopagite." *Revue des sciences philosophiques et théologiques* 28 (1939): 204–21.

Rorem, Paul. *Pseudo-Dionysius: A Commentary on the Texts and an Introduction to Their Influence.* New York: Oxford University Press, 1993.

Bernard of Clairvaux (1090–1153)

Abbot, ecclesiastical statesman, mediator between warring armies, counselor of popes and kings, champion of orthodoxy, Bernard of Clairvaux was unquestionably the most influential person in Europe in the first half of the twelfth century. But it is perhaps in the stamp he left on Christian spirituality that his most enduring influence is to be found. As already noted in our General Introduction, at one point in the history of Western Christianity love became equated with the very essence of the spiritual life, and if we had to assign the beginning of that movement to one person, that person would have to be Bernard. The passages from his writings included in this anthology are intended above all to illustrate this centrality of love in his mystical theology.

Born the third son of a noble family near Dijon in 1090, Bernard received a broad, humanistic education at Chatillon and then, in the year 1112 and to his parents' dismay, convinced thirty of his relatives and friends to join him in entering the new and struggling reform monastery of Citeaux, a few miles south of his home. This sudden influx breathed new life into a community that had seemed to be on the verge of extinction. A continuing stream of candidates led to the founding of many daughter houses, including the one at Clairvaux, over which Bernard was named abbot after having been a monk for only three years. Gradually Bernard attained a wide reputation for holiness and wisdom and so became more and more involved in the ecclesiastical and political issues of the entire continent. These often drew him away from his monastery for long periods of time and once led him to complain in a letter to his Cistercian confrere Pope Eugene III that "I am a kind of Chimera of my age, living neither as a religious nor as a layman" (*Ep.* 250.4). Toward the end of his life, the failure of the Crusade that he had preached at the request of the same pope brought much abuse upon him, so that in the eyes of many he died under a cloud of failure. It was, however, only another twenty-one years before he was canonized by Pope Alexander III, and in 1830 he was officially declared a doctor of the church.

It is instructive to compare the writings of Bernard with those of his close friend William of St. Thierry. In some ways the two men were kindred spirits; they shared the same monastic ideal and communicated or dedicated some of their works to each other. But there were also some important differences, the recognition of which can help us better appreciate Bernard's unique place in the history of Christian spirituality. Perhaps the most significant contrast between the two men was the one summed up in the following words at the congress held at Dijon in 1953 to commemorate the eighth centenary of Bernard's death: "In his work as a whole, St. Bernard was interested less in knowledge than in love, whereas William of St. Thierry was more concerned with joining the one to the other and so arriving at a full knowledge of God."[1] The basic reason for Bernard's proportionately greater emphasis on love was his double conviction that all the disorder and sinfulness of human life is ultimately due to the turning of the will from God to self *(voluntas propria)* and that love alone engages a person at a sufficiently deep level to bring about true conversion to God. As he writes in his treatise On Loving God *(De diligendo Deo)*: "It [love] alone can turn the mind from love of itself and the world and direct it to God. Neither fear nor love of self can convert the soul. They change the appearance of one's deeds from time to time, but

---

[1]Jacques Hourlier, O.S.B., "Saint Bernard et Guillaume de Saint Thierry dans le 'Liber de amore,'" in S. *Bernard théologien: Actes du Congrès de Dijon,* 2d ed. (Rome, 1955), 229.

never one's character....Love truly converts souls because it makes them willing" (*On Loving God,* XII.34; henceforth *Dil.*)

For Bernard, the way to overcome immoderate self-love is not simply to hear and heed the commandment "You shall love your neighbor as yourself." Rather, one must first love God, "so that in him you can love your neighbor too" (*Dil.* VIII.25), and the most effective way to arrive at this love is to reflect not only on God's love for us in general (which even non-Christians can and should do), but on the surpassing love revealed to us in Jesus Christ: "The faithful know how utterly they stand in need of Jesus and him crucified. They wonder at and reach out to that supreme love of his which surpasses all knowledge....The more surely you know yourself loved, the easier you will find it to love in return" (*Dil.* III.7). Knowing himself thus loved, Bernard responded with lyrical expressions of his own love for Christ, as in the following lines from his fifteenth sermon on the Song of Songs: "Write what you will, I shall not relish it unless it tells of Jesus. Talk or argue about what you will, I shall not relish it if you exclude the name of Jesus. Jesus to me is honey in the mouth, music in the ear, a song in the heart" (*Sermons on the Song of Songs,* 15.6; henceforth *SC*).

Here is that new note of affectionate love for Jesus that has led so many commentators to speak, with good reason, of Bernard's "affective mysticism." The experiences of the Word's presence that elicited such love from Bernard are movingly described by him in a famous passage from the seventy-fourth sermon on the Song of Songs that we have included in this anthology. At such times, he writes, it is not by any of the five senses but only by the warmth of his heart that he knows the Word is present, and when he afterward suffers the departure of the Word "and all these things become dim and weak and cold," then "I shall not cease to cry, as if after someone who is leaving, begging him with a burning desire to return; I will beseech him to give me the joy of his salvation and return to me" (*SC* 74.7).

As has been suggested by Andrew Louth, we see in such passages from Bernard a shift in the understanding of the spiritual life.[2] For Augustine (and for Bernard's friend William), the love of God and the knowledge of God go closely together, being united in wisdom *(sapientia)*, the contemplation of eternal reality. For Bernard, on the other hand, wisdom is characterized primarily not by the harmonious union of these two components but rather "by peace of mind and spiritual sweetness"; he even defines wisdom in affective terms as "a taste for goodness" *(SC* 85.7,8). To be sure, neither here nor elsewhere in his writings does Bernard radically disdain knowledge or understanding, but their place in the whole process of turning to and being united with God is nevertheless significantly reduced when compared with their place in Augustine's works. We are still far from the sharp dichotomy between thought and feeling, theology and devotion, which was to become so marked in many writers of the late Middle Ages, but in Bernard's affective mysticism we already sense something of the shape of things to come.

---

[2]Andrew Louth, "Bernard and Affective Mysticism," in *The Influence of St. Bernard: Anglican Essays,* ed. Sister Benedicta Ward (Oxford: SLG Press, 1976), 1–10.

ON LOVING GOD

VII.22. 1 said before that God is the cause of loving God. I spoke the truth, for he is both the efficient and the final cause. He himself provides the occasion. He himself creates the longing. He himself fulfils the desire. He himself causes himself to be (or rather, to be made) such that he should be loved. He hopes to be so happily loved that no one will love him in vain. His love both prepares and rewards ours (cf. 1 Jn 4:19). Kindly, he leads the way. He repays us justly. He is our sweet hope. He is riches to all who call upon him (Rm 10:12). There is nothing better than himself. He gave himself in merit. He keeps himself to be our reward. He gives himself as food for holy souls (Wis 3:13). He sold himself to redeem the captives.

Lord, you are good to the soul which seeks you. What are you then to the soul which finds? But this is the most wonderful thing, that no one can seek you who has not already found you. You therefore seek to be found so that you may be sought for, sought so that you may be found. You can be sought and found, but not forestalled. For even if we say, "In the morning my prayer will forestall you" (Ps 87:14), it is certain that every prayer which is not inspired is half-hearted. Now let us see where our love begins, for we have seen where it finds its end.

VIII.23. Love is one of the four natural passions. They are well enough known; there is no need to name them. It is clearly right that what is natural should be at the service of the Lord of

All selections in this chapter are from *Bernard of Clairvaux: Selected Works*, trans. G. R. Evans, The Classics of Western Spirituality (New York: Paulist Press, 1987). Translation slightly modified. Reprinted with permission of the publisher.

nature. That is why the first and great commandment is, "You shall love the Lord your God" (Mt 22:37).

THE FIRST DEGREE OF LOVE:
WHEN ONE LOVES ONESELF FOR ONE'S OWN SAKE

But because nature has become rather frail and weak, we are driven by necessity to serve nature first. This results in bodily love, by which a person loves himself for his own sake. He does not yet know anything but himself, as it is written, "First came what is animal, then what is spiritual" (1 Cor 15:46). This love is not imposed by rule but is innate in nature. For who hates his own flesh? (Eph 5:29). But if that same love begins to get out of proportion and headstrong, as often happens, and it ceases to be satisfied to run in the narrow channel of its needs, but floods out on all sides into the fields of pleasure, then the overflow can be stopped at once by the commandment, "You shall love your neighbor as yourself" (Mt 22:39)....

25. But to love one's neighbour with perfect justice it is necessary to be prompted by God. How can you love your neighbour with purity if you do not love him in God? But one who does not love God cannot love in God. You must first love God, so that in him you can love your neighbour too (Mk 12:30–1).

God therefore brings about your love for him, just as he causes other goods. This is how he does it: He who made nature also protects it. For it was so created that it needs its creator as its protector, so that what could not have come into existence without him cannot continue in existence without him. So that no rational creature might be in ignorance of this fact and (dreadful thought) claim for himself the gifts of the Creator, that same Creator willed by a high and saving counsel that we should endure tribulation; then when we fail and God comes to our aid and sets us free, we will honour God as he deserves. For this is what he says, "Call upon me in the day of tribulation. I will deliver you, and you shall honour me" (Ps 49:15). And so in that way it comes about that one who is a bodily animal (1 Cor 2:14) and does not know how to love anything but himself, begins to love God for his own benefit, because he learns from frequent experience that in God he can do everything which is good for him (Phil 4:13), and that without him he can do nothing (Jn 15:5).

THE SECOND DEGREE OF LOVE:
WHEN ONE LOVES GOD FOR ONE'S OWN GOOD

IX.26. One therefore loves God, but as yet he loves him for his own sake, not God's. Nevertheless the wise person ought to know what he can do by himself and what he can do only with God's help; then you will avoid hurting him who keeps you from harm.

If a person has a great many tribulations and as a result frequently turns to God and frequently experiences God's liberation, surely even if he had a breast of iron or a heart of stone (Ezek 11:19; 36:26), must he not soften towards the generosity of the redeemer and love God not only for his own benefit, but for God himself?

THE THIRD DEGREE OF LOVE:
WHEN ONE LOVES GOD FOR GOD'S SAKE

One's frequent needs make it necessary for him to call upon God often, and to taste by frequent contact, and to discover by tasting how sweet the Lord is (Ps 33:9). It is in this way that the taste of his own sweetness leads us to love God in purity more than our need alone would prompt us to do. The Samaritans set us an example when they said to the woman who told them the Lord was there, "Now we believe, not because of your words, but because we have heard him for ourselves and we know that truly he is the Saviour of the world" (Jn 4:42). In the same way, I urge, let us follow their example and rightly say to our flesh, "Now we love God not because he meets your needs; but we have tasted and we know how sweet the Lord is" (Ps 33:9).

There is a need of the flesh which speaks out, and the body tells by its actions of the kindnesses it has experienced. And so it will not be difficult for one who has had that experience to keep the commandment to love his neighbour (Mk 12:31). He truly loves God, and therefore he loves what is God's. He loves chastely, and to the chaste it is no burden to keep the commandments; the heart grows purer in the obedience of love, as it is written (1 Pet 1:22). Such a person loves justly and willingly keeps the just law.

This love is acceptable because it is given freely. It is chaste because it is not made up of words or talk, but of truth and action (1 Jn 3:18). It is just because it gives back what it has received. For one who loves in this way loves as he is loved. One loves, seeking in return not what is his own (1 Cor 13:5), but what is Jesus Christ's, just as he has sought not his own but our good, or rather, our very selves (2 Cor 12:14). One who says, "We trust in the Lord for he is good" (Ps 117:1) loves in this way. One who trusts in the Lord not because he is good to him but simply because he is good, truly loves God for God's sake and not for his own. One of whom it is said, "He will praise you when you do him favours" (Ps 48:19), does not love him in this way. That is the third degree of love, in which God is already loved for his own sake.

THE FOURTH DEGREE OF LOVE:
WHEN ONE LOVES ONESELF FOR THE SAKE OF GOD

27. Happy is he who has been found worthy to attain to the fourth degree, where one loves oneself only for God's sake. "O God, your justice is like the mountains of God" (Ps 35:7). That love is a mountain, and a high mountain of God. Truly, "a rich and fertile mountain" (Ps 67:16). "Who will climb the mountain of the Lord?" (Ps 23:3). "Who will give me wings like a dove, and I shall fly there and rest?" (Ps 54:7). That place was made a place of peace and it has its dwelling-place in Sion (Ps 75:3). "Alas for me, my exile has been prolonged!" (Ps 119:5). When will flesh and blood (Mt 16:17), this vessel of clay (2 Cor 4:7), this earthly dwelling (Wis 9:15) grasp this? When will it experience this kind of love, so that the mind, drunk with divine love and forgetting itself, making itself like a broken vessel (Ps 30:13), may throw itself wholly on God and, clinging to God (1 Cor 6:17), become

one with him in spirit and say, "My body and my heart have fainted, O God of my heart; God, my part in eternity" (Ps 72:26)? I should call him blessed and holy to whom it is given to experience even for a single instant something which is rare indeed in this life. To lose yourself as though you did not exist and to have no sense of yourself, to be emptied out of yourself (Phil 2:7) and almost annihilated, belongs to heavenly, not to human love.

And if indeed any mortal is rapt for a moment or is, so to speak, admitted for a moment to this union, at once the world presses itself on him (Gal 1:4), the day's wickedness troubles him, the mortal body weighs him down, bodily needs distract him, he fails because of the weakness of his corruption and—more powerfully than these—brotherly love calls him back. Alas, he is forced to come back to himself, to fall again into his affairs, and to cry out wretchedly, "Lord, I endure violence; fight back for me" (Is 38:14), and, "Unhappy man that I am, who will free me from the body of this death?" (Rom 7:24).

28. But since Scripture says that God made everything for himself (Prov 16:4; Rev 4:11), there will be a time when he will cause everything to conform to its Maker and be in harmony with him. In the meantime, we must make this our desire: that as God himself willed that everything should be for himself, so we, too, will that nothing, not even ourselves, may be or have been except for him, that is according to his will, not ours. The satisfaction of our needs will not bring us happiness, not chance delights, as does the sight of his will being fulfilled in us and in everything which concerns us. This is what we ask every day in prayer when we say, "Your will be done, on earth as it is in heaven" (Mt 6: 10). O holy and chaste love! O sweet and tender affection! O pure and sinless intention of the will—the more pure and sinless in that there is no mixture of self-will in it, the more sweet and tender in that everything it feels is divine.

To love in this way is to become like God. As a drop of water seems to disappear completely in a quantity of wine, taking the wine's flavour and colour; as red-hot iron becomes indistinguishable from the glow of fire and its own original form disappears; as air suffused with the light of the sun seems transformed into the brightness of the light, as if it were itself light rather than merely lit up; so, in those who are holy, it is necessary for human affection to dissolve in some ineffable way, and be poured into the will of God. How will God be all in all (1 Cor 15:26), if anything human remains in one? The substance remains, but in another form, with another glory, another power. When will this be? Who will see this? Who will possess it? "When shall I come and when shall I appear in God's presence?" (Ps 41:3). O Lord my God, "My heart said to you, 'My face has sought you. Lord, I will seek your face'" (Ps 26:8). Shall I see your holy temple? (Ps 26:4).

29. I think that cannot be until I do as I am bid: "Love the Lord your God with all your heart and with all your soul and with all your strength" (Mk 12:30). Then the mind will not have to think of the body. The soul will no longer have to give the body life and feeling, and its power will be set free of these ties and be strengthened by the power of God. For it is impossible to draw together all that is in you and turn towards the face of God as long as the care of the weak and miserable body demands one's attention. So it is in a spiritual and immortal body, a perfect body, beautiful and at peace and subject to the spirit in all things, that the soul hopes to attain the fourth degree of love, or rather, to be caught up in it; for it lies in God's power to give it to whom he will. It is not to be obtained by human effort. That, I say, is when one will easily reach the fourth degree: when no entanglements of the flesh hold him back and no troubles disturb him, as he hurries with great speed and eagerness to the joy of the Lord (Mt 25:21, 23).

But do we not think that the holy martyrs received this grace while they were still in their victorious bodies—at least in part? They were so moved within by the great force of their love that they were able to expose their bodies to outward torments and think nothing of them. The sensation of outward pain could do no more than whisper across the surface of their tranquility; it could not disturb it.

XI.30. But what of those who are already free of the body? We believe that they are wholly immersed in that sea of eternal light and bright eternity.

WHAT IS IMPOSSIBLE FOR SOULS BEFORE THE RESURRECTION

It is not in dispute that they want their bodies back; if they thus desire and hope for them, it is clear that they have not wholly turned from themselves, for it is evident that they are still clinging to something which is their own, even if their desires return to it only a very little. Until death is swallowed up in victory (1 Cor 15:54), and the everlasting light invades the farthest bounds of night and shines everywhere—so that heavenly glory gleams even in bodies—these souls cannot wholly remove themselves and transport themselves to God. They are still too much bound to their bodies, if not in life and feeling, certainly in natural affection. They do not wish to be complete without them, and indeed they cannot be.

And so before the restoration of their bodies souls will not lose themselves, as they will when they are perfect and reach their highest state. If they did so the soul would be complete without its body, and would cease to want it. The body is not laid down nor resumed except for the good of the soul. "Precious in God's sight is the death of his saints" (Ps 115:15). If death is precious, what must life be, and such a life as that? It need not be surprising that the glorified body should seem to confer something on the soul, for it was of use to it when it was weak and mortal. O how truly did he speak who said that all things work together for good to those who love God (Rm 8:28). Its weak body helps the soul to love God; it helps it when it is dead; it helps it when it is resurrected, first in producing fruits of patience, secondly in bringing peace, thirdly in bringing completeness. Truly the soul does not want to be perfected without that which it feels has served it well in every condition.

31. It is clear that the flesh is a good and faithful companion to the good spirit. It helps it if it is burdened, or if it does not help, it relieves it; at any rate, it is an aid and not a burden. The first

state is full of labour, but fruitful (Mt 3:8); the second is a time of waiting, but without weariness; the third is glorious. Listen to the Bridegroom in the Song holding out this threefold invitation: "Eat," he says, "and drink, friends; be intoxicated, dearest" (Sg 5:1). He calls those who are labouring in the body to eat. Those who have set aside their bodies he calls to drink. Those who have resumed their bodies, he encourages to drink their fill. These he calls "dearest," for they are filled to overflowing with love. For there is this difference between these and those others he calls "friends," not "dearest," so that those who groan because they are still labouring in the flesh are held dear for the love they have; those who are free from the weight of the flesh are more dear because they are made more ready and quicker to love. More than both are they called "dearest" (and so they are) (1 Jn 3:1) who, having received the second garment, are in their resurrected bodies in glory. They burn the more eagerly and fiercely with love for God because nothing is left to them which can trouble them or hold them back in any way.

SERMON 74
ON THE SONG OF SONGS

1. "Return," she says (Sg 2:17). It is clear that he whom she calls to come back is not present. But he was there, and not long before. Indeed, she seems to be calling him back as he is leaving. She calls him back urgently, and that is a sign of the great love she bears him and of his great loveliness. Who are these who are so wrapped up in love, these unwearying lovers who are driven on by a love which will not let them rest?

It is my task to carry out my promise and to show how these words apply to the Word and the soul. But to do so worthily—or indeed at all—I tell you that I need the help of the Word himself.

That Word ought to be expounded by someone far, far more experienced, who knows more about that holy and mysterious love than I. But I must do my duty—and what you ask. I see the danger, but I ignore it because you force me to (2 Cor 12:11). You oblige me to walk in great things and in wonders which are beyond me (Ps 130:1). O how I fear that I shall suddenly hear, "Why do you speak of my delights and let my secret out in your talk?" (cf. Ps 49:16). Hear me, then, as a man who is afraid to speak, but is not able to be silent. That fear of mine may perhaps excuse my boldness; and if you are perhaps edified, that will excuse me further—as perhaps, too, will these tears I shed.

"Return," she says. Good. He was going away; he is called back. Who will explain to me the mystery of this change? Who will give a worthy account of the Word's coming and going? Surely the Bridegroom is not inconstant? Where can he come from or go to, he who fills heaven and earth? (Jer 23:24). How can he who is spirit move from place to place? How can you say that there is any movement of any kind in God? He is unchanging.

2. Let him who is able understand (Mt 19:12). But let us go on carefully (Eph 5:15) and with pure hearts (Prov 11:20) to expound this holy and mysterious utterance (Is 23:3), and do as Scripture does in speaking of the wisdom which is hidden in the mystery (1 Cor 2:7); it speaks of God in images we can understand, in comparisons with things familiar to the senses. By putting what is precious, the unknown and unseen things of God (Rom 1:20) in common vessels (2 Cor 4:7), it brings them within the grasp of human minds.

Let us, then, follow the way of this pure Word (Ps 11:7) and say that the Word of God, God himself, the soul's Bridegroom, comes to the soul as he wishes and leaves it again (1 Cor 12:11). But let us understand that this is only how it feels to the soul; there is no movement of the Word. When the soul is aware of grace, she knows that the Word is with her. When she is not, she seeks him who is absent, and begs him to come to her, saying with the Prophet, "My face has sought you; your face, Lord, will I seek" (Ps 26:8). How could she not? For when so sweet a Bridegroom leaves her, she cannot desire or even think of any other. So she longs for him in his absence, and calls him back as he leaves. So then, the Word is recalled, and by the soul's desire, by that soul which has once tasted his sweetness (Is 26:8). Is longing not a cry? It is a loud one! Then, "the Lord has heard the desire of the poor," says Scripture (Ps 9:38). When the Word goes away, then, the one and continuous cry of the soul, its endless desire, is a repeated "Return," until he comes.

3. And now give me a soul which the Word, the Bridegroom, often visits, to which familiarity has brought courage, which hungers for what it has tasted, and whose contempt for all but him has freed from all other preoccupations. I will unhesitatingly attribute to her the voice and name of Bride, and I shall consider everything this passage says to be applicable to her. For that is how the speaker is portrayed. For she proves that she has deserved

the presence of him whom she calls back, even if not his constant presence. Otherwise she would call him, not recall him. For the word "return" is a word of recall.

And perhaps he has withdrawn so that he might the more eagerly be called back and embraced more closely. For once he made as if to go further not because he wished to do so, but because he wanted to hear them say, "Stay with us till morning, for the evening draws on" (Lk 24:28–29). And again, when the Apostles were in a boat and were labouring at the oars, he walked on the water, and seemed to be passing them by; yet he was not going by, but only testing their faith and encouraging their prayers (Mk 6:48). Then, as the Evangelist says, they were troubled and cried out, thinking he was a ghost (Mk 6:49). This holy pretence, this saving contrivance, which the incarnate Word then showed, the same Word still makes as spirit, in his spiritual way, when he wants to stir the soul which loves him. He pretends to pass by, but he goes only to be recalled, for the Word is not irrevocable. He comes and goes as he pleases, as if visiting the soul at dawn (Jb 7:18), and suddenly putting it to the test. His going is part of his purpose; his return is at his will. Both are in perfect wisdom. Only he knows his reasons.

4. Now it is agreed that his comings and goings are the alterations in the soul of which he speaks when he says, "I go away and come to you again" (Jn 14:28), and "A little while and you shall not see me and again a little while and you shall see me" (Jn 16:17). O little and little! Such a long time! Dear Lord, you say it is only for a little while that we do not see you. What you say must be true, yet it is too long, far too long. Both are true: it is a little while in terms of our deserts, and a long time in terms of our desire. You can find both in the prophet: "If he delays, wait for him; for he will come and not delay" (Hab 2:3). How can he not be long, if he delays, unless he comes more quickly than we deserve and yet more slowly than we desire? The loving soul is carried away by longing, swept away by desire; she does not think of what she deserves. She closes her eyes to his majesty and sees only the pleasure he brings; she trusts in his saving grace (Ps 11:6), and puts her faith in him. Boldly and without shame she calls the Word back, and trustingly she asks to have his

delights again. She calls him with the freedom we associate not with a Lord but with a lover. "Return, my Beloved." And she adds, "Be like a fawn or a doe on the mountains of Bethel" (Sg 2:17). We shall come back to that later.

5. Now bear with my foolishness for a little while (2 Cor 11:1). I want to tell you, for I promised, about my own experience. It is not important (2 Cor 12:1). But I do so in the hope that it may benefit you, and if it does I shall be content in my foolishness. If not, my foolishness will be plain enough.

I tell you that the Word has come even to me—I speak in my foolishness—and that he has come more than once (2 Cor 11:17). Yet however often he has come, I have never been aware of the moment of his coming. I have known he was there; I have remembered his presence afterwards; sometimes I had an inkling that he was coming. But I never felt it, nor his leaving me (Ps 120:8). And where he comes from when he enters my soul, or where he goes when he leaves it, and how he enters and leaves, I frankly do not know. As it says, "You do not know where he comes from, nor where he goes" (Jn 3:8). That is not surprising, for of him was it said, "Your footsteps will not be known" (Ps 76:20). He did not enter by the eyes, for he has no colour; nor by the ears, for he made no sound; nor by the nostrils, for he is not mingled with the air, but the mind. He did not blend into the air; he created it. His coming was not tasted by the mouth, for he was not eaten or drunk; nor could he be touched, for he is impalpable. So by what route did he enter?

Or perhaps he did not enter at all, because he did not come from outside? For he is not one of those who are without (1 Cor 5:12). Yet he does not come from within me, for he is good (Ps 51:11), and I know that there is no good in me. I have climbed up to the highest that is in me, and see! The Word is far, far above. A curious explorer, I have plumbed my own depths, and he was far deeper than that. If I looked outwards, I saw him far beyond. If I looked inward, he was further in still. And I knew that what I had read was true, that "in him we live and move and have our being" (Acts 17:28). But blessed is he in whom he has his being, who lives for him and is moved by him.

6. You ask me then how I knew he was present, he whose ways cannot be traced (Rm 11:33). He is life and power (Heb 4:12), and as soon as he enters in he stirs my sleeping soul. He moves and soothes and pierces my heart (Sg 4:9), which was as hard as stone and riddled with disease (Sir 3:27; Ezek 11:19; 36:26). And he begins to root up and destroy, to build and to plant, to water the dry places and light the dark corners (cf. Jer 1:10), to open what was closed, set what was cold on fire, to make the crooked straight and the rough places smooth (Is 40:4), so that my soul may bless the Lord and all that is within me praise his holy name (Ps 102:1).

And so when the Bridegroom, the Word, came to me, he never made any sign that he was coming; there was no sound of his voice, no glimpse of his face, no footfall. There was no movement of his by which I could know his coming; none of my senses showed me that he had flooded the depths of my being. Only by the warmth of my heart, as I said before, did I know that he was there, and I knew the power of his might because my faults were purged and my body's yearnings brought under control. And when my secret faults were revealed (Ps 18:13) and made visible, I have been amazed at the depth of his wisdom. At the slightest sign of amendment of life, I have experienced the goodness of his mercy. In the remaking and renewing of the spirit of my mind (Eph 4:23), that is, the inner man, I perceived the excellence of his glorious beauty (Ps 49:2); and when I contemplate all these things I am filled with awe of his manifold greatness (Ps 150:2).

7. But when the Word has left me, and all these things become dim and weak and cold, as though you had taken the fire from under a boiling pot, I know that he has gone. Then my soul cannot help being sorrowful until he returns, and my heart grows warm within me, and I know he is there.

With such an experience of the Word, is it surprising if I speak the words of the Bride and call him back when he absents himself, when even if I do not burn with an equal desire, I burn with a desire like hers? It will be natural to me as long as I live to speak "Return," the word of recall, to call back the Word.

As often as he slips away from me, so often will I seek him, and I shall not cease to cry, as if after someone who is leaving (Jdg 18:23), begging him, with a burning desire of the heart, to return (Ps 20:3); 1 will beseech him to give me the joy of his salvation (Ps 50:14) and return to me.

I tell you, children, nothing else gives me joy when he is not with me, who alone is the source of my joy. And I pray that he may not come empty-handed (Is 55:11) but full of grace and truth (Jn 1:14), as is his way, as he did yesterday and the day before (Gen 31:5). In this he is like a roe or a fawn (Sg 2:17), for his truth is like a roe's clear eyes and his grace like the gaiety of a fawn.

I need both: truth, so that I cannot hide from him, and grace, so that I do not wish to hide. If either were lacking, his severity might seem heavy without the one and his gaiety frivolous without the other. Truth without grace is bitter; and without the restraint of truth, devotion can be capricious, immoderate and over-confident. How many people have received grace and not benefited, because they did not accept the truth at the same time to temper it? As a result they have been too complacent in their possession of it (Is 42:1), without regard to the truth. They have not imitated the full-grown roe, but behaved like gay and giddy young fawns. So it is that they have lost the grace they wanted to enjoy by itself. It could be said, too late, to them, "Go, then, and learn what it is to serve the Lord in fear, and rejoice in him with awe" (Ps 2:11).

The holy soul once said in her abundance, "I shall never be moved" (Ps 29:7–8), when suddenly she felt the Word turn his face away from her, and she was not only moved but thrown into confusion. And so she sadly learned that she needed not only the gift of devotion but also the gravity of truth. Therefore the fullness of grace lies not in grace alone, nor in truth alone. What profit is it to know what you ought to do if you cannot do it? I have known many who were sadder for knowing the truth, for they did not have the excuse of ignorance when they knew what the Truth wanted them to do and did not do it.

9. So neither is sufficient without the other. I have not put it strongly enough. Neither is of any use without the other. How do

we know that? Scripture says, "If anyone knows what is good and does not do it, it counts as sin in him" (Jam 4:17). And again, "A servant who knows his master's will and does not do it as he should, will be soundly beaten" (Lk 12:47). That is said of truth. What is said of grace? It is written, "And after the sop Satan entered into him" (Jn 13:27). The reference is to Judas who, having received the gift of grace, did not walk in the truth with the Lord of truth (or rather, with truth as his mistress), but let the devil find a foothold in him (Eph 4:27)....

Both grace and truth are found in the Bridegroom. "Grace and truth came by Jesus Christ" (Jn 1:17), says John the Baptist. If the Lord Jesus knocks at my door with one but not the other—for he is the Word of God, the soul's Bridegroom—he will enter not as a Bridegroom but as a judge. Perish the thought! "Do not enter into judgment with your servant" (Ps 142:2). Let him enter as a bringer of peace, joyous and glad; but may he come grave and adult, too, to purify my joy and restrain my overconfidence with the stern face of truth. Let him enter as a leaping fawn and a sharp-eyed roe, to pass over my blameworthiness at a bound, and look on my faults with pity. Let him enter as one coming down from the mountains of Bethel, full of joy and radiance, descending from the Father (Jn 15:26), sweet and gentle (Ps 85:5), deigning to become the Bridegroom of the soul that seeks him and to be known as such (Lam 3:25), he who is God, blessed above all for ever (Rm 9:5).

Selected Bibliography

TEXTS

Edition used:
Bernard of Clairvaux: Selected Works. Translated by G. R. Evans. The Classics of Western Spirituality. New York: Paulist Press; London: SPCK, 1987.

Other sources:
On Loving God. Translated by Robert Walton. Kalamazoo, Mich.: Cistercian Publications, 1995.

On the Song of Songs. Translated by Kilian Walsh, O.C.S.O., and Irene M. Edmonds. 4 vols. Kalamazoo, Mich.: Cistercian Publications, 1971–80.

STUDIES

Casey, Michael. *Athirst for God: Spiritual Desire in Bernard of Clairvaux's Sermons on the Song of Songs.* Kalamazoo, Mich.: Cistercian Publications, 1987.

Gilson, Etienne. *The Mystical Theology of St. Bernard.* Translated by A. H. C. Downes. London and New York: Sheed and Ward, 1940. Reprint. Kalamazoo, Mich.: Cistercian Publications, 1990.

Leclercq, Jean. *Saint Bernard mystique.* Paris and Brussels: Desclée, 1948.

Sommerfeldt, John R., ed. *Bernardus Magister: Papers Celebrating the Nonacentenary of the Birth of Saint Bernard of Clairvaux (1090–1990).* Kalamazoo, Mich.: Cistercian Publications, 1992.

Ward, Sister Benedicta, ed. *The Influence of St. Bernard: Anglican Essays.* Oxford: SLG Press, 1976.

Francis of Assisi
(c.1182–1226)
and
Clare of Assisi
(c.1193–1253)

Francis, the most popular saint in the Roman calendar and one who accomplished a revolution both in religion and in culture, was an uneducated man from a small hill-town in northern Umbria. Until his time, Christian piety had mostly been directed at the indwelling God as revealed in Jesus' message. Jesus as a historical individual had rarely been an object of devotion, though Christians had always prayed to the *divine Word* incarnated in him. Francis turned his loving attention to Jesus' human nature, with its strictly individual features, and to the environment in which he lived and taught. That Francis started the custom of building crèches for the infant Jesus is not certain, but the custom began in his time and perfectly reflects the particular nature of his piety. He perceived the eternal Christ as a child in the house of Nazareth, as a companion of young fishermen at the lake, as a traveling preacher, and as the Man of Sorrows who died on the cross and was then physically raised from the grave.

Francis's insight into the concreteness of the incarnation transformed the view of the natural realm in which this incarnation had occurred. Each part of nature now received a divine significance—not only men and women, but also animals, the sun, the moon, the water and wind, as is seen so vividly in our first selection, the well-known "Canticle of Brother Sun." All elements of the cosmos symbolized the God who had assumed them into his own human nature. This symbolic naturalism changed the culture of the Middle Ages, evoking a new interest in the natural processes that eventually was to give rise, mostly through Francis's followers (such as Roger Bacon), to the scientific movement. In Francis's own time it created a new attitude to nature and, particularly, an aesthetic sensitivity to it. Cimabue, reputed to have painted Francis's portrait, stood at the origin of that splendid line of Tuscan artists—Giotto, Duccio, the Lorenzettis, Martini—who transferred the new sense of the physically concrete and individual to their canvases. It was also Francis's spirit that permeated the early humanist poets, beginning with Dante and continuing with Petrarch and Boccaccio. It was as if a new spring had revealed the world for the first time to our eyes and ears.

Francis formed a tradition that he hardly understood himself and that he had no intention of challenging. Thinkers, not only those of his own Franciscan order, were to draw the theological and philosophical conclusions from his simple, mystical vision. This vision was neither speculative nor esoteric; it consisted of a practical grasp of the principle of universal love for all those creatures in whose midst God had chosen to dwell. Love, of course, had been an ancient Christian theme. No one had written about it more exuberantly than Bernard. Yet even in the Cistercian's lyrical prose, the object of love remained purely divine. Bernard speaks mainly of loving God's *Word*, whereas for Francis the *humanity* of Christ stands in the very center of mystical love. In this humanity the entire world becomes sanctified.

The aspect of Christ's earthly life that had a special attraction for Francis was his poverty, preached insistently by the saint to his early followers and earning for him the appellation *Il Poverello*. After his death, varying interpretations of religious poverty led to sharp dissension and even formal division within the ranks of the friars. The preservation of Francis's own ideal was due largely to the courage and perseverance not of a friar but of a woman, Clare of Assisi, the first woman to write a religious rule. "While the friars were accepting papal indults that relaxed their practice of poverty, Clare was courageously clinging to the primitive ideals and challenging the Holy See to allow her and her sisters to maintain the charism of poverty, which she had received from Francis himself."[1]

It is uncertain just when Clare first met Francis, but this probably occurred a year or two before Holy Week of 1212, when she offered to Francis her commitment to follow his way of living the gospel. Soon other women joined her at the church of San Damiano, the first of the edifices that Francis had repaired with his own hands. There Clare remained with her "Poor Ladies" for the remaining forty-two years of her life. During this time she struggled mightily for papal approbation of the strict form of poverty that she had incorporated into her rule. When the papal bull of approval finally came, she lay on her deathbed—it is said that she kissed the document many times. Clare died two days later, August 11, 1253, and was canonized by Pope Alexander IV in 1255.

Without derogating from the historical importance of her rule, it is nevertheless above all in her letters to Agnes of Prague that we most clearly find the mystical dimension of Clare's life. Agnes, daughter of the king of Bohemia and the queen of Hungary, could have married into the royalty of Europe but chose instead to enter the monastery of the Poor Ladies at Prague. Even before her entry she had begun a correspondence with Clare, whose four surviving letters from Assisi span a period of nineteen years, the last written just months before Clare's death. Our selections, from the third and fourth letters, contain fervent exhortations for Agnes to rejoice in the calling she has received, to "taste the hidden sweetness which God Himself has reserved from the beginning for those who love Him" (Letter 3). In both of these

---

[1] Regis Armstrong, O.F.M. Cap., and Ignatius Brady, O.F.M., trans., *Francis and Clare: The Complete Works*, The Classics of Western Spirituality (New York: Paulist Press, 1982), 173.

letters Clare uses the image of a mirror, which we have already seen in Gregory of Nyssa and which became so popular among many later mystics. In her final letter Clare singles out three virtues that may be contemplated in Christ the mirror (humility, poverty, and charity) and moves at once to phrases drawn from that book of the Bible that has been especially beloved by mystical writers from the time of Origen up to the present: the Song of Songs. Quoting 1:3, Clare urges Agnes to "cry out: 'Draw me after You! We will run in the fragrance of Your perfumes,' O heavenly Spouse!"

Here, the mirror imagery gives way to bridal imagery, which has been even more favored by the Christian mystics. Clare regularly addresses Agnes as "spouse of the King of all ages," "bride of the Lamb," and "queen of the Eternal King." This spousal relationship was, of course, lived out by Agnes within the monastic enclosure at Prague, just as it was by Clare in Assisi, for there was no other option for religious women at that time. Clare was, however, fully aware that her commitment to follow the Franciscan way within the cloister involved no less a responsibility for the church as a whole than did the more active form of life led by the friars in their preaching and pastoral care. The same may be said of the Poor Clares of our own day, women who "have remained stable, unassuming beacons of the poverty and contemplation that are at the heart of the Franciscan ideal."[2]

---

[2]Ibid., 185.

FRANCIS OF ASSISI: SELECTED WRITINGS

THE CANTICLE OF BROTHER SUN

Most High, all-powerful, good Lord,
Yours are the praises, the glory, the honor, and all blessing.
To You alone, Most High, do they belong,
and no man is worthy to mention Your name.
Praised be You, my Lord, with all your creatures,
especially Sir Brother Sun,
Who is the day and through whom You give us light.
And he is beautiful and radiant with great splendor;
and bears a likeness of You, Most High One.
Praised be You, my Lord, through Sister Moon and the
stars,
in heaven You formed them clear and precious and
beautiful.
Praised be You, my Lord, through Brother Wind,
and through the air, cloudy and serene, and every kind of
weather
through which You give sustenance to Your creatures.
Praised be you, my Lord, through Sister Water,
which is very useful and humble and precious and chaste.
Praised be You, my Lord, through Brother Fire,

From *Francis and Clare: The Complete Works*, trans. Regis J. Armstrong, O.F.M. Cap., and Ignatius Brady, O.F.M., The Classics of Western Spirituality (New York: Paulist Press, 1982), 38–39, 61, 104–6. Reprinted with permission of the publisher.

119

through whom You light the night
and he is beautiful and playful and robust and strong.
Praised be You, my Lord, through our Sister Mother Earth,
who sustains and governs us,
and who produces varied fruits with colored flowers and
    herbs.
Praised be You, my Lord, through those who give pardon
    for Your love
and bear infirmity and tribulation.
Blessed are those who endure in peace
for by You, Most High, they shall be crowned.
Praised be You, my Lord, through our Sister Bodily Death,
from whom no living man can escape.
Woe to those who die in mortal sin.
Blessed are those whom death will find in Your most holy
    will,
for the second death shall do them no harm.
Praise and bless my Lord and give Him thanks
and serve Him with great humility.

A PRAYER OF ST. FRANCIS

Almighty, eternal, just, and merciful God,
grant us in our misery [the grace]
    to do for You alone
        what we know You want us to do,
        and always
    to desire what pleases You.
Thus,
    inwardly cleansed,
    interiorly enlightened,
    and inflamed by the fire of the Holy Spirit,
may we be able to follow
    in the footprints of Your beloved Son,
    our Lord Jesus Christ.

And,
by Your grace alone,
may we make our way to You,
Most High,
Who live and rule
in perfect Trinity and simple Unity,
and are glorified
God all-powerful
forever and ever. Amen.

THE PRAYER INSPIRED BY THE OUR FATHER

O OUR most holy FATHER,
Our Creator, Redeemer, Consoler, and Savior
WHO ARE IN HEAVEN:
In the angels and in the saints,
Enlightening them to love, because You, Lord, are light
Inflaming them to love, because you, Lord, are love
Dwelling [in them] and filling them with happiness,
Because You, Lord, are the Supreme Good, the Eternal
Good
from Whom comes all good
without Whom there is no good.
HALLOWED BE YOUR NAME:
May our knowledge of You become ever clearer
That we may know the breadth of Your blessings
the length of Your promises
the height of Your majesty
the depth of Your judgments
YOUR KINGDOM COME:
So that You may rule in us through Your grace
and enable us to come to Your kingdom
where there is an unclouded vision of You
a perfect love of You
a blessed companionship with You
an eternal enjoyment of You

YOUR WILL BE DONE ON EARTH AS IT IS IN HEAVEN:
That we may love You with our whole heart by always
    thinking of You
    with our whole soul by always desiring You
    with our whole mind by directing all our intentions to
        You and by seeking Your glory in everything
    and with our whole strength by spending all our
        energies and affections
        of soul and body
        in the service of Your love
        and of nothing else
and may we love our neighbors as ourselves
    by drawing them all with our whole strength to Your love
    by rejoicing in the good fortunes of others as well as our
        own
    and by sympathizing with the misfortunes of others
    and by giving offense to no one
GIVE US THIS DAY:
In memory and understanding and reverence
    of the love which [our Lord Jesus Christ] had for us
    and of those things which He said and did and suffered
        for us
OUR DAILY BREAD:
Your own Beloved Son, our Lord Jesus Christ
AND FORGIVE US OUR TRESPASSES:
Through Your ineffable mercy
through the power of the Passion of Your Beloved Son
    together with the merits and intercession of the Blessed
        Virgin Mary
        and all Your chosen ones
AS WE FORGIVE THOSE WHO TRESPASS AGAINST US:
And whatever we do not forgive perfectly,
do you, Lord, enable us to forgive to the full
so that we may truly love [our] enemies
and fervently intercede for them before You
returning no one evil for evil

and striving to help everyone in You
AND LEAD US NOT INTO TEMPTATION
Hidden or obvious
Sudden or persistent
BUT DELIVER US FROM EVIL
Past, present and to come.
Glory to the Father and to the Son and to the Holy Spirit
As it was in the beginning, is now, and will be forever. Amen.

CLARE OF ASSISI: LETTERS TO BLESSED AGNES OF PRAGUE

THE THIRD LETTER

To the lady [who is] most respected in Christ and the sister loved more than all [other] human beings, Agnes, sister of the illustrious king of Bohemia, but now the sister and spouse of the Most High King of Heaven: Clare, the most lowly and unworthy handmaid of Christ and servant of the Poor Ladies: the joys of redemption in *the Author of salvation* (Heb 2:10) and every good thing that can be desired.

I am filled with such joys at your well-being, happiness, and marvelous progress through which, I understand, you have advanced in the course you have undertaken to win the prize of heaven (cf. Phil 3:14). And I sigh with such happiness in the Lord because I know you see that you make up most wonderfully what is lacking both in me and in the other sisters in following the footprints of the poor and humble Jesus Christ.

I can rejoice truly—and no one can rob me of such joy— because I now possess what under heaven I have desired. For I see that, helped by a special gift of wisdom from the mouth of God Himself and in an awe-inspiring and unexpected way, you have brought to ruin the subtleties of our crafty enemy and the pride that destroys human nature and the vanity that infatuates human hearts.

From *Francis and Clare: The Complete Works,* trans. Regis J. Armstrong, O.F.M. Cap., and Ignatius Brady, O.F.M., The Classics of Western Spirituality (New York: Paulist Press, 1982), 199–201, 203–6. Reprinted with permission of the publisher.

I see, too, that by humility, the virtue of faith, and the strong arms of poverty, you have taken hold of that *incomparable treasure hidden in the field* of the world and in the hearts of men (cf. Mt 13:44), with which you have purchased that field of Him by Whom all things have been made from nothing. And, to use the words of the Apostle himself in their proper sense, I consider you a *co-worker of God* Himself (cf. 1 Cor 3:9; Rm 16:3) and a support of the weak members of His ineffable Body. Who is there, then, who would not encourage me to rejoice over such marvelous joys?

Therefore, dearly beloved, may you too *always rejoice in the Lord* (Phil 4:4). And may neither bitterness nor a cloud [of sadness] overwhelm you, O dearly beloved Lady in Christ, joy of the angels and crown of your sisters!

Place your mind before the mirror of eternity!
Place your soul in the *brilliance of glory!*
Place your heart in *the figure of the* divine *substance!*
And *transform* your whole being *into the image* of the
    Godhead Itself through contemplation
So that you too may feel what His friends feel
    as they taste *the hidden sweetness*
    which God Himself has reserved
    from the beginning
    for those who love Him

Since you have cast aside all [those] things which, in this deceitful and turbulent world, ensnare their blind lovers, love Him totally Who gave himself totally for Your love. His beauty the sun and moon admire; and of His gifts there is no limit in abundance, preciousness, and magnitude. I am speaking of Him Who is the Son of the Most High, Whom the Virgin brought to birth and remained a virgin after his birth. Cling to His most sweet Mother who carried a Son Whom the heavens could not contain; and yet she carried Him in the little enclosure of her holy womb and held Him on her virginal lap.

Who would not dread the treacheries of the enemy of mankind, who, through the arrogance of momentary and deceptive glories, attempts to reduce to nothing that which is greater than heaven itself? Indeed, is it not clear that the soul of the faithful person, the most worthy of all creatures because of the grace of God, is greater than heaven itself? For the heavens with the rest of creation cannot contain their Creator. Only the faithful soul is His dwelling place and [His] throne, and this [is possible] only through the charity which the wicked do not have. [He Who is] the Truth has said: *Whoever loves me will be loved by My Father, and I too shall love him, and We shall come to him and make our dwelling place with him* (Jn 14:21).

Therefore, as the glorious Virgin of virgins carried [Christ] materially in her body, you, too, by *following in His footprints* (cf. 1 Pet 2:21), especially [those] of poverty and humility, can, without any doubt, always carry Him spiritually in your chaste and virginal body. And you will hold Him by Whom you and *all things are held together* (cf. Wis 1:7; Col 1:17), [thus] possessing that which, in comparison with the other transitory possessions of this world, you will possess more securely....

THE FOURTH LETTER

To her who is the half of her soul and the special shrine of her heart's deepest love, to the illustrious Queen and Bride of the Lamb, the eternal King: to the Lady Agnes, her most dear mother, and, of all the others, her favorite daughter: Clare, an unworthy servant of Christ and *a useless* handmaid (Lk 17:10) of His handmaids in the monastery of San Damiano of Assisi: health and [a prayer] that she may sing *a new song* with the other most holy virgins before the throne of God and of the Lamb and *follow the lamb wherever He may go* (cf. Rev 14:3–4).

O mother and daughter, spouse of the King of all ages, if I have not written to you as often as your soul and mine as well desire and long for, do not wonder or think that the fire of love for you glows less sweetly in the heart of your mother. No, this is the difficulty: the lack of messengers and the obvious dangers of the roads. Now, however, as I write to your love, I rejoice and exult with you in *the joy of the Spirit* (1 Thess 1:6), O bride of Christ, because, since you have totally abandoned the vanities of this world, like another most holy virgin, Saint Agnes, you have been marvelously espoused to *the spotless lamb Who takes away the sins of the world* (1 Pt 1:19; Jn 1:29).

> Happy, indeed, is she to whom it is given to share this sacred banquet,
> to cling with all her heart to Him
> > Whose beauty all the heavenly hosts admire unceasingly,
> > Whose love inflames our love,
> > Whose contemplation is our refreshment,
> > Whose graciousness is our joy,
> > Whose gentleness fills us to overflowing,
> > Whose remembrance brings a gentle light,
> > Whose fragrance will revive the dead,
> > Whose glorious vision will be the happiness of all the citizens of the heavenly Jerusalem.

Inasmuch as this vision is *the splendor of eternal glory* (Heb 1:3), *the brilliance of eternal light and the mirror without blemish* (Wis 7:26), look upon that mirror each day, O queen and spouse of Jesus Christ, and continually study your face within it, so that you may adorn yourself within and without with beautiful robes and cover yourself with the flowers and garments of all the virtues, as becomes the daughter and most chaste bride of the Most High King. Indeed, blessed poverty, holy humility, and ineffable charity are reflected in that mirror, as, with the grace of God, you can contemplate them throughout the entire mirror.

Look at the parameters of this mirror, that is, the poverty of Him Who was placed in a manger and wrapped in swaddling clothes. O marvelous humility, O astonishing poverty! The King of the angels, the Lord of heaven and earth, is laid in a manger! Then, at the surface of the mirror, dwell on the holy humility, the blessed poverty, the untold labors and burdens which He endured for the redemption of all mankind. Then, in the depths of this same mirror, contemplate the ineffable charity which led Him to suffer on the wood of the Cross and die thereon the most shameful kind of death. Therefore, that Mirror, suspended on the wood of the Cross, urged those who passed by to consider, saying: *"All you who pass by the way, look and see if there is any suffering like My suffering!"* (Lam

1:12). Let us answer Him with one voice and spirit, as He said: *Remembering this over and over leaves my soul downcast within me* (Lam 3:20)! From this moment, then, O queen of our heavenly King, let yourself be inflamed more strongly with the fervor of charity!

[As you] contemplate further His ineffable delights, eternal riches and honors, and sigh for them in the great desire and love of your heart, may you cry out:

> *Draw me after You!*
> *We will run in the fragrance of Your perfumes,*
>   O heavenly Spouse!
> I will run and not tire,
>   until *You bring me into the wine-cellar*
>   until Your *left hand is under my head*
>   and Your *right hand will embrace me* happily
>   [and] *You will kiss me with the happiest kiss of Your*
>   *mouth*

In this contemplation, may you remember your poor little mother, knowing that I have inscribed the happy memory of you indelibly on the tablets of my heart, holding you dearer than all the others.

What more can I say? Let the tongue of the flesh be silent when I seek to express my love for you; and let the tongue of the Spirit speak, because the love that I have for you, O blessed daughter, can never be fully expressed by the tongue of the flesh, and even what I have written is an inadequate expression.

I beg you to receive my words with kindness and devotion, seeing in them at least the motherly affection which in the fire of charity I feel daily toward you and your daughters, to whom I warmly commend myself and my daughters in Christ. On their part, these very daughters of mine, especially the most prudent virgin Agnes, our [blood-]sister, recommend themselves in the Lord to you and your daughters.

Farewell, my dearest daughter, to you and to your daughters until we meet at the throne *of the glory of the great God* (Tit 2:13), and desire [this] for us....

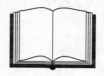

Selected Bibliography

TEXTS

Edition used:
Francis and Clare: The Complete Works. Translated by Regis J. Armstrong, O.F.M. Cap., and Ignatius C. Brady, O.F.M. The Classics of Western Spirituality. New York: Paulist Press; London: SPCK, 1982.

Other sources:
Clare of Assisi: Early Documents. Edited and translated by Regis J. Armstrong. New York: Paulist Press, 1988.

St. Francis of Assisi: Writings and Early Biographies. English Omnibus of Sources for the Life of St. Francis. Edited by Marion A. Habig. Chicago: Franciscan Herald Press, 1983.

STUDIES

Bartoli, Marco. *Clare of Assisi.* Translated by Sister Frances Teresa. Quincy, Ill.: Franciscan Press, 1993.

Johnson, Timothy J. "Visual Imagery and Contemplation in Clare of Assisi's 'Letters to Agnes of Prague.'" *Mystics Quarterly* 19 (1993): 161–72.

Manselli, Raoul. *St. Francis of Assisi.* Translated by Paul Duggan. Chicago: Franciscan Herald Press, 1988.

McGinn, Bernard. "Was St. Francis a Mystic?" In *Doors of Understanding: Conversations on Global Spirituality in Honor of Ewert Cousins,* ed. Steven Chase, 145–74. Quincy, Ill.: Franciscan Press, 1997.

Peterson, Ingrid. "Clare of Assisi's Mysticism of the Poor Cruci-fied." *Studies in Spirituality* 4 (1994): 51–78.

Pozzi, Giovanni. "The Canticle of Brother Sun: From Grammar to Prayer." *Greyfriars Review* 4 (1990): 1–21.

Schlosser, Marianne. "Mother, Sister, Bride: The Spirituality of St. Clare." *Greyfriars Review* 5 (1991): 233–49.

Schmucki, Octavian. "The Mysticism of St. Francis in the Light of His Writings." *Greyfriars Review* 3 (1989): 241–66.

Bonaventure
(c.1217–74)

Offering his readers a rare glimpse into his own past, Bonaventure writes in the prologue to the longer of his two lives of St. Francis:

When I was a boy, as I still vividly remember, I was snatched from the jaws of death by his [Francis's] invocation and merits....I recognize that God saved my life through him, and I realize that I have experienced his power in my very person. This, then, is my principal reason for undertaking this task, that I may gather together the accounts of his virtues...so that they may not be lost when those who lived with this servant of God die.[1]

Besides praising the power of Francis's intercession, Bonaventure also, and even more insistently, extolled the saint as a living example of how to adhere totally to God through a contemplative way of life. What the Poor Man of Assisi lived, Bonaventure the theologian reflected upon with intellectual acumen and fervent devotion, leaving us a doctrine that in the opinion of the great medievalist Etienne Gilson, "marks...the culminating point of Christian mysticism and constitutes the completest synthesis it has ever achieved."[2]

---

[1]Bonaventure, *The Life of St. Francis*, Prologue, in *Bonaventure: The Soul's Journey into God; The Tree of Life; The Life of St. Francis*, trans. Ewert Cousins (New York: Paulist Press; London, SPCK, 1978), 182–83.

[2]Etienne Gilson, *The Philosophy of St. Bonaventure*, trans. Dom Illtyd Trethowan and F. J. Sheed (London and New York: Sheed and Ward, 1938), 494.

Bonaventure was born near Viterbo, probably in 1217. After joining the Roman province of the Franciscans as a young man, he was sent to Paris to complete his education. There he studied under the English Franciscan master Alexander of Hales and began a lifelong friendship with Thomas Aquinas, who joined Bonaventure in helping defend the mendicant ideal of the Franciscans and Dominicans against the attacks of secular masters. Bonaventure himself began teaching in Paris in 1248 and continued doing so until 1257, when he was elected minister general of the entire Franciscan Order, a position he held for the next sixteen years. Much of his work during this period was focused on the delicate task of trying to reconcile sharply divergent factions within the Order, but he also found time to write works of spiritual theology that have become classics, including *The Soul's Journey into God* (whose final two chapters were chosen for this anthology), *The Tree of Life* (meditations on the life of Christ developed within a theological framework), and *The Triple Way* (a systematic treatment of the stages of the spiritual life). He was made a cardinal in 1273 and died the following year at the Council of Lyons. He was canonized in 1482 and declared a doctor of the church in 1588.

The new devotion of twelfth-century humanism eventually came to rest in Francis, and it was Bonaventure who assigned this new spirituality of creation its place in a traditional mystical theology. One of the best ways to illustrate the extent of this newness is to contrast Bonaventure with the greatest medieval mystical writer before him—Bernard of Clairvaux. For the Cistercian, meditation on the humanity of Christ and on his passion is a profitable but still rather imperfect kind of devotion, belonging to the realm of *amor carnalis* rather than that of *amor rationalis* or *amor spiritualis*. Not surprisingly, meditation on other aspects of the sensible world has even less place in Bernard's mystical theology. His early biographers make much of the fact that Bernard's mental asceticism was such that whatever sensations were produced by exterior stimuli seemed to leave no trace in his memory; it was said that he did not even know the structure of the oratory to which he went every day to pray. In Gilson's striking phrase, "the walls of his mysticism are as bare as the walls of a Cistercian chapel."[3]

Bonaventure's mysticism is of a very different order, in part because of the influence of the mystical treatises of Hugh and Richard of St. Victor, to whom he owed so much, but even more because of the powerful example of his spiritual father, Francis. How very unlike Bernard, for example, is Bonaventure in the following passage from *The Life of St. Francis:*

> Who can describe the fervent charity which burned within Francis, the friend of the Bridegroom?...Aroused by all things to the love of God, he rejoiced in all the works of the Lord's hands, and from these joy-producing manifestations he rose to their life-giving principle and cause. In beautiful things he saw Beauty itself, and through his vestiges imprinted on creation he followed his Beloved everywhere, making from all things a ladder by which he could climb up and embrace him who is utterly desirable.[4]

Equally great is the contrast with Bernard as regards loving contemplation of the crucifixion of Christ. For Bonaventure, such contemplation is not some beginning step to be later transcended through *amor spiritualis* but is a distinguishing mark of his entire mystical theology. As he writes in the prologue to *The Soul's Journey into God* (where he is commenting on the vision Francis saw on the occasion of receiving the stigmata):

> The six wings of the seraph can rightly be taken to symbolize the six levels of illumination by which, as if by six steps or stages, the soul can pass over to peace through ecstatic elevations of Christian wisdom. There is no other path but through the burning love of the Crucified.[5]

---

[3]Ibid., 488.
[4]Bonaventure, *The Life of St. Francis,* 9.1, in Cousins, *Bonaventure,* 262–63.
[5]Bonaventure, *The Soul's Journey into God,* Prologue, in Cousins, Bonaventure, 54. Henceforth cited in the text by chapter and section number.

The prevalence of such passages and the prominence they give to Christ crucified in the description of mystical union distinguish the mysticism of Bonaventure from that of all his predecessors.[6]

As an aid to understanding the two chapters we have selected from *The Soul's Journey into God* for this anthology, something should be said about the overall structure of the treatise. The first six of its seven chapters deal with six steps or degrees of ascent to mystical union with God: in the first two the mind turns outside itself to find God through his vestiges in the universe (chap. 1) and in the world of the senses (chap. 2); in the next two the mind turns within itself to contemplate God both through his image imprinted on our natural powers of memory, understanding, and will (chap. 3) and in this image reformed and purified by the theological virtues of faith, hope, and charity (chap. 4); and in the last two the mind rises above itself to consider the divine Unity through its primary name, "being" (chap. 5), and also the blessed Trinity through its name, "the good" (chap. 6). Having here reached "the perfection of its illuminations," the mind is drawn on to mystical ecstasy, the subject of chapter seven.

Bonaventure begins his sixth chapter by writing that the good itself is the principal foundation for contemplating the emanations of the Trinity, since (as Dionysius holds) the good is diffusive of itself. As Bonaventure proceeds with his reflections, it might at times seem as though he is claiming to prove the Trinity by natural reason, but in fact he is only offering what might be called proofs of congruency. He next expresses wonder not only at the coincidence of opposites found among the essential attributes and properties of the triune God but also at the union of opposites in the person of Jesus Christ:

> The eternal is joined with temporal man,
> born of the Virgin in the fulness of time,
> the most simple with the most composite,

---

[6]On this point, see Philotheus Boehner, O.F.M., Introduction to *Ininerarium Mentis in Deum*, vol. 2 of *Works of Saint Bonaventure* (St. Bonaventure, N.Y.: Franciscan Institute, 1956), 16.

the most actual with the one who suffered supremely and
  died,
the most perfect and immense with the lowly,
the supreme and all-inclusive one
with a composite individual distinct from others,
that is, the man Jesus Christ. (6.5)

Here the power of the intellect is at its limit. Just as God
rested after the sixth day of creation, so now there is nothing
remaining for the mind except "the day of rest on which through
mystical ecstasy the mind's discernment comes to rest from all the
work which it has done" (6.7). This ecstasy is described in terms
borrowed explicitly and at length from *The Mystical Theology* of
Pseudo-Dionysius; it occurs in darkness, and consists in the
embrace of a Good that transcends thought and would be altogether unattainable were it not for the grace of Christ, who will
bestow this gift upon "him who is enflamed in his very marrow by
the fire of the Holy Spirit whom Christ sent into the world" (7.4).
"This fire," he says some lines later, "is God...and Christ enkindles it in the heat of his burning passion....Let us, then, die and
enter into the darkness....With Christ crucified, let us pass out of
this world to the Father" (7.6).

From this brief overview of Bonaventure's mysticism, it
should be clear that he, perhaps more than any other mystic in this
anthology, resists any kind of overly neat categorization. Image
mysticism, apophatic mysticism, trinitarian mysticism, love mysticism—all four are very prominent in *The Soul's Journey into God*.
This, however, is in no sense a problem, but rather a way of cor-
roborating Gilson's claim that Bonaventure provides the most
complete synthesis that Christian mysticism has ever achieved.

THE SOUL'S JOURNEY INTO GOD

Chapter Six

ON CONTEMPLATING THE MOST HOLY TRINITY IN ITS NAME WHICH IS GOOD

1. After considering the essential attributes of God,
the eye of our intelligence
should be raised to look upon
the most blessed Trinity,
so that the second Cherub
may be placed alongside the first.
Now just as being itself is the root principle
of viewing the essential attributes,
and the name
Through which the others become known,
so the good itself is
the principal foundation
for contemplating the emanations.

2. See, then, and observe
that the highest good is without qualification
that than which no greater can be thought.
And it is such
that it cannot rightly be thought

From *Bonaventure: The Soul's Journey into God; The Tree of Life; The Life of St. Francis*,
trans. Ewert Cousins, The Classics of Western Spirituality (New York: Paulist Press, 1978),
102–16. Reprinted with permission of the publisher.

not to be,
since to be is in all ways better than not to be;[1]
it is such
that it cannot rightly be thought of unless it be thought of
as three and one.
For good is said to be
self-diffusive;[2]
therefore the highest good must be
most self-diffusive.
But the greatest self-diffusion cannot exist unless it is
actual and intrinsic,
substantial and hypostatic,
natural and voluntary,
free and necessary,
lacking nothing and perfect.
Therefore, unless there were eternally in the highest good
a production which is actual and consubstantial,
and a hypostasis as noble as the producer,
as is the case in a producing by way of generation and spiration,
so that it is from an eternal principle eternally coproducing
so that there would be a beloved
and a cobeloved,
the one generated and the other spirated,
and this is
the Father and the Son and the Holy Spirit—
unless these were present,
it would by no means be the highest good
because it would not diffuse itself in the highest degree.
For the diffusion in time in creation
is no more than a center
or point
in relation to the immensity of the divine goodness.
Hence another diffusion can be conceived
greater than this,

[1]Cf. Anselm, *Proslogion*, c. 2–5, 15.
[2]Cf. Dionysius, *De caelesti hierarchia*, IV, 1; *De divinis nominibus*, IV, 1, 20.

namely, one in which
the one diffusing communicates to the other
his entire substance and nature.
Therefore it would not be the highest good
if it could lack this,
either in reality or in thought.
If, therefore, you can behold with your mind's eye
the purity of goodness,
which is the pure act
of a principle loving in charity
with a love
that is both free and due and a mixture of both,
which is the fullest diffusion
by way of nature and will,
which is a diffusion by way of the Word,
in which all things are said,
and by way of the Gift, in which other gifts are given,
then you can see
that through the highest communicability of the good,
there must be
a Trinity of the Father and the Son and the Holy Spirit.
From supreme goodness,
it is necessary that there be in the Persons
supreme communicability;
from supreme communicability, supreme consubstantiality;
from supreme consubstantiality, supreme configurability;
and from these supreme coequalilty
and hence supreme coeternity;
finally, from all of the above, supreme mutual intimacy,
by which one is necessarily in the other
by supreme interpenetration
and one acts with the other
in absolute lack of division
of the substance, power and operation
of the most blessed Trinity itself.

3. But when you contemplate these things,
do not think
that you comprehend the incomprehensible.
For you still have something else to consider
in these six properties
which strongly leads our mind's eye
to amazement and admiration.
For here is
supreme communicability with individuality of persons,
supreme consubstantiality with plurality of hypostases,
supreme configurability with distinct personality,
supreme coequality with degree,
supreme coeternity with emanation,
supreme mutual intimacy with mission.
Who would not be lifted up in admiration
at the sight of such marvels?
But we understand with complete certitude
that all these things are in the most blessed Trinity
if we lift up our eyes
to the superexcellent goodness.
For if there is here
supreme communication and true diffusion,
there is also here
true origin and true distinction;
and because the whole is communicated and not merely part,
whatever is possessed is given,
and given completely.
Therefore, the one emanating and the one producing
are distinguished by their properties
and are one in essence.
Since, then, they are distinguished by their properties,
they have
personal properties and plurality of hypostases
and emanation of origin
and order, not of posteriority but of origin,
and a sending forth,

not involving a change of place but free inspiration
by reason of the producer's authority
which the sender has in relation to the one sent.
Moreover, because they are one in substance,
there must be unity
in essence, form, dignity, eternity, existence and unlimitedness.
Therefore, when you consider these in themselves one by one,
you have matter for contemplating the truth;
when you compare them with one another,
you have reason to be lifted up to the highest wonder.
Therefore, that your mind may ascend
through wonder to wondering contemplation,
these should be considered together.

4. For the Cherubim who faced each other
also signify this.
the fact that they faced each other,
With their faces turned toward the Mercy Seat,[3]
is not without a mystical meaning,
so that what Our Lord said in John
might be verified:
*This is eternal life,
that they may know you, the only true God,
and Jesus Christ, whom you have sent.*[4]
For we should wonder
not only at the essential and personal properties of God
in themselves
but also in comparison with
the superwonderful union of God and man
in the unity of the Person of Christ.

5. For if you are the Cherub
contemplating God's essential attributes,
and if you are amazed

---

[3]Exod 25:20.
[4]John 17:3.

because the divine Being is both
first and last,
eternal and most present,
utterly simple and the greatest or boundless,
totally present everywhere and nowhere contained,
most actual and never moved,
most perfect and having nothing superfluous or lacking,
and yet immense and infinite without bounds,
supremely one and yet all-inclusive,
containing all things in himself,
being all power, all truth, all goodness—
if you are this Cherub,
look at the Mercy Seat and wonder
that in him there is joined
the First Principle with the last,
God with man, who was formed on the sixth day;[5]
the eternal is joined with temporal man,
born of the Virgin in the fullness of time,
the most simple with the most composite,
the most actual with the one who suffered supremely and died,
the most perfect and immense with the lowly,
the supreme and all-inclusive one
with a composite individual distinct from others,
that is, the man Jesus Christ.

6. But if you are the other Cherub
contemplating the properties of the Persons,
and you are amazed that communicability exists with
individuality,
consubstantiality with plurality,
configurability with personality,
coequality with order,
coeternity with production,
mutual intimacy with sending forth,
because the Son is sent by the Father

---

[5] Cf. Gen 1:26.

and the Holy Spirit by both,
who nevertheless is with them and never departs from them—
if you are this Cherub,
look at the Mercy Seat and wonder
that in Christ
personal union exists
with a trinity of substances and a duality of natures;
that complete agreement exists
with a plurality of wills;
that mutual predication of God and man exists
with a plurality of properties;
that coadoration exists
with a plurality of excellence,
that coexaltation above all things exists
with a plurality of dignity;
That codomination exists
with a plurality of powers.

7. In this consideration is
the perfection of the mind's illumination
when, as if on the sixth day of creation,
it sees man made to the image of God.[6]
For if an image is an expressed likeness,
when our mind contemplates
in Christ the Son of God,
who is the image of the invisible God by nature,
our humanity
so wonderfully exalted, so ineffably united,
when at the same time it sees united
the first and the last,
the highest and the lowest,
the circumference and the center,
the Alpha and the Omega,[7]
the caused and the cause,

[6]Ibid.
[7]Apoc 1:8, 21:6, 22:13.

the Creator and the creature,
that is, *the book written within and without,*[8]
it now reaches something perfect.
It reaches the perfection of its illuminations
on the sixth stage,
as if with God on the sixth day of creation;
nor does anything more remain
except the day of rest on which
through mystical ecstasy
the mind's discernment comes to rest
from all the work which it has done.[9]

[8] Apoc 5:1; Ezech 2:9.
[9] Gen 2:2.

Chapter Seven

ON SPIRITUAL AND MYSTICAL ECSTASY
IN WHICH REST IS GIVEN TO OUR INTELLECT
WHEN THROUGH ECSTASY OUR AFFECTION
PASSES OVER ENTIRELY INTO GOD

1. We have, therefore, passed through
these six considerations.
They are like
the six steps of the true Solomon's throne,
by which we arrive
at peace,
where the true man of peace
rests in a peaceful mind
as in the interior Jerusalem.

They are also like
the six wings of the Seraph[1]
by which the mind of the true contemplative
can be borne aloft,
filled with illumination of heavenly wisdom.
They are also like the first six days,
in which the mind has been trained so that it may reach
the Sabbath of rest.

After our mind has beheld God
outside itself
through his vestiges and in his vestiges,
within itself
through his image and in his image,
and above itself
through the similitude of the divine Light shining above us
and in the Light itself,

---

[1] Although the critical text has "Cherub," we have read "Seraph," since Bonaventure is clearly referring to the six-winged Seraph of Francis's vision (cf. prologue, 2–3), which serves as the symbolic matrix of the entire treatise.

insofar as this is possible in our state as wayfarers
and through the exercise of our mind,
when finally in the sixth stage
our mind reaches that point
where it contemplates
in the First and Supreme Principle
and in the *mediator of God and men*,[2]
Jesus Christ,
those things whose likeness can in no way be found
in creatures
and which surpass all penetration
by the human intellect,
it now remains for our mind,
by contemplating these things,
to transcend and pass over not only this sense world
but even itself.
In this passing over,
Christ is the *way and the door*;[3]
Christ is the ladder and the vehicle,
like the Mercy Seat placed above the ark of God[4]
and the *mystery hidden from eternity*.[5]

2. Whoever turns his face fully to the Mercy Seat
and with faith, hope and love,
devotion, admiration, exultation,
appreciation, praise and joy
beholds him hanging upon the cross,
such a one makes the Pasch, that is, the Passover,
with Christ.
By the staff of the cross
he passes over the Red Sea,[6]
going from Egypt into the desert,

---

[2]1 Tim 2:5.
[3]Cf. John 14:6, 10:7.
[4]Cf. Exod 25:21.
[5]Eph 3:9.
[6]Cf. Exod 12:11.

145

where he will taste the *hidden manna;*[7]
and with Christ
he rests in the tomb,
as if dead to the outer world,
but experiencing,
as far as is possible in this wayfarer's state,
what was said on the cross
to the thief who adhered to Christ:
Today you shall be with me in paradise.[8]

3. This was shown also
to blessed Francis,
when in ecstatic contemplation
on the height of the mountain—
where I thought out these things I have written—
there appeared to him
a six-winged Seraph fastened to a cross,
as I and several others heard
in that very place
from his companion who was with him then.[9]
There he passed over into God in ecstatic contemplation
and became an example of perfect contemplation
as he had previously been of action,
like another Jacob and Israel,[10]
so that through him,
more by example than by word,
God might invite all truly spiritual men
to this kind of passing over
and spiritual ecstasy.

4. In this passing over,
if it is to be perfect,
all intellectual activities must be left behind

---

[7]Apoc 2:17.
[8]Luke 23:43.
[9]Cf. Bonaventure's *Life of St. Francis*, XIII,3.
[10]Cf. Gen 35:10.

and the height of our affection
must be totally transferred and transformed
into God.
this, however, is mystical and most secret,
which *no one knows*
except him *who receives it,*[11]
no one receives
except him who desires it,
and no one desires except him
who is inflamed in his very marrow by the fire of the Holy Spirit
whom Christ sent into the world.[12]
And therefore the Apostle says that
this mystical wisdom is revealed
by the Holy Spirit.[13]

5. Since, therefore, in this regard
nature can do nothing
and effort can do but little,
little importance should be given to inquiry,
but much to unction;
little importance should be given to the tongue,
but much to inner joy;
little importance should be given to words and to writing,
but all to the gift of God,
that is, the Holy Spirit;
little or no importance should be given to creation,
but all to the creative essence,
the Father, Son and Holy Spirit,
saying with Dionysius
to God the Trinity:
"Trinity,
superessential, superdivine and supereminent

---

[11]Apoc 2:17.
[12]Cf. Luke 12:49.
[13]Cf. 1 Cor 2:10ff.

overseer of the divine wisdom of Christians,
direct us into
the super-unknown, superluminous and most sublime
summit
of mystical communication.
There
new, absolute and unchangeable mysteries of theology
are hidden
in the superluminous darkness
of a silence
teaching secretly in the utmost obscurity
which is supermanifest—
a darkness which is super-resplendent
and in which everything shines forth
and which fills to overflowing
invisible intellects
with the splendors of invisible goods
that surpass all good."[14]
This is said to God.
But to the friend to whom these words were written,
let us say with Dionysius:
"But you, my friend,
concerning mystical visions,
with your journey more firmly determined,
leave behind
your senses and intellectual activities,
sensible and invisible things,
all nonbeing and being;
and in this state of unknowing
be restored,
insofar as is possible,
to unity with him
who is above all essence and knowledge.
For transcending yourself and all things,
by the immeasurable and absolute ecstasy of a pure mind,

---

[14]Dionysius, *De mystica theologia*, I, 1.

leaving behind all things
and freed from all things,
you will ascend
to the superessential ray
of the divine darkness."[15]

6. But if you wish to know how these things come about,
Ask grace not instruction,
desire not understanding,
the groaning of prayer not diligent reading,
the Spouse not the teacher,
God not man,
darkness not clarity,
not light but the fire
that totally inflames and carries us into God
by ecstatic unctions and burning affections.
This fire is God,
and *his furnace is in Jerusalem;*[16]
and Christ enkindles it
in the heat of his burning passion,
which only he truly perceives who says:
My soul chooses hanging and my bones death.[17]
Whoever loves this death
can see God
because it is true beyond doubt that
man will not see me and live.[18]
Let us, then, die
and enter into the darkness;
let us impose silence
upon our cares, our desires and our imaginings.
With Christ crucified
let us pass *out of this world to the Father*[19]

[15]Ibid.
[16]Isa 31:9.
[17]Job 7:15.
[18]Exod 33:20.
[19]John 13:1.

so that when the Father is shown to us,
we may say with Philip:
It is enough for us.[20]
Let us hear with Paul:
My grace is sufficient for you.[21]
Let us rejoice with David saying:
My flesh and my heart have grown faint;
You are the God of my heart,
and the God that is my portion forever.
Blessed be the Lord forever
and all the people will say:
Let it be; let it be.
Amen.[22]

Here Ends the Soul's Journey into God.

---

[20]John 14:8.
[21] 2 Cor 12:9.
[22]Ps 72:26, 105:48.

Selected Bibliography

TEXTS

Edition used:
Bonaventure: The Soul's Journey into God; The Tree of Life; The Life of St. Francis. Translated by Ewert Cousins. The Classics of Western Spirituality. New York: Paulist Press; London, SPCK, 1978.

Other sources:
Itinerarium Mentis in Deum. Edited and translated by Philotheus Boehner, O.F.M. St. Bonaventure, N.Y.: Franciscan Institute, 1956.

The Works of Bonaventure. Translated by José de Vinck. 5 vols. Paterson, N.J.: St. Anthony Guild Press, 1960–70.

STUDIES

Bougeral, Jacques Guy, O.F.M. *Introduction to the Works of Bonaventure.* Translated by José de Vinck. Paterson, N.J.: St. Anthony Guild Press, 1964.

Cousins, Ewert H. "Bonaventure's Mysticism of Language." In *Mysticism and Language,* ed. Steven Katz, 236–57. New York: Oxford University Press, 1992.

Dreyer, Elizabeth. "Bonaventure the Franciscan: An Affective Spirituality." In *Spiritualities of the Heart,* ed. Annice Callahan, 33–44. New York: Paulist Press, 1990.

Hayes, Zachary. *The Hidden Center: Spirituality and Speculative Christology in St. Bonaventure.* New York: Paulist Press, 1981.

Tavard, George, A. A. "St. Bonaventure as Mystic and Theologian." In *The Heritage of the Early Church*, ed. David Neiman and Margaret Schatkin, 289–306. Orientalia Christiana Analecta, 195. Rome, 1973.

Meister Eckhart
(c.1260–c.1329)

Today Eckhart may well be the most-quoted Christian mystic. His name appears not only in theological studies but perhaps even more in philosophical, literary, and historical ones. We may doubt, however, whether his popularity is matched by a correct understanding of his thought. Symptomatic for what is at least a one-sided presentation of it is that, until recent years, the bold German sermons received all the attention while the Latin works remained unread. Two volumes of the Classics of Western Spirituality, as well as a few monographs, have begun to remedy the lack of balance. A more thorough acquaintance with his work reveals Aristotelian-Thomist sources as well as the obvious influence of Neoplatonic (Christian) ones. Their simultaneous presence gives Eckhart's thought a complexity unparalleled in the ecstatic tradition. On the one hand, the Meister places God beyond Being (in Neoplatonic fashion), while, on the other, he defines God as *esse simpliciter*—Being-as-such (a Thomist position). Clearly, Being for Eckhart means not the supreme intelligible, or the act of existing, but that ultimately real that lies beyond all names. Indeed, with the concept of Being, Eckhart attempts to surpass even Dionysius's One (which he regards as still a category of cognition) and to overcome the very opposition between transcendence and immanence, for it is the point in which God and the ground of the soul coincide.

Nor should we be surprised by this prevalence of Thomist terminology in the writings of a Dominican friar who lived only a few decades after Thomas and consistently claimed to be a disciple of the Angelic Doctor. Far from being an outsider, Eckhart enjoyed lifelong esteem in his order. Born near Erfurt in Thuringia, he joined the Dominicans at an early age, studied in Cologne and Paris, and lectured in the theology faculties at Paris, Strasbourg, and Cologne. Eckhart enjoyed a great success as a preacher—especially in Cologne. He was appointed to several positions of authority, including that of general vicar of the Dominican provinces of Saxony and Bohemia. Though given to the highest theological speculation, he nevertheless seems to have been a quite practical person, gifted with a great deal of common sense. Moreover, honoring the Dominican ideal of *contemplata tradere,* he literally "preached" mysticism in sermons that, however sublime and often abstruse, were nevertheless directed to all devout believers, not to a few privileged souls. Though his spirituality decidedly belongs to the intellectual type introduced by Dionysius, many of his most spiritual sermons deal with moral virtues—poverty, humility, resignation—preparing the soul to pass beyond all cognitive endeavor.

His efforts to stress the total transcendence of God as well as his total immanence resulted more in dynamic tension than in balanced synthesis. Toward the end of his life his doctrine came under severe attack by the archbishop of Cologne, whose assembled theologians condemned a number of theses attributed to Eckhart. His defense combines denials of ever having held some of the theses with somewhat disingenuously innocuous interpretations of others. Pope John XXII, in his bull *In agro dominico,* ratified the Cologne condemnations. But some of the members of the papal commission (possibly John XXII's own successor, Benedict XII) appear to have felt serious misgivings about the juridical procedure. Awaiting the verdict at the papal court in Avignon, Eckhart died having professed his loyalty to the church and, according to the bull, "revoked and deplored the twenty-six articles that he admitted that he had preached." At the time of this writing Rome appears to be considering lifting the condemnations (which contain some clear misreadings of his work) and restoring him to full ecclesiastical honor.

Eckhart took apophatic theology to an unprecedented extreme where it surpassed even the Persons in the Trinity. The mystical journey leads "into the simple ground, into the quiet desert, into which distinction never gazed, not the Father, nor the Son, nor the Holy Spirit" (Sermon 48). The innermost ground of the Godhead leaves no room for distinctions. At the same time, Eckhart's theology of the Image may well count as one of the first important trinitarian spiritual theologies in Latin Christianity and was to give the main impulse to trinitarian mysticism in the Rhineland and Flanders. Indeed, more than his negation, his doctrine of the birth of the Son in the soul was singled out for doctrinal criticism by both the Cologne and the Avignon commissions. In his *Commentary on Genesis* Eckhart had written: "In one and the same time in which He was God and in which He begat His coeternal Son as God equal to Himself in all things, He also created the world." Eckhart defended himself against charges of having held the eternity of creation by distinguishing the eternal *now* of God's creative activity and the temporal result of that creative act. Whether his reply adequately settles the matter or not, his intention to present the creature as in some manner eternally present in the divine *Image* of the Son is clear enough. His sixth sermon, a daring speculation on the birth of the Son in the soul, fully highlights the central importance of the theology of the Image in Eckhart's mysticism. In fact, most of the texts here reproduced reflect that theology. Especially the famous Sermon 52 on spiritual poverty points the way toward a decreation that would allow the divine Image to occupy the empty space.

Eckhart never fully integrated the two aspects of God's essence and God's manifestation. This failure may well be responsible for some of the doctrinal difficulties he brought upon himself. His theology moves, often abruptly, between the extremes of religious atheism and pantheism without lapsing into either one, but also without ever achieving a harmonious synthesis. This unsurmounted dualism renders his doctrine as controversial today as in his own time, but its dynamic opposition of the two major tendencies of Western mysticism also conveys to that doctrine its striking power.

SERMON SIX

Justi vivent in aeternum (Wis 5:16)

"The just will live forever, and their reward is with God." See exactly what this means; though it may sound simple and commonplace, it is really noteworthy and excellent.

"The just will live." Which are the just? Somewhere it is written: "That man is just who gives everyone what belongs to him";[1] those who give God what is his, and the saints and the angels what is theirs, and their fellow man what is his.

Honor belongs to God. Who are those who honor God? Those who have wholly gone out of themselves, and who do not seek for what is theirs in anything, whatever it may be, great or little, who are not looking beneath themselves or above themselves or beside themselves or at themselves, who are not desiring possessions or honors or ease or pleasure or profit or inwardness or holiness or reward or the kingdom of heaven, and who have gone out from all this, from everything that is theirs, these people pay honor to God, and they honor God properly, and they give him what is his.

People ought to give joy to the angels and the saints. What, does this amaze you? Can a man in this life give joy to those who are in everlasting life? Yes, indeed, he can! Every saint has such great delight and such unspeakable joy from every good work;

The three sermons in this chapter are from *Meister Eckhart: The Essential Sermons, Commentaries, Treatises, and Defense,* trans Edmund College, O.S.A., and Bernard McGinn, the Classics of Western Spirituality (New York Paulist Press, 1981), 185–89, 197–203. Reprinted with permission of the publisher.
[1]Justinian, *Institutes* I, 1.

from a good will or an aspiration they have such great joy that no tongue can tell, no heart can think how great is the joy they have from this. Why is that? Because their love for God is so immeasurably great, and they have so true a love for him, that his honor is dearer to them than their blessedness. And not only the saints or the angels, for God himself takes such delight in this, just as if it were his blessedness; and his being depends upon it, and his contentment and his well-being. Yes, mark this well: If we do not want to serve God for any other reason than the great joy they have in this who are in everlasting life, and that God himself has, we could do it gladly and with all our might.

And one ought also to give help and support to those who are in purgatory, and improvement and edification to those who are still living.

Such a man is just in one way, and so in another sense are all those who accept all things alike from God, whatever it may be, great or small, joy or sorrow, all of it alike, less or more, one like the other. If you account anything more than something else, you do wrong. You ought to go wholly out from your own will.

Recently I had this thought: If God did not wish as I do, then I would still wish as he does. There are some people who want to have their own will in everything; that is bad, and there is much harm in it. Those are a little better who do want what God wants, and want nothing contrary to his will; if they were sick, what they would wish would be for God's will to be for them to be well. So these people want God to want according to their will, not for themselves to want according to his will. One has to endure this, but still it is wrong. The just have no will at all; what God wills is all the same to them, however great distress that may be.

For just men, the pursuit of justice is so imperative that if God were not just, they would not give a fig for God; and they stand fast by justice, and they have gone out of themselves so completely that they have no regard for the pains of hell or the joys of heaven or for any other thing. Yes, if all the pains that those have who are in hell, men or devils, or all the pains that have ever been or ever will be suffered on earth were to be joined on to justice, they would not give a straw for that, so fast do they stand by God and by justice. Nothing is more painful or hard for a just man than what is contrary to justice. In what way? If one thing gives them joy and another sorrow, they are not just; but if on one occasion they are joyful, then they are always joyful; and if on one occasion they are more joyful and on others less, then they are wrong. Whoever loves justice stands so fast by it that whatever he loves, that is his being; nothing can deflect him from this, nor does he esteem anything differently. Saint Augustine says: "When the soul loves, it is more properly itself than when it gives life."[2] This sounds simple and commonplace, and yet few understand what it means, and still it is true. Anyone who has discernment in justice and in just men, he understands everything I am saying.

"The just will live." Among all things there is nothing so dear or so desirable as life. However wretched or hard his life may be, a man still wants to live. It is written somewhere that the closer anything is to death, the more it suffers. Yet however wretched life may be, still it wants to live. Why do you eat? Why do you sleep? So that you live. Why do you want riches or honors? That you know very well; but why do you live? So as to live; and still you do not know why you live. Life is in itself so desirable that we desire it for its own sake. Those in hell are in everlasting torment, but they would not want to lose their lives, not the devils or the souls of men, for their life is so precious that it flows without any medium from God into the soul. And because it flows from God without medium they want to live. What is life? God's being is my life. If my life is God's being, then God's existence must be my existence and God's is-ness is my is-ness, neither less nor more.

They live eternally "with God," directly close to God, not beneath or above. They perform all their works with God, and God with them. Saint John says: "The Word was with God" (Jn 1:1). It was wholly equal, and it was close beside, not beneath there or above there, but just equal. When God made man, he

---

[2]This is actually from Bernard of Clairvaux, *Of Precept and Dispensation* 20.60.

made woman from man's side, so that she might be equal to him. He did not make her out of man's head or his feet, so that she would be neither woman nor man for him, but so that she might be equal. So should the just soul be equal with God and close beside God, equal beside him, not beneath or above.

Who are they who are thus equal? Those who are equal to nothing, they alone are equal to God. The divine being is equal to nothing, and in it there is neither image nor form. To the souls who are equal, the Father gives equally, and he withholds nothing at all from them. Whatever the Father can achieve, that he gives equally to this soul, yes, if it no longer equals itself more than anything else, and it should not be closer to itself than to anything else. It should desire or heed its own honor, its profit and whatever may be its own, no more than what is a stranger's. Whatever belongs to anyone should not be distant or strange to the soul, whether this be evil or good. All the love of this world is founded on self-love. If you had forsaken that, you would have forsaken the whole world.

The Father gives birth to his Son in eternity, equal to himself. "The Word was with God, and God was the Word" (Jn 1:1); it was the same in the same nature. Yet I say more: He has given birth to him in my soul. Not only is the soul with him, and he equal with it, but he is in it, and the Father gives his Son birth in the soul in the same way as he gives him birth in eternity, and not otherwise. He must do it whether he likes it or not. The Father gives birth to his Son without ceasing; and I say more: He gives me birth, me, his Son and the same Son. I say more: He gives birth not only to me, his Son, but he gives birth to me as himself and himself as me and to me as his being and nature. In the innermost source, there I spring out in the Holy Spirit, where there is one life and one being and one work. Everything God performs is one; therefore he gives me, his Son, birth without any distinction. My fleshly father is not actually my father except in one little portion of his nature, and I am separated from him; he may be dead and I alive. Therefore the heavenly Father is truly my Father, for I am his Son and have everything that I have from him, and I am the same Son and not a different one.

Because the Father performs one work, therefore his work is me, his Only-Begotten Son without any difference.

"We shall be completely transformed and changed into God" (2 Cor 3:18). See a comparison. In the same way, when in the sacrament bread is changed into the Body of our Lord, however many pieces of bread there were, they still become one Body. Just so, if all the pieces of bread were changed into my finger, there would still not be more than one finger. But if my finger were changed into the bread, there would be as many of one as of the other. What is changed into something else becomes one with it. I am so changed into him that he produces his being in me as one, not just similar. By the living God, this is true! There is no distinction.

The Father gives his Son birth without ceasing. Once the Son has been born he receives nothing from the Father because he has it all, but what he receives from the Father is his being born. In this we ought not to ask for something from God as if he were a stranger. Our Lord said to his disciples: "I have not called you servants, but friends" (Jn 15:14). Whoever asks for something from someone else is a servant, and he who grants it is a master. Recently I considered whether there was anything I would take or ask from God. I shall take careful thought about this, because if I were accepting anything from God, I should be subject to him as a servant, and he in giving would be as a master. We shall not be so in life everlasting.

Once I said here, and what I said is true: If a man obtains or accepts something from outside himself, he is in this wrong. One should not accept or esteem God as being outside oneself, but as one's own and as what is within one; nor should one serve or labor for any recompense, not for God or for his honor or for anything that is outside oneself, but only for that which one's own being and one's own life is within one. Some simple people think that they will see God as if he were standing there and they here. It is not so. God and I, we are one. I accept God into me in knowing; I go into God in loving. There are some who say that blessedness consists not in knowing but in willing. They are wrong; for if it consisted only in the will, it would not be one. Working and becoming are one. If a carpenter does not work, nothing becomes of the house. If the axe is not doing anything, nothing is becoming anything. In this working God and I are one; he is working and I am becoming. The fire changes anything into itself that is put into it and this takes on fire's own nature. The wood does not change the fire into itself, but the fire changes the wood into itself. So are we changed into God, that we shall know him as he is (1 Jn 3:2). Saint Paul says: "So shall we come to know him, I knowing him just as he knows me" (1 Cor 13:12), neither less nor more, perfectly equal. "The just will live forever, and their reward is with God," perfectly equal.

That we may love justice, for its own sake and for God, without asking return, may God help us to this. Amen.

SERMON FORTY-EIGHT

Ein meister sprichet: alliu glichiu dinc minnent sich under einander.

An authority says: "All things that are alike love one another and unite with one another, and all things that are unlike flee from one another and hate one another."[1] And one authority says that nothing is so unlike as are heaven and earth.[2] The kingdom of earth was endowed by nature with being far off from heaven and unlike it. This is why earth fled to the lowest place and is immovable so that it may not approach heaven. Heaven by nature apprehended that the earth fled from it and occupied the lowest place. Therefore heaven always pours itself out fruitfully upon the kingdom of earth; and the authorities maintain that the broad and wide heaven does not retain for itself so much as the width of a needle's point, but rather bestows it upon the earth. That is why earth is called the most fruitful of all created things that exist in time.

I say the same about the man who has annihilated himself in himself and in God and in all created things; this man has taken possession of the lowest place, and God must pour the whole of himself into this man, or else he is not God. I say in the truth, which is good and eternal and enduring, that God must pour out the whole of himself with all his might so totally into every man who has utterly abandoned himself that God withholds nothing of his being or his nature or his entire divinity, but he must pour all

---

[1] Of the possible sources indicated by Quint in his critical edition, the closest is Thomas Aquinas, STh IaIIae.29.1.
[2] The "authority" seems to be Aristotle, *On Heaven and Earth*, passim.

163

of it fruitfully into the man who has abandoned himself for God and has occupied the lowest place.

As I was coming here today I was wondering how I should preach to you so that it would make sense and you would understand it. Then I thought of a comparison: If you could understand that, you would understand my meaning and the basis of all my thinking in everything I have ever preached. The comparison concerns my eyes and a piece of wood. If my eye is open, it is an eye; if it is closed, it is the same eye. It is not the wood that comes and goes, but it is my vision of it. Now pay good heed to me! If it happens that my eye is in itself one and simple (Mt 6:22), and it is opened and casts its glance upon the piece of wood, the eye and the wood remain what they are, and yet in the act of vision they become as one, so that we can truly say that my eye is the wood and the wood is my eye. But if the wood were immaterial, purely spiritual as is the sight of my eye, then one could truly say that in the act of vision the wood and my eye subsisted in one being. If this is true of physical objects, it is far truer of spiritual objects. You should know that my eye has far more in common with the eye of a sheep which is on the other side of the sea and which I never saw, than it has in common with my ears, with which, however, it shares its being, and that is because the action of the sheep's eye is also that of my eye. And so I attribute to both more in common in their action than I do to my eyes and my ears, because their actions are different.

Sometimes I have spoken of a light that is uncreated and not capable of creation and that is in the soul. I always mention this light in my sermons; and this same light comprehends God without a medium, uncovered, naked, as he is in himself, and this comprehension is to be understood as happening when the birth takes place. Here I may truly say that this light may have more unity with God than it has with any power of the soul, with which, however, it is one in being. For you should know that this light is not nobler in my soul's being than is the feeblest or crudest power, such as hearing or sight or anything else which can be affected by hunger or thirst, frost or heat; and the simplicity of my being is the cause of that. Because of this, if we take the powers as they are in our being, they are all equally noble; but if we take them as they work, one is much nobler and higher than another.

That is why I say that if a man will turn away from himself and from all created things, by so much will you be made one and blessed in the spark in the soul, which has never touched either time or place. This spark rejects all created things, and wants nothing but its naked God, as he is in himself. It is not content with the Father or the Son or the Holy Spirit, or with the three Persons so far as each of them persists in his properties. I say truly that this light is not content with the divine nature's generative or fruitful qualities. I will say more, surprising though this is. I speak in all truth, truth that is eternal and enduring, that this same light is not content with the simple divine essence in its repose, as it neither gives nor receives; but it wants to know the source of this essence, it wants to go into the simple ground, into the quiet desert, into which distinction never gazed, not the Father, nor the Son, nor the Holy Spirit. In the innermost part, where no one dwells, there is contentment for that light, and there it is more inward than it can be to itself, for this ground is a simple silence, in itself immovable, and by this immovability all things are moved, all life is received by those who in themselves have rational being.

May that enduring truth of which I have spoken help us that we may so have rational life. Amen.

SERMON FIFTY-TWO

Beati pauperes spiritu, quoniam ipsorum est regnum caelorum
(Mt 5:3)

Blessedness opened its mouth to wisdom and said: "Blessed are the poor in spirit, for the kingdom of heaven is theirs" (Mt 5:3).

All angels and all saints and all who were ever born must keep silent when the Wisdom of the Father speaks, for all the Wisdom of the angels and of all created beings is mere folly before the unfathomable Wisdom of God. It has said that the poor are blessed.

Now there are two kinds of poverty. There is an external poverty, which is good and is greatly to be esteemed in a man who voluntarily practices it for the love of our Lord Jesus Christ, for he himself used it when he was on earth. I do not now want to say anything more about this poverty. But there is a different poverty, an inward poverty, and it is of this that we must understand that our Lord is speaking: "Blessed are the poor in spirit."

Now I beg you to be disposed to what I say, for I say to you in everlasting truth that if you are unlike this truth of which we want to speak, you cannot understand me. Various people have asked me what poverty may be in itself and what a poor man may be. Let us try to answer this.

Bishop Albert says that a poor man is one who does not find satisfaction in all the things God created;[1] and this is well said. But we can put it even better, and take poverty in a higher sense. A poor man wants nothing, and knows nothing, and has nothing.

---

[1] Albert the Great, *Commentary on Matthew* 5.3.

166

Let us now talk about these three points; and I beg you for the sake of God's love that you understand this truth, if you can, and if you do not understand it, do not burden yourself with it, for the truth I want to expound is such that there will be few good people to understand it.

First let us discuss a poor man as one who wants nothing. There are some people who do not understand this well. They are those who are attached to their own penances and external exercises, which seem important to people. God help those who hold divine truth in such low esteem! Such people present an outward picture that gives them the name of saints; but inside they are donkeys, for they cannot distinguish divine truth. These people say that a man is poor who wants nothing; but they interpret it in this way, that a man ought to live so that he never fulfills his own will in anything, but that he ought to comport himself so that he may fulfill God's dearest will. Such people are in the right, for their intention is good. For this let us commend them. May God in his mercy grant them the kingdom of heaven. But I speak in the divine truth when I say that they are not poor men, nor do they resemble poor men. They have great esteem in the sight of men who know no better, but I say that they are donkeys who have no understanding of divine truth. They deserve the kingdom of heaven for their good intention, but of the poverty of which we want to talk they know nothing.

If someone asks me now what kind of poor man he is who wants nothing, I reply in this way. So long as a man has this as his will, that he wants to fulfill God's dearest will, he has not the poverty about which we want to talk. Such a person has a will with which he wants to fulfill God's will, and that is not true poverty. For if a person wants really to have poverty, he ought to be as free of his own created will as he was when he did not exist. For I tell you by the truth that is eternal, so long as you have a will to fulfill God's will, and a longing for God and for eternity, then you are not poor; for a poor man is one who has a will and longing for nothing.

When I stood in my first cause, I then had no "God," and then I was my own cause. I wanted nothing, I longed for nothing, for I was an empty being, and the only truth in which I rejoiced was in the knowledge of myself. Then it was myself I wanted and nothing else. What I wanted I was, and what I was I wanted; and so I stood, empty of God and of everything. But when I went out from my own free will and received my created being, then I had a "God," for before there were any creatures, God was not "God," but he was what he was. But when creatures came to be and received their created being, then God was not "God" in himself, but he was "God" in the creatures.

Now I say that God, so far as he is "God," is not the perfect end of created beings. The least of these beings possesses in God as much as he possesses. If it could be that a fly had reason and could with its reason seek out the eternal depths of the divine being from which it issued, I say that God, with all that he has as he is "God," could not fulfill or satisfy the fly. So therefore let us pray to God that we may be free of "God," and that we may apprehend and rejoice in that everlasting truth in which the highest angel and the fly and the soul are equal—there where I was established, where I wanted what I was and was what I wanted. So I say: If a man is to become poor in his will, he must want and desire as little as he wanted and desired when he did not exist. And in this way a man is poor who wants nothing.

Next, a man is poor who knows nothing. Sometimes I have said that a man ought to live so that he did not live for himself or for the truth or for God. But now I say something different and something more, that a man who would possess this poverty ought to live as if he does not even know that he is not in any way living for himself or for the truth or for God. Rather, he should be so free of all knowing that he does not know or experience or grasp that God lives in him. For when man was established in God's everlasting being, there was no different life in him. What was living there was himself. So I say that a man should be set as free of his own knowing as he was when he was not. Let God perform what he will, and let man be free.

Everything that ever came from God is directed into pure activity. Now the actions proper to a man are loving and knowing. The question is: In which of these does blessedness most consist? Some authorities have said that it consists in knowing, others say that it consists in loving; others that it consists in knowing and loving, and what they say is better. But I say that it does not consist in either knowing or loving, but that there is that in the soul from which knowing and loving flow; that something does not know or love as do the powers of the soul. Whoever knows this knows in what blessedness consists. That something has neither before nor after, and it is not waiting for anything that is to come, for it can neither gain nor lose. So it is deprived of the knowledge that God is acting in it; but it is itself the very thing that rejoices in itself as God does in himself. So I say that a man ought to be established, free and empty, not knowing or perceiving that God is acting in him; and so a man may possess poverty. The authorities say that God is a being, and a rational one, and that he knows all things. I say that God is neither being nor rational, and that he does not know this or that.[2] Therefore God is free of all things, and therefore he is all things. Whoever will be poor in spirit, he must be poor of all his own knowledge, so that he knows nothing, not God or created things or himself. Therefore it is necessary for a man to long not to be able to know or perceive God's works. In this way a man can be poor of his own knowledge.

Third, a man is poor who has nothing. Many people have said that it is perfection when one possesses no material, earthly things, and in one sense this is indeed true, if a man does this voluntarily. But this is not the sense in which I mean it.

I have said just now that a man is poor who does not want to fulfill God's will, but who lives so that he may be free both of his own will and of God's will, as he was when he was not. About this poverty I say that it is the highest poverty. Second, I say that a man is poor who knows nothing of God's works in him. A man who is so established is as free of knowing and perceiving as God is free of all things, and this is the purest poverty. But a third form is the most intimate poverty, on which I now want to speak; and this is when a man has nothing.

---

[2] "This or that," that is, particular things.

Now pay great attention and give heed! I have often said, and great authorities say, that a man should be so free of all things and of all works, both interior and exterior, that he might become a place only for God, in which God could work. Now I say otherwise. If it be the case that man is free of all created things and of God and of himself, and if it also be that God may find place in him in which to work, then I say that so long as that is in man, he is not poor with the most intimate poverty. For it is not God's intention in his works that man should have in himself a place for God to work in. Poverty of spirit is for a man to keep so free of God and of all his works that if God wishes to work in the soul, he himself is the place in which he wants to work; and that he will gladly do. For if he finds a man so poor as this, then God performs his own work, and the man is in this way suffering God to work, and God is his own place to work in, and so God is his own worker in himself. Thus in this poverty man pursues that everlasting being which he was and which he is now and which he will evermore remain.

It is Saint Paul who says: "All that I am, I am by God's grace" (1 Cor 15:10). But if what I say transcends grace and being and understanding and will and longing, how then can Paul's words be true? People show that what Paul said is true in this way. That the grace of God was in him was necessarily so, for it was God's grace working in him that brought what was accidental to the perfection of the essential. When grace had finished and had perfected its work, then Paul remained what he was.

So I say that man should be so poor that he should not be or have any place in which God could work. When man clings to place, he clings to distinction. Therefore I pray to God that he may make me free of "God," for my real being is above God if we take "God" to be the beginning of created things. For in the same being of God where God is above being and above distinction, there I myself was, there I willed myself and committed myself to create this man. Therefore I am the cause of myself in the order of my being, which is eternal, and not in the order of my becoming, which is temporal. And therefore I am unborn, and in the manner in which I am unborn I can never die. In my unborn manner I have been eternally, and am now, and shall eternally remain. What I am in the order of having been born, that will die and perish, for it is mortal, and so it must in time suffer corruption. In my birth all things were born and I was the cause of myself and of all things; and if I would have wished it, I would not be nor would all other things be. And if I did not exist, "God" would also not exist. That God is "God," of that I am a cause; if I did not exist, God too would not be "God." There is no need to understand this.

A great authority says that his breaking through is nobler than his flowing out;[3] and that is true. When I flowed out from God, all things said: "God is." And this cannot make me blessed, for with this I acknowledge that I am a creature. But in the breaking-through, when I come to be free of will of myself and of God's will and of all his works and of God himself, then I am above all created things, and I am neither God nor creature, but I am what I was and what I shall remain, now and eternally. Then I received an impulse that will bring me up above all the angels. Together with this impulse, I receive such riches that God, as he is "God," and as he performs all his divine works, cannot suffice me; for in this breaking-through I receive that God and I are one. Then I am what I was, and then I neither diminish nor increase, for I am then an immovable cause that moves all things. Here God finds no place in man, for with this poverty man achieves what he has been eternally and will evermore remain. Here God is one with the spirit, and that is the most intimate poverty one can find.

Whoever does not understand what I have said, let him not burden his heart with it; for as long as a man is not equal to this truth, he will not understand these words, for this is a truth beyond speculation that has come immediately from the heart of God. May God help us so to live that we may find it eternally. Amen.

---

[3]The "great authority" may be Eckhart himself.

COMMENTARY ON THE
BOOK OF WISDOM

"And since it is one, it can do all things" (Wis 7:27a)

144. The wise man makes two statements about Wisdom: first, that it is one; second, a hint that because it is one it can do all things. As far as Wisdom being one is concerned, I have amply treated the matter [in commenting on] Deuteronomy 6 and Galatians 3, "God is one." It should be noted in the case of this text that when God is said to be one by Moses speaking in God's name, this is not the only thing that God intended to teach Israel (that is, those who see God). He intimated something deeper to us, beyond the fact that God is one and not many as the sun is one and not many, though this is also true.

We must understand that the term "one" is the same as indistinct,[1] for all distinct things are two or more, but all indistinct things are one. Furthermore, there is an indistinction that concerns God's nature, both because he is infinite, and also because he is not determined by the confines or limits of any genera or beings. But it is the nature of any created being to be determined and limited by the fact that it is created, as we read in Chapter 11, "You have ordered all things in measure, and number and weight" (Wis 11:21). Therefore, saying that God is one is to say

From *Meister Eckhart: Teacher and Preacher,* ed. and trans. Bernard McGinn with the collaboration of Frank Tobin and Elvira Borgstädt, The Classics of Western Spirituality (New York: Paulist Press, 1986), 166–71. Reprinted with permission of the publisher.
[1]"Indistinct," that is, "not-to-be-distinguished."

that God is indistinct from all things, which is the property of the highest and first existence and its overflowing goodness. For this reason later in the same eleventh chapter there follows, "You love all things which are" (Wis 11:25).

145. A further, third argument. God is one which is indistinct. This signifies the highest divine perfection by which nothing exists or is able to exist without him or distinct from him. This is most clear if in place of the word "God" we use the word "existence." God is existence. It is clear that existence is indistinct from everything which exists and that nothing exists or can exist that is distinct and separated from existence. John 1 says, "All things were made through him and without him nothing was made" (Jn 1:3); and Augustine speaking to God says, "You were with me and I was not with you."[2] "You were with me," because indistinct from all things; "I was not with you," because I am distinct as something created. Therefore, here where the discussion concerns Wisdom which is "one," the fullness and purity of its own existence is shown, and also the goodness by which it loves all things, and thirdly its highest and primal perfection, as well as the imperfection of every created thing in that they are made from it and without it are nothing in themselves.

146. From these observations the common understanding according to the literal sense of the text "God is one" (Gal 3:20) is well proven. This is the first way. It is impossible for there to be two infinite things. This is immediately evident to anyone who understands the terms, because the infinite is that outside of which there is nothing. But God, as contained and limited by no genus or comprehended by no limits, is infinite, as said above. Therefore, he is one and unique. The second argument runs thus. It is impossible for there to be two or more indistinct things, for the indistinct and the One are the same, as was also said above. But God is indistinct and the Indistinct Itself. Therefore, it is impossible for there to be many gods.

Yet a third argument comes from the fact that God is Existence Itself (Ex 3:14). Granted this, it follows that it is impossible

---

[2]Augustine, *Conf.* 10.27.

for there to be two or more gods. Rather, if two gods are admitted, there will not be two gods: Either none or one of them will be God. Again, it would follow that there will be two acts of existence in any creature, and consequently any being will [actually] be two beings. The conclusion of all these premises will be clear enough to one who understands the terms. Nevertheless, the consequence has been demonstrated [in the explanation] of Galatians 3, "God is one" (Gal 3:20).

147. Again, the statement that Wisdom is one is proven from the nature of this term, that is, "one." Indeed, the first three proofs are derived from the nature of the term Wisdom or God. Therefore, it should be recognized now that the term "one" is a negative word but is in reality affirmative. Moreover, it is the negation of negation which is the purest form of affirmation and the fullness of the term affirmed. Fullness, superabundance, and "what is said by way of superabundance belong to the One alone," as the Philosopher says.[3]

148. Still, the One descends totally into all things which are beneath it, which are many and which are enumerated. In these individual things the One is not divided, but remaining the incorrupt One, it flows forth into every number and informs it with its own unity. So, the One is necessarily found prior to any duality or plurality both in reality and understanding. Thus the term "one" adds nothing beyond existence, not even conceptually, but only according to negation. This is not so in the case of "true" and "good." For this reason it is most immediately related to existence in that it signifies the purity and core and height of existence itself, something which even the term "existence" does not do. The term "one" signifies Existence Itself in itself along with the negation and exclusion of all nonbeing, which [nonbeing], I say, every negation entails. Every negation denies the existence of a thing whose very existence bespeaks privation. The negation of negation (which the term "one" signifies) denotes that everything which belongs to the term is present in the signified and everything which is opposed to it is absent. This is necessarily the One.

---

[3]Aristotle, *Top.* 5.5.

It is impossible for any being or nature to be multiplied unless something of its nature is either lacking to a second being or there is something added to the second being from another source, or both together, that is, there is both lack and addition.[4]

149. It is therefore evident from all the premises that unity or the One most properly belongs to God, even more than the terms "the True" and "the Good," and this is what is said here of Wisdom ("since it is one"), and in Galatians 3, "God is one" (Gal 3:20). The sense is not only that God is one, but also that he is the only one or that he is alone. "God," he says, "is one," that is, he is the one God. Macrobius says this plainly in the first book of his *Commentary on the Dream of Scipio,* a good bit before the middle, in these words: "The One which is called the Monad, that is, unity, is not a number, but the source and origin of all number. The beginning and the end of all things, itself not knowing beginning nor end, it refers to the supreme God. You would seek it in vain in an inferior stage below God. Since it is one, it cannot be numbered itself; nevertheless, it creates innumerable kinds of genera from itself and contains them within itself."[5] Thus far the words of Macrobius, from which it is clear that God is one and is one Wisdom, as it says here, "since it is one, it can do all things."

150. From Macrobius's words, especially the last sentence, it is seen that the One, in that it is one, is formally distinguished from number as an opposed principle. This is the greatest distinction. Therefore Boethius in his *Trinity* says, "That is truly one in which there is no number,"[6] as if we were to say, "That is truly gold in which there is nothing foreign or opposed to gold."

151. The One itself also gives number existence, for number is a multitude composed of unities. The One even conserves number and multitude in existence; "Every multitude participates in the One," as Proclus says.[7] And this is what Macrobius states: "Unity cannot be numbered itself." Observe the opposition and

---

[4]The meaning of this convoluted sentence is that there can be only one "One."
[5]Macrobius, *Comm. on the Dream of Scipio* 1.6.7.
[6]Boethius, *Trinity* 2.
[7]Proclus, *Elements of Theology,* prop. 1.

distinction. There follows: "It creates innumerable kinds from itself and contains them within itself." Observe the indistinction.

152. From these two points I form two new arguments to prove from the nature of the One that God, Wisdom, is one. The first is this: "The One is that in which there is no number." But in God there is no number, as Macrobius says here. The reason is that number is a falling away, and falling away does not pertain to God, since he is the First and also since he is existence. Therefore, God is one. This second [argument] is this. The One and the Many are opposed. But in God there is no number (as was said and proved above), because there is no falling away in him and because he is the First and is existence. Therefore, God is one.

153. What Augustine says in *True Religion,* Chapter 11, speaks to this: "All agree that what is preferred to everything else is God." Immediately prior to this he says, "All created things eagerly compete [in describing] the excellence of God."[8] From this it is evident that there is no falling away or retreat in him; consequently, there is neither number nor multitude. Therefore, God is one, for that is one in which there is no number. Again, [the same follows] because the One and the Many are opposed.

154. Accordingly, it should be noted that nothing is so distinct from number and the thing numbered or what is numerable (the created thing, that is) as God is. And yet nothing is so indistinct.

The first proof is because the indistinct is more distinguished from the distinct than any two distinct things are from each other. For example, something not colored is further from a colored thing than two colored things are from each other. But indistinction belongs to God's nature; distinction to the created thing's nature and idea, as was said above. Therefore, God is most distinct from each and every created thing.

Further, the second argument goes this way. Nothing is further from something than its opposite. But God and the creature are opposed as the One and Unnumbered is opposed to number,

---

[8]The text is actually from Augustine, *Christ. Doct.* 1.7.7.

the numerated, and the numerable. Therefore, nothing is as distinct from any created being.

The third argument goes thus. Everything which is distinguished by indistinction is the more distinct the more indistinct it is, because it is distinguished by its own indistinction. Conversely, it is the more indistinct the more distinct it is, because it is distinguished by its own distinction from what is indistinct. Therefore, it will be the more indistinct insofar as it is distinct and vice versa, as was said.[9] But God is something indistinct which is distinguished by his indistinction, as Thomas says in Ia, q.7, a.1, at the end. For God is a sea of infinite substance, and consequently indistinct, as Damascene says.[10]

155. On the other hand, it must be noted that nothing is so one and indistinct as God and every created being. There is a threefold reason for this, as proven before in the opposite sense.

First, because nothing is as indistinct as being and existence, potency and its act, form and matter. This is how God and every creature are related. Second, nothing is so much one and indistinct as a thing that is composed and that from which, through which, and in which it is composed and subsists. But, as said above, number or multitude, the numbered or the numerable as such, is composed and subsists from unities. Therefore, nothing is as indistinct as the one God or Unity and the numbered created thing. The third argument is this. Nothing is as indistinct from anything as from that from which it is indistinguished by its own distinction. But everything that is numbered or created is indistinguished from God by its own distinction, as said above. Therefore, nothing is so indistinct and consequently one, for the indistinct and the One are the same. Wherefore, God and any creature whatever are indistinct. The text of Romans 11 speaks to this: "From him, through him and in him are all things" (Rom 11:36). Therefore, the first principal point is evident, namely that Wisdom is one, as it says here, "since it is one."

---

[9]To facilitate understanding of this difficult dialectical text, one can substitute "transcendent" for "distinct" and "immanent" for "indistinct."
[10]John Damascene, *Orthodox Faith* 1.9.

156. The second principal point follows, namely that because it is one "it can do all things." For it would not be able to do anything were it not one, much less do all things. It should be recognized that insofar as a thing is more simple and more unified, it is more powerful and more strong, able to do more things. The reason is that every composite thing draws its power and strength from the other things composing it. Clearly, therefore, power and strength in a composite being are alien to it insofar as it is composite, but are proper to simple beings. This is what we want, because the simpler a thing is, the more powerful and strong it is, able to work in more things and upon more things. That with us the more composite beings are more perfect is not against our position, but in its favor. This happens not because they are more composite (for as such they are later and dependent), but because there are more simple things that compose them. A thing is more powerful, able to work more things, insofar as power descends upon it from many [simple] sources.

157. In summary, the argument may be briefly put in this way. The more a thing is one, the more powerful it is, as said. Therefore, what is simply one, and it alone, can do all things. The *Topics* say: "When more results in more, then what is simple results in simplicity."[11] But Wisdom is simply one, as it says here. Therefore, it can do all things. This is the meaning of "Since it is one, it can do all things."

Furthermore, the second argument—from the *Book of Causes*—runs thus, "Every unified power is more infinite,"[12] able to work more things and in more things. But the Wisdom which is God is especially one in that it is the First. Therefore, it is simply infinite and is able to do all things.

Further, the third argument runs this way. Form and act are always directed to one thing and exist in one thing. What is potential and material is in potency to many things, but in a passive and negative way. Each thing acts insofar as it is in act and is one. Therefore, the more anything is one, the more it will be in act, as was said. Then

---

[11]Aristotle, *Top.* 2.11 and 5.8.
[12]*Book of Causes*, prop. 17(16).

the conclusion is as before. Divine Wisdom, "since it is one," has power and ability to act in that it is one and through the fact that it is one. Because it is simply and especially one, as being the First, it has the power to do all things. "It has the power," because it is one; "it has the power to do all things," because it is the First One. It also follows that nothing else can do all things.

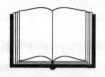

Selected Bibliography

TEXTS

Edition used:
Meister Eckhart: The Essential Sermons, Commentaries, Treatises, and Defense. Translated by Edmund Colledge, O.S.A., and Bernard McGinn. The Classics of Western Spirituality. New York: Paulist Press; London, SPCK, 1981.

Other sources:
Meister Eckhart: Sermons and Treatises. Translated by M. O'C. Walshe. 3 vols. London and Dulverton: Element Books, 1991 and 1992.

Meister Eckhart: Teacher and Preacher. Translated by Bernard McGinn, Frank Tobin, and Elvira Borgstädt. The Classics of Western Spirituality. New York: Paulist Press; London, SPCK, 1986.

STUDIES

Caputo, John. "Fundamental Themes in Meister Eckhart's Mysticism." *The Thomist* 42 (1978): 197–225.

Kelley, C. F. *Meister Eckhart on Divine Knowledge.* New Haven, Conn.: Yale University Press, 1977.

McGinn, Bernard. "The God Beyond God: Theology and Mysticism in the Thought of Meister Eckhart." *Journal of Religion* 61 (1981): 1–19.

Schürmann, Reiner. *Meister Eckhart: Mystic and Philosopher.* Bloomington, Ind., and London: Indiana University Press, 1978.

Selected Bibliography

Tobin, Frank. *Meister Eckhart: Thought and Language.* Philadelphia: University of Pennsylvania Press, 1986.

Woods, Richard, O.P. *Eckhart's Way.* The Way of the Christian Mystics, 2. Wilmington, Del.: Michael Glazier, 1986.

Jan van Ruusbroec
(1293–1381)

The greatest of the Flemish mystics, Jan van Ruusbroec was conversant not only with the main currents of mystical theology in the medieval Low Countries and the Rhineland but also with the patristic heritage of both the East and the West. His personal appropriation of this legacy, together with a keen sensitivity to the needs of all the members of the church of his day and a rare gift for describing the highest levels of mystical experience, enabled Ruusbroec to produce treatises of unsurpassed beauty, perspicuity, and synthetic power.

Ordained a priest in Brussels at the age of twenty-four, Ruusbroec spent the next twenty-six years of his life there, serving as a chaplain at the large collegiate church of St. Gudula (which has since become a cathedral church under the new title of St. Michael). Although his early biographers are silent about most details of his life during this period, we do know that he began writing his first treatises out of a conscious desire to combat an unorthodox movement of quietistic and sometimes pantheistic tendencies that is generally known as the movement of the Free Spirit. These early works, however, are by no means written in a primarily polemical style. On the contrary, they are marked above all by a profoundly positive presentation of all that was best in the Christian spiritual tradition, from the humblest ascetic strivings in what he called "the active life," through those diverse stages of fervent longing for God that he termed collectively "the interior life," up to that rare state of the most intimate union with God that he named the contemplative or "God-seeing life."

Altogether Ruusbroec completed five treatises during his years in Brussels (including his masterpiece, *The Spiritual Espousals*) and had begun a sixth when, with two like-minded priests, he retired in 1343 to a more solitary, forested setting at Groenendaal, about ten kilometers southeast of the city. Others were soon attracted to join the original group of three, and on March 10, 1349, they were clothed in the habit of the canons regular of St. Augustine, with Ruusbroec being named prior of the community under the man whom the bishop of Cambrai appointed provost. It was in this setting that he spent the final thirty-two years of his life. When not engaged in community duties he would regularly go out alone into the forest and there compose further mystical treatises on wax tablets, which he would then bring back to the monastery to be copied by others. Some of these later treatises were written in the first instance for a Poor Clare nun in Brussels, another was an attempt to clarify some passages from an earlier work that had puzzled and even disturbed some of his Carthusian friends at a nearby charter-house, and a final treatise seems to be a posthumous collection of writings that Ruusbroec had left unfinished at the time of his death in 1381. He was buried in the monastery chapel, but his remains were later removed to the church in Brussels where he had long served as a chaplain. He was beatified in 1909 and his feast day is observed in the diocese of Mechelen-Brussels on the anniversary of his death, December 2.

As is the case with all the introductions to the mystics in this anthology, we can here discuss only some of the most fundamental points that might help bring the reader to a fuller understanding of the texts themselves. For Ruusbroec, the Trinity is the very essence of the spiritual life. What cannot be emphasized too strongly is that for him, as for the Flemish mystics in general, the inner life of the Trinity is marked by a twofold movement: at one pole there is a movement toward "the dark silence" and toward rest in the "superessential Unity" (terminology reminiscent of Pseudo-Dionysius, Eckhart, and other followers of the *via negativa*), while at the other pole there is, simultaneously, a movement outward in the generation of the Son by the Father and the breathing forth of the Holy Spirit as the bond of love between them both. Of equal importance is Ruusbroec's claim that our being created in the divine image means precisely that we partake of this same simultaneous interplay between repose and activity, rest and work. In other words, the soul's relation to God partakes in the very movements that are within the triune God.

Only if this is clearly understood will the reader be able to attain a firm grasp of our first two selections from Ruusbroec and of their interrelationship. In the first selection (drawn, like the second, from the final part of book two of *The Spiritual Espousals*), Ruusbroec writes of various ways of meeting God: "with intermediary" (referring above all to the gifts of God and our response to them through virtuous activity) and "without intermediary" (referring to a "blissful unity [where] we will constantly rest in a state transcending ourselves and all things"). Since the second selection deals with three manners or modes of meeting God "without intermediary," one might assume that it will be concerned only with various forms of that blissful rest already referred to. But of the three modes that Ruusbroec ascribes to this union without intermediary, the second is explicitly said to be "*with* intermediary," while the third is in large measure based on the intermediary of virtuous activity. This is not, however, in any way a sign of inconsistency on Ruusbroec's part, but is rather one more manifestation of his basic principle that such realities are complementary and concomitant rather than separated from one another by temporal succession. As Paul Henry observes in a long and carefully reasoned essay on Ruusbroec's Trinitarian mysticism:

> The reader familiar with other mystics, such as St. Teresa of Avila, for whom the spiritual "marriage" comes after the "full union" and the latter comes after the state of "quiet," will derive [from Ruusbroec] an impression of confusion and of disorder. But in fact *the concomitance of "intermediary"*

mystical states at even the highest level is only a consistent corollary of his doctrine of the complementarity of divine moments [in the Trinity].[1]

Ruusbroec himself makes the same point with all possible clarity at the end of our second selection: "Anyone who does not possess both rest and activity in one and the same exercise has not attained this righteousness."

Our final selection from Ruusbroec reproduces in its entirety the third and last book of *The Spiritual Espousals,* the most important of his many descriptions of the contemplative life. He himself was well aware that his attempt to articulate the nature of the deepest possible experience of union with God would appear overly bold and even unorthodox to persons who had not themselves experienced such union. He was in fact posthumously attacked by Jean Gerson, the late-fourteenth-century chancellor of the University of Paris, for such statements as that the contemplative life means "to be God with God, without intermediary or any element of otherness which could constitute an obstacle or impediment." A careful reading of such statements in their full context, however, shows clearly enough that Ruusbroec is writing of mystical *consciousness,* of how a true contemplative may no longer "feel" or "perceive" any distinction from God. He is, in other words, writing as a phenomenologist of mystical experience and is not making claims of ontological identity with God.

A final point to be made concerning Ruusbroec's description of the contemplative life is that here, too, is to be found that same dialectical relationship between rest and activity that we noted earlier. He speaks of a state of darkness that, in itself, sounds as utterly formless and ineffable as anything ever written by the most rigorous advocate of the *via negativa,* but for Ruusbroec this state of darkness is in no sense absolute. Rather, "in this darkness an incomprehensible light is born and shines forth; this is the Son of God, in whom a person becomes able to see and to contemplate

---

[1] Paul Henry, "La mystique trinitaire du bienheureux Jean Ruusbroec: II," *Recherches de science religieuse* 41 (1953): 62.

eternal life." So, too, "the eternal state of rest" in which even the divine Persons give way before the essential Unity is not utterly divorced from all activity, for it is at all times the very ground of what the mystic calls "the active meeting of the Father and the Son, in which we are lovingly embraced by means of the Holy Spirit in eternal love." In sum, even if the notes of ineffability, modelessness, rest, and Unity predominate in the final paragraphs of *The Spiritual Espousals,* they always remain in dialectical relationship with the notes of effability, distinctness, activity, and Trinity. This could hardly be more beautifully expressed than by the words with which Ruusbroec concludes his entire treatise: "That we might blissfully possess the essential Unity and clearly contemplate the Unity in the Trinity—may the divine love grant us this, for it turns no beggar away. Amen. Amen."

From this, it should be clear why Louis Cognet, the highly respected twentieth-century historian of spirituality, spoke of Ruusbroec's work as "one of the most exceptional achievements that Western mysticism has produced,"[2] and why Evelyn Underhill regarded him as "one of the greatest—perhaps the very greatest—of the mystics of the Church."[3]

---

[2]Louis Cognet, *Introduction aux mystiques rhéno-flamands* (Paris: Desclée, 1968), 281.
[3]Evelyn Underhill, *The Mystics of the Church* (Cambridge, England, 1925; Greenwood, S.C.: Attic Press, 1975), 148.

THE SPIRITUAL ESPOUSALS

BOOK TWO: THE INTERIOR LIFE

Part Four: "To Meet Him."

I have now shown you how a free and uplifted person becomes able to see by the help of God's grace in interior exercises. This is the first thing that Christ requires and desires of us when he says, "See." As regards the second and third points (when he says, "The Bridegroom is coming. Go out."), I have described three manners in which Christ comes interiorly, of which the first manner has four different modes; I have also shown how we are to go out through exercises that are in accordance with all the ways in which God interiorly enkindles, teaches, and moves us by his coming. It remains for us to consider the fourth and last point, which is a meeting with Christ our Bridegroom. All of our interior, spiritual seeing, whether in grace or in glory, and all of our going out through the practice of virtue in various exercises are all for the purpose of meeting and being united with Christ our Bridegroom, for he is our eternal rest and the goal and reward of all our activity.

A. INTRODUCTORY REMARKS
ON THE VARIOUS WAYS OF MEETING GOD

As you know, every meeting is an encounter between two persons coming from different places which are separate from and

From *John Ruusbroec: The Spiritual Espousals and Other Works*, trans. James A. Wiseman, O.S.B., The Classics of Western Spirituality (New York: Paulist Press, 1985), 116–21, 132–36, 145–52. Reprinted with permission of the publisher.

set over against one another. Now Christ comes from above as an almighty Lord and generous Benefactor, while we come from below as poor servants who can do nothing of ourselves but have need of everything. Christ comes to us from within outward, while we come to him from without inward. It is this which gives rise to a spiritual meeting. This coming, this meeting between ourselves and Christ, occurs in two ways, namely, with intermediary and without intermediary.

Natural union with God, without intermediary

Now understand and note carefully that the unity of our spirit exists in two ways, namely, as it is in its essential being and as it is in its activity. According to its essential being, you should know that the spirit receives Christ's coming in its bare nature without intermediary and without interruption, for the being and life that we are in God, in our eternal image, is immediately and indivisibly united with the being and life that we possess in ourselves and that we are according to our essential being. For this reason the spirit, in the most intimate and highest part of its being, in its bare nature, ceaselessly receives the imprint of its eternal image and of the divine resplendence and becomes an eternal dwelling place of God. God possesses this dwelling place with his eternal presence and constantly comes to it afresh with new resplendence radiating anew from his eternal birth.[1] Where he comes, there he is present, and where he is present, there he comes. But he will never come where he has never been, for in him there is nothing fortuitous or changeable. Everything in which he is present is also present in him, for he never goes outside himself.

For this reason the spirit possesses God essentially in its bare nature, and God possesses the spirit, for it lives in God and God in it. In the highest part of its being it is also capable of receiving

---

[1]This teaching about the birth of Christ in the soul, even more prominent in the writings of Eckhart, has its roots in the earliest Christian theology and is found in many of the Greek Fathers. The best modern study of the doctrine, from its beginnings up to Eckhart, is Hugo Rahner, "Die Gottesgeburt," in *Symbole der Kirche* (Salzburg: Otto Muller, 1964), 13–87.

God's resplendence without intermediary, together with all that God can accomplish. By means of the resplendence of its eternal image, which shines within it both essentially and personally, the spirit immerses itself in the divine being as regards the highest part of its own vital being and there possesses in an enduring way its eternal blessedness. It then flows out again with all other creatures through the eternal birth of the Son and is established in its created being by the free will of the Holy Trinity. It here bears a likeness to the image of the sublime Trinity and Unity, according to which it was made. In its creatureliness it ceaselessly receives the imprint of its eternal image, just like a spotless mirror in which the image always remains and in which knowledge of it is ceaselessly renewed with fresh clarity each time you look at it. This essential unity of our spirit with God does not subsist in itself but remains in God, flows forth from God, depends upon God, and turns back to God as to its eternal cause. Accordingly it has never been separated from God and never will be, for this unity exists within us in our bare nature, and if a creature were to be separated from God in this respect it would fall into pure nothingness. This unity transcends time and place and is ceaselessly active according to God's own manner of acting, but it passively receives the imprint of its eternal image inasmuch as it is like God but is in itself a creature. This is the nobility which we naturally possess in the essential unity of our spirit, which is at this level naturally united with God. This renders us neither holy nor blessed, for all persons, both good and bad, possess this unity within themselves; it is, however, the first principle of all holiness and blessedness. This, then, is the meeting and union between God and our spirit in our bare nature.

Meeting God with intermediary

Now pay careful attention to the meaning of my words, for if you understand well what I now wish to say as well as what I have already said, then you will have understood all the divine truth which any creature could teach you—and much more besides. In this same unity our spirit also exists in a second way, namely, as it is in its activity. In this respect it subsists in itself as being. This is the originating source of the higher powers and the beginning and end of all creaturely activity which is performed in a creaturely manner, whether in the natural or the supernatural order. Nevertheless the unity is not active insofar as it is unity; it is the powers of the soul which act, but in whatever way they act they derive their power and potency from their originating source, that is, from the unity of the spirit, where the spirit subsists in its personal mode of being.

In this unity the spirit must always be either like God by means of grace and virtue or else unlike God because of mortal sin. This is because human beings have been created to the likeness of God, that is, in the grace of God, for grace is a deiform light which shines through us and makes us like God, so that without this light which makes us like God we cannot attain supernatural union with him. Even though we cannot lose God's image or our natural unity with God, if we lose our likeness to him, which is his grace, then we will suffer damnation.

For this reason, whenever God finds in us some capacity for receiving his grace, he wishes out of gratuitous goodness to give us life and make us like himself by means of his gifts. This happens whenever we turn to him with all our will, for in one and the same moment Christ comes to us and enters within us with intermediary and without intermediary (that is, with his gifts and above all gifts), and we come to him and enter within him with intermediary and without intermediary (that is, with our virtues and above all virtues). He imprints his image and likeness upon us, namely, himself and his gifts, delivers us from our sins, sets us free, and makes us like himself.

Meeting God without intermediary

In this same activity whereby God delivers us from sin, sets us free, and makes us like himself in charity, the spirit immerses itself in blissful love. Here there occurs a meeting and a union which are without intermediary and supernatural, and in this is found our highest blessedness. Although from God's side it is natural that he bestows gifts out of love and gratuitous goodness, from our side this is something accidental and supernatural, for previously we were strangers and unlike him, while afterward we attained a likeness to God and unity with him. This meeting and unity which the loving spirit attains in God and possesses without intermediary must take place in the essential ground of our being; it therefore remains a deep mystery to our understanding, unless the understanding apprehends it essentially in an utterly simple way.

In this blissful unity we will constantly rest in a state transcending ourselves and all things. All natural and supernatural gifts flow forth from this unity, and yet the loving spirit rests in this unity above all gifts. Here there is nothing but God and the spirit united with God without intermediary. In this unity we are received by the Holy Spirit, and we ourselves receive the Holy Spirit, the Father, the Son, and the divine nature in its entirety, for God cannot be divided. The spirit's inclination to blissful enjoyment seeks rest in God above all likeness. In the spirit's essential being, this inclination obtains and possesses in a supernatural way all that the spirit ever received there in a natural way.

All good persons possess this, but its nature remains hidden to them all their lives if they are not interiorly fervent and empty of all creatures. In the very moment in which a person turns from sin, he is received by God in the essential unity of his being, the topmost part of his spirit, so that he might rest in God now and forevermore. He also receives grace and a likeness to God in the ground of his powers, so that he might constantly grow and increase in new virtues. As long as this likeness exists through charity and the practice of virtue, just so long does this unity in rest perdure, for it cannot be lost except through mortal sin.

The absolute necessity of God's grace and our response to it

Now all holiness and blessedness lie in the spirit's being led, by means of likeness and the mediation of grace or glory, to a state of rest in the essential unity. The grace of God is the path we must always follow if we are to arrive at that bare being in which God gives himself to us without intermediary in all his richness. Sinners

191

and the damned spirits are in darkness precisely because they lack God's grace, which would have enlightened them, instructed them, and led them to this blissful unity. Nevertheless the essential being of the spirit is so noble that the damned cannot will their own annihilation, but sin causes such a state of darkness and unlikeness and raises so great a barrier between the spirit's powers and the essential being where God dwells that the spirit cannot attain union in its own being, which would be the spirit's proper place of eternal rest if it were not for sin. Whoever lives apart from sin lives in the likeness and grace of God and has God as his own possession. Grace is therefore necessary, for it drives away sin, prepares the way for us, and makes our entire life fruitful.

For this reason Christ is constantly coming to us through the mediation of grace and manifold gifts, while we in turn go to him through the mediation of our virtues and various exercises. The more interior the gifts he bestows and the more finely wrought his movements within us, the more interior and delightful will be the exercises of our spirit, as you have already heard concerning all the ways which have previously been described. There is in all this a constant renewal, for God is always giving new gifts and our spirit is always turning back to God in accordance with the ways in which it has been called and gifted by God, and in this encounter it constantly receives new and higher gifts. In this way a person is constantly advancing to a higher form of life.

This active meeting is always with intermediary, since God's gifts, together with our virtues and the activity of our spirit, constitute this intermediary. Such mediation is necessary for all persons and all spirits, for without the mediation of God's grace and of our freely willed and loving conversion no one can be saved....

C. MEETING GOD WITHOUT INTERMEDIARY, IN THREE DIFFERENT MODES

Now understand well what follows: The measureless illumination of God which, together with his incomprehensible resplendence, is a cause of all gifts and virtues is the same incomprehensible light which transforms and pervades our spirit's inclination toward blissful enjoyment. It does this in a way which is devoid of all particular form, since it occurs in incomprehensible light. In this light the spirit immerses itself in a rest of pure bliss, for this rest is modeless and fathomless. It cannot be known except through itself, for if we could know and comprehend it by ourselves it would lapse into some particular form or measure and would then not be able to satisfy us; instead, this rest would become an eternal state of restlessness. For this reason the simple, loving inclination of our spirit, immersed in rest, produces in us a blissful love, and such love is fathomless. Here, God's deep calls to deep (cf. Ps 42:8), that is, calls to all who are united with the Spirit of God in blissful love. This call is an overflow of essential resplendence, and this essential resplendence, enveloping us in fathomless love, makes us lose ourselves and flow forth into the wild darkness of the Godhead. Thus united—one with the Spirit of God, without intermediary—we are able to meet God with God and endlessly possess our eternal blessedness with him and in him. This most interior way of life is practiced in three manners or modes.

The first mode: emptiness

Sometimes a person living the interior life turns within himself in a simple way in accordance with his inclination toward blissful enjoyment. This occurs above and beyond all activity and all virtue, by means of a simple, inward act of gazing in blissful love. Here such a person meets God without intermediary, and an ample light, shining from out of God's Unity, reveals to him darkness, bareness, and nothingness. He is enveloped by the darkness and falls into a modeless state, as though he were completely lost; through the bareness he loses the power of observing all things in their distinctness and becomes transformed and pervaded by a simple resplendence; in the nothingness all his activity fails him, for he is overcome by the activity of God's fathomless love, while in the inclination of his spirit toward blissful enjoyment he overcomes God and becomes one spirit with him (cf. 1 Cor 6:17).

Through this unity in the Spirit of God such a person enters a state of blissful savor and there possesses God's essential being. Being immersed in his own essential being, this person becomes filled with the fathomless delights and riches of God. From out of these riches there flow into the unity of the higher powers an embrace and a fullness of felt love, and from this fullness of felt love there flows into the heart and into the corporeal powers a felt and deeply penetrating savor. By means of this influx such a person becomes interiorly unable to move and powerless over himself and all his activity. In the inmost part of his being, in both soul and body, he neither knows nor feels anything except a unique resplendence accompanied by a felt sense of well-being and a penetrating savor.

This is the first mode, which is characterized by emptiness, for it empties a person of all things, lifts him up above all virtues and activities, unites him with God, and provides a firm and stable basis for the most fervent interior exercises which a person can practice. When, therefore, any restlessness or any virtuous practice sets up an obstacle or interposes images between a good person and the bare introversion which he desires, then he will be hindered in this mode, since it consists in transcending all things to enter a state of emptiness. This is the first mode in the practice of the most interior exercises.

The second mode: active desire

At times this interiorly fervent person turns to God in a way characterized by desire and activity, so that he might give God glory and honor and might offer him both himself and all his works, letting them be consumed in the love of God. At such times he meets God with intermediary, namely, the intermediary of the gift of savorous wisdom. This gift is the ground and source of all virtue, for it urges and moves every good person toward virtue in accordance with the degree of his love. It sometimes touches an interior person so deeply and enkindles his love so intensely that all God's gifts and all that God can bestow apart from himself are too small and unsatisfying and serve only to increase his restlessness. Such a person has an interior perception or feeling in the ground of his being, where all virtues have their beginning and end, where with ardent desire he offers God all these virtues, and where love has its abode. Here the hunger and thirst of love are so great that he surrenders himself at every moment and is unable to work any further, but rather transcends his activity and comes to nought in love. He hungers and thirsts for the taste of God and at each sudden illumination of God is seized by him and touched by him anew in love. Though living he dies; though dying he comes back to life. In this way the yearning hunger and thirst of love are constantly renewed within him.

This is the second mode, one which is characterized by desire. In it, love stands in a state of likeness and yearningly desires to be united with God. This mode is more honorable and more beneficial to us than the first since it is the cause of the first, for no one can enter a state of rest transcending activity unless he has previously loved in a way characterized by desire and activity. For this reason God's grace and our active love must both precede and follow, that is, must be practiced both before and after, for without works of love we cannot merit or attain God nor can we retain what we have gained by means of the works of love. Therefore no one should be empty of activity if he is master of himself and can give himself to the works of love. But whenever a good person lingers somewhat over any of God's gifts or over any creature, he will be hindered in this most interior exercise, for it is a hunger which cannot be satisfied by anything or anyone except God alone.

The third mode: both resting and working in accordance with righteousness

From these first two modes there arises the third, which is an interior life in accordance with righteousness. You should understand that God comes ceaselessly to us both with intermediary and without intermediary and calls us both to blissful enjoyment and to activity in such a way that the one will not be hindered by the other but rather constantly strengthened by it. An interior person therefore possesses his life in these two ways, that is, in rest and in activity, and in each he is whole and undivided, for he is completely in God when he blissfully rests and is completely in himself when he actively loves. He is exhorted and called by God at all times to renew both his rest and his activity, and his spirit's righteousness wishes to pay at each instant whatever God asks of it. For this reason the spirit turns inward both actively and with blissful enjoyment each time it experiences God's sudden illumination. In this way it is constantly renewed in all the virtues and becomes more deeply immersed in blissful rest, for each time God bestows something on us he gives himself as well as his gifts, while in each of its inward movements the spirit gives itself as well as all its works. By means of God's simple illumination and the spirit's inclination to be blissfully immersed in love, the spirit is united with God and is ceaselessly transported into a state of rest. In addition, by means of the gifts of understanding and of savorous wisdom, it is actively touched and at all times enlightened and enkindled in love.

To a person in this state there is spiritually revealed and held out before him all that one could desire. He is hungry and thirsty, for he sees angelic food and heavenly drink; he works intensely in love, for he sees his rest; he is a pilgrim and sees his fatherland; he strives for victory in love, for he sees his crown. Consolation, peace, joy, beauty, riches, and everything else that brings delight are revealed in God to the enlightened reason without measure in spiritual likenesses. Through this revelation and God's touch love remains active, for this righteous person has established for himself a truly spiritual life in both rest and activity; such a life will continue forever, though after this present life it will be transformed into a higher state.

It is in all this that a person's righteousness consists. He goes toward God with fervent interior love through his eternal activity, enters into God with his blissful inclination toward eternal rest, remains in God, and nevertheless goes out to creatures in virtue and righteousness through a love which is common to all. This is the highest point of the interior life. Anyone who does not possess both rest and activity in one and the same exercise has not attained this righteousness, while a person who has attained it cannot be hindered when he turns inward, for he does so both actively and in blissful enjoyment.

A person is, however, like a double mirror, receiving images on both sides, for in the higher part of his being he receives God with all his gifts and in the lower part he receives corporeal images through the senses. Now he can turn inward whenever he wishes and so practice righteousness without hindrance. But in this life a person is inconstant and accordingly often turns outward; without necessity or the direction of his enlightened reason he gets caught up in the activities of the senses and so falls into daily faults. Still, in the loving inward movement of a righteous person these daily faults are just like a drop of water in a red-hot furnace. With this I conclude the description of the interior life....

BOOK THREE: THE CONTEMPLATIVE LIFE

A fervent lover of God who possesses God in blissful rest, who possesses himself in dedicated and active love, and who possesses his entire life in virtues and righteousness will—by means of these three points and the hidden revelation of God—enter the contemplative life. Indeed, God freely desires to choose this fervent and righteous lover and raise him to a state of superessential contemplation in the divine light in accordance with the divine mode of being. This contemplation establishes us in a state of purity which transcends all our understanding, for it is a special adornment and heavenly crown and is, in addition, an eternal reward for all our virtues and for our entire life. No one can attain this through knowledge or subtle reasoning or through any exercises; the only persons who can attain divine contemplation are those whom God wishes to unite with himself in his Spirit and to enlighten through himself—no one else can attain this.

The hidden divine nature is eternally active in contemplation and love as regards the Persons and is constantly in a state of blissful enjoyment insofar as the Persons are embraced in the Unity of

197

the divine being.[2] All interior spirits are one with God through their loving immersion in this embrace, which takes place within God's essential Unity; they are that same oneness which the divine being is in itself according to the mode of blessedness. In this sublime Unity of the divine nature, the heavenly Father is the origin and beginning of every work which is wrought in heaven and on earth. In the hidden depths in which our spirit is immersed, he speaks the words: "See, the bridegroom is coming. Go out to meet him." We wish to explain and clarify these words as they relate to the state of superessential contemplation, which is the ground of all holiness and of all the life which can ever be lived.

Few persons can attain this divine contemplation because of their own incapacity and because of the hidden, mysterious nature of the light in which one contemplates. For this reason no one can properly or thoroughly understand its meaning through any learning or subtle reflections of his own, for all words and all that can be learned or understood in a creaturely manner are alien to and far beneath the truth which I mean. However, a person who is united with God and enlightened in this truth can understand the truth through itself. To comprehend and understand God as he is in himself, above and beyond all likenesses, is to be God with God, without intermediary or any element of otherness which could constitute an obstacle or impediment. I therefore beseech everyone who does not understand this or feel it in the blissful unity of his spirit not to take offense at it but simply to let it be as it is. What I want to say is true; Christ, the eternal truth, said it himself at many places in his teaching, if only we are able to manifest and express it

---

[2] For a proper understanding of book three of the *Espousals*, it is important to note the constant allusions to the dialectical relationship between work and rest, a relationship so very evident in the two clauses of this particular sentence of Ruusbroec. As regards God's own life, the active pole of the dialectic is characterized by such notes as the distinctions among the three Persons, the begetting of the Son, the breathing forth of the Holy Spirit, and the Father and the Son's love of all things in the Spirit. On the other hand, the pole of blissful rest is characterized by the Persons' being embraced in the divine Unity, "beyond the distinction of Persons," in a state of "essential bareness" where all names and distinctions "pass away into simple ineffability, without mode and without reason." As noted in the introduction to this chapter, much of the strength of Ruusbroec's mystical theology lies in his insistence that both poles are always present, both in God's life and in the life of contemplatives.

well. Whoever, then, wishes to understand it must have died to himself and be living in God and must turn his gaze to that eternal light which is shining in the ground of his spirit, where the hidden truth is revealing itself without intermediary.

Part One: "See."

Our heavenly Father wishes us to see, for he is the Father of light (cf. Jas 1:17). Accordingly, in the hidden depths of our spirit he eternally, ceaselessly, and without intermediary utters a single, fathomless word, and only that word. In this word he gives utterance to himself and all things. This word, which is none other than "See," is the generation and birth of the Son, the eternal light, in whom all blessedness is seen and known.

If our spirit is to contemplate God with God without intermediary in this divine light, three things are necessary. The first is that a person must be exteriorly well ordered, interiorly unhindered, and as empty of all his exterior works as if he were not even performing them, for if he is interiorly disturbed through any virtuous work he will be troubled by images, and as long as this lasts he will not be able to contemplate. Secondly, he must interiorly cleave to God with devoted intention and love, just as if he were a burning, glowing fire which can never be extinguished. As long as he feels himself to be in this state, he will be able to contemplate. Thirdly, he must lose himself in a state devoid of particular form or measure, a state of darkness in which all contemplatives blissfully lose their way and are never again able to find themselves in a creaturely way.

In the abyss of this darkness in which the loving spirit has died to itself, God's revelation and eternal life have their origin, for in this darkness an incomprehensible light is born and shines forth; this is the Son of God, in whom a person becomes able to see and to contemplate eternal life. This divine light is shed upon a person in the simple being of his spirit, where the spirit receives the resplendence which is God himself above and beyond all gifts and creaturely activity in the empty idleness of the spirit, where the spirit has lost itself in blissful love and receives God's resplendence without intermediary.

The spirit ceaselessly becomes the very resplendence which it receives. See, this hidden resplendence, in which a person contemplates all that he desires in accordance with his spirit's mode of emptiness, is so great a resplendence that the loving contemplative neither sees nor feels in the ground of his being, in which he is at rest, anything other than an incomprehensible light. In the simple bareness which envelops all things, he feels and finds himself to be nothing other than the same light with which he sees.

This is the first point, describing how a person is made capable of seeing in the divine light. Blessed are the eyes that see in this way, for they possess eternal life.

Part Two: "The Bridegroom Is Coming."

When we have thus become able to see, we can joyfully contemplate the eternal coming of our Bridegroom, which is the second point of which we wish to speak. What is this eternal coming of our Bridegroom? It is a new birth and a new illumination which knows no interruption, for the ground out of which the resplendence shines forth and which is the resplendence itself is both living and fruitful. The revelation of the eternal light is therefore ceaselessly renewed in the hidden depths of the spirit. See, all creaturely activity and all exercises of virtue must here cease, for here God works himself alone in the most sublime nobility of the spirit, where there is only an eternal contemplating of and gazing at the light with the light and in the light. The coming of the Bridegroom is so fast that he has always come and is always abiding with fathomless richness and yet is personally and ceaselessly coming anew with such new resplendence that it seems as if he had never previously come. This is because his coming occurs beyond time in an eternal now, which is ever received with new pleasure and new joy.

See, the delight and joy which the Bridegroom brings at his coming is fathomless and without measure, for it is his very self. For this reason the spirit's eyes, with which it contemplates and gazes at its Bridegroom, are opened so wide that they will never again be closed, for the spirit's gaze and contemplation remain eternally caught up in God's hidden revelation, and the spirit's capacity for comprehending is opened so wide for the coming of the Bridegroom that the spirit itself becomes the very breadth which it comprehends. In this way God is comprehended and seen with God; in this lies all our blessedness.

This is the second point, describing how we ceaselessly receive the eternal coming of our Bridegroom into our spirit.

Part Three: "Go Out."

A. OUR ETERNAL BEING IN GOD BEFORE OUR CREATION IN TIME

The Spirit of God now speaks within our own spirit in its hidden immersion: "Go out, into a state of eternal contemplation and blissful enjoyment after God's own manner." All the richness which is in God by nature is something which we lovingly possess in God—and God in us—through the infinite love which is the Holy Spirit. In this love a person savors all that he can desire. By means of this love we have died to ourselves and through a loving immersion of ourselves have gone out into a state of darkness devoid of particular form. There the spirit is caught up in the embrace of the Holy Trinity and eternally abides within the super-essential Unity in a state of rest and blissful enjoyment. In this same Unity, considered now as regards its fruitfulness, the Father is in the Son and the Son in the Father, while all creatures are in them both. This is beyond the distinction of Persons, for here we can only make distinctions of reason between fatherhood and sonship in the living fecundity of the divine nature.

This is the origin and beginning of an eternal going forth and an eternal activity which is without beginning, for it is a beginning without beginning. Since the almighty Father has perfectly comprehended himself in the ground of his fruitfulness, the Son, who is the Father's eternal Word, goes forth as another Person within the Godhead. Through this eternal birth all creatures have gone forth eternally before their creation in time. God has thus seen and known them in himself—as distinct in his living ideas and as different from himself, though not different in every respect, for all that is in God is God.

This eternal going forth and this eternal life which we eternally have and are in God apart from ourselves is a cause of our created being in time. Our created being depends upon this eternal being and is one with it in its essential subsistence. This eternal being and life which we have and are in God's eternal wisdom is like God, for it both abides eternally and without distinction in the divine essence and, through the birth of the Son, flows forth eternally as a distinct entity, its distinctness being in accordance with God's eternal idea of it. In these two ways it is so like God that he ceaselessly knows and expresses himself in this likeness as regards both the divine essence and the Persons. Although there are here distinctions and differences of a rational kind, this likeness is nevertheless one with the very image of the Holy Trinity which is the wisdom of God, in which God contemplates himself and all things in an eternal now that has no before or after. He sees himself and all things in a single act of seeing; this is God's image and likeness as well as our image and likeness, for in this act God expresses both himself and all things. In this divine image all creatures have an eternal life apart from themselves, as in their eternal Exemplar.

B. ATTAINING OUR ETERNAL IMAGE IN THE CONTEMPLATIVE LIFE

It is to this eternal image and likeness that the Holy Trinity has created us. God therefore wills that we go out from ourselves into this divine light, supernaturally pursuing this image which is our own life and possessing it with him both actively and blissfully in a state of eternal blessedness. We will find that the bosom of the Father is our own ground and origin, in which our life and being have their beginning. From out of this ground, that is, from out of the Father and all that lives in him, there shines an eternal resplendence, which is the birth of the Son. In this resplendence, that is, in the Son, the Father is himself revealed together with all that lives in him, for he gives to the Son all that he is and all that he has, with the single exception of the property of fatherhood, which he retains himself. For this reason all that in the Father lives still concealed in unity lives also in the Son as having flowed forth in open manifestation; so too, the simple ground of our eternal image constantly abides in a state of darkness devoid of particular form, while the infinite resplendence which shines forth from there reveals and manifests the hidden mystery of God in particular forms.

All persons who have been raised above their creaturely state into the contemplative life are one with this divine resplendence and are this resplendence itself. Through this divine light—and as regards their uncreated being—they see, feel, and find themselves to be the same simple ground from out of which the resplendence shines without measure in a divine way and in which it eternally abides devoid of particular form according to the simplicity of the divine essence. For this reason interior, contemplative persons will go out in accordance with the mode of their contemplation, above and beyond reason and distinction and their own created being. Through an eternal act of gazing accomplished by means of the inborn light, they are transformed and become one with that same light with which they see and which they see. It is in this way that contemplatives pursue the eternal image to which they have been created; they contemplate God and all things without distinction in a simple act of seeing in the divine resplendence.

This is the noblest and most beneficial contemplation which a person can attain in this life, for in such contemplation a person remains free and master of himself in the best possible way. With each loving movement within, he is able to grow in nobility of life beyond anything that is humanly understandable: He remains free and master of himself in the practice of the interior life and of virtue; in addition, his gazing into the divine light raises him above all interiority, all virtue, and all acquisition of merit, for it is the crown and reward to which we aspire and which we now have and possess in a certain way, for the contemplative life is a heavenly life. If, however, we were set free from this present exile, we would have a still greater capacity in our creatureliness to receive this resplendence, and then God's glory would in every respect shine through us in a better and nobler way.

All this is the way above all ways in which a person goes out into a state of divine contemplation and an eternal act of gazing and in which he is transformed and formed over in the divine resplendence.

Part Four: "To Meet Him."

This going forth of a contemplative also takes place in love, for by means of blissful love he transcends his creaturely state and finds and savors the riches and delight which God is himself and which he causes ceaselessly to flow forth into the hidden depths of the spirit, where the spirit bears a likeness to God's own nobility.[3]

When an interior, contemplative person has thus attained his eternal image and, in this purity and by means of the Son, has possessed the Father's bosom, then he is enlightened with divine truth. He continually receives the eternal birth and goes out into a state of divine contemplation in accordance with the mode of the light. Here arises the fourth and last point, which is a meeting in love; it is in this more than in than anything else that our highest blessedness resides.

You should know that the heavenly Father, as a living ground and with all that lives in him, has turned actively toward his Son as toward his own eternal wisdom and that this same wisdom,

---

[3]The close parallelism between this fourth part of book three and the preceding third part should be noted. In part three, Ruusbroec writes that contemplatives "are transformed and become one with that same light with which they see and which they see," that light being the Son of God. In part four, there is a similar transformation—only this time through the Holy Spirit—whereby a person's spirit is "raised above itself and...made one with the Spirit of God," who is the love of the Father and Son. These two transformations are clearly on the level of what the mystic calls an "active meeting," characterized by distinction of Persons. In the same two parts of the book there is also a meeting or union that is not active but "blissful," occurring "beyond distinction." In part three, contemplatives are said to feel themselves to be the same simple ground from out of which the divine resplendence shines forth but which itself is in a state of darkness, devoid of particular form, while in part four contemplatives are described as encompassed in "that dark stillness in which all lovers lose their way."

together with all that lives in it, has actively turned back toward the Father, that is, toward that same ground from which it comes forth. In this meeting between the Father and the Son there arises the third Person, the Holy Spirit, who is the love of them both and who is one with them in the same nature. In a way characterized by both activity and blissful enjoyment, the Spirit embraces and penetrates the Father and Son and all that lives in both of them with such great riches and joy that all creatures must remain silent before this, for the incomprehensible wonder which resides in this love eternally transcends the understanding of all creatures. But when a person understands this wonder and savors it without amazement, then has his spirit been raised above itself and been made one with the Spirit of God; it savors and sees—without measure, like God himself—the riches which it has itself become in the Unity of the living ground where it possesses itself in accordance with the mode of its uncreated being.

Now this blessed meeting is actively renewed in us without ceasing in accordance with God's own mode of being, for the Father gives himself to the Son and the Son to the Father in an eternal sense of well-being and a loving embrace. This is constantly renewed in the bond of love, for just as the Father ceaselessly sees all things anew in the birth of the Son, so too are all things loved anew by the Father and Son in the flowing forth of the Holy Spirit. This is the active meeting of the Father and the Son, in which we are lovingly embraced by means of the Holy Spirit in eternal love.

Now this active meeting and this loving embrace are in their ground blissful and devoid of particular form, for the fathomless, modeless being of God is so dark and so devoid of particular form that it encompasses within itself all the divine modes and the activity and properties of the Persons in the rich embrace of the essential Unity; it thereby produces a divine state of blissful enjoyment in this abyss of the ineffable. Here there is a blissful crossing over and a self-transcending immersion into a state of essential bareness, where all the divine names and modes and all the living ideas which are reflected in the mirror of divine truth all pass away into simple ineffability, without mode and without reason. In this fathomless abyss of simplicity all things are encompassed in a state of blissful blessedness, while the ground itself remains completely uncomprehended, unless it be through the essential Unity. Before this the Persons must give way, together with all that lives in God, for here there is nothing other than an eternal state of rest in a blissful embrace of loving immersion.

This is that modeless being which all fervent interior spirits have chosen above all things, that dark stillness in which all lovers lose their way. But if we could prepare ourselves through virtue in the ways I have shown, we would at once strip ourselves of our bodies and flow into the wild waves of the Sea, from which no creature could ever draw us back.

That we might blissfully possess the essential Unity and clearly contemplate the Unity in the Trinity—may the divine love grant us this, for it turns no beggar away. Amen. Amen.

Selected Bibliography

TEXTS

Edition used:
John Ruusbroec: The Spiritual Espousals and Other Works.
Translated by James A. Wiseman, O.S.B. The Classics of Western
Spirituality. New York: Paulist Press; London, SPCK, 1985.

Other sources:
The Spiritual Espousals. Translated by Helen Rolfson, O.S.F. Collegeville, Minn.: Liturgical Press, 1995.

Opera Omnia. Edited by the Ruusbroecgenootschap. Tielt and
Leiden, 1981; Turnhout, 1988–. A critical edition of the original
text is accompanied by an English translation.

STUDIES

Dupré, Louis. *The Common Life: The Origins of Trinitarian Mysticism and Its Development by Jan Ruusbroec.* New York: Crossroad, 1984.

Mommaers, Paul. *The Land Within: The Process of Possessing
and Being Possessed by God According to the Mystic Jan van
Ruusbroec.* Chicago: Franciscan Herald Press, 1975.

Mommaers, Paul, and Norbert De Paepe, eds. *Jan van Ruusbroec:
The Sources, Content, and Sequels of His Mysticism.* Mediaevalia
Lovaniensia, ser. 1, stud. 12. Louvain, 1984.

Teasdale, Wayne. "Ruysbroeck's Mystical Theology." Parts 1, 2.
American Benedictine Review 35 (1984): 82–96, 176–93.

Verdeyen, Paul. *Ruusbroec and His Mysticism.* Translated by
André Lefevere. Collegeville, Minn.: Liturgical Press, 1995.

207

Gregory Palamas
(1296–1359)

Gregory Palamas is a controversial figure. Proclaimed a saint by the Synod of Constantinople in 1368, he became for many in the Latin Church the paragon of what separated them from the East. Even within the Orthodox Church resistance to his theology remained fierce during his lifetime and never entirely subsided. Yet whatever interpretation theologians may give to his distinction between God's essence and God's energies, the mystical insight behind it should be a source of inspiration to the West as well as to the East. Palamas's main contribution lies in his attempt to provide a theological justification for the direct experience of God that some of his contemporaries claimed to enjoy and that all mystics in one form or another aspire to.

Unfortunately, his theology as articulated in the *Triads* (three essays written at different stages of the same controversy) is highly polemical and often tediously repetitive. The Calabrian monk Barlaam (who resided in Constantinople), in defending the Orthodox interpretation of the Creed, had concluded that theology could reach only "dialectical," that is, probable rather than absolutely certain conclusions, since the divine mystery remains inaccessible to the human mind. His main antagonists were the hesychast monks who claimed that, in the practice of the Jesus Prayer (a constant repetition of the word "Jesus" or of a one-phrase invocation of Jesus' name), both body and mind were transformed by the divine light and the direct presence of God. Palamas himself, though born of a noble family close to the Byzantine Court, had joined the monastic community of the "Great Lavra" on Mount Athos, where he assiduously practiced the hesychastic prayer. When Barlaam attacked the hesychasts' claim of a "spiritual knowledge" of God, Palamas rose to their defense. To him the issue concerned the very essence of faith. His defense became heatedly polemical after Barlaam branded the hesychasts with the name of the condemned sect of the Messalians (who had held that we may "see" God with our eyes). At this point Palamas felt it necessary to distinguish God's essence (which is and remains unknown, as Greek theologians had persistently maintained) from God's energies. These energies, which transform the praying person, are themselves uncreated. Not only Barlaam but also some Greek theologians objected that no such distinction could be made between God's essence and energies. Whatever did not belong to the essence had to be created.

To most Latin theologians that principle settled the case, until the question of "uncreated grace" emerged in occidental theology in recent times. Is grace merely a creation, an "accident," as Scholastics would claim, or is it a form of "theosis," a transformation of one's entire being, as the Greek fathers and a number of Western mystics since Eckhart and Ruusbroec had implied? Palamas's expression may not be theologically the most felicitous, for it is hard to see how God's energies can be distinguished from God's nature. Yet the mystical vision upon which this expression is based remains profound and convincing. John Meyendorff perceptively describes it:

> The darkness of the cloud surrounding God is not an empty darkness. While eliminating all perceptions of the senses, or of the mind, it nevertheless places man before a Presence, revealed to a transfigured mind and purified body....The theological principle presupposed by Palamas is that God, even when he communicates himself to the purified body and mind, remains transcendent in his

essence. In this, Palamas follows St. Gregory of Nyssa, who spoke of mystical experience in terms of an experience of divine inexhaustibility, and used the term "tension" *(epektasis)* to describe it.[1]

The image of light, symbol of God's glory, illuminating both the mind and the body, originated in a spiritual reading of the gospel pericope of Jesus' transfiguration on Mount Thabor.

The contrast between light and darkness, introduced in the Fourth Gospel, pervades the entire Eastern spirituality. Yet for Greek theologians darkness itself assumes a positive, spiritual meaning: it is the cloud that surrounds God's nature and subtracts it from our understanding. Even as the divine light transformed the body of Jesus, so it transforms those who become united with him. Yet that light itself was nothing less than the divine glory itself shining through his human appearance. Palamas insists throughout the *Triads* that this divine light does not originate in the mind's natural aptitude. The mind is not capable of understanding God in any way; only uncreated grace can enable it to experience God's glory. Even as the apostles' eyes and minds were transformed by grace, so our bodies and minds may be transformed beyond their natural capacities to receive the divine light. Only in this light can we see the Light (Ps 36). "For it is in light that light is seen, and that which sees operates in a similar light, since this faculty has no other way in which to work....If it sees itself, it sees light; if it beholds the object of its vision, that too is light; and if it looks at the means by which it sees, again it is light" (*Triads* 2.3.36). The Thaboric light is not knowledge, in the ordinary sense, though it is refracted into cognition both in the mind and in the senses.

The tension in Palamas's mystical theology arises from the fact that it supports a direct experience of God, translatable into language, while remaining within the confines of a strictly negative

---

[1] *Gregory Palamas: The Triads*, ed. with an introduction by John Meyendorff, The Classics of Western Spirituality (New York: Paulist Press, 1983), 14.

theology. This paradox has inhered in Neoplatonic mysticism since the beginning. For Plotinus, the One stands beyond all knowledge, yet remains immediately present to the lower hypostases and may even be directly experienced by the soul. What distinguishes Palamas's theology is that its basis lies in experience rather than in speculation. As such, it remains a rich—yet in the West inadequately explored—source of inspiration.

THE TRIADS

A. TEXTS ON APOPHATIC THEOLOGY AS POSITIVE EXPERIENCE

I.iii.4. The human mind also, and not only the angelic, transcends itself, and by victory over the passions acquires an angelic form. It, too, will attain to that light[1] and will become worthy of a supernatural vision of God, not seeing the divine essence, but seeing God by a revelation appropriate and analogous to Him. One sees, not in a negative way—for one does see something—but in a manner superior to negation. For God is not only beyond knowledge, but also beyond unknowing;[2] His revelation itself is also truly a mystery of a most divine and extraordinary kind, since the divine manifestations, even if symbolic, remain unknowable by reason of their transcendence. They appear, in fact, according to a law which is not appropriate to either human or divine nature—being, as it were, for us yet beyond us—so that no name can properly describe them.

From *Gregory Palamas: The Triads,* ed. John Meyendorff, trans. Nicholas Gendle, The Classics of Western Spirituality (New York: Paulist Press, 1983), 32–40, 57–63. Reprinted with permission of the publisher.
[1]That is, the divine uncreated light of Thabor, God Himself in His outward manifestation (or *energies*).
[2]A key idea in Palamas, deriving ultimately from Pseudo-Dionysius. The Divine Reality transcends not only the positive concepts we may hold of God (cataphatic theology) but also the negations of the apophatic way. The "knowledge" of the utterly unknowable God is a supremely positive experience, not a cognitive void, for it is the superabundance of light and being in God that dazzles the created mind. God, as Dionysius says, is beyond unknowabililty, beyond the human antithesis of affirmation and negation. Similarly the vision of such a God must be ineffable, yet it is less misleading to say what it is not than what it is.

And this God indicated when, in reply to Manoe's question, "What is your name?," He replied, "It is marvellous" (Jdg 13:17–18); for that vision, being not only incomprehensible but also unnameable, is no less wonderful, However, although vision be beyond negation, yet the words used to explain it are inferior to the negative way. Such explanations proceed by use of examples or analogies, and this is why the word "like," pointing to a simile, appears so often in theological discourse, for the vision itself is ineffable, and surpasses all expression.

5. So, when the saints contemplate this divine light within themselves, seeing it by the divinising communion of the Spirit, through the mysterious visitation of perfecting illuminations— then they behold the garment of their deification, their mind being glorified and filled by the grace of the Word, beautiful beyond measure in His splendour;[3] just as the divinity of the Word on the mountain glorified with divine light the body conjoined to it. For "the glory which the Father gave Him," He Himself has given to those obedient to Him, as the Gospel says, and "He willed that they should be with Him and contemplate His glory" (Jn 17:22, 24).

How can this be accomplished corporeally, now that He Himself is no longer corporeally present after His ascension to the heavens? It is necessarily carried out in a spiritual fashion, for the mind becomes supercelestial, and as it were the companion of Him who passed beyond the heavens for our sake, since it is manifestly yet mysteriously united to God, and contemplates supernatural and ineffable visions, being filled with all the immaterial knowledge of a higher light. Then it is no longer the sacred symbols accessible to the senses that it contemplates, nor yet the variety of Sacred Scripture that it knows; it is made

---

[3]The vision of God for Palamas is not an intellectual grasp of an external object, but an interior participation in the life of the Holy Spirit: to see God is to share in this life, i.e., to become divinized. This involves a complete transfiguration of the whole person, body and soul together.

beautiful by the creative and primordial Beauty, and illumined by the radiance of God.[4]

In the same way, according to the revealer and interpreter of their hierarchy,[5] the ranks of supracosmic spirits above are hierarchically filled, in a way analogous to themselves, not only with the first-given knowledge and understanding, but with the first light in respect of the sublimest triadic initiation. Not only do they [the angels] participate in, and contemplate, the glory of the Trinity, but they likewise behold the manifestation of the light of Jesus, revealed to His disciples on Thabor. Judged worthy of this vision, they are initiated into Him, for He is Himself deifying light: They truly draw near to Him, and enjoy direct participation in His divinising rays. This is why the blessed Macarius calls this light "the food of the supracelestial beings."[6] And here is what another theologian says: "All the intelligible array of supracosmic beings, immaterially celebrating this light, give us a perfect proof of the love which the Word bears towards us."[7] And the great Paul, at the moment of encountering the invisible and supracelestial visions that are in Christ, was "ravished"[8] and became himself supracelestial, without his mind needing to pass beyond the heavens by actually changing place. This "ravishment" denotes a mystery of an entirely different order, known only to those who have experienced it. But it is not necessary to mention that we ourselves have heard the testimony of Fathers who have had this experience, so as not to expose these things to calumny. But what has already been said should suffice to demonstrate easily to the unconvinced that there is indeed an intellectual illumination, visible to those whose hearts have been purified, and utterly different from knowledge, though productive of it....

---

[4] That is, the transfigured spiritual intellect is able to apprehend directly the transcendent realities figured forth symbolically in Scripture and the liturgy.

[5] That is, Pseudo-Dionysius, the author of *The Celestial Hierarchy.*

[6] Macarius, Hom. 12.14.

[7] St. Andrew of Crete, Hom. 7 on the Transfiguration.

[8] 2 Cor 12:2. Paul's ecstasy is frequently cited by the Greek fathers as a paradigm of mystical experience.

18. Do you now understand that in place of the intellect, the eyes and ears, they acquire the incomprehensible Spirit and by Him hear, see and comprehend? For if all their intellectual activity has stopped, how could the angels and angelic men see God except by the power of the Spirit? This is why their vision is not a sensation, since they do not receive it through the senses; nor is it intellection, since they do not find it through thought or the knowledge that comes thereby, but after the cessation of all mental activity. It is not, therefore, the product of either imagination or reason; it is neither an opinion nor a conclusion reached by syllogistic argument.

On the other hand, the mind does not acquire it simply by elevating itself through negation. For, according to the teaching of the Fathers, every divine command and every sacred law has as its final limit purity of heart; every mode and aspect of prayer reaches its term in pure prayer;[9] and every concept which strives from below towards the One Who transcends all and is separated from all comes to a halt once detached from all created beings. However, it is erroneous to say that over and above the accomplishment of the divine commands, there is nothing but purity of heart. There are other things, and many of them: There is the pledge of things promised in this life, and also the blessings of the life to come, which are rendered visible and accessible by this purity of heart. Thus, beyond prayer, there is the ineffable vision, and ecstasy in the vision, and the hidden mysteries. Similarly, beyond the stripping away of beings, or rather after the cessation [of our perceiving or thinking of them] accomplished not only in words, but in reality, there remains an unknowing which is beyond knowledge; though indeed a darkness, it is yet beyond radiance, and, as the great Denys says, it is in this dazzling darkness that the divine things are given to the saints.

---

[9]A technical phrase deriving from Evagrius, "pure prayer" means the state of undifferentiated consciousness when the mind is "naked" of all images and earthly notions. But, Palamas insists, it is not enough to abstract oneself from creation; the mind must be emptied of contingent things so as to be filled with divine ones.

Thus the perfect contemplation of God and divine things is not simply an abstraction; but beyond this abstraction, there is a participation in divine things, a gift and a possession rather than just a process of negation. But these possessions and gifts are ineffable: If one speaks of them, one must have recourse to images and analogies—not because that is the way in which these things are seen, but because one cannot adumbrate what one has seen in any other way. Those, therefore, who do not listen in a reverent spirit to what is said about these ineffable things, which are necessarily expressed through images, regard the knowledge that is beyond wisdom as foolishness; trampling under foot the intelligible pearls, they strive also to destroy as far as possible by their disputations those who have shown them to them.

19. As I have said, it is because of their love of men that the saints speak, so far as this is possible, about things ineffable, rejecting the error of those who in their ignorance imagine that, after the abstraction from beings, there remains only an absolute inaction, not an inaction surpassing all action. But, I repeat, these things remain ineffable by their very nature. This is why the great Denys says that after the abstraction from beings, there is no word but "an absence of words"; he also says, "After every elevation, we will be united with the Inexpressible."[10] But, despite this inexpressible character, negation alone does not suffice to enable the intellect to attain to superintelligible things. The ascent by negation is in fact only an apprehension of how all things are distinct from God; it conveys only an image of the formless contemplation and of the fulfillment of the mind in contemplation, not being itself that fulfillment.[11]

But those who, in the manner of angels, have been united to that light celebrate it by using the image of this total abstraction. The mystical union with the light teaches them that this light is superessentially transcendent to all things. Moreover, those judged

---

[10]Both quotations are from *The Mystical Theology,* chap. 3.

[11]The cardinal point about the *via negativa* is that it is neither a species of agnosticism nor itself the vision of God, but rather a necessary preliminary process of mental detachment from created things which provides an image of the otherness of divine ones.

worthy to receive the mystery with a faithful and prudent ear can also celebrate the divine and inconceivable light by means of an abstraction from all things. But they can only unite themselves to it and see if they have purified themselves by fulfillment of the commandments and by consecrating their mind to pure and immaterial prayer, so as to receive the supernatural power of contemplation.

20. What then shall we call this power which is an activity neither of the senses nor of the intellect? How else except by using the expression of Solomon, who was wiser than all who preceded him: "a sensation intellectual and divine."[12] By adding those two adjectives, he urges his hearer to consider it neither as a sensation nor as an intellection, for neither is the activity of the intelligence a sensation, nor that of the senses an intellection. The "intellectual sensation" is thus different from both. Following the great Denys, one should perhaps call it union, and not knowledge. "One should realise," he says, "that our mind possesses both an intellectual power which permits it to see intelligible things, and also a capacity for that union which surpasses the nature of the intellect and allies it to that which transcends it."[13] And again: "The intellectual faculties become superfluous, like the senses, when the soul becomes deiform, abandoning itself to the rays of the inaccessible light in an unknown union by blind advances."[14] In this union, as St. Maximus puts it, "the saints by beholding the light of the hidden and more than ineffable glory themselves become capable of receiving blessed purity, together with the celestial powers."[15]

Let no one think that these great men are referring here to the ascent through the negative way. For the latter lies within the powers of whoever desires it; and it does not transform the soul so as to bestow on it the angelic dignity. While it liberates the understanding from other beings, it cannot by itself effect union with transcendent things. But purity of the passionate part of the soul effectively liberates the mind from all things through impassibility,

---

[12]In fact, the phrase "divine sensation" is an Origenist version of Prov. 2:5.
[13]*The Divine Names* 7.1.
[14]Ibid. 4.11.
[15]Cf. *Chapters on Knowledge* 2.70, 76.

and unites it through prayer to the grace of the Spirit; and through this grace the mind comes to enjoy the divine effulgence, and acquires an angelic and godlike form.

21. This is why the Fathers, following the great Denys, have called this state "spiritual sensation," a phrase appropriate to, and somehow more expressive of, that mystical and ineffable contemplation. For at such a time man truly sees neither by the intellect nor by the body, but by the Spirit, and he knows that he sees supernaturally a light which surpasses light. But at that moment he does not know by what organ he sees this light, nor can he search out its nature, for the Spirit through whom he sees is untraceable. This was what Paul said when he heard ineffable words and saw invisible things: "I know not whether I saw out of the body or in the body" (2 Cor 12:2). In other words, he did not know whether it was his intellect or his body which saw.

Such a one does not see by sense perception, but his vision is as clear as or clearer than that by which the sight clearly perceives sensibilia. He sees by going out of himself, for through the mysterious sweetness of his vision he is ravished beyond all objects and all objective thought, and even beyond himself.[16]

Under the effect of the ecstasy, he forgets even prayer to God. It is this of which St. Isaac speaks, confirming the great and divine Gregory: "Prayer is the purity of the intellect which is produced with dread only from the light of the Holy Trinity."[17] And again, "Purity of spiritual mind is what allows the light of the Holy Trinity to shine forth at the time of prayer....The mind then transcends prayer, and this state should not properly be called prayer, but a fruit of the pure prayer sent by the Holy Spirit. The mind does not pray a definite prayer, but finds itself

---

[16]*Ecstasis* in the Greek fathers need not imply any kind of paranormal psychological state of loss of consciousness. It is (literally) a "going-out" from oneself, a self-transcendence under the influence of love and divine grace. It enables a supernatural mode of cognition of divine things, which is mystical knowledge, after one has ceased to know and see through the functions of the discursive intellect and the senses.

[17]Isaac of Nineveh, Hom. 32.

in ecstasy in the midst of incomprehensible realities. It is indeed an ignorance superior to knowledge."[18]

This most joyful reality, which ravished Paul and made his mind go out from every creature but yet return entirely to himself—this he beheld as a light of revelation, though not of sensible bodies; a light without limit, depth, height or lateral extension. He saw absolutely no limit to his vision and to the light which shone round about him; but rather it was as it were a sun infinitely brighter and greater than the universe, with himself standing in the midst of it, having become all eye.[19] Such, more or less, was his vision.

22. This is why the great Macarius says that this light is infinite and supercelestial.[20] Another saint, one of the most perfect, saw the whole universe contained in a single ray of this intelligible sun—even though he himself did not see this light as it is in itself, in its full extent, but only to that extent that he was capable of receiving it.[21] By this contemplation and by his supraintelligible union with this light, he did not learn what it is by nature, but he learnt that it really exists, is supernatural and superessential, different from all things; that its being is absolute and unique, and that it mysteriously comprehends all in itself. This vision of the Infinite cannot permanently belong to any individual or to all men.

He who does not see understands that he is himself incapable of vision because not perfectly conformed to the Spirit by a total purification, and not because of any limitation in the Object of vision. But when the vision comes to him, the recipient knows well that it is that light, even though he sees but dimly; he knows this from the impassible joy akin to the vision which he experiences, from the peace which fills his mind, and the fire of love for God which burns in him. The vision is granted him in proportion to his

---

[18]Ibid.

[19]The image of becoming "all eye," entirely subsumed in the vision that consumes and unites, goes back to Plotinus.

[20]Cf. Macarius-Symeon, *De libert. mentis* 21.

[21]An episode in Gregory the Great's *Life* of St. Benedict, whose biography was popular among Byzantine monks. At a time of theological tension between Latins and Greeks, it is pleasing to find Palamas describing a Western saint as "one of the most perfect."

practice of what is pleasing to God, his avoidance of all that is not, his assiduity in prayer, and the longing of his entire soul for God; always he is being borne on to further progress and experiencing even more resplendent contemplation. He understands then that his vision is infinite because it is a vision of the Infinite, and because he does not see the limit of that brilliance; but, all the more, he sees how feeble is his capacity to receive the light.

23. But he does not consider that the vision of which he has been deemed worthy is simply the Divine Nature. Just as the soul communicates life to the animated body—and we call this life "soul," while realising that the soul which is in us and which communicates life to the body is distinct from that life—so God, Who dwells in the God-bearing soul, communicates the light to it. However, the union of God the Cause of all with those worthy transcends that light. God, while remaining entirely in Himself, dwells entirely in us by His superessential power; and communicates to us not His nature, but His proper glory and splendour.[22]

The light is thus divine, and the saints rightly call it "divinity," because it is the source of deification. It is not only "divinity," but "deification-in-itself"[23] and thearchy. While it appears to produce a distinction and multiplication within the one God, yet it is nonetheless the Divine Principle, more-than-God, and more-than-Principle. The light is one in the one divinity, and therefore is itself the Divine Principle, more-than-God and more-than-Principle, since God is the ground of subsistence of divinity. Thus the doctors of the Church, following the great Areopagite Denys, call "divinity" the deifying gift that proceeds from God. So when Gaius asked Denys how God could be beyond the thearchy, he

---

[22]This touches on the cardinal doctrine of Palamas, that God, utterly and permanently unknowable and inaccessible in His essence, yet comes to us and shares His life with us in His energies. Palamas insists that the energies *are* God, personally present, not just a created grace in us, yet he also affirms that the energies are distinct from the essence, without implying division in God.

[23]The language in this paragraph is Dionysian. The light, energy, or grace is indeed "divinity," a communication of the life of God, yet God as the source of that life may be termed "beyond being," or even "beyond divinity."

replied in his letter: "If you consider as 'divinity' the reality of the deifying gift which divinises us, and if this Gift is the principle of divinisation, then He Who is above all principle is also above what you thus call 'divinity.'"[24] So the Fathers tell us that the divine grace of the suprasensible light is God. But God in his nature does not simply identify Himself with this grace, because He is able not only to illumine and deify the mind, but also to bring forth from nonbeing every intellectual essence.

B. TEXTS ON DEIFICATION IN CHRIST

II iii. 8. The monks know that the essence of God transcends the fact of being inaccessible to the senses, since God is not only above all created things, but is even beyond Godhead. The excellence of Him Who surpasses all things is not only beyond all affirmation, but also beyond all negation; it exceeds all excellence that is attainable by the mind. This hypostatic light, seen spiritually by the saints, they know by experience to exist, as they tell us, and to exist not symbolically only, as do manifestations produced by fortuitous events; but it is an illumination immaterial and divine, a grace invisibly seen and ignorantly known.[25] What it is, they do not pretend to know.[26]

9. ...This light is not the essence of God, for that is inaccessible and incommunicable; it is not an angel, for it bears the marks of the Master. Sometimes it makes a man go out from the body or else, without separating him from the body, it elevates him to an ineffable height. At other times, it transforms the body, and communicates its own splendour to it when, miraculously, the light which deifies the body becomes accessible to the bodily eyes. Thus indeed did the great Arsenius appear when engaged in hesychastic combat; similarly

---

[24]Epistle 2.
[25]A classic example of deliberately paradoxical language, of the kind common in Gregory of Nyssa and Pseudo-Dionysius (cf. "learned ignorance" and "sober drunkenness") when referring to mystical knowledge or experience.
[26]The divine subject of such illumination constitutes an overwhelming experiential impact, yet permanently defies intellectual analysis. True mystical cognition is darkness to the discursive mind, since it is by definition ineffable and incomprehensible.

Stephen, whilst being stoned, and Moses, when he descended from
the mountain. Sometimes the light "speaks" clearly, as it were with
ineffable words, to him who contemplates it. Such was the case with
Paul. According to Gregory the Theologian, "It descends from the
elevated places where it dwells, so that He who in His own nature
from eternity is neither visible to nor containable by any being may
in a certain measure be contained by a created nature."[27] He who has
received this light, by concentrating upon himself, constantly perceives in his mind that same reality which the children of the Jews
called manna, the bread that came down from on high....

10. ...The hesychasts in fact never claim that this light is an angel.
Having been initiated by the teaching of the Fathers, they know
that the vision of angels takes place in various ways, according to
the capacities of those who behold it: sometimes in the form of a
concrete essence, accessible to the senses, and visible even to creatures full of passions and totally foreign to all initiation; sometimes
under the form of an ethereal essence which the soul itself can only
see in part; sometimes as a true vision, which only those who are
purified and who see spiritually are worthy to behold. But you,[28]
who have not been initiated into these different modes of seeing
angels, think to show that the angels are invisible to one another
not because they are incorporeal, but in their essence; and implic-
itly you class the contemplators of God with Balaam's ass, which
also is said to have seen an angel (Num 22:25, 27)!

11. Elsewhere you claim that the mind contemplates God "not in
some other hypostasis; but when purified at once of passions and
ignorance, in beholding itself, it sees God in itself, since it is made in
His image."[29] You also believe that those who claim to see in this way

---

[27]Gregory Nazianzen, Hom. 45.11.

[28]Addressing Barlaam directly, who was prepared to accept the hesychasts' claim to have
seen the divine light if this were admitted to be an angel.

[29]The vision of God in the mirror of the purified soul is a commonplace of patristic spiritual
teaching. The doctrine stems from the biblical view of man as created in the divine image
and therefore originally capable of reflecting the splendor of God Himself. But, as a result
of the Fall, the image has become tarnished and corroded, and must undergo restoration
and cleaning in order once again to mediate the vision of God.

the very essence of the mind under the form of light are in accord with the most mystical Christian tradition. But hesychasts know that the purified and illuminated mind, when clearly participating in the grace of God, also beholds other mystical and supernatural visions—for in seeing itself, it sees more than itself. It does not simply contemplate some other object, or simply its own image, but rather the glory impressed on its own image by the grace of God. This radiance reinforces the mind's power to transcend itself, and accomplish that union with those better things which is beyond understanding. By this union, the mind sees God in the Spirit in a manner transcending human powers....

15. It is our purpose to communicate the teaching on the light of grace of those long-revered saints whose wisdom comes from experience, proclaiming that "such is the teaching of Scripture." Thus we set forth as a summary the words of Isaac, the faithful interpreter of these things: "Our soul," he affirms, "possesses two eyes, as all the Fathers tell us.... Yet the sight which is proper to each 'eye' is not for the same use: with one eye, we behold the secrets of nature, that is to say, the power of God, His wisdom and providence towards us, things comprehensible by virtue of the greatness of His governance. With the other eye, we contemplate the glory of His holy nature, since it pleases God to introduce us to the spiritual mysteries."[30]

Since then these are eyes, what they see is a light; but since each possesses a power of vision designed for a particular use, a certain duality appears in the contemplation of this light, since each eye sees a different light, invisible to the other eye. As the divine Isaac has explained, the one is the apprehension of the power, wisdom and providence of God, and in general, knowledge of the Creator through the creatures; the other is contemplation, not of the divine nature...but of the glory of His nature, which the Saviour has bestowed on His disciples, and through them, on all

---

[30]Isaac of Nineveh, Hom. 72. He contrasts two kinds of religious knowledge: "natural contemplation" *(physike theoria)*, knowledge of God in creation; and direct vision of God's uncreated energies or glory *(theologia* in the strict sense).

who believe in Him and have manifested their faith through their works. This glory He clearly desired them to see, for He says to the Father, "I will that they contemplate the glory You have given Me, for You have loved Me since the foundation of the world" (Jn 17:24). And again, "Glorify Me, Father, with that glory I have had from You since before the world began" (Jn 17:5).

Thus to our human nature He has given the glory of the God-head, but not the divine nature; for the nature of God is one thing, His glory another, even though they be inseparable one from another. However, even though this glory is different from the divine nature, it cannot be classified amongst the things subject to time, for in its transcendence "it is not," because it belongs to the divine nature in an ineffable manner.

Yet it is not only to that human composite which is united to His hypostasis[31] that He has given this glory which transcends all things, but also to His disciples. "Father," He says, "I have given them the glory which You gave Me, so that they may be perfectly one" (Jn 17:22–23). But He wishes also that they should see this glory, which we possess in our inmost selves and through which properly speaking we see God.

16. How then do we possess and see this glory of the divine nature? Is it in examining the causes of things and seeking through them the knowledge of the power, wisdom and providence of God? But, as we have said, it is another eye of the soul which sees all this, which does not see the divine light, "the glory of his nature" (in St. Isaac's words). This light is thus different from the light synonymous with knowledge Therefore, not every man who possesses the knowledge of created things, or who sees through the mediation of such knowledge has God dwelling in him; but he merely possesses knowledge of creatures, and from this by means of analogy he infers the existence of God. As to him who mysteriously possesses and sees this light, he knows and possesses God in himself, no

---

[31]That is, the created (and therefore composite) human nature united to Christ as Second Person *(hypostasis)* of the Trinity. Participation in Christ's divine glory is not limited to His own individual humanity, but is shared by those incorporated into His Body by grace.

longer by analogy, but by a true contemplation, transcendent to all creatures, for he is never separated from the eternal glory.

Let us not, then, turn aside incredulous before the super-abundance of these blessings; but let us have faith in Him who has participated in our nature and granted it in return the glory of His own nature, and let us seek how to acquire this glory and see it. How? By keeping the divine commandments. For the Lord has promised to manifest Himself to the man who keeps them, a manifestation He calls His own indwelling and that of the Father, saying, "If anyone loves Me, he will keep My word, and My Father will love him, and We will come to him and will make our abode with him" (Jn 14:23), and "I will manifest Myself to him" (Jn 14:21). And it is clear that in mentioning His "word," He means His commandments, since earlier He speaks of "commandments" in place of "word": "He who possesses and keeps My commandments, that is the man who loves Me" (Jn 14:21).

17. We have here a proof...that this contemplation of God is not a form of knowledge,[32] even though Barlaam's greatest desire is that the opposite should be true. For our own part, if we refuse to call this contemplation "knowledge," it is by reason of its transcendence—just as we also say that God is not being, for we believe Him to be above being....

18. ...But let us also hear what certain saints...have to say of the glory of God mysteriously and secretly visible to the initiated alone. Let us look first at the eyewitnesses and apostles of our one God and Father Jesus Christ, from Whom all paternity in the fulness of Holy Church is derived. And, first among them, let us listen to their leader Peter, who says, "It is not by following improbable fables that we have come to know the power and presence of Our Lord Jesus Christ, but because we have ourselves become witnesses of His greatness" (2 Pet 1:16). And here is

---

[32] In the sense of a field of human knowledge naturally accessible to the reason. Infused illumination is different in kind from that sort of knowledge, and as such is "not-knowledge" or "learned ignorance." It is in this respect that Palamas affirms that "contemplation is not knowledge."

another apostolic eyewitness of this glory: "Keeping themselves awake, Peter and his companions beheld the glory of Christ" (Lk 9:32). What glory? Another evangelist testifies: "His face shone like the sun, and His garments became white like the light" (Mt 17:2), showing them that He was Himself the God Who, in the Psalmist's words, "wraps himself in light as in a mantle" (Ps 104:2).

But, after having testified to his vision of Christ's glory on the holy mountain—of a light which illumines, strange though it may be, the ears themselves (for they contemplated also a luminous cloud from which words reverberated)—Peter goes on to say, "This confirms the prophetic word" (2 Pet 1:19). What is this prophetic word which the vision of light confirms for you, O contemplators of God? What if not that verse that God "wraps Himself in light as in a mantle"? He continues, "You would do well to pay attention to that prophetic word, as to a lamp which shines in a dark place till the day dawns." What day, if not that which dawned in Thabor? "Let the morning star arise!" What star, if not that which illuminated Peter there, and also James and John? And where will that star rise, but "in your hearts"?

Do you not see how this light shines even now in the hearts of the faithful and perfect? Do you not see how it is superior to the light of knowledge? It has nothing to do with that which comes from Hellenic studies, which is not worthy to be called light, being but deception or confounded with deception, and nearer to darkness than light. Indeed, this light of contemplation even differs from the light that comes from the holy Scriptures, whose light may be compared to "a lamp that shines in an obscure place," whereas the light of mystical contemplation is compared to the star of the morning which shines in full daylight, that is to say, to the sun.[33]

---

[33]That is, the truth of Scripture is not self-explanatory, but remains an "obscure light" until the Holy Spirit illuminates our hearts to perceive its inner meaning. By contemplation, the inner eye is purified and we are assimilated to Christ, who is all truth. Thus the hesychast is able to see the divine light directly ("in full daylight"), not only as mediated through the veils of Scripture.

Selected Bibliography

TEXTS

Edition used:
Gregory Palamas: The Triads. Translated by Nicholas Gendle. The Classics of Western Spirituality. New York: Paulist Press; London: SPCK, 1983.

Other sources:
Défense des saints hésychastes: Introduction, texte critique, traduction et notes. Edited by J. Meyendorff. Spicilegium Sacrum Lovaniense, fasc. 30–31. 2d ed. Louvain, 1973.

Treatise on the Spiritual Life. Translated by Daniel M. Rogich. Minneapolis, Minn.: Light and Life Publishing Co., 1994.

STUDIES

Chrestou, P. "Gregory Palamas." In *Festschrift Honoring the Six Hundredth Anniversary of the Death of St. Gregory Palamas,* ed. P. Chrestou, 255–71. Thessaloniki, 1960.

Krivochéine, Basile. "The Ascetic and Theological Teaching of Gregory Palamas." Parts 1–4. *Eastern Churches Quarterly* 3 (1938–39): 26–33, 71–84, 138–56, 193–214.

Mantzarides, G. I. *The Deification of Man: St. Gregory Palamas and the Orthodox Tradition.* Crestwood, N.Y.: St. Vladimir's Seminary Press, 1984.

Meyendorff, John. *St. Gregory Palamas and Orthodox Spirituality.* Translated by Adele Fiske. Crestwood, N.Y.: St. Vladimir's Seminary Press; London: Faith Press, 1974.

————. *A Study of Gregory Palamas.* Translated by G. Lawrence. 2d ed. Crestwood, N.Y.: St. Vladimir's Seminary Press, 1974.

Ware, Kallistos. "The Debate About Palamism." *Eastern Churches Review* 9 (1977): 45–63.

Julian of Norwich
(c.1342–c.1416)

The suspicion with which the writings of women mystics have often been viewed surely discouraged some women from writing at all, while those who did publish their reflections regularly did so only with diffidence and self-depreciation. Such disparagement appears at times in the writings of Julian of Norwich, who protests that she has no pretensions of being a teacher, "for I am a woman, ignorant, weak, and frail."[1] Fortunately for us, she did not allow such diffidence to keep her from writing down her revelations or "showings," for she was convinced that she had received them "by the revelation of him who is the sovereign teacher" (135) and that they would lead her fellow Christians to a deeper knowledge and love of God.

Of Julian's life we know little more than may be gleaned from her *Showings*. Born toward the end of 1342 or the beginning of 1343, she writes that as a young woman she had desired three graces: recollection of Christ's passion; a bodily sickness; and the three "wounds" of contrition, compassion for the sufferings of Christ, and longing for God. She had forgotten about the first two of these desires when, toward the middle of May 1373, she suddenly

---

[1] *Julian of Norwich: Showings*, trans. Edmund Colledge, O.S.A., and James Walsh, S.J., The Classics of Western Spirituality (New York: Paulist Press, 1978), 135. All subsequent citations of this work will be given in the text, the numbers being page references.

fell so ill that after three days she received the last rites of the church and prepared for imminent death. After two more days, however, she suddenly recovered and thereupon thought to wish for the second of the three wounds, "for I wished that his [Christ's] pains might be my pains, with compassion that would lead to longing for God" (180). With this, she suddenly began having (in the course of a single day) a series of sixteen revelations, which, after some initial hesitation, she concluded had truly been given her by God. Some time later—we do not know just when—she began living as an anchoress in a cell attached to the church of St. Julian in Norwich, apparently taking for herself the name of that saint in accordance with anchoritic custom.[2] During her many years of living in this anchorhold she wrote two versions of her showings: the first a relatively short text in which she primarily limits herself to the description of what she had experienced; and twenty years later a much longer text containing extended reflections on its meaning. It is above all in virtue of this longer text that she has come to be regarded not simply as a visionary possessed of rare literary gifts for describing her experiences but as a mystical theologian of the highest order, able to correlate her experiences with the teaching of scripture and the Christian mystical tradition in a way that is comprehensive, sane, and in some respects strikingly original.

Before we consider her teaching itself, something should be said about the nature of her revelations. Anyone reading her description of the first showing, in which she "saw the red blood running down from under the crown, hot and flowing freely and copiously, a living stream, just as it was at the time when the crown of thorns was pressed on his blessed head" (181), might be led to expect that the remaining fifteen were also of this sort, which in traditional theological language would be called imaginative visions. In fact, only five others are of this type, while a second category is made up of what Julian calls "words formed in my understanding" (traditionally called locutions), and a third is

---

[2] For a helpful description of the way of life of a medieval anchoress, see Margaret Wade Labarge, "Women Who Prayed: Recluses and Mystics," chap. 6 in *A Small Sound of the Trumpet: Women in Medieval Life* (Boston: Beacon Press, 1986).

comprised of those intellectual visions (her term is "spiritual vision") of which Augustine had written centuries before in *The Literal Meaning of Genesis* and which Teresa of Avila and John of the Cross would discuss with such acumen two centuries after Julian. Our first selection from the *Showings* is Julian's account of just such a vision of the glorified Christ, one which she herself recalls a number of times in her work as she tries to fathom all that was intended there in the constantly repeated words of Christ: "I am he, I am he, I am he who is highest" (223).

Since only the briefest of summaries of Julian's mystical theology is possible here, it may be best to focus first on a pair of contrasted terms that keep recurring in the other chapters from the long text included in this anthology—the terms *substance* and *sensuality*. Although she understandably does not attempt to give a precise, scholastic definition of these terms, by "substance" she seems to mean what other mystical writers have called the "ground" of the soul, that aspect of our being which is in immediate contact with God and which, even though "a creature in God" (285), is so like its Creator that Julian "saw no difference between God and our substance, but, as it were, all God" (285). The other element of the human person according to her theological anthropology is what she calls "sensuality" or "the sensual soul" *(sensualyte)*, designating by this term all that depends on the body; she speaks, for example, of that moment "when our soul is breathed into our body, at which time we are made sensual" (286). Certainly there is nothing negative or pejorative about sensuality for Julian, for she writes, "I saw very surely that our substance is in God, and I also saw that God is in our sensuality, for in the same instant and place in which our soul is made sensual, in that same instant and place exists the city of God, ordained for him from without beginning" (287). It is sin alone that has disrupted the original harmony between our substance and our sensuality, but if from one point of view sin is "incomparably worse, more vile and painful than Hell," since it is so unnatural, so much "in opposition to our fair nature" (304), from another point of view it is a *felix culpa,* since "the goodness of [God's] mercy and grace

231

opposed that wickedness and turned everything to goodness and honor for all who will be saved" (295).

This mercy and grace were, of course, manifested above all in the incarnation and redemption, but it is precisely in her magnificent treatment of these themes that Julian shows herself to be not simply a Christocentric mystic but one of the most profound trinitarian mystics in the history of the church. Already in commenting on her first vision of the thorn-crowned head of Christ, Julian had said that "where Jesus appears, the blessed Trinity is understood" (181). Later in the work, as part of her lengthy reflections on the meaning of the fourteenth showing, she declares that the words of the glorified Christ in the twelfth revelation ("I am he, I am he...") are in fact to be understood not simply of the second Person of the Trinity but of the triune God *in toto*:

> As truly as God is our Father, so truly is God our Mother, and he revealed that in everything, and especially in these sweet words where he says: I am he; that is to say: I am he, the power and goodness of fatherhood; I am he, the wisdom and lovingness of motherhood; I am he, the light and grace which is all blessed love; I am he, the Trinity; I am he, the unity; I am he, the supreme goodness of every kind of thing; I am he who makes you to love; I am he who makes you to long; I am he, the endless fulfillment of all true desires. (296)

Our final point by way of introduction to Julian concerns her declaration at the beginning of the passage just quoted that God is "truly...our Mother." This theme, and particularly her attribution of motherhood to Jesus, is very prominent in the chapters here presented. Recent scholarship has shown that the allusions to God's motherhood in scripture had already been elaborated by some of the fathers of the church and that the motherhood of Jesus was a favorite subject of many Cistercian writers of the twelfth century.[3]

---

[3]See Ritamary Bradley, "Patristic Background of the Mother Similitude in Julian of Norwich," *Christian Scholar's Review* 8 (1978): 101–13, and Caroline Walker Bynum, "Jesus as Mother and Abbot as Mother: Some Themes in Twelfth-Century Cistercian Writing," chap. 4 in *Jesus as Mother: Studies in the Spirituality of the High Middle Ages* (Berkeley and Los Angeles: University of California Press, 1983).

Seldom, however, had this theme received the extended treatment that it has in Julian's *Showings,* nor had the obviously maternal aspects of Christ as the one who feeds us in the Eucharist and saves us from perishing through his own suffering and death been complemented in the writings of Julian's predecessors by a parallel emphasis on the maternal aspects of Christ's role (as eternal Wisdom) in our *creation.* In Julian, the creative and redemptive works of "Jesus our Mother" are regularly brought together, as when she writes that "Jesus is our true Mother in nature by our first creation, and he is our true Mother in grace by his taking our created nature. All the lovely works and all the sweet loving offices of beloved motherhood are appropriated to the second person..." (296).[4]

Even with good, modern English translations now available, reading Julian is not particularly easy, which is perhaps one reason why, at least up to the present time, her *Showings* have not been as widely read as the works of other major fourteenth-century mystics. But those who take the time to read her carefully and reflectively will understand why Thomas Merton once wrote that she "is without doubt one of the most wonderful of all Christian voices. She gets greater and greater in my eyes as I grow older....I think that Julian of Norwich is, with Newman, the greatest English theologian."[5]

---

[4]On this point, see J. P. H. Clark, "Nature, Grace and the Trinity in Julian of Norwich," *Downside Review* 100 (1982): 211.

[5]From a letter of Merton's quoted in Robert Llewelyn, *All Shall Be Well: The Spirituality of Julian of Norwich for Today* (New York: Paulist Press, 1982), 137.

SHOWINGS (LONG TEXT)

The Twenty-Sixth Chapter

And after this our Lord showed himself to me, and he appeared to me more glorified than I had seen him before, in which I was taught that our soul will never have rest till it comes into him, acknowledging that he is full of joy, familiar and courteous and blissful and true life. Again and again our Lord said: I am he, I am he, I am he who is highest. I am he whom you love. I am he in whom you delight. I am he whom you serve. I am he for whom you long. I am he whom you desire. I am he whom you intend. I am he who is all. I am he whom Holy Church preaches and teaches to you. I am he who showed himself before to you. The number of the words surpasses my intelligence and my understanding and all my powers, for they were the most exalted, as I see it, for in them is comprehended I cannot tell what; but the joy which I saw when they were revealed surpasses all that the heart can think or the soul may desire. And therefore these words are not explained here, but let every man accept them as our Lord intended them, according to the grace God gives him in understanding and love....

The Fifty-Eighth Chapter

God the blessed Trinity, who is everlasting being, just as he is eternal from without beginning, just so was it in his eternal purpose

From *Julian of Norwich: Showings,* trans. Edmund Colledge, O.S.A., and James Walsh, S.J., The Classics of Western Spirituality (New York: Paulist Press, 1978), 223–24, 293–305. Reprinted with permission of the publisher.

to create human nature, which fair nature was first prepared for his own Son, the second person; and when he wished, by full agreement of the whole Trinity he created us all once. And in our creating he joined and united us to himself, and through this union we are kept as pure and as noble as we were created. By the power of that same precious union we love our Creator and delight in him, praise him and thank him and endlessly rejoice in him. And this is the work which is constantly performed in every soul which will be saved, and this is the godly will mentioned before.

And so in our making, God almighty is our loving Father, and God all wisdom is our loving Mother, with the love and the goodness of the Holy Spirit, which is all one God, one Lord. And in the joining and the union he is our very true spouse and we his beloved wife and his fair maiden, with which wife he was never displeased; for he says: I love you and you love me, and our love will never divide in two.

I contemplated the work of all the blessed Trinity, in which contemplation I saw and understood these three properties: the property of the fatherhood, and the property of the motherhood, and the property of the lordship in one God. In our almighty Father we have our protection and our bliss, as regards our natural substance, which is ours by our creation from without beginning; and in the second person, in knowledge and wisdom we have our perfection, as regards our sensuality, our restoration and our salvation, for he is our Mother, brother and saviour; and in our good Lord the Holy Spirit we have our reward and our gift for our living and our labour, endlessly surpassing all that we desire in his marvelous courtesy, out of his great plentiful grace. For all our life consists of three: In the first we have our being, and in the second we have our increasing, and in the third we have our fulfillment. The first is nature, the second is mercy, and the third is grace.

As to the first, I saw and understood that the high might of the Trinity is our Father, and the deep wisdom of the Trinity is our Mother, and the great love of the Trinity is our Lord; and all these we have in nature and in our substantial creation. And furthermore I saw that the second person, who is our Mother, substantially the same beloved person, has now become our mother sensually, because we are double by God's creating, that is to say substantial and sensual. Our substance is the higher part, which we have in our Father, God almighty; and the second person of the Trinity is our Mother in nature in our substantial creation, in whom we are founded and rooted, and he is our Mother of mercy in taking our sensuality. And so our Mother is working on us in various ways, in whom our parts are kept undivided; for in our Mother Christ we profit and increase, and in mercy he reforms and restores us, and by the power of his Passion, his death and his Resurrection he unites us to our substance. So our Mother works in mercy on all his beloved children who are docile and obedient to him, and grace works with mercy, and especially in two properties, as it was shown, which working belongs to the third person, the Holy Spirit. He works, rewarding and giving. Rewarding is a gift for our confidence which the Lord makes to those who have laboured; and giving is a courteous act which he does freely, by grace, fulfilling and surpassing all that creatures deserve.

Thus in our Father, God almighty, we have our being, and in our Mother of mercy we have our reforming and our restoring, in whom our parts are united and all made perfect man, and through the rewards and the gifts of grace of the Holy Spirit we are fulfilled. And our substance is in our Father, God almighty, and our substance is in our Mother, God all wisdom, and our substance is in our Lord God, the Holy Spirit, all goodness, for our substance is whole in each person of the Trinity, who is one God. And our sensuality is only in the second person, Christ Jesus, in whom is the Father and the Holy Spirit; and in him and by him we are powerfully taken out of hell and out of the wretchedness on earth, and gloriously brought up into heaven, and blessedly united to our substance, increased in riches and nobility by all the power of Christ and by the grace and operation of the Holy Spirit.

The Fifty-Ninth Chapter

And we have all this bliss by mercy and grace, and this kind of bliss we never could have had and known, unless that property of goodness which is in God had been opposed, through which we have this bliss. For wickedness has been suffered to rise in opposition to that goodness; and the goodness of mercy and grace opposed that wickedness, and turned everything to goodness and honour for all who will be saved. For this is that property in God which opposes good to evil. So Jesus Christ, who opposes good to evil, is our true Mother. We have our being from him, where the foundation of motherhood begins, with all the sweet protection of love which endlessly follows.

As truly as God is our Father, so truly is God our Mother, and he revealed that in everything, and especially in these sweet words where he says: I am he; that is to say: I am he, the power and goodness of fatherhood; I am he, the wisdom and the lovingness of motherhood; I am he, the light and the grace which is all blessed love: I am he, the Trinity; I am he, the unity; I am he, the great supreme goodness of every kind of thing; I am he who makes you to love; I am he who makes you to long; I am he, the endless fulfilling of all true desires. For where the soul is highest, noblest, most honourable, still it is lowest, meekest and mildest.

And from this foundation in substance we have all the powers of our sensuality by the gift of nature, and by the help and the furthering of mercy and grace, without which we cannot profit. Our great Father, almighty God, who is being, knows us and loved us before time began. Out of this knowledge, in his most wonderful deep love, by the prescient eternal counsel of all the blessed Trinity, he wanted the second person to become our Mother, our brother and our saviour. From this it follows that as truly as God is our Father, so truly is God our Mother. Our Father wills, our Mother works, our good Lord the Holy Spirit confirms. And therefore it is our part to love our God in whom we have our being, reverently thanking and praising him for our creation, mightily praying to our Mother for mercy and pity, and to our Lord the Holy Spirit for help and grace. For in these three is all our life: nature, mercy and grace, of which we have mildness, patience and pity, and hatred of sin and wickedness; for the virtues must of themselves hate sin and wickedness.

And so Jesus is our true Mother in nature by our first creation, and he is our true Mother in grace by his taking our created nature. All the lovely works and all the sweet loving offices of beloved motherhood are appropriated to the second person, for in him we have this godly will, whole and safe forever, both in nature and in grace, from his own goodness proper to him.

I understand three ways of contemplating motherhood in God. The first is the foundation of our nature's creation; the second is his taking of our nature, where the motherhood of grace begins; the third is the motherhood at work. And in that, by the same grace, everything is penetrated, in length and in breadth, in height and in depth without end; and it is all one love.

The Sixtieth Chapter

But now I should say a little more about this penetration, as I understood our Lord to mean: How we are brought back by the motherhood of mercy and grace into our natural place, in which we were created by the motherhood of love, a mother's love which never leaves us.

Our Mother in nature, our Mother in grace, because he wanted altogether to become our Mother in all things, made the foundation of his work most humbly and most mildly in the maiden's womb. And he revealed that in the first revelation, when he brought that meek maiden before the eye of my understanding in the simple stature which she had when she conceived; that is to say that our great God, the supreme wisdom of all things, arrayed and prepared himself in this humble place, all ready in our poor flesh, himself to do the service and the office of motherhood in everything. The mother's service is nearest, readiest and surest: nearest because it is most natural, readiest because it is most loving, and surest because it is truest. No one ever might or could perform this office fully, except only him. We know that all our mothers bear us for pain and for death. O, what is that? But our true Mother Jesus, he alone bears us for joy and for endless life, blessed may he be. So he carries us within him in love and travail, until the full time when he wanted to suffer the sharpest thorns and cruel pains that ever were or will be, and at the last he died. And when he had finished, and had borne us so for bliss, still all this could not satisfy his wonderful love. And he revealed this in these great surpassing words of love: If I could suffer more, I would suffer more. He could not die any more, but he did not want to cease working; therefore he must needs nourish us, for the precious love of motherhood has made him our debtor.

The mother can give her child to suck of her milk, but our precious Mother Jesus can feed us with himself, and does, most courteously and most tenderly, with the blessed sacrament, which is the precious food of true life; and with all the sweet sacraments he sustains us most mercifully and graciously, and so he meant in these blessed words, where he said: I am he whom Holy Church preaches and teaches to you. That is to say: All the health and the life of the sacraments, all the power and the grace of my word, all the goodness which is ordained in Holy Church for you, I am he.

The mother can lay her child tenderly to her breast, but our tender Mother Jesus can lead us easily into his blessed breast through his sweet open side, and show us there a part of the godhead and of the joys of heaven, with inner certainty of endless bliss. And that he revealed in the tenth revelation, giving us the same understanding in these sweet words which he says: See how I love you, looking into his blessed side, rejoicing.

This fair lovely word "mother" is so sweet and so kind in itself that it cannot truly be said of anyone or to anyone except of him and to him who is the true Mother of life and of all things. To the property of motherhood belong nature, love, wisdom and knowledge, and this is God. For though it may be so that our bodily bringing to birth is only little, humble and simple in comparison with our spiritual bringing to birth, still it is he who does it in the creatures by whom it is done. The kind, loving mother who knows and sees the need of her child guards it very tenderly, as the nature and condition of motherhood will have. And always as the child grows in age and in stature, she acts differently, but she does not change her love. And when it is even older, she allows it to be chastised to destroy its faults, so as to make the child receive virtues and grace. This work, with everything which is lovely and good, our Lord performs in those by whom it is done. So he is our Mother in nature by the operation of grace in the lower part, for love of the higher part. And he wants us to know it, for he wants to have all our love attached to him; and in this I saw that every debt which we owe by God's command to fatherhood and motherhood is fulfilled in truly loving God, which blessed love Christ works in us. And this was revealed in everything, and especially in the great bounteous words when he says: I am he whom you love.

The Sixty-First Chapter

And in our spiritual bringing to birth he uses more tenderness, without any comparison, in protecting us. By so much as our soul is more precious in his sight, he kindles our understanding, he prepares our ways, he eases our conscience, he comforts our soul, he illumines our heart and gives us partial knowledge and love of his blessed divinity, with gracious memory of his sweet humanity and his blessed Passion, with courteous wonder over his great surpassing goodness, and makes us to love everything which he loves for love of him, and to be well satisfied with him and with all his works. And when we fall, quickly he raises us up with his loving embrace and his gracious touch. And when we are strengthened by his sweet working, then we willingly choose him by his grace, that we shall be his servants and his lovers, constantly and forever.

And yet after this he allows some of us to fall more heavily and more grievously than ever we did before, as it seems to us. And then we who are not all wise think that everything which we have undertaken was all nothing. But it is not so, for we need to fall, and we need to see it; for if we did not fall, we should not know how feeble and how wretched we are in ourselves, nor, too, should we know so completely the wonderful love of our Creator.

For we shall truly see in heaven without end that we have sinned grievously in this life; and notwithstanding this, we shall truly see that we were never hurt in his love, nor were we ever of less value in his sight. And by the experience of this falling we shall have a great and marvelous knowledge of love in God without end; for enduring and marvelous is that love which cannot and will not be broken because of offences.

And this was one profitable understanding; another is the humility and meekness which we shall obtain by the sight of our fall, for by that we shall be raised high in heaven, to which raising we might never have come without that meekness. And therefore we need to see it; and if we do not see it, though we fell, that would not profit us. And commonly we first fall and then see it; and both are from the mercy of God.

The mother may sometimes suffer the child to fall and to be distressed in various ways, for its own benefit, but she can never suffer any kind of peril to come to her child, because of her love. And though our earthly mother may suffer her child to perish, our heavenly Mother Jesus may never suffer us who are his children to perish, for he is almighty, all wisdom and all love, and so is none but he, blessed may he be.

But often when our falling and our wretchedness are shown to us, we are so much afraid and so greatly ashamed of ourselves that we scarcely know where we can put ourselves. But then our courteous Mother does not wish us to flee away, for nothing would be less pleasing to him; but he then wants us to behave like a child. For when it is distressed and frightened, it runs quickly to its mother; and if it can do no more, it calls to the mother for help with all its might. So he wants us to act as a meek child, saying: My kind Mother, my gracious Mother, my beloved Mother, have mercy on me. I have made myself filthy and unlike you, and I may not and cannot make it right except with your help and grace.

And if we do not then feel ourselves eased, let us at once be sure that he is behaving as a wise Mother. For if he sees that it is

241

profitable to us to mourn and to weep, with compassion and pity he suffers that until the right time has come, out of his love. And then he wants us to show a child's characteristics, which always naturally trusts in its mother's love in well-being and in woe. And he wants us to commit ourselves fervently to the faith of Holy Church, and find there our beloved Mother in consolation and true understanding, with all the company of the blessed. For one single person may often be broken, as it seems to him, but the entire body of Holy Church was never broken, nor ever will be without end. And therefore it is a certain thing, and good and gracious to will, meekly and fervently, to be fastened and united to our mother Holy Church, who is Christ Jesus. For the flood of mercy which is his dear blood and precious water is plentiful to make us fair and clean. The blessed wounds of our saviour are open and rejoice to heal us. The sweet gracious hands of our Mother are ready and diligent about us; for he in all this work exercises the true office of a kind nurse, who has nothing else to do but attend to the safety of her child.

It is his office to save us, it is his glory to do it, and it is his will that we know it; for he wants us to love him sweetly and trust in him meekly and greatly. And he revealed this in these gracious words: I protect you very safely.

The Sixty-Second Chapter

For at that time he revealed our frailty and our falling, our trespasses and our humiliations, our chagrins and our burdens and all our woe, as much as it seemed to me could happen in this life. And with that he revealed his blessed power, his blessed wisdom, his blessed love, and that he protects us at such times, as tenderly and as sweetly, to his glory, and as surely to our salvation as he does when we are in the greatest consolation and comfort, and raises us to this in spirit, on high in heaven, and turns everything to his glory and to our joy without end. For his precious love, he never allows us to lose time; and all this is of the natural goodness of God by the operation of grace.

God is essence in his very nature; that is to say, that goodness which is natural is God. He is the ground, he is the substance, he is very essence or nature, and he is the true Father and the true Mother of natures. And all natures which he has made to flow out of him to work his will, they will be restored and brought back into him by the salvation of man through the operation of grace. For all natures which he has put separately in different creatures are all in man, wholly, in fullness and power, in beauty and in goodness, in kingliness and in nobility, in every manner of stateliness, preciousness and honour.

Here we can see that we are all bound to God by nature, and we are bound to God by grace. Here we can see that we do not need to seek far afield so as to know various natures, but to go to Holy Church, into our Mother's breast, that is to say into our own soul, where our Lord dwells. And there we should find everything, now in faith and understanding, and afterwards truly, in himself, clearly, in bliss.

But let no man or woman apply this particularly to himself, because it is not so. It is general, because it is our precious Mother Christ, and for him was this fair nature prepared for the honour and the nobility of man's creation, and for the joy and the bliss of man's salvation, just as he saw, knew and recognized from without beginning.

The Sixty-Third Chapter

Here we may see that truly it belongs to our nature to hate sin, and truly it belongs to us by grace to hate sin, for nature is all good and fair in itself, and grace was sent out to save nature and destroy sin, and bring fair nature back again to the blessed place from which it came, which is God, with more nobility and honour by the powerful operation of grace. For it will be seen before God by all his saints in joy without end that nature has been tried in the fire of tribulation, and that no lack or defect is found in it.

So are nature and grace of one accord; for grace is God, as uncreated nature is God. He is two in his manner of operation, and one in love, and neither of these works without the other, and they are not separated. And when we by the mercy of God and with his help reconcile ourselves to nature and to grace, we shall see truly that sin is incomparably worse, more vile and painful than hell. For it is in opposition to our fair nature, for as truly as sin is unclean, so truly is sin unnatural. All this is a horrible thing to see for the loving soul which would wish to be all fair and shining in the sight of God, as nature and grace teach. But do not let us be afraid of this, except insofar as fear may be profitable; but let us meekly lament to our beloved Mother, and he will sprinkle us all with his precious blood, and make our soul most pliable and most mild, and heal us most gently in the course of time, just as it is most glory to him and joy to us without end. And from this sweet and gentle operation he will never cease or desist, until all his beloved children are born and brought to birth; and he revealed that when he gave understanding of the spiritual thirst which is the longing in love which will last till the day of judgment.

So in our true Mother Jesus our life is founded in his own prescient wisdom from without beginning, with the great power of the Father and the supreme goodness of the Holy Spirit. And in accepting our nature he gave us life, and in his blessed dying on the Cross he bore us to endless life. And since that time, now and ever until the day of judgment, he feeds us and fosters us, just as the great supreme lovingness of motherhood wishes, and as the natural need of childhood asks. Fair and sweet is our heavenly Mother in the sight of our soul, precious and lovely are the children of grace in the sight of our heavenly Mother, with gentleness and meekness and all the lovely virtues which belong to children by nature. For the child does not naturally despair of the mother's love, the child does not naturally rely upon itself, naturally the child loves the mother and either of them the other.

These, and all others that resemble them, are such fair virtues, with which our heavenly Mother is served and pleased. And I understood no greater stature in this life than childhood, with its feebleness and lack of power and intelligence, until the time that our gracious Mother has brought us up into our Father's bliss. And there it will truly be made known to us what he means in the sweet words when he says: All will be well, and you will see it yourself that every kind of thing will be well. And then will the bliss of our motherhood in Christ be to begin anew in the joys of our Father, God, which new beginning will last, newly beginning without end.

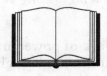

Selected Bibliography

TEXTS

Edition used:
Julian of Norwich: Showings. Translated by Edmund Colledge, O.S.A., and James Walsh, S.J. The Classics of Western Spirituality. New York: Paulist Press; London: SPCK, 1978.

Other sources:
Revelations of Divine Love. Translated by Clifton Wolters. Harmondsworth and New York: Penguin, 1966.

Revelation of Love. Translated by John Skinner. Garden City, N.Y.: Doubleday, Image Books, 1997.

STUDIES

Baker, Denise Nowakowski. *Julian of Norwich's "Showings": From Vision to Book*. Princeton, N.J.: Princeton University Press, 1994.

Jantzen, Grace. *Julian of Norwich: Mystic and Theologian*. New York: Paulist Press, 1988.

Lichtmann, Maria R. "Julian of Norwich and the Ontology of the Feminine." *Studia Mystica* 13 (1990): 53-65.

Llewelyn, Robert. *All Shall Be Well: The Spirituality of Julian of Norwich for Today*. New York: Paulist Press, 1985.

Nuth, Joan M. *Wisdom's Daughter: The Theology of Julian of Norwich*. New York: Crossroad, 1991.

Pelphrey, Brant. *Julian of Norwich. The Way of the Christian Mystics*. Wilmington, Del.: Michael Glazier, 1988.

The Cloud
of Unknowing
(fourteenth century)

The anonymous writer of *The Cloud of Unknowing* belongs, together with Pseudo-Dionysius and Eckhart, to the more radical branch of negative theology. Contrary to the other two, however, his approach is practical rather than theoretical. Negative theology, a mode of speaking of God as being beyond the names we commonly attribute to God, began with the third-century Greek philosopher Plotinus, who based it on a few obscure passages in Plato. Christians soon accepted it as part of spiritual theology but qualified the negation, claiming that God's self-revelation was indeed in scripture and in the person of Jesus Christ. The author of *The Cloud*—most likely a priest in a religious order, possibly a Carthusian—explored negative theology's application as a method of prayer. He considers "dark contemplation" a normal step in the development of a devout person who for years has practiced religious virtue and meditated on the mysteries of the Christian faith. There comes a time when such a person will make no more progress by following traditional methods of meditation. To him or her, the author presents a different mode of praying, one that is no longer led by a desire to know but by one to love without knowledge. In another short essay, *The Book of Privy*

Counseling, the author explains the transition. This latter treatise is not directed to a general, spiritual readership but to a person ready for contemplative prayer:

> You have reached a point where your further growth in perfection demands that you do not feed your mind with meditations on the multiple aspects of your being. In the past these meditations helped you to understand something of God....But now it is important that you seriously concentrate on the effort to abide continually in the deep center of your spirit, offering to God that naked blind awareness of your being which I call your first fruit. (chap. 5)

The Cloud, then, is not a philosophical treatise on negative theology, as some of Plotinus's and Proclus's writings were. Nor is it even a theological one, as Eckhart's Latin works were. It is intended to assist a person in finding a mode of contemplation unencumbered by the discursive method of meditation. Yet behind the practical advice lies an original, remarkable theology. The obvious question occurs: How may the soul communicate with a God whom it does not know at all? *The Cloud* answers this in a twofold way. First, its author draws attention to the fact that all faith is by its very nature "obscure." The believer can never claim to possess a full understanding of the Christian mysteries but can darkly intuit in and through these mysteries what lies beyond all understanding. The contemplative presupposes these mysteries, is inspired by them, but then in the actual exercise of faith leaves them behind. A second part of the answer is that the receptive soul is moved by "the blind stirring" of love. The soul responds to a mysterious desire for God in a love that surpasses our knowledge of God and, in fact, actually leads to a new, "dark" knowledge. The author considered this "stirring" crucial for his doctrine and actually devoted a separate short treatise to it, *An Epistle of Discretion of Stirrings.*

This blind link of love may well be *The Cloud's* most original and most valuable teaching about the Christian meaning of negative theology. Through it the author achieved a unique synthesis between Dionysius's negative theology and the kind of love mysticism that, in

248

the West, had originated with Bernard. How keenly he was aware of the full significance of both sources appears from the fact that he translated (very freely and not very accurately) works of Bernard as well as of Dionysius. *The Cloud's* main authority is unquestionably Dionysius's *Mystical Theology,* which the author paraphrased under the title *Deonise Hid Divinite.* He refers to Dionysius and defines the mystical life in his terms. Having asserted that by the knowledge of created things a person can never reach the uncreated, he adds: "But by the failing of it [knowledge], he can. For where his understanding fails is in nothing except God alone; and it was for this reason that Saint Denis said, 'The truly divine knowledge of God is that which is known by unknowing'" (chap. 71). Indeed, unknowing itself here appears as a means to purify the soul and thus to prepare it for the union of love.

While Dionysius led him *to* love, Bernard instructed him about *the ways* of love. The author "translated" two sermons of Bernard under the title *A Treatise of Discretion of Spirits.* He also wrote a paraphrase of Richard of Saint Victor's famous work on love mysticism, *A Treatise of Discretion of the Study of Wisdom that Men Call Benjamin.* By means of an analogy of the patriarch Benjamin's birth, Richard explicates the dialectic between knowledge and love that *The Cloud* presupposes. Benjamin, who stands for contemplation, is the son of Rachel, who stands for reason. Indeed, the soul must have some knowledge of itself and its relation to God before contemplation is possible. Yet once Benjamin is born, his mother Rachel dies. In contemplation proper, discursive reason vanishes altogether and the dark knowledge of God's love becomes the soul's only light. Love, then, transforms *apophatic* mysticism into *kataphatic,* one that can and does speak of God.

This interpretation considerably altered the traditional reading of Dionysius and initiated a dispute concerning the nature of mysticism that was to culminate in the fifteenth century: Does mystical contemplation consist in the mind's pure *understanding,* that is, in a knowledge free of images and concepts but still a knowledge? Or is it ecstatic love *without* understanding? Chancellor Gerson had claimed that mystical love always contains an intellectual element, for how could the soul love what it does not know? Others, especially the Carthusians, attacked this position, claiming that it betrayed Dionysius's thought, the core of which was entirely affective, not cognitive. Though one may doubt whether their interpretation of Dionysius was right, it seems certain that the scholastic notion of mysticism as "pure intelligence" (embraced by Gerson in his *Mystical Theology*) leaves out an element that had been prominent in mystical writers since Eckhart and Ruusbroec and was to be given even stronger emphasis by John of the Cross. It was precisely this element that the author of *The Cloud* developed in his idea of "blind stirring." Somewhat earlier, Ruusbroec had described the mystical union as an immediate (that is, without any intermediary) presence of God that reveals itself to the soul in God's *touching* it. John of the Cross will speak even more explicitly of a *toque sustancial,* a touching of the soul's substance. Such a touch does create a light, but it is a "blinding" or "incomprehensible" light that cannot be compared to ordinary understanding. It is in fact, as Ruusbroec writes, God's own brightness. The author of *The Cloud* thus stands at a turning point in the tradition of negative theology. He inverts the relation between knowledge and affection, with love now being the cause rather than the effect of mystical contemplation.

The author assumes that the practice of naked contemplation is in principle accessible to all Christians who seriously apply themselves to it. At the same time, he insists that contemplative prayer is an entirely gratuitous gift of God. No one earns it.

"It is in the nature of this gift that one who receives it receives also the aptitude for it. No one can have the aptitude without the gift itself. The aptitude for this work is one with the work" (chap. 34). Yet contrary to most Catholic theories of mysticism of the past two centuries, the author of *The Cloud* does not conclude from the gratuitousness of the gift that contemplative prayer is an exceptional, exclusively "supernatural" gift. It is both natural and supernatural: supernatural insofar as God works "in the depths of the spirit," for no one would desire it if God did not attract him or her to it. Yet it is natural insofar as the person who desires it also possesses the aptitude to practice it. Hence contemplation, however supernatural in origin, is not an exceptional grace reserved to only a few. The considerable popularity of *The Cloud* in our own time surely reflects our contemporaries' awareness of this.

THE CLOUD OF UNKNOWING

CHAPTER III
How this exercise is to be made; how it is worth more than all other exercises.

Lift up your heart to God with a humble impulse of love; and have himself as your aim, not any of his goods. Take care that you avoid thinking of anything but himself, so that there is nothing for your reason or your will to work on, except himself. Do all that in you lies to forget all the creatures that God ever made, and their works, so that neither your thought nor your desire be directed or extended to any of them, neither in general nor in particular. Let them alone and pay no attention to them. This is the work of the soul that pleases God most. All saints and angels take joy in this exercise, and are anxious to help it on with all their might. All the devils are furious when you undertake it, and make it their business, insofar as they can, to destroy it. We cannot know how wonderfully all people dwelling on earth are helped by this exercise. Yes, and the souls in purgatory are eased of their pain, and you yourself are purified and made virtuous, much more by this work than by any other. Yet it is the easiest exercise of all and most readily accomplished when a soul is helped by grace in this felt desire; otherwise, it would be extraordinarily difficult for you to make this exercise. Do not hang back then, but labour in it until you experience the desire. For when you first begin to undertake

From *The Cloud of Unknowing,* ed. James Walsh, S.J., The Classics of Western Spirituality (New York: Paulist Press, 1981), 119–23, 127–41. Reprinted with permission of the publisher.

it, all that you find is a darkness, a sort of cloud of unknowing; you cannot tell what it is, except that you experience in your will a simple reaching out to God. This darkness and cloud is always between you and your God, no matter what you do, and it prevents you from seeing him clearly by the light of understanding in your reason, and from experiencing him in sweetness of love in your affection. So set yourself to rest in this darkness as long as you can, always crying out after him whom you love. For if you are to experience him or to see him at all, insofar as it is possible here, it must always be in this cloud and in this darkness. So if you labour at it with all your attention as I bid you, I trust, in his mercy, that you will reach this point.

CHAPTER IV
The brief nature of this exercise; it cannot be attained by intellectual study or through the imaginative faculty.

To prevent you from making mistakes in this exercise, and from thinking that it is other than it actually is, I am going to tell you a little more about it, as I believe it to be. It is an exercise that does not need a long time before it can be truly done, as some men seem to think; for it is the shortest possible of all exercises that men can imagine. It is neither longer nor shorter than an atom. The atom, if we follow the definition of good philosophers in the science of astronomy, is the smallest particle of time. It is so little that, because of its littleness, it is indivisible and almost unperceivable. It is the time of which it is written: "All time is given to you, it shall be asked of you how you have spent it." And it is right that you should give account of it, for it is neither longer nor shorter but exactly equal to each single stirring that is in the chief working power of your soul, that is, your will. For as many choices and desires, no more and no less, as there can be and are in your will in one hour, so are there atoms in an hour. If you were reformed by grace according to the primal state of man's soul as it was before sin, you would always, by the help of that grace, be in control of that impulse or of those impulses. None of them would go unheeded, but all would reach out to the preeminent and supreme object of your will and your desire, which is God himself.

He fits himself exactly to our souls by adapting his Godhead to them; and our souls are fitted exactly to him by the worthiness of our creation after his image and his likeness. He, by himself alone, and no one but he, is fully sufficient, and much more so, to fulfil the will and the desire of our souls. And our soul, because of his reforming grace, is wholly enabled to comprehend by love the whole of him who is incomprehensible to every created knowing power: that is, to the souls of angels and of men. I speak of their knowing and not of their loving; that is why I call their souls in this case knowing powers.

Now all rational creatures, angels and men alike, have in them, each one individually, one chief working power, which is called a knowing power, and another chief working power called a loving power; and of these two powers, God, who is the maker of them, is always incomprehensible to the first, the knowing power. But to the second, which is the loving power, he is entirely comprehensible in each one individually; in so much that one loving soul of itself, because of love, would be able to comprehend him who is entirely sufficient, and much more so, without limit, to fill all the souls of men and angels that could ever exist. This is the everlastingly wonderful miracle of love, which shall never have an end. For he shall ever work it and shall never cease to do so. Let him understand it who can do so by grace; for the experience of this is endless happiness, and its contrary is endless suffering....

Whoever hears this exercise read or spoken of may think that he can or ought to achieve it by intellectual labour; and so he sits and racks his brains how it can be achieved, and with such ingenious reasonings he does violence to his imagination, perhaps beyond its natural ability, so as to fashion a false way of working which fits neither body nor soul. Truly such a man, whoever he be, is perilously deluded; and so much so that unless God in his great goodness show him his wondrous mercy, and quickly lead him away from his imaginings, to put himself meekly under direction of those experienced in the exercise, he shall be overcome by frenzies or else fall into other great mischief, spiritual sins and the devil's deceits; and through these he may easily be robbed of body and soul for all eternity. So for the love of God, take care in this exercise and do not labour with your senses or with your imagination in any way at all. For I tell you truly, this exercise cannot be achieved by their labour; so leave them and do not work with them.

Now when I call this exercise a darkness or a cloud, do not think that it is a cloud formed out of the vapours which float in the air, or a darkness such as you have in your house at night, when your candle is out. For such a darkness or such a cloud you can certainly imagine by subtle fancies, as though it were before your eyes, even on the clearest day of summer; and likewise, on the darkest night of winter, you can imagine a clear shining light. But leave such false-hood alone. I mean nothing of that sort. When I say "darkness," I mean a privation of knowing, just as whatever you do not know or have forgotten is dark to you, because you do not see it with your spiritual eyes. For this reason, that which is between you and your God is termed, not a cloud of the air, but a cloud of unknowing.

CHAPTER V
During this exercise, all creatures and all the works of creatures, past, present or future, must be hidden in the cloud of forgetting.

If ever you come to this cloud, and live and work in it as I bid you, just as this cloud of unknowing is above you, between you and your God, in the same way you must put beneath you a cloud of forgetting, between you and all the creatures that have ever been made. It seems to you, perhaps, that you are very far from him, because this cloud of unknowing is between you and your God. However, if you give it proper thought, you are certainly much further away from him when you do not have the cloud of forgetting between you and all the creatures that have ever been made. Whenever I say "all the creatures that have ever been made," I mean not only the creatures themselves, but also all their works and circumstances. I make no exceptions, whether they are bodily creatures or spiritual, nor for the state or activity of any creature, whether these be good or evil. In short, I say that all should be hid under the cloud of forgetting.

For though it is very profitable on some occasions to think of the state and activities of certain creatures in particular, nevertheless in this exercise it profits little or nothing. Being mindful or thinking of any creature that God ever made, or of any of their works either, is a sort of spiritual light. The eye of your soul is opened on it and fixed upon it, like the eye of the bowman upon the eye of the target that he is shooting at. I have one thing to say to you: Everything that you think of is above you during this time, and between you and your God. Insofar as there is anything in your mind except God alone, in that far you are further from God.

Yes, and if one may say it courteously and fittingly, in this exercise it is of little or no profit to think of the kindness or the worthiness of God, or of our Lady or the saints or angels in heaven, or even of the joys of heaven; that is to say, with a special concentration upon them, as though you wished by that concentration to feed and increase your purpose. I believe that it would in no wise be so in this case and in this exercise, for though it is good to think of the kindness of God and to love him and to praise him for that, yet it is far better to think upon his simple being and to love him and praise him for himself.

CHAPTER VI
*A short appreciation of this exercise by means
of question and answer.*

But now you put me a question and say: "How might I think of him in himself, and what is he?" And to this I can only answer thus: "I have no idea." For with your question you have brought me into that same darkness, into that same cloud of unknowing where I would you were yourself. For a man may, by grace, have the fulness of knowledge of all other creatures and their works, yes, and of the works of God's own self, and he is well able to reflect on them. But no man can think of God himself. Therefore, it is my wish to leave everything that I can think of and choose for my love the thing that

I cannot think. Because he can certainly be loved, but not thought. He can be taken and held by love but not by thought. Therefore, though it is good at times to think of the kindness and worthiness of God in particular, and though this is a light and a part of contemplation, nevertheless, in this exercise, it must be cast down and covered over with a cloud of forgetting. You are to step above it stalwartly but lovingly, and with a devout, pleasing, impulsive love strive to pierce that darkness above you. You are to smite upon that thick cloud of unknowing with a sharp dart of longing love. Do not leave that work for anything that may happen.

CHAPTER VII
How to deal with all thoughts during this exercise, particularly those which result from one's own investigation, knowledge and natural acumen.

If any thought should rise and continue to press in, above you and between you and that darkness, and should ask you and say: "What do you seek and what would you have?" you must say that it is God whom you would have. "Him I covet, him I seek, and nothing but him." And if the thought should ask you who that God is, you must answer that it is the God who made you and ransomed you, and with his grace has called you to his love. And say: "You have no part to play." So say to the thought: "Go down again." Tread it down quickly with an impulse of love, even though it seems to you to be very holy; even though it seems that it could help you to seek him. Perhaps the thought will bring to your mind a variety of excellent and wonderful instances of his kindness; it will say that he is most sweet and most loving, gracious and merciful. The thought will want nothing better than that you should listen to it; for in the end it will increase its chattering more and more until it brings you lower down to the recollection of his passion. There it will let you see the wonderful kindness of God; it looks for nothing better than that you should listen to it. For soon after that he will let you see your former wretched state of life; and perhaps as you see and think upon it, the thought will bring to

257

your mind some place in which you used to live. And so at the end, before you are even aware of it, your concentration is gone, scattered about you know not where. The cause of this dissipation is that in the beginning you deliberately listened to the thought, answered it, took it to yourself and let it continue unheeded.

Yet what it said was nonetheless both good and holy. Yes indeed, so holy that if any man or woman should think to come to contemplation without many sweet meditations of this sort, on their own wretched state, on the passion, the kindness and the great goodness and the worthiness of God, they will certainly be deceived and fail in their purpose. At the same time, those men and women who are long practised in these meditations must leave them aside, put them down and hold them far under the cloud of forgetting, if they are ever to pierce the cloud of unknowing between them and their God.

Therefore, when you set yourself to this exercise, and experience by grace that you are called by God to it, then lift up your heart to God by a humble impulse of love, and mean the God who made you and ransomed you, and has in his grace called you to this exercise. Have no other thought of God; and not even any of these thoughts unless it should please you. For a simple reaching out directly towards God is sufficient, without any other cause except himself. If you like, you can have this reaching out, wrapped up and enfolded in a single word. So as to have a better grasp of it, take just a little word, of one syllable rather than of two; for the shorter it is the better it is in agreement with this exercise of the spirit. Such a one is the word "God" or the word "love." Choose which one you prefer, or any other according to your liking—the word of one syllable that you like best. Fasten this word to your heart, so that whatever happens it will never go away. This word is to be your shield and your spear, whether you are riding in peace or in war. With this word you are to beat upon this cloud and this darkness above you. With this word you are to strike down every kind of thought under the cloud of forgetting; so that if any thought should press upon you and ask you what you would have, answer it with no other word but with this one.

If the thought should offer you, out of its great learning, to analyse that word for you and to tell you its meanings, say to the thought that you want to keep it whole, and not taken apart or unfastened. If you will hold fast to this purpose, you may be sure that the thought will not stay for very long. And why? Because you will not allow it to feed itself on the sort of sweet meditations that we mentioned before.

CHAPTER VIII
An accurate treatment, by question and answer, of certain doubts that may arise during this exercise; the suppression of rational investigation, knowledge and intellectual acumen; distinguishing the various levels and divisions of the active and contemplative lives.

But now you will ask, "What is this thought that presses upon me in this work, and is it a good or an evil thing?" "If it is an evil thing," you say, "then I am very much surprised, because it serves so well to increase a man's devotion; and at times I believe that it is a great comfort to listen to what it has to say. For I believe that sometimes it can make me weep very bitterly out of compassion for Christ in his passion, and sometimes for my own wretched state, and for many other reasons. All these, it seems to me, are very holy and do me much good. And therefore I believe that these thoughts can in no way be evil; and if it is good, and their sweet tales do me so much good, then I am very surprised why you bid me put them deep down under the cloud of forgetting!"

This strikes me as being a very good question. And so I must reflect in order to answer it as well as my feebleness permits. First, when you ask me what this thought is that presses so hard upon you in this exercise, offering to help you in this work, I answer that it is a well-defined and clear sight of your natural intelligence imprinted upon your reason within your soul. And when you ask me whether it is good or evil, I say that it must of necessity be always good in its nature, because it is a ray of God's likeness. But the use of it can be both good and evil. It is good when it is illuminated by grace, so that

259

you may see your wretched state, the passion, the kindness and the wonderful works of God in his creatures, bodily and spiritual. And so it is no wonder that it increases your devotion as much as you say. But the use of it is evil when it is swollen with pride, and with the curiosity which comes from the subtle speculation and learning, such as theologians have, which makes them want to be known not as humble clerics and masters of divinity or of devotion, but proud scholars of the devil and masters of vanity and falsehood. And in other men and women, whether they be religious or seculars, the use and exercise of this natural understanding is evil when it is swollen with proud and clever learning of worldly things and earthly ideas, for the coveting of worldly honours and rich possessions, and the pleasure and vainglory which comes from men's flatterings.

Next, you ask me why you should put down such thoughts under the cloud of forgetting, since it is true that they are good of their kind, and when well used they do you so much good and greatly increase your devotion. My answer is that you must clearly understand that there are two kinds of lives in holy Church. One is the active life, and the other is the contemplative life. The active life is the lower and the contemplative life is the higher. Active life has two degrees, a higher and a lower; and the contemplative life also has two degrees, a lower and a higher. Further, these two lives are so joined together that though in part they are different, neither of them can be lived fully without having some part in the other. For the higher part of the active life is the same as the lower part of the contemplative life. Hence, a man cannot be fully active unless he is partly a contemplative, nor can he be fully contemplative here below unless he is in some way active. It is the nature of the active life both to be begun and ended in this life. Not so, however, of the contemplative life, which is begun in this life and shall last without end. That is why the part that Mary chose shall never be taken away. The active life is troubled and anxious about many things; but the contemplative sits in peace, intent only on one thing.

The lower part of the active life consists in good and honest corporal works of mercy and of charity. The higher part of the active life, and the lower part of the contemplative, consists in good spiritual meditations and earnest consideration of a man's own wretched state with sorrow and contrition, of the passion of Christ and of his servants with pity and compassion, and of the wonderful gifts, kindness, and works of God in all his creatures, corporeal and spiritual, with thanksgiving and praise. But the higher part of contemplation, insofar as it is possible to possess it here below, consists entirely in this darkness and in this cloud of unknowing, with a loving impulse and a dark gazing into the simple being of God himself alone.

In the lower part of the active life, a man is outside himself and beneath himself. In the higher part of the active life, and the lower part of the contemplative life, a man is within himself and on a par with himself. But in the higher part of the contemplative life, a man is above himself and under his God. He is above himself, because he makes it his purpose to arrive by grace whither he cannot come by nature: that is to say, to be knit to God in spirit, in oneness of love and union of wills.

One can understand that it is impossible for a man to come to the higher part of the active life unless he leaves, for a time, the lower part. In the same way, a man cannot come to the higher part of the contemplative life unless he leaves for a time the lower part. It would be a wrong thing for a man engaged on meditation, and a hindrance to him, to turn his mind to the outward corporal works which he had done or should do, even though in themselves they are very holy works. In the same way, it would be very inappropriate and a great hindrance to a man who ought to be working in this darkness and in this cloud of unknowing, with an affective impulse of love to God for himself alone, to permit any thought or any meditation on God's wonderful gifts, kindness or his work in any of his creatures, bodily or spiritual, to rise up in his mind so as to press between him and his God, even if they should be very holy thoughts, and give him great happiness and consolation.

This is the reason why I bid you put down any such clear and insinuating thought, and cover it up with a thick cloud of forgetting, no matter how holy it might be, and no matter how well it might promise to help you in your endeavour. Because it is love alone that can reach God in this life, and not knowing. For as long as the soul dwells in this mortal body, the clarity of our understanding in the contemplation of all spiritual things, and especially of God, is always mixed up with some sort of imagination; and because of it this exercise of ours would be tainted, and it would be very surprising if it did not lead us into great error.

CHAPTER IX
During this exercise, the calling to mind of the holiest creature
God ever made is a hindrance rather than a help.

The intense activity, therefore, of your understanding, which will always press upon you when you set yourself to this dark contemplation, must always be put down. For if you do not put it down it will put you down; so much so that when you imagine that you can best abide in this darkness, and that nothing is in your mind except God alone, if you take a close look, you will find that your mind is occupied, not with this darkness, but with a clear picture of something beneath God. If this is in fact so, then indeed that thing is above you for the moment, and between you and your God. So set yourself to put down such clear pictures, no matter how holy or how pleasant they may be.

One thing I must tell you. This blind impulse of love towards God for himself alone, this secret love beating on this cloud of unknowing, is more profitable for the salvation of your soul, more worthy in itself, and more pleasing to God, and to all the saints and angels in heaven; yes and of more use to all your friends both bodily and spiritually, whether they are alive or dead. And it is better for you to experience this spiritually in your affection than it is to have the eye of your soul opened in contemplation either in seeing all the angels and the saints in heaven, or in hearing all the mirth or the melody that is amongst those who are in bliss.

Nor need you be surprised at what I say; for if you could once see it as clearly as you can come by grace to touch it and to experience it in this life, you would think as I do. But take it for granted that no man shall ever have such clear sight here in this life; but the feeling—that a man can have through grace, when God deigns to grant it. So lift up your love to that cloud; or rather, if I am to speak more truthfully, let God draw your love up to that cloud; and try, through the help of his grace, to forget every other thing.

A simple awareness of anything under God, which forces itself upon your will and consciousness, puts you further away from God than you would be if it did not exist; it hinders you and makes you less able to feel, by experience, the fruit of his love. How much more, then, do you think that an awareness which is drawn to yourself knowingly and deliberately, will hinder you in your purpose? And if the consciousness of any particular saint or pure spiritual thing hinders you so much, how do you think that the consciousness of any living person in this wretched life or any corporal or worldly thing will hinder you and be an obstacle to you in this exercise?

I am not saying that any such simple, sudden thought of any good and pure spiritual thing under God which presses against your will or your understanding, or is willfully drawn into your mind deliberately in order to increase your devotion, is therefore evil, even though it is a hindrance to this sort of exercise; and God forbid that you should understand it so! But I do say that in spite of its goodness and holiness, in this exercise it is more of a hindrance than a help—I mean during the time of the exercise. For certainly, he who seeks to have God perfectly will not take his rest in the consciousness of any angel or any saint that is in heaven.

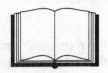

Selected Bibliography

TEXTS

Edition used:
The Cloud of Unknowing. Translated by James Walsh, S.J. The Classics of Western Spirituality. New York: Paulist Press; London: SPCK, 1981.

Other sources:
The Cloud of Unknowing and Other Works. Translated by Clifton Wolters. Harmondsworth and New York: Penguin, 1978.

The Cloud of Unknowing and The Book of Privy Counseling. Edited by William Johnston. Garden City, N.Y.: Doubleday, Image Books, 1996.

STUDIES

Clark, John P. H. *"The Cloud of Unknowing."* In *An Introduction to the Medieval Mystics of Europe,* ed. Paul Szarmach, 273–91. Albany, N.Y.: SUNY Press, 1984.

Egan, Harvey, S.J. "Mystical Crosscurrents." *Communio* 7 (1980): 4–20.

Johnston, William, S.J. *The Mysticism of The Cloud of Unknowing.* New York: Harper & Row, 1967.

Knowles, David, O.S.B. "The Excellence of The Cloud." *Downside Review* 52 (1934): 71–92.

Strolle, Charles. "The Primacy of Love in *The Cloud of Unknowing.*" *Review for Religious* 40 (1981): 736–58.

Catherine of Siena
(1347–80)

In 1962, the same year that the Second Vatican Council was convened, a remarkable statue was erected along Rome's Via della Conciliazione, the colonnaded avenue that leads to the Basilica of St. Peter, where the council fathers met. The sculpture depicts Catherine of Siena, co-patron of Italy (together with Francis of Assisi) and one of only thirty-three persons to have been declared a doctor of the church. To the right of the statue itself are four bas-relief scenes from Catherine's life, the first of which shows her dictating to two Dominican friars, each with pen in hand. The dictation was not a mere convenience, as it might be for a modern business executive. Having received no formal education as a child, Catherine was unable to write. That this unlettered woman should nevertheless rank as one of the greatest teachers in the history of the church is a striking example of the kind of paradox that regularly marks the lives of the Christian mystics.

Born in Siena in 1347 as the twenty-third child of Giacomo and Lapa di Benincasa, Catherine prepared for what eventually became a life of intense involvement in matters of church and state by living for some years in strict retirement in a small room at home. Emerging from this domestic retreat in her early twenties, she began working among the sick and poor of her native city and soon drew to herself a band of devoted followers, including some priests of the Dominican Order, to which she herself was affiliated by the simple vows of a tertiary. At this period the popes were residing at Avignon, and it was in large measure due to Catherine's personal intervention that Gregory XI returned to Rome in 1376, thereby ending the papal "Babylonian Captivity." This modest success on Catherine's part was, however, soon overshadowed by the still greater trial of the Great Schism, when two or at times three men all claimed the papal throne. In part because of the fatigue brought on by her unsuccessful attempts to end the schism, Catherine died at a relatively young age in 1380.

Three years earlier she had begun dictating the work that was originally called simply *The Book (Il Libro)* but that has subsequently come to be known as the *Dialogue,* a fitting designation for a treatise that takes the form of a conversation between Catherine and God the Father. As might be expected in a work composed by dictation over a period of some ten months, parts of the *Dialogue* are repetitious. As might also be expected from the fact that Catherine suffered so much from the trials and disorders afflicting the church of her day, the book contains many harsh denunciations of sin and vice. But the great strength of the work, and the reason why it is rightly regarded as one of the masterpieces of Christian literature, is Catherine's sure grasp of the basic doctrines of the faith (much of which she would have learned from regular participation in the liturgy) and of their practical import for the conduct of one's life. As will be evident from our selection from the *Dialogue,* her basic insight is God's love for humanity, a love manifested above all in the saving death of Christ, whom Catherine calls "the Way" or "the Bridge" between God and ourselves. As she wrote in one of her letters, "The way has been made. It is the doctrine of Christ crucified. Whoever walks along this way...reaches the most perfect light."

Like all great mystics of the Christian tradition, Catherine never divorced this emphasis on God's love for humanity from our call to show a similar love to our fellow human beings. This is most explicitly taught in our selection from chapter 78 of the *Dialogue,* where she not only speaks of a stage of "giving birth to charity in the person of her neighbor" and of a still higher stage of "perfect union" with God but also insists that these two stages can never be separated: "These two stages are linked together, for the one is never found without the other any more than charity for me [God the Father] can exist without charity for one's neighbors or the latter without charity for me."

In Catherine's life there were, to be sure, many of the extraordinary phenomena that are popularly associated with mysticism. Already at the age of six she had a vision of Christ blessing her and later claimed that her life had thereby been changed irrevocably. Moreover, her associates declared that parts of her *Dialogue* were dictated while she was in a state of ecstasy. Such phenomena, however, are altogether secondary to what makes Catherine a preeminent mystical doctor, namely, her sure grasp of the heart of the good news, her zealous attempts to bring others to live according to the gospel (whether those she addressed were popes or simply persons about whom we know nothing more than their names), and the fidelity with which she herself lived out the union of love of God and neighbor.

Nowhere is this last-named point more evident than in the letter we have selected for this anthology, one of the most famous letters in world literature. A young man, Niccolò di Toldo, had foolishly voiced some criticism of the Sienese government and, to his surprise and dismay, was condemned to death for such disrespectful language. Terrified by the ordeal facing him, he was restored to a state of calm and even joyful acceptance of his fate by Catherine, who described the change in Niccolò in this letter addressed to her Dominican confessor, Raymond of Capua. Beginning her letter with stark references to the saving blood of Christ, in which she even wishes to see Raymond "plunged and drowned," she then moves to a description of Niccolò's final hours and of the way she received into her hands his severed head on the scaffold, herself now splattered with *his* blood. She likewise describes a vision of Christ that she beheld at this time, in which the Savior's open side received the blood that had just been shed, blood "that now possessed merit through the blood of God's Son." Catherine's imagery may be shocking to our contemporary sensibilities, but the shock can be salutary, even as it can be beneficial to ponder the bas-relief placed next to the one mentioned at the beginning of this introduction. This second scene shows Catherine ready to receive Niccolò's head, with the swordsman standing in the background poised to strike. If anyone should ever think that a mystic's life is normally passed in retirement from the more violent and sanguinary aspects of human activity, this scene alone would suffice to disabuse one of the notion.

THE DIALOGUE

73. Up to now I have shown you in many ways how the soul rises up from imperfection and comes to perfect love, and what she does after she has attained the love of friendship and filial love.

I told you that she came this far by dint of perseverance and shutting herself up in the house of self-knowledge. (But this self-knowledge must be seasoned with knowledge of me, or it would end in confusion.) For through self-knowledge the soul learns contempt for her selfish sensual passion and for pleasure in her own consolation. And from contempt grounded in humility she draws patience, which will make her strong in the face of the devil's attacks and other people's persecutions, and strong in my presence when for her own good I take away her spiritual pleasure. With this power she will endure it all.

And if difficulties make her selfish sensuality want to rise up against reason, her conscience must use [holy] hatred to pronounce judgment and not let any impulse pass uncorrected. Indeed the soul who lives in [holy] hatred finds self-correction and self-reproach in everything—not only in those [movements] which are against reason but often even in those which come from me. This is what my gentle servant Gregory meant when he said that a holy and pure conscience makes sin where there is no sin. In other words, the soul in the purity of her conscience sees guilt even where there was no guilt.

From *Catherine of Siena: The Dialogue*, trans. Suzanne Noffke, O.P., The Classics of Western Spirituality (New York: Paulist Press, 1980), 135–37, 144–47, 363–66. Reprinted with permission of the publisher.

Now the soul who would rise up from imperfection by awaiting my providence in the house of self-knowledge with the lamp of faith ought to do and does just as the disciples did. They waited in the house and did not move from there, but persevered in watching and in constant humble prayer until the coming of the Holy Spirit.

This, as I have told you, is what the soul does when she has risen from imperfection and shuts herself up at home to attain perfection. She remains watching, gazing with her mind's eye into the teaching of my Truth. She is humbled, for in constant prayer (that is, in holy and true desire) she has come to know herself, and in herself she has come to know my affectionate charity.

74. Now it remains to say how one can tell that a soul has attained perfect love. The sign is the same as that given to the holy disciples after they had received the Holy Spirit. They left the house and fearlessly preached my message by proclaiming the teaching of the Word, my only-begotten Son. They had no fear of suffering. No, they even gloried in suffering. It did not worry them to go before the tyrants of the world to proclaim the truth to them for the glory and praise of my name.

So it is with the soul who has waited for me in self-knowledge: I come back to her with the fire of my charity. In that charity she conceived the virtues through perseverance when she stayed at home, sharing in my power. And in that power and virtue she mastered and conquered her selfish sensual passion.

In that same charity I shared with her the wisdom of my Son, and in that wisdom she saw and came to know, with her mind's eye, my truth and the delusions of spiritual sensuality, that is, the imperfect love of one's own consolation. And she came to know the malice and deceit the devil works on the soul who is bound up in that imperfect love. So she rose up in contempt of that imperfection and in love for perfection.

I gave her a share in this love, which is the Holy Spirit, within her will by making her will strong to endure suffering and to leave her house in my name to give birth to the virtues for her neighbors. Not that she abandons the house of self-knowledge, but the virtues

270

conceived by the impulse of love come forth from that house. She gives birth to them as her neighbors need them, in many different ways. For the fear she had of not showing herself lest she lose her own consolations is gone. After she has come to perfect, free love, she lets go of herself and comes out, as I have described

And this brings her to the fourth stage. That is, after the third stage, the stage of perfection in which she both tastes and gives birth to charity in the person of her neighbor, she is graced with a final stage of perfect union with me. These two stages are linked together, for the one is never found without the other any more than charity for me can exist without charity for one's neighbors or the latter without charity for me. The one cannot be separated from the other. Even so, neither of these two stages can exist without the other....

78. Now I would not refrain from telling you with what delight these souls enjoy me while still in their mortal bodies. For having arrived at the third stage, as I have told you, they now reach the fourth. Not that they leave the third. The two are joined together, nor can the one exist without the other any more than charity for me without charity for your neighbor. But there is a fruit that comes from this third stage, from the soul's perfect union with me. She receives strength upon strength until she no longer merely suffers with patience, but eagerly longs to suffer for the glory and praise of my name.

Such souls glory in the shame of my only-begotten Son, as my trumpeter the glorious Paul said: "I glory in the hardships and shame of Christ crucified." And in another place he says, "I bear in my body the marks of Christ crucified." So these also run to the table of the most holy cross, in love with my love and hungry for the food of souls. They want to be of service to their neighbors in pain and suffering, and to learn and preserve the virtues while bearing the marks of Christ in their bodies. In other words, their anguished love shines forth in their bodies, evidenced in their contempt for themselves and in their delight in shame as they endure difficulties and suffering however and from whatever source I grant them.

271

To such very dear children as these, suffering is a delight and pleasure is wearisome, as is every consolation or delight the world may offer them. And not only what the world gives them through my dispensation (for my kindness sometimes constrains the world's servants to hold them in reverence and help them in their physical needs) but even the spiritual consolation they receive from me, the eternal Father—even this they scorn because of their humility and contempt for themselves. It is not, however, the consolation, my gift and grace, that they scorn, but the pleasure their soul's desire finds in that consolation. This is because of the true humility they have learned from holy hatred, which humility is charity's governess and wet nurse, and is learned in truly knowing themselves and me. So you see how virtue and the wounds of Christ crucified shine forth in their bodies and spirits.

To such as these it is granted never to feel my absence. I told you how I go away from others (in feeling only, not in grace) and then return. I do not act thus with these most perfect ones who have attained great perfection and are completely dead to every selfish impulse. No, I am always at rest in their souls both by grace and by feeling. In other words, they can join their spirits with me in loving affection whenever they will. For through loving affection their desire has reached such union that nothing can separate it [from me]. Every time and place is for them a time and place of prayer. For their conversation has been lifted up from the earth and has climbed up to heaven. In other words, they have shed every earthly affection and sensual selfishness and have risen above themselves to the height of heaven by the stairway of virtue, having climbed the three stairs that I symbolized for you in the body of my only-begotten Son.

At the first step they put off love of vice from the feet of their affection. At the second they taste the secret and the love of his heart and there conceive love in virtue. At the third step of spiritual peace and calm they prove their virtue, and rising up from imperfect love they come to great perfection. Thus have these found rest in the teaching of my Truth. They have found table and food and waiter, and they taste this food through the teaching of Christ crucified, my only-begotten Son.

I am their bed and table. This gentle loving Word is their food, because they taste the food of souls in this glorious Word and because he himself is the food I have given you: his flesh and blood, wholly God and wholly human, which you receive in the sacrament of the altar, established and given to you by my kindness while you are pilgrims and travelers, so that you may not slacken your pace because of weakness, nor forget the blessing of the blood poured forth for you with such burning love, but may be constantly strengthened and filled with pleasure as you walk. The Holy Spirit, my loving charity, is the waiter who serves them my gifts and graces.

This gentle waiter carries to me their tender loving desires, and carries back to them the reward for their labors, the sweetness of my charity for their enjoyment and nourishment. So you see, I am their table, my Son is their food, and the Holy Spirit, who proceeds from me the Father and from the Son, waits on them.

You see, then, how they feel me constantly present to their spirits. And the more they have scorned pleasure and been willing to suffer, the more they have lost suffering and gained pleasure. Why? Because they are enflamed and on fire in my charity, where their own will is consumed. So the devil is afraid of the club of their charity, and that is why he shoots his arrows from far off and does not dare come near. The world strikes at the husk of their bodies, but though it thinks it is hurting, it is itself hurt, for the arrow that finds nowhere to enter returns to the one who shot it. So it is with the world and its arrows of insult and persecution and grumbling: When it shoots them at my most perfect servants, they find no place at all where they can enter because the soul's orchard is closed to them. So the arrow poisoned with the venom of sin returns to the one who shot it.

You see, they cannot be struck from any side, because what may strike the body cannot strike the soul, which remains at once happy and sad: sad because of her neighbor's sin, happy because of the union [with me] and the loving charity she has received for herself.

These souls follow the spotless Lamb, my only-begotten Son, who was both happy and sad on the cross. He was sad as he carried the cross of his suffering body and the cross of his longing to make satisfaction for the sin of humankind. And he was happy because his divine nature joined with his human nature could not suffer and made his soul always happy by showing itself to him unveiled. This is why he was at once happy and sad, because his flesh bore the pain the Godhead could not suffer—nor even his soul, so far as the superior part of his intellect was concerned.

So it is with these very dear children. When they have attained the third and fourth stage they are sad as they carry their actual and spiritual cross by actually enduring physical pain as I permit it, and the cross of desire, their crucifying sorrow at the offense done to me and the harm done to their neighbors. They are happy, I say, because the delight of charity that makes them happy can never be taken away from them, and in this they receive gladness and blessedness. Therefore their sadness is called not "distressing sadness" that dries up the soul, but "fattening sadness" that fattens the soul in loving charity, because sufferings increase and strengthen virtue, make it grow and prove it.

So their suffering is fattening, not distressing, because no sadness or pain can drag them out of the fire. They are like the burning coal that no one can put out once it is completely consumed in the furnace, because it has itself been turned into fire. So it is with these souls cast into the furnace of my charity, who keep nothing at all, not a bit of their own will, outside of me, but are completely set afire in me. There is no one who can seize them or drag them out of my grace. They have been made one with me and I with them. I will never withdraw from their feelings. No, their spirits always feel my presence within them, whereas of the others I told you that I come and go, leaving in terms of feeling, not in terms of grace, and I do this to bring them to perfection. When they reach perfection I relieve them of this lover's game of going and coming back. I call it a "lover's game" because I go away for love and I come back for love—no, not really I, for I am your unchanging and unchangeable God; what goes and comes back is the feeling my charity creates in the soul....

167. *Now that soul had seen the truth and the excellence of obedience with the eye of her understanding, and had known it by the light of most holy faith; she had heard it with feeling and tasted it with anguished longing in her will as she gazed into the divine majesty. So she gave him thanks, saying:*

Thanks, thanks be to you, eternal Father, that you have not despised me, your handiwork, nor turned your face from me, nor made light of these desires of mine. You, Light, have disregarded my darksomeness; you, Life, have not considered that I am death; nor you, Doctor, considered these grave weaknesses of mine. You, eternal Purity, have disregarded my wretched filthiness; you who are infinite have overlooked the fact that I am finite, and you, Wisdom, the fact that I am foolishness.

For all these and so many other endless evils and sins of mine, your wisdom, your kindness, your mercy, your infinite goodness have not despised me. No, in your light you have given me light. In your wisdom I have come to know the truth; in your mercy I have found your charity and affection for my neighbors. What has compelled you? Not my virtues, but only your charity.

Let this same love compel you to enlighten the eye of my understanding with the light of faith, so that I may know your truth, which you have revealed to me. Let my memory be great enough to hold your favors, and set my will ablaze in your charity's fire. Let that fire burst the seed of my body and bring forth blood; then with that blood, given for love of your blood, and with the key of obedience, let me unlock heaven's gate.

I heartily ask the same of you for every reasoning creature, all and each of them, and for the mystic body of holy Church. I acknowledge and do not deny that you loved me before I existed, and that you love me unspeakably much, as one gone mad over your creature.

O eternal Trinity! O Godhead! That Godhead, your divine nature, gave the price of your Son's blood its value. You, eternal

Trinity, are a deep sea: The more I enter you, the more I discover, and the more I discover, the more I seek you. You are insatiable, you in whose depth the soul is sated yet remains always hungry for you, thirsty for you, eternal Trinity, longing to see you with the light in your light. Just as the deer longs for the fountain of living water, so does my soul long to escape from the prison of my darksome body and see you in truth. O how long will you hide your face from my eyes?

O eternal Trinity, fire and abyss of charity, dissolve this very day the cloud of my body! I am driven to desire, in the knowledge of yourself that you have given me in your truth, to leave behind the weight of this body of mine and give my life for the glory and praise of your name. For by the light of understanding within your light I have tasted and seen your depth, eternal Trinity, and the beauty of your creation. Then, when I considered myself in you, I saw that I am your image. You have gifted me with power from yourself, eternal Father, and my understanding with your wisdom—such wisdom as is proper to your only-begotten Son; and the Holy Spirit, who proceeds from you and from your Son, has given me a will, and so I am able to love.

You, eternal Trinity, are the craftsman; and I your handiwork have come to know that you are in love with the beauty of what you have made, since you made of me a new creation in the blood of your Son.

O abyss! O eternal Godhead! O deep sea! What more could you have given me than the gift of your very self?

You are a fire always burning but never consuming; you are a fire consuming in your heat all the soul's selfish love; you are a fire lifting all chill and giving light. In your light you have made me know your truth: You are that light beyond all light who gives the mind's eye supernatural light in such fullness and perfection that you bring clarity even to the light of faith. In that faith I see that my soul has life, and in that light receives you who are Light.

In the light of faith I gain wisdom in the wisdom of the Word your Son; in the light of faith I am strong, constant, persevering; in the light of faith I have hope: It does not let me faint along the way. This light teaches me the way, and without this light I would be walking in the dark. This is why I asked you, eternal Father, to enlighten me with the light of most holy faith.

Truly this light is a sea, for it nourishes the soul in you, peaceful sea, eternal Trinity. Its water is not sluggish; so the soul is not afraid because she knows the truth. It distills, revealing hidden things, so that here, where the most abundant light of your faith abounds, the soul has, as it were, a guarantee of what she believes. This water is a mirror in which you, eternal Trinity, grant me knowledge; for when I look into this mirror, holding it in the hand of love, it shows me myself, as your creation, in you, and you in me through the union you have brought about of the Godhead with our humanity.

This light shows you to me, and in this light I know you, highest and infinite Good: Good above every good, joyous Good, Good beyond measure and understanding! Beauty above all beauty; Wisdom above all wisdom—indeed you are wisdom itself! You who are the angels' food are given to humans with burning love. You, garment who cover all nakedness, pasture the starving within your sweetness, for you are sweet without trace of bitterness.

O eternal Trinity, when I received with the light of most holy faith your light that you gave me, I came to know therein the way of great perfection, made smooth for me by so many wonderful explanations. Thus I may serve you in the light, not in the dark; and I may be a mirror of a good and holy life; and I may rouse myself from my wretched life in which, always through my own fault, I have served you in darkness. I did not know your truth, and so I did not love it. Why did I not know you? Because I did not see you with the glorious light of most holy faith, since the cloud of selfish love darkened the eye of my understanding. Then with your light, eternal Trinity, you dispelled the darkness.

But who could reach to your height to thank you for so immeasurable a gift, for such generous favors, for the teaching of truth that you have given me? A special grace, this, beyond the common grace you give to other creatures. You willed to bend down to my need and that of others who might see themselves mirrored here.

You responded, Lord; you yourself have given and you yourself answered and satisfied me by flooding me with a gracious light, so that with that light I may return thanks to you. Clothe, clothe me with yourself, eternal Truth, so that I may run the course of this mortal life in true obedience and in the light of most holy faith. With that light I sense my soul once again becoming drunk! Thanks be to God! Amen.

LETTER 9

To: *Fra Raimondo of Capua, O.P.*
Date: Probably June 1375, from Siena.

Beloved father and dearest son in Christ Jesus, I, Catherine, servant and slave of the servants of Christ, write and recommend myself to you in the precious blood of the Son of God, desiring to see you plunged and drowned in that sweet blood, all aglow with his burning charity....

So that my soul may indeed exult to see you drowned in this way, I want you, like one who draws water in a bucket, that is, in your boundless desire, to pour the water over your brethren who are all members with us in the one body, the sweet Bride. And be sure you keep at it, whatever trick the devil may play (and I know you have been and will be troubled in this way), until we actually see their sweet and loving desires flowing like blood.

Come, father, this is no time for sleep. The news is such that I simply cannot rest. Already I have taken a man's head in my hands, and been so deeply moved that my heart can hardly conceive it or my tongue relate it and I am sure no eye has seen or ear heard the like.

God's will was at work (as it had been in the mystery of what went before) but I will not go into all the details as it

---

From *I, Catherine: Selected Writings of St. Catherine of Siena*, ed. and trans. Kenelm Foster, O.P., and Mary John Ronayne, O.P. (London: Collins, 1980), 71–75. Reprinted with permission of HarperCollins Publishers Ltd.

would take too long. Well! I went to see the person you know about and my visit helped him so much that he went to confession and made a good preparation. He made me promise, for the love of God, to be with him at the end. I gave him my word, and kept it. So, early that morning before the [curfew] bell rang, I went to him and he was much consoled. I took him to hear mass and he received holy communion, which he had never done before. His own will was conformed and subject to God's, but he was still fearful that he might not be strong when it came to the point. However God, in his boundless and burning goodness, deceived him, as it were, by instilling into him such love and affection for *me* (in God) that he did not know how to be without *Him*. He kept saying: "Stay with me and don't leave me; then I shall be all right and die happy"—and all the time he leaned his head on my breast. I was aware of sudden joy, of the odour of his blood in some way mingled with that of my own, which I hope to shed for sweet Jesus my bridegroom. As my own yearning increased and I sensed his fear, I said to him: "Courage, dearest brother. We shall soon be at the wedding. *You* will be going to it bathed in the sweet blood of God's Son and with the sweet name of Jesus [on your lips]. Don't let it slip from your mind for an instant. I shall be waiting for you at the place of execution." Think of it, father (and son). At that, his heart lost all fear, the sadness on his face turned to joy and he kept rejoicing and exulting and saying: "How have I been given so much grace that my soul's delight will be waiting for me at the blessed place of my execution?" (He had reached the point of being able to call the place "blessed"!) Then he said: "I shall go with joy and courage and the time in between will seem like a thousand years, thinking that you will be there waiting for me." He said such lovely things that one could almost burst at the goodness of God.

So I waited for him at the place of execution. All the time I waited I was praying and sensing the presence of Mary and of Catherine, virgin and martyr. Before he arrived, I lay down and placed my own head on the block, but I did not quite have what I wanted. So I begged, indeed forced Mary to get me the grace I wanted, which was that I might give him light and peace of heart at the moment of death, and then see him going to God. I was so absorbed in the assurance I received that my prayer would be granted that I saw no one in the crowd around me.

At last he arrived, as meek as a lamb. When he saw me, he began to laugh and wanted me to make the sign of the Cross over him. I did so and then said: "Down with you to the wedding, brother! You will soon be in the life that never ends." He laid himself down with great meekness; then I stretched out his neck and bent over him, speaking to him of the blood of the Lamb. His lips murmured only "Jesus" and "Catherine," and he was still murmuring when I received his head into my hands, while my eyes were fixed on the divine Goodness and I said: *"I will."*

Then I saw the God-Man as one sees the light of the sun. His side was open to receive into his own the blood that had just been shed; a fire of holy desire, which his grace had poured into and concealed in that soul, was now received into the fire of his own divine Charity. After receiving the blood and the desire, he received the soul itself and plunged it into the mercy-filled storehouse of his open side. Thus did the First Truth show that his reception was due entirely to God's grace and mercy and to nothing else. How indescribably moving it was to see God's goodness; to see the gentleness and love with which he waited to welcome that soul—with the eyes of his mercy fixed on it—as it left the body and was plunged into his open side, bathed in its own blood that now possessed merit through the blood of God's Son. When he had been thus received by God in his almighty power, the Son, who is wisdom and incarnate Word, gave him a share in the crucified love with which, in obedience to the Father, he himself had endured his own painful and shameful death for the benefit of all mankind. Then the hands of the Holy Spirit sealed him into that open side.

But he did such a lovely thing—one last gesture that would melt a thousand hearts (and no wonder, seeing that he was already experiencing the divine sweetness). He looked back, like a bride who pauses on the bridegroom's threshold to look back and bow her thanks to her escort.

When he had gone, my own soul was serenely at peace, and so impregnated with the scent of blood that I could not bear to remove the blood itself that had splashed onto me. Alas, poor me, I can say no more. I was so envious, seeing myself left behind....

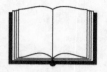

Selected Bibliography

TEXTS

Editions used:
Catherine of Siena: The Dialogue. Translated by Suzanne Noffke, O.P. The Classics of Western Spirituality. New York: Paulist Press; London: SPCK, 1980.

I, Catherine: Selected Writings of St. Catherine of Siena. Translated by Kenelm Foster, O.P., and Mary Joan Ronayne, O.P. London: Collins, 1980.

Another source:
The Prayers of Catherine of Siena. Translated by Suzanne Noffke, O.P. New York: Paulist Press, 1983.

STUDIES

Fatula, Mary Ann, O.P. *Catherine of Siena's Way. The Way of the Christian Mystics.* Wilmington, Del.: Michael Glazier, 1987.

Foster, Kenelm, O.P. "St. Catherine's Teaching on Christ." *Life of the Spirit* 16 (1962): 310–23.

O'Driscoll, Mary. "Catherine the Theologian." *Spirituality Today* 40 (1988): 4–17.

Perrin, Joseph Marie. *Catherine of Siena.* Translated by Paul Barrett. Westminster, Md.: Newman, 1965.

Raymond of Capua. *The Life of Catherine of Siena by Raymond of Capua.* Translated by Conleth Kearns. Wilmington, Del.: Michael Glazier, 1980.

Ignatius of Loyola
(1491–1556)

Only in recent years have we witnessed serious efforts to restore Ignatius to the place of honor he deserves in the development of Western mysticism. Formerly the man tended to disappear behind his formidable accomplishment: the inspiration and organization of that most versatile of all religious orders, the Society of Jesus, with its legions of saints, scholars, spiritual directors, teachers, and missionaries. Often the spiritual writings of this poor stylist were eclipsed by those of his more eloquent followers. Ignatius wrote little and, we must confess, badly. Moreover, he succeeded in destroying all but one small part of his diaries. Still we may justifiably claim that his mystical vision stands at the origin of one of the greatest outbursts of spiritual energy in the history of the Catholic Church.

His early years as a Basque soldier serving in the emperor's army held little promise of any spiritual future, active or contemplative. Only after having been wounded in the defense of the Pamplona fortress and finding nothing better to read than Ludolph the Saxon's *Life of Christ* and Jacobus de Voragine's *Golden Legend* (the lives of the saints) did the prospect of any but a military career first appear worth considering.

A little more than a year later he received his first great mystical revelation in Manresa on the bank of the River Cardoner:

As he sat there, the eyes of his understanding began to open. It was not that he beheld any vision, but rather, he comprehended, understood many things about the spiritual life as well as about faith and learning. This took place with an illumination so great that all these things appeared to be something new.[1]

It was what the schools have come to call an intellectual vision, that is, a sudden insight without sense impression or dominating image. In Elmer O'Brien's well-chosen words, "It was not knowledge delimited and defined and accorded in concepts: his inability then or later to express it in so many words is sufficient indication that it was a question of a direct experience in the order of knowing quite as that of other mystics is a direct *experience* in the order of loving."[2] Thus began a mystical life that would become ever more continuous until in the final years of Ignatius' life it was virtually uninterrupted. The constant presence of God, far from distracting him from what he understood to be his task, inspired him even in the details of its organization. But not until he had articulated the various aspects of his vision in the *Spiritual Exercises* could it effectively coordinate his apostolic activity. This mighty spiritual synthesis he wrought in the solitude of Manresa (1522–23).

For a long time the *Spiritual Exercises* enjoyed a rather dubious reputation among writers on contemplative prayer. As late as the beginning of the twentieth century some dismissed it as a mere technique, perhaps useful for bringing the recently converted to an elementary form of prayer but clearly not conducive to higher contemplation. Fortunately, such evaluations no longer appear in print today. Yet some of the difficulties that gave rise to them remain. The *Spiritual Exercises,* for all its simplicity, is an exceedingly difficult book to read. Indeed, it is not a book to read at all, but a manual of instructions about how to behave while entering into, and progressing in, the spiritual life. What Ignatius provides in the dry form of "annotations" and "points" for meditation

[1]Ignacio de Loyola, *Obras Completas* (Madrid: Biblioteca de autores Christianos, 1952), 50. *Saint Ignatius' Own Story as Told to Luis González de Cámara,* trans. William J. Young, S.J. (Chicago: Henry Regnery, 1956).
[2]*Varieties of Mystic Experience* (New York: Holt, Rinehart and Winston, 1964), 249.

constitutes in fact an effective method for opening the aspirant to receive the contemplative grace he or she is capable of receiving and not to prevent its effect in any way. The method delicately balances between eliciting the kind of active endeavor ("exercise") without which no spiritual life is possible and cautioning the exercitant to become utterly passive when divine grace invites him or her. Throughout, the work bears the mark of Ignatius' own mystical progress.

Since the *Spiritual Exercises* is essentially a process, its individual parts taken separately will not convey their full meaning, nor will they attain their intended effect. The three outlines of meditations, then, which we reproduce in the following selection, must be interpreted as way-stations or cardinal moments of that process. In the "Foundation" the "facts" of human life are reduced to their stark simplicity in order to awaken exercitants from their distracted existence. The meditation on the divine King, the centerpiece of the *Spiritual Exercises,* already conceived in Manresa, must turn the exercitants' entire life to one, spiritual purpose. The "contemplation to attain divine love" allows exercitants to return to the world they have abandoned without being distracted from their adopted spiritual goal. The terms of the *Spiritual Exercises* are carefully chosen and serve a purpose in the overall attempt to lead retreatants into less discursive prayer. "Contemplation" differs from "meditation." Frequently, in the course of either, Ignatius suggests an "application of the senses," as when he invites exercitants in the meditation on hell "to see in imagination the great fires," "to hear the wailing, the screaming, cries and blasphemies," "to smell the smoke, the brimstone, the corruption, rottenness," "to taste bitter things, as tears, sadness, and remorse of conscience," "with the sense of touch to feel how the flames surround and burn souls." Concrete presentations such as these may not be to the modern taste, but the idea behind them remains an essential part of contemplative life. They play a particularly significant role in the meditations on the life of Christ. Commentators have rightly pointed out the similarity that links them to the Christocentric tradition initiated by Francis, which, through the *Meditations on the Life of Christ* (formerly attributed to Bonaventure), found their way into Ludolph the Saxon's *Life of Christ.* Yet in the context of the *Spiritual Exercises* the applications of the senses fulfill a different, more self-conscious function. They appear in places where a direct exposure to the human Christ is expected to have a maximum impact upon retreatants' "election" of an appropriate state of perfection. At the same time, they are intended to introduce exercitants to a more contemplative mode of praying.

The meditation on the divine King, placed at a strategic position after the "Foundation" and the purgation of the "first week," when candidates are ready for a positive illumination, also betrays the impact of an earlier work of piety. On the title page of the Spanish translation of *The Golden Legend,* which Ignatius read during his convalescence, Christ appears as the King of Kings. His cross is described as a "royal standard," and Christ himself invites Christians to follow him in the "conquest of the world."[3] Yet again, Ignatius transforms the metaphor in a sense at once more practical and more contemplative. Its practical aim consists in leading candidates, now in a state of holy "indifference," to follow Christ alone. Beyond that immediate goal, however, the meditation aims at establishing a bond of prayerful and affective intimacy with the Christ whose life, death, and resurrection retreatants are about to contemplate.

Finally, the "contemplation to attain divine love" fully reveals Ignatius' intentions. That a "contemplation," unrelated to any direct plan of action, should conclude the *Spiritual Exercises* shows that the ultimate purpose of the exercises consists in bringing generous Christians to a point where they may live in the constant presence of God and work under the exclusive guidance of God's Spirit, whatever the circumstances of their task may be. In a few dry sentences Ignatius here sketches what John of the Cross was to announce and develop poetically in the *Spiritual Canticle:* "The soul is able to see in that tranquil wisdom how all the

[3]Robert W. Gleason, S.J., Introduction to *The Spiritual Exercises of Saint Ignatius,* trans. Anthony Mottola (New York: Doubleday, Image Books, 1964), 19.

creatures...raise their voice in testimony to that which God is. She sees that each one after its manner exalts God, since it has God in itself according to its capacity" (*Sp. Cant.*, st. 14/ 15). Even while stating this contemplative ideal, Ignatius keeps it united with the world of action. This mysticism of creation may well, and, in the case of the Society (which he had foremost in his mind) *must* allow, the retreatant to become a "contemplative *in action*." Precisely this unique combination of contemplation with an apostolic orientation made great men of action out of great contemplatives—missionaries like Francis Xavier or Peter Canisius; philosophers and scientists like Francisco Suarez, Joseph Maréchal, Karl Rahner, Petavius, Pierre Teilhard de Chardin; spiritual directors like Louis Lallemant, Balthasar Alvarez, Jean de Caussade.

Our final selection consists of a passage taken from Ignatius' *Spiritual Diary*. The entries in this journal (of which only seventy pages have been preserved) are extremely short, written in "telegram style," and clearly not destined to be read by others. Only the entries here reproduced, between February 19 and 29, 1544, describe at any length the nature of the experience. Together with the few visions Ignatius reported to Gonzalez de Cámara in his narrated autobiography they permit us to conclude that this reticent man of action was one of the giants of contemplation in the Western Church.

AUTOBIOGRAPHY

27. ...God treated him at this time [1522, at Manresa] just as a schoolmaster treats a child whom he is teaching. Whether this was because of his lack of education and of brains, or because he had no one to teach him, or because of the strong desire God himself had given him to serve him, he believed without doubt and has always believed that God treated him in this way. Indeed, if he were to doubt this, he would think he offended his Divine Majesty. Something of this can be seen from the five following points.

28. FIRST. He had great devotion to the Most Holy Trinity, and so each day he prayed to the three Persons separately. But as he also prayed to the Most Holy Trinity, the thought came to him: Why did he say four prayers to the Trinity? But this thought gave him little or no difficulty, being hardly important. One day while saying the Office of Our Lady on the steps of the same monastery, his understanding began to be elevated so that he saw the Most Holy Trinity in the form of three musical keys.[1] This brought on so many tears and so much sobbing that he could not control himself. That morning, while going in a procession that set out from there, he could not hold back his tears until dinnertime; nor after eating could he stop talking about the Most Holy Trinity, using

---

All selections in this chapter are from *Ignatius of Loyola: The Spiritual Exercises and Selected Works,* ed. George E. Ganss, S.J., The Classics of Western Spirituality (New York: Paulist Press, 1991), 79–81, 130, 146–48, 176–77, 245–52. Reprinted with permission of the publisher.
[1]He means keys as on a piano. Each produces its own sound, but the three sounds together are one harmony.

many comparisons in great variety and with much joy and consolation. As a result, the effect has remained with him throughout his life of experiencing great devotion while praying to the Most Holy Trinity.

29. SECOND. Once, the manner in which God had created the world was presented to his understanding with great spiritual joy. He seemed to see something white, from which rays were coming, and God made light from this. But he did not know how to explain these things, nor did he remember too well the spiritual enlightenment that God was imprinting on his soul at the time.

THIRD. At Manresa too, where he stayed almost a year, after he began to be consoled by God and saw the fruit which he bore in dealing with souls, he gave up those extremes he had formerly practiced, and he now cut his nails and his hair. One day in this town while he was hearing Mass in the church of the monastery mentioned above, at the elevation of the Body of the Lord, he saw with interior eyes something like white rays coming from above. Although he cannot explain this very well after so long a time, nevertheless, what he saw clearly with his understanding was how Jesus Christ our Lord was there in that Most Holy Sacrament.

FOURTH. Often and for a long time, while at prayer, he saw with interior eyes the humanity of Christ. The form that appeared to him was like a white body, neither very large nor very small, but he did not see any distinction of members. He saw it at Manresa many times. If he should say twenty or forty, he would not dare judge it a lie. He has seen this another time in Jerusalem and yet another while traveling near Padua. He has also seen Our Lady in a similar form, without distinguishing parts. These things he saw strengthened him then and always gave him such strength in his faith that he has often thought to himself: If there were no Scriptures to teach us these matters of faith, he would be resolved to die for them, solely because of what he has seen.

30. FIFTH. Once he was going out of devotion to a church situated a little more than a mile from Manresa; I believe it is called St. Paul's, and the road goes by the river. As he went along

occupied with his devotions, he sat down for a little while with his face toward the river, which ran down below. While he was seated there, the eyes of his understanding began to be opened; not that he saw any vision, but he understood and learnt many things, both spiritual matters and matters of faith and of scholarship, and this with so great an enlightenment that everything seemed new to him. The details that he understood then, though there were many, cannot be stated, but only that he experienced a great clarity in his understanding. This was such that in the whole course of his life, after completing sixty-two years, even if he gathered up all the various helps he may have had from God and all the various things he has known, even adding them all together, he does not think he had got as much as at that one time.

THE SPIRITUAL EXERCISES

[23] PRINCIPLE AND FOUNDATION

Human beings are created to praise, reverence, and serve God our Lord, and by means of this to save their souls.

The other things on the face of the earth are created for the human beings, to help them in working toward the end for which they are created.

From this it follows that I should use these things to the extent that they help me toward my end, and rid myself of them to the extent that they hinder me.

To do this, I must make myself indifferent[1] to all created things, in regard to everything which is left to my freedom of will and is not forbidden. Consequently, on my own part I ought not to seek health rather than sickness, wealth rather than poverty, honor rather than dishonor, a long life rather than a short one, and so on in all other matters.

I ought to desire and elect only the thing which is more conducive to the end for which I am created....

---

[1] "Indifferent": undetermined to one thing or option rather than another; impartial; unbiased, with decision suspended; undecided. It implies interior freedom from disordered inclinations. Variously nuanced by contexts, it is a key technical term of Ignatius' spirituality and very frequent throughout his writings. In no way does it mean unconcerned or unimportant.

[91–100] THE CALL OF THE TEMPORAL KING, AS AN AID TOWARD CONTEMPLATING THE LIFE OF THE ETERNAL KING.[2]

The Preparatory Prayer will be as usual.

The First Prelude. A composition by imagining the place. Here it will be to see with the eyes of the imagination the synagogues, villages, and castles through which Christ our Lord passed as he preached.

The Second Prelude is to ask for the grace which I desire. Here it will be to ask grace from our Lord that I may not be deaf to his call, but ready and diligent to accomplish his most holy will.

The First Point. I will place before my mind a human king, chosen by God our Lord himself, whom all Christian princes and all Christian persons reverence and obey.

The Second Point. I will observe how this king speaks to all his people, saying, "My will is to conquer the whole land of the infidels. Hence, whoever wishes to come with me has to be content with the same food I eat, and the drink, and the clothing which I wear, and so forth. So too he or she must labor with me during the day, and keep watch in the night, and so on, so that later they may have a part with me in the victory, just as they shared in the toil.

The Third Point. I will consider what good subjects ought to respond to a king so generous and kind; and how, consequently, if someone did not answer his call, he would be scorned and upbraided by everyone and accounted as an unworthy knight.

---

[2]Here begins the Second Week of the *Exercises,* during which the exercitant will engage in exercises characteristic of the illuminative way or stage of spiritual development, especially by contemplating Christ, the Divine Light who has come into the world. Ignatius' introduction to all the remaining weeks is his classic contemplation on "The Kingdom."...It presents Christ as the realization of the ideal of the Principle and Foundation and is often called a Second Foundation for the rest of the *Exercises,* to which it gives an explicit Christological orientation. Its aim is to stir up enthusiasm and desire to follow Christ in love and to accept his invitation to share in his saving mission.

THE SECOND PART

The second part of this exercise consists in applying the above parable of a temporal king to Christ our Lord, according to the three points just mentioned.

The First Point. If we give consideration to such a call from the temporal king to his subjects, how much more worthy of consideration it is to look on Christ our Lord, the eternal King, and all the world assembled before him. He calls to them all, and to each one in particular he states: "My will is to conquer the whole world and all my enemies, and thus to enter into the glory of my Father. Therefore, whoever wishes to come with me must labor with me, so that through following me in the pain he or she may follow me also in the glory."

The Second Point. This will be to reflect that all those who have judgment and reason will offer themselves wholeheartedly for this labor.

The Third Point. Those who desire to show greater devotion and to distinguish themselves in total service to their eternal King and universal Lord will not only offer their persons for the labor, but go further still. They will work against their human sensitivities and against their carnal and worldly love, and they will make offerings of greater worth and moment and say:

"Eternal Lord of all things, I make my offering, with your favor and help. I make it in the presence of your infinite Goodness, and of your glorious Mother, and of all the holy men and women in your heavenly court. I wish and desire, and it is my deliberate decision, provided only that it is for your greater service and praise, to imitate you in bearing all injuries and affronts, and any poverty, actual as well as spiritual, if your Most Holy Majesty desires to elect and receive me into such a life and state."

First Note. This exercise will be made twice during the day, that is, on rising in the morning and an hour before the noonday or the evening meal.

Second Note. During the Second Week, and also the following weeks, it is profitable to spend occasional periods in reading from *The Imitation of Christ,* the Gospels, or lives of the saints....

[230–37] CONTEMPLATION TO ATTAIN LOVE.[3]

Note. Two preliminary observations should be made.

First. Love ought to manifest itself more by deeds than by words.

Second. Love consists in a mutual communication between the two persons. That is, the one who loves gives and communicates to the beloved what he or she has, or a part of what one has or can have; and the beloved in return does the same to the lover. Thus, if one has knowledge, one gives it to the other who does not; and similarly in regard to honors or riches. Each shares with the other.

The Usual Preparatory Prayer.

The First Prelude. A composition. Here it is to see myself as standing before God our Lord, and also before the angels and saints, who are interceding for me.

The Second Prelude is to ask for what I desire. Here it will be to ask for interior knowledge of all the great good I have received, in order that, stirred to profound gratitude, I may become able to love and serve his Divine Majesty in all things.

The First Point.[4] I will call back into my memory the gifts I have received—my creation, redemption, and other gifts particular to myself. I will ponder with deep affection how much God our Lord has done for me, and how much he has given me of what he

---

[3]This justly renowned contemplation, coming in the Fourth Week and directed toward increasing the exercitant's love of God, is the conclusion and apt climax of the spiritual experience of the *Exercises.* Love of God is the greatest of the virtues (1 Cor 13:13), and one who thinks he loves God but does not love his neighbor is in error (1 Jn 4:20).

[4]The four points overlap somewhat; they view the gifts of God from many angles rather than in a logical order. Some find it helpful to contemplate God in point 1 as the giver of all gifts; in 2, as present in all the creatures and conserving their existence; in 3, as cooperating in their activities; and in 4, as the preeminent Source of all the good present in creatures. The prayer "Take, Lord, and receive" *(Suscipe)* is one of the most famous of Ignatius' prayers and one regularly associated with him.

possesses, and consequently how he, the same Lord, desires to give me even his very self, in accordance with his divine design.

Then I will reflect on myself, and consider what I on my part ought in all reason and justice to offer and give to his Divine Majesty, namely, all my possessions, and myself along with them. I will speak as one making an offering with deep affection and say:

"Take, Lord, and receive all my liberty, my memory, my understanding, and all my will—all that I have and possess. You, Lord, have given all that to me. I now give it back to you, O Lord. All of it is yours. Dispose of it according to your will. Give me your love and your grace, for that is enough for me."

The Second Point. I will consider how God dwells in creatures; in the elements, giving them existence; in the plants, giving them life; in the animals, giving them sensation; in human beings, giving them intelligence; and finally, how in this way he dwells also in myself, giving me existence, life, sensation, and intelligence; and even further, making me his temple, since I am created as a likeness and image of his Divine Majesty. Then once again I will reflect on myself, in the manner described in the first point, or in any other way I feel to be better. This same procedure will be used in each of the following points.

The Third Point. I will consider how God labors and works for me in all the creatures on the face of the earth; that is, he acts in the manner of one who is laboring. For example, he is working in the heavens, elements, plants, fruits, cattle, and all the rest—giving them their existence, conserving them, concurring with their vegetative and sensitive activities, and so forth. Then I will reflect on myself.

The Fourth Point. I will consider how all good things and gifts descend from above; for example, my limited power from the Supreme and Infinite Power above; and so of justice, goodness, piety, mercy, and so forth—just as the rays come down from the sun, or the rains from their source. Then I will finish by reflecting on myself, as has been explained. I will conclude with a colloquy and an Our Father.

THE SPIRITUAL DIARY

The Trinity. 1st.[1]

18. Tuesday [February 19]

...the intense love I felt toward the Holy Trinity...gave me confidence and I determined to say the Mass of the Holy Trinity, so as to see afterward what I would do.... Then with devotion and spiritual confidence, I decided to say successively six or more Masses of the Holy Trinity.

On the way to Mass and just before it, I was not without tears. During the Mass there were many and very peaceful tears, and very many insights into the Holy Trinity. These enlightened my understanding to such a degree that it seemed to me I could not learn so much by hard study. Later when I reviewed the matter again I thought that I had understood more in my experiencing or seeing than I would even if I should study all my life.

As soon as Mass was over I offered a short prayer with the words: "Eternal Father, confirm me; Son, and so on, confirm me." Tears streamed down my face, and my will to persevere in saying their Masses grew stronger (and I consented according to whatever number I would determine later). With much intense sobbing I drew much closer to his Divine Majesty and felt more assured in my increased love of him.

In general, during Mass and before it the insights were about the appropriation[2] of the prayers of the Mass when one is address-

---

[1]This refers to the first of the "six or more Masses of the Holy Trinity" that he promises to say, immediately below.

[2]Appropriation: attributing to one Person of the Trinity what is common to the three.

ing God, or the Father, or the Son, and so on while attending to the operations of the Divine Persons and their processions,[3] more by experiencing with feeling or contemplating than by understanding. Since all these things corroborated what had been done, I was encouraged for the future.

On that same day, even when I was walking in the city with great interior joy and when I saw three rational creatures, or three animals, or three other things, and so forth, I saw them as images reminding me of the Holy Trinity.

The Trinity. 2nd.

19. Wednesday [February 20].

Before starting my prayer I felt a devout eagerness to do so. After beginning, I experienced much warm or bright and mild devotion. I had no insights but was drawn rather to a confidence of soul which did not terminate in any one Divine Person.

Then, confirming myself about the past, I recognized the evil spirit there. That is to say, he was the one who wanted to make me doubt and become indignant against the Most Holy Trinity, as was stated in chapter 17.

With this recognition I felt a new interior impulse to tears. Likewise later on, before and during Mass, I experienced a greatly increased, quiet, and tranquil devotion, along with tears and some insights.

I also felt or believed, both before and after Mass, that I should not continue further; or, the desire to proceed left me—especially after Mass because of that great peace or satisfaction of soul. For it seemed unnecessary to continue the Masses of the Most Holy Trinity, unless as a thanksgiving or fulfillment of my promise;[4] but not out of any need to confirm what had been decided.

---

[3]Processions: the theological explanation that the Father produces the Son (who proceeds from him by generation from the divine intellect), and the Father and the Son produce the Holy Spirit (who is the act of love proceeding from the divine will). Ignatius contemplates these divine operations as they are in God.

[4]This refers to his promise to say six or more Masses of the Trinity. On February 19 and 20 Ignatius seemingly felt confirmed in his election of having no fixed revenue for the Society of Jesus.

The Trinity. 3rd.
20. Thursday [February 21].
Throughout the whole time of my prayer, I felt continual and very great devotion, warm brightness, and spiritual relish. I seemed somehow drawn partly upward.

Then while I was making my preparation in my room, at the altar, and while vesting, there were some interior spiritual impulses drawing me to tears. In this state I finished Mass and remained in great spiritual repose.

Throughout Mass there were tears in greater abundance than the preceding day. Once or several times I was unable to speak, experiencing spiritual insights to such an extent that I seemed to understand that there was, so to speak, nothing to be known about this matter of the Holy Trinity.

The reason for this is the following. Previously I had been trying to find devotion in the Trinity, and I neither desired nor adapted myself to seeking or finding the Trinity in prayers to the Father. For such prayers to the Father did not seem to me to be consolation or visitation pertaining to the Holy Trinity. But during this Mass I was knowing, or experiencing, or contemplating—the Lord knows—that to speak to the Father was to recognize that he was one Person of that Holy Trinity. This brought me to love that Person's whole self; and that all the more because the other two Persons were by their very essence present in that One. I experienced the same recognition about prayer to the Son, and again about prayer to the Holy Spirit. I rejoiced that when I perceived consolations from any One of them I recognized them with joy as coming from all Three. To have untied this knot, or whatever else it might be called, seemed so important to me that I kept on saying about myself: "And you, who are you? Where did you come from? How could you merit this? And whence did this come to pass?" and the like.

The Trinity. 4th.
21. Friday [February 22].
During the whole of my usual prayer I experienced much help from grace that was warm and in part bright. There was

much devotion, even though on my part I sometimes found it easy to fall into distractions. However, the assistance of the grace did not cease. Later while I was preparing the altar, there were certain motions toward tears, and I repeated often: "I am not worthy to call upon the name of the Holy Trinity." This thought and repetition moved me to greater interior devotion. While I was vesting, this consideration and others with it opened my soul still more to tears and sobs. I began Mass and continued to the Gospel, which I read with much devotion and great assistance from warm grace. Later this grace seemed to struggle, like fire with water, with some thoughts <about salvation, sometimes expelling and sometimes conserving them>.

The Trinity. 5th.
22. Saturday [February 23].

In my customary prayer I found nothing at its beginning, but from the middle on there was much devotion and satisfaction of soul, with some manifestation of bright clarity.

While I was preparing the altar the thought of Jesus came to me, and an urge to follow him. Deeply in my soul I thought that since he is the head of the Society, that very fact is a greater argument for proceeding in total poverty than all the other human reasons—even though it also seemed that all the other reasons which I had considered in the deliberations favored the same conclusion. This thought moved me to devotion and to tears, and to such a firmness that even if I were not to find tears at Mass or in my Masses and the like, this sentiment seemed sufficient to make me remain firm in time of temptations or tribulations.

As I went to vest, these thoughts increased and appeared to be a confirmation, although I did not receive consolations in this regard. The fact that Jesus showed himself or made his presence felt seemed to me to be in some way a work of the Most Holy Trinity; and I remembered the occasion when the Father placed me with the Son.[5]

---

[5]He is referring to a mystical experience he had at La Storta, near Rome, in November 1537. It is recounted in chapter 10 of his autobiography.

As I finished vesting the name of Jesus imprinted itself so intensely within me and I was so fortified or seemingly confirmed for the future that tears and sobs came upon me with a new force. As I began Mass, <overwhelming> motions of copious grace and devotion continued to help me, along with peaceful, continual tears. Even when Mass was finished, a great devotion and impulses to tears lasted until I had unvested.

During Mass I experienced diverse sentiments in confirmation of what has been stated. At the moment when I held the Blessed Sacrament in my hands, a voice and an intense emotion surged within me never to leave him for all heaven or all the world or the like. I felt new motions, devotion, and spiritual joy. I added "for my part, doing whatever was in my power." I made this addition because of my companions who had signed.[6]

Later during the day whenever I thought of Jesus or memory of him came to my mind, I had a certain deep perception or intellectual seeing which brought continual devotion and confirmation.

Mass of the Day [Quinquagesima Sunday].
23. Sunday [February 24].

In my customary prayer, from the beginning up to its very end, I experienced continual assistance from much internal, gentle grace and I was full of warm and very sweet devotion. While I was preparing the altar and vesting, the Name of Jesus was represented to me with much love and confirmation. Amid tears and sobs my will to follow him became stronger.

During the entire Mass I experienced continuous and very great devotion along with many tears, so that often I could not speak. All the devotions and sentiments terminated in Jesus. Therefore I could not apply them to the other Persons except, so to speak, inasmuch as the First Person was the Father of such a Son. In regard to that, spiritual responses came to mind: "What a Father! And what a Son!"

---

[6]Nearly three years earlier Ignatius' six companions had signed the agreement that fixed revenues would be permitted to the sacristies of the Society. Ignatius now had the embarrassing task of opposing this decision, and he was firmly resolved to do so.

After Mass, during prayer I experienced that same perception of the Son. Whereas I had sought confirmation from the Holy Trinity, I now perceived that it was being communicated to me by Jesus, who was showing himself to me and giving me such interior strength and sure confirmation that I had no fear for the future. The thought came to me to beg Jesus to obtain pardon from the Holy Trinity for me. Thereupon I had increased devotion along with tears and sobbing, and the hope of obtaining this grace. I found myself very strong and confirmed for the future.

Then at the fire[7] a fresh representation of Jesus came to me along with great devotion and impulse to tears. Later as I was walking along the street Jesus represented himself to me and I experience strong motions and tears. After I spoke to [Cardinal] Carpi and was returning home I similarly felt great devotion. After the meal, especially after I passed through the door of the vicar, in the house of Trana, while perceiving or seeing Jesus I experienced many interior motions amid many tears. I asked and begged Jesus to obtain for me pardon from the Most Holy Trinity, and all this time a feeling of great confidence remained in me that I would obtain it.

All through these hours I found in myself such intense love and such perception or seeing of Jesus that I thought that in the future nothing could come and separate me from him, or make me doubt about the graces or confirmation I had received.

St. Matthias.

24. Monday [February 25].

During the first prayer I had much devotion, and later even more with warmth and the assistance of copious grace. Yet on my side, because of some disturbances that I suffered from others, I found myself easily distracted. I did not ask or seek confirmation, but I desired reconciliation with the three Divine Persons. Then when I was vested to say Mass but did not know

---

[7] I.e., near the fire-pan of burning coals that was in the room.

to whom to commend myself or where to begin, and while Jesus was communicating himself to me, this thought came to my mind: "I want to move forward and start the prayer 'I confess to God' *(Confiteor Deo),* just as Jesus said in the Gospel of the day [Matt. 11:25] 'I confess to you' *(Confiteor tibi,* and so on)."

Immediately I moved forward into that prayer of confession, with new devotion and not without impulses to shed tears. I entered into the Mass with great devotion, warmth, tears, and occasional loss of speech. In the prayers to the Father, it seemed to me that Jesus was presenting them, or that he was accompanying into the Father's presence those which I was saying. I deeply perceived or saw this in a way that cannot be explained....

The First Day of Lent [Ash Wednesday].
26. Wednesday [February 27].

...Upon entering the chapel, during prayer I perceived deeply in my heart, or more precisely I saw beyond my natural powers, the Most Holy Trinity and Jesus. He was representing me, or placing me, or serving as my mediator with the Most Holy Trinity in order that intellectual vision might be granted to me. At this perception and sight I was covered with tears and love terminating chiefly on Jesus. Toward the Trinity too I felt a respect of affectionate awe closer to reverential love than to anything else.

Then when I thought of praying to the Father, with similar deep feeling I perceived Jesus exercising the same role. Deeply within myself it seemed that in the presence of the Father and the Holy Trinity Jesus was doing it all.

I began Mass with many tears and through the whole Mass I continually had much devotion and tears. Likewise at one moment I saw in a remarkable way the same vision of the Holy Trinity as at first.[8] All the while my love for the Divine Majesty was growing greater still. Several times I lost the power of speech.

When Mass was finished and I was in prayer and later near the fire, several times I experienced very intense devotion terminating in

---

[8]Ignatius is probably referring to his vision of the Trinity at Manresa, as recounted in his autobiography, par. 28.

Jesus, and that not without special interior impulses to tears or something more.

In writing this I find my intellect being drawn to see the Holy Trinity in such a way that I seem to see the three Persons, though not distinctly as before. At the time of Mass, when saying "Lord Jesus Christ, Son of the Living God" and so on *(Domine Iesu Christe, fili Dei vivi)*, it seemed to me that in spirit I saw Jesus in the same way as I described the first time, as something white, that is, his humanity. But now in this second time, deeply in my soul I was seeing him in another way, that is to say, I perceived not the humanity alone, but that in his whole self he is my God,[9] and so forth. There was a fresh outpouring of tears, great devotion, and the like.

The Trinity. 7th.
27. Thursday [February 28].

During the whole of my customary prayer there was much devotion and much helping grace, warm, bright, and loving. When I entered the chapel I felt a fresh devotion. After kneeling down I had a manifestation or vision of Jesus at the feet of the Most Holy Trinity and, with this, motions and tears. This vision was not as long or as clear as the past one on Wednesday, although it seemed to be of the same kind. Later during Mass there were tears, much devotion, and some profitable sentiments. After Mass I was not without tears.

Of the Wounds.
28. Friday [February 29].

During my customary prayer, from the beginning to its very end, there was very great and very bright devotion which covered my sins and would not allow me to think about them. Outside the house, in the church before Mass, I had a vision of the heavenly fatherland or of its Lord, in the form of an insight into the Three Persons, and into the Second and Third Persons as being in the

---

[9]Here too there is continuity with the visions at Manresa, but there is also a progression. At Manresa his attention was more on "the humanity of Christ" like a white body, and here on Christ as God and man.

Father. During Mass at times there was much devotion, but without insights or any motions to tears.

When Mass was finished I had the same vision of the fatherland or of its Lord without the distinction of Persons, but clearly, just as I did on many other occasions, sometimes more clearly and sometimes less. All day long there was special devotion.

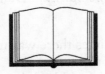

Selected Bibliography

TEXTS

Edition used:
Ignatius of Loyola: Spiritual Exercises and Selected Works. Edited by George E. Ganss, S.J. The Classics of Western Spirituality. New York: Paulist Press; London: SPCK, 1991.

Other sources:
St. Ignatius' Own Story as Told to Luis González de Cámara. Translated by William J. Young, S.J. Chicago: Loyola University Press, 1980.

The Spiritual Exercises of St. Ignatius. Translated by Anthony Mottola. Garden City, N.Y.: Doubleday, Image Books, 1964.

STUDIES

Buckley, Michael. "The Contemplation to Attain Love." *The Way Supplement,* no. 24 (Spring 1975): 92–105.

Dalmases, Cándido de. *Ignatius of Loyola, Founder of the Jesuits: His Life and Work*. St. Louis: Institute of Jesuit Sources, 1985.

Dister, John E., S.J., ed. *A New Introduction to the Spiritual Exercises of St. Ignatius*. Collegeville, Minn.: Liturgical Press, 1993.

Dupré, Louis. "Ignatian Humanism and Its Mystical Origins." *Communio* 18 (1991): 164–82.

Egan, Harvey, S.J. *The Spiritual Exercises and the Ignatian Mystical Horizon*. St. Louis: Institute of Jesuit Sources, 1976.

Rahner, Hugo, S.J. *The Spirituality of St. Ignatius Loyola: An Account of Its Historical Development*. Translated by Francis J. Smith, S.J. Westminster, Md.: Newman, 1953.

Teresa of Avila
(1515–82)

Entering the town of Avila on the Castilian plateau of central Spain where Teresa was born and lived most of her life, one cannot but be struck by its similarity with the birthplace of another doctor of the church—Siena. Safely snuggled within elegantly fortified walls, both compact cities appear to have endowed their native saints with a sense of security and a clearly defined identity. Their physical dwelling, quite naturally, came to symbolize God's presence in the soul. There the similarity between Teresa's and Catherine's living conditions ends. Teresa's family, well-to-do, belonged to the lower nobility. Her father's father had converted from Judaism, as many Jews had done after the laws of Ferdinand and Isabella. But in his case, more than moral pressure appears to have been involved, for both his sons became unusually devout Christians. Teresa's paternal uncle played a significant role both in her decision to enter a convent and, later, in her conversion to a life of genuine piety. The *Reconquista* was still in the air, even though the Catholic kings had recently (1492) and forcefully united the peninsula in the Christian faith. The seven-year-old Teresa, apparently not fully acquainted with the latest political developments, once left home with her brother to go "to the land of the Moors" in order "to be decapitated" and thus find the shortest path to heaven. This early drive to heroic sanctity soon gave way to an interest in the more profane heroism of chevaleresque novels. The young teenager started work on such a novel herself, but this premature expression of her literary inclinations never reached completion. All such mundane activities came abruptly to a halt when her father brought her, much against her will, at age seventeen, to a convent of Augustinian nuns. After less than two years Teresa became sick and left the convent school for a prolonged stay with her uncle. While reading to him St. Jerome's *Letters* she, surprisingly enough, decided to enter a convent. Her father, though deeply pious, drew the line at that point. Teresa, in her characteristically dramatic, somewhat Quixotic style, eloped to the Carmelite Convent of the Incarnation in Avila. In retrospect we may find it difficult to appreciate this grand gesture made in order to join a community as open to the world as a dovecote: the nuns spent much of their time in the parlor gossiping with city acquaintances and frequently returned to their families for special care or even for a good meal.

To one such excursion from the convent Teresa owed what could be called her second conversion—not yet the definitive one! Shortly after her profession she fell seriously ill. Was her sickness psychosomatic? Possibly, but the forceful treatment of her "wonder doctor" would have sufficed to kill a healthy patient. Once more she ended in her uncle's home, and again a book from his well-stocked spiritual library deeply touched her. Francisco de Osuna's *Third Spiritual Alphabet* initiated her into the method of "recollection." Franciscans had devised a mode of interior prayer that would enable lay men and women to practice in the world the kind of mental discipline professed religious were expected to practice in their monasteries. Concentrating on the imitation of Christ as a means to total union with God, recollection was intended to bring the soul from discursive meditation to passive contemplation. In Spain, Francisco de Osuna had been one of its most effective expositors. The reform movement inspired by the new piety had affected religious orders as well. Occasionally it had shown some affinity with the so-called *Alumbrados* who, favoring interior abandonment to God's will over any traditional form of piety, tended to discredit discursive or liturgical prayer altogether. Ecclesiastical authorities, suspecting some link with the emerging Reformation in northern Europe, became increasingly suspicious. After the Council of Trent, fear led to repressive action. The Spanish Inquisitor General placed a number of devotional works on the Index of Forbidden Books—among them Francisco de Osuna's *Third Alphabet.* Teresa, distressed about seeing some of her favorite authors being taken out of circulation, felt comforted only when the Lord promised her a living book instead.

But much had occurred between her recovery and this event of her forty-fourth year. The facts, as filtered through her own penitent autobiography, may have been somewhat distorted but appear essentially trustworthy. Having passed through a prolonged period of desolation she seems to have become discouraged in pursuing internal prayer and, in her outward conduct, to have followed the rather relaxed standards of discipline that prevailed at the Incarnation, including the frequent visits to the parlor for hours of idle conversation. In 1554, when thirty-nine years old, she experienced her definitive conversion. There appear to have been two stages: the first one occurred when she was suddenly struck by the sight of a statue of Christ after his flagellation, tied to a pole and mocked by soldiers; the second was occasioned by the reading of Augustine's conversion. An interior life that had lain dormant during the preceding years instantly blossomed. The subterranean development of her spiritual life during the "infertile" period allowed her to enter immediately into the passive state of prayer.

With these events, as narrated in her *Life,* begins an episode often distressing, but occasionally comical—troubles with spiritual directors. The first to whom she confided her particular experiences promptly informed her that they all came from the devil. The next one, relenting somewhat on the source, nevertheless advised her to resist passive recollection. Fortunately, all such interpretations and counsels turned out to be marvelously ineffective while Teresa kept waiting for God's Providence to send her the right confessor. Eventually she did indeed encounter confessors, mostly Jesuits, who fully realized the extraordinary nature of the person they were called to direct. One of them, Balthasar Alvarez, a very articulate mystic himself, left a remarkable diary of his own spiritual experience. Teresa respected him well enough, but by that time she had become highly critical of these men appointed by authority to guide her along a path totally unfamiliar to them. She sums up her twenty years of travails with incapable confessors: "Through them I suffered so much that I now wonder how I could endure it." Nor were there many books on prayer left to assist her after most of the good ones had been removed from the library. Thus Teresa found herself compelled to seek her own way. In the process of doing so she took others along, because she wrote—easily and well.

But before introducing Teresa's writings, we must say something about her activities. Despairing of her ability to lead a genuinely contemplative life in the company of so many women hostile to any tightening of convent discipline, Teresa conceived the plan of founding an unsubsidized house where cloister, poverty, and prayer would be enforced according to the original rule of the Carmel. Despite almost universal resistance in the beginning, she obtained permission in 1562 to move with four postulants to a small house in Avila. There matters rested for several years; Teresa had no intention of founding another "branch" of Carmelites. But during a visit to her new foundation of Saint Joseph, the Superior General in 1567 granted Teresa authority to start "as many houses as she had hairs on her head." That decision transformed the life of the woman who had pursued a strictly cloistered life into one of traveling thousands of miles, by two-wheel cart and by mule, of sleeping in dubious, mostly untidy inns, bothered by "fleas, poltergeists, and all the inconveniences of travel," of suffering from extreme heat and cold, from fever and angina. By one of those ironical twists of fortune to which saints appear to be particularly prone, the authorities, anxious to halt, at least temporarily, her controversial foundations, appointed her prioress of her former convent. The unreformed nuns received their unelected prioress with howls of indignation. Defusing the explosive situation, Teresa placed a statue of the Virgin on the prioress's seat and exclaimed, "Mary will be our prioress; I shall be a sister among sisters." Not only did she survive the opposition of her former fellow sisters at Incarnation, she "converted" the entire convent! The confessor who assisted her in this turmoil was John of the Cross, a man who was to suffer as much as Teresa in the course of reforming the male Carmel.

Under such uncontemplative circumstances Teresa wrote her books on contemplation. They reveal a person of extraordinary religious sensitivity, endowed with an earthly realism and a refreshing ability to see the comical side of her own and other people's struggle through life. Having always been an avid reader and being capable of expressing even the subtlest experiences in words, she would have seemed predestined to become a writer. That she actually became one, however, we owe in the first place to some of her more "enlightened" directors, who ordered her to write. Once she started, there was no way of stopping her. Among her works: a spiritual autobiography, reports on her foundations, and, while her *Life* was "at the Inquisition" for examination, a treatise on prayer that was to formulate her experience in an impersonal, objective mode. About this final project she felt plenty of misgivings, which she unambiguously expressed to Father Jeronimo Gracian, who had suggested the writing:

> There are more than enough books written on prayer already.
> For the love of God, let me get on with my spinning and go to
> the choir and do my religious duties like the other sisters. I
> am not meant for writing. I have neither the health nor the
> wits for it.

The overcoming of her resistance resulted in that accomplished spiritual masterpiece *The Interior Castle*. In it Teresa attempted to be systematic and impersonal. She did not altogether succeed in the former and, fortunately for us, completely failed in the latter.

In judging her work we should remain aware of the circumstances of its composition: Teresa was surrounded by all the cares and confusion accompanying what amounted to the erection of a new religious order, ceaselessly traveled under conditions hard to imagine today, and constantly was plagued by ill health. She herself occasionally reminds the reader of the fragmented, improvised composition of her work:

> God help me in this task which I have embarked upon. I had quite forgotten what I was writing about, for business matters and ill health forced me to postpone continuing it until a more suitable time, and, as I have a poor memory, it will all be very confused for I cannot read it through again. (*The Interior Castle*, 4.2.1).

Yet, precisely this marvelous directness defines her unique and inimitable writing style.

No writings in this collection have proven more resistant to being anthologized than Teresa's. One should read them from one end to the other—repetitions, excursions, inconsistencies, and all. We would render a disservice if the reader were to consider the following excerpts to be more than an invitation to read the whole work from which they were taken—and some others as well.

The image of an interior castle came to Teresa in a vision of "a most beautiful crystal globe, made in the shape of a castle, and containing seven mansions, in the seventh and innermost of which was the King of Glory, in the greatest splendor, illuming and beautifying them all." Teresa herself in her description of the first mansion alludes to the word of John 14:2: "In my Father's house are many mansions." The first three prepare the higher spiritual life by means of prayer, pious readings, and the practice of love. In the fourth mansion the prayer of quiet introduces the mystical grace. That grace proper consists of a state of infused contemplation, described in mansions five and six. Initially the soul's faculties are asleep, as the silkworm lies dormant in the cocoon before turning into a butterfly. In the sixth mansion Teresa describes the development of the mystical life up to the permanent union—the mystical betrothal. Here also occurs that very painful purgation of the soul John of the Cross refers to as the dark night. The work concludes with the short seventh mansion wherein the soul is permanently transformed into God—the spiritual marriage.

THE INTERIOR CASTLE

The Fifth Dwelling Places

CHAPTER ONE

Begins to deal with how the soul is united to God in prayer. Tells how one discerns whether there is any illusion.

1. O Sisters, how can I explain the riches and treasures and delights found in the fifth dwelling places? I believe it would be better not to say anything about these remaining rooms, for there is no way of learning how to speak of them; neither is the intellect capable of understanding them nor can comparisons help in explaining them; earthly things are too coarse for such a purpose.

Send light from heaven, my Lord, that I might be able to enlighten these Your servants—for You have been pleased that some of them ordinarily enjoy these delights—so that they may not be deceived by the devil transforming himself into an angel of light. For all their desires are directed toward pleasing You.

2. And although I have said "some," there are indeed only a few who fail to enter this dwelling place of which I shall now speak. There are various degrees, and for that reason I say that most enter these places. But I believe that only a few will experience some of the things that I will say are in this room. Yet even if

From *The Collected Works of St. Teresa of Avila*, vol. 2, trans. Kieran Kavanaugh, O.C.D., and Otilio Rodriguez, O.C.D. (Washington, D.C.: Institute of Carmelite Studies, 1980), 335–40, 366–69, 405–8, 432–38. Reprinted with permission of the publisher. Copyright © 1980 by Washington Province of Discalced Carmelites, ICS Publications 2131 Lincoln Rd., N.E., Washington, D.C. 20002-1199.

souls do no more than reach the door, God is being very merciful to them; although many are called few are chosen. So I say now that all of us who wear this holy habit of Carmel are called to prayer and contemplation. This call explains our origin; we are the descendants of men who felt this call, of those holy fathers on Mount Carmel who in such great solitude and contempt for the world sought this treasure, this precious pearl of contemplation that we are speaking about. Yet few of us dispose ourselves that the Lord may communicate it to us. In exterior matters we are proceeding well so that we will reach what is necessary; but in the practice of the virtues that are necessary for arriving at this point we need very, very much and cannot be careless in either small things or great. So, my Sisters, since in some way we can enjoy heaven on earth, be brave in begging the Lord to give us His grace in such a way that nothing will be lacking through our own fault; that He show us the way and strengthen the soul that it may dig until it finds this hidden treasure. The truth is that the treasure lies within our very selves. This is what I would like to know how to explain, if the Lord would enable me to do so.

3. I said "strengthen the soul" so that you will understand that bodily strength is not necessary for those to whom God does not give it. He doesn't make it impossible for anyone to buy His riches. He is content if each one gives what he has. Blessed be so great a God. But reflect, daughters, that He doesn't want you to hold on to anything, for if you avoid doing so you will be able to enjoy the favors we are speaking of. Whether you have little or much, He wants everything for Himself, and in conformity with what you know you have given you will receive greater or lesser favors. There is no better proof for recognizing whether our prayer has reached union or not. Don't think this union is some kind of dreamy state like the one I mentioned before.[1] I say "dreamy state" because it seems that the soul is as though asleep; yet neither does it really think it is asleep nor does it feel awake. There is no need here to use any technique to suspend the mind since all the faculties are asleep in this state—and truly asleep—to

---

[1] She is referring to the "prayer of recollection" as discussed in IV, ch. 3, no. 11.

the things of the world and to ourselves. As a matter of fact, during the time that the union lasts the soul is left as though without its senses, for it has no power to think even if it wants to. In loving, if it does love, it doesn't understand how or what it is it loves or what it would want. In sum, it is like one who in every respect has died to the world so as to live more completely in God. Thus the death is a delightful one, an uprooting from the soul of all the operations the latter can have while being in the body. The death is a delightful one because in truth it seems that in order to dwell more perfectly in God the soul is so separated from the body that I don't even know if it has life enough to breathe. (I was just now thinking about this, and it seems to me that it doesn't—at least if it does breathe, it is unaware that it is doing so.) Nonetheless, its whole intellect would want to be occupied in understanding something of what is felt. And since the soul does not have the energy to attain to this, it is so stunned that, even if it is not completely lost, neither a hand nor a foot stirs, as we say here below when a person is in such a swoon that we think he is dead....

5. ...This union is above all earthly joys, above all delights, above all consolations, and still more than that. It doesn't matter where those spiritual or earthly joys come from, for the feeling is very different, as you will have experienced. I once said that the difference is like that between feeling something on the rough outer covering of the body or in the marrow of the bones. And that was right on the mark, for I don't know how to say it better.

6. It seems to me that you're still not satisfied, for you will think you can be mistaken and that these interior things are something difficult to examine. What was said will be sufficient for anyone who has experienced union. Yet, because the difference between union and the previous experience is great, I want to mention a clear sign by which you will be sure against error or doubts about whether the union is from God. His Majesty has brought it to my memory today, and in my opinion it is the sure sign. In difficult matters, even though it seems to me that I understand and that I speak the truth, I always use this expression "it

seems to me." For if I am mistaken, I'm very much prepared to believe what those who have a great deal of learning say....

7. I have had a great deal of experience with learned men, and have also had experience with half-learned, fearful ones; these latter cost me dearly. At least I think that anyone who refuses to believe that God can do much more or that He has considered and continues to consider it good sometimes to communicate favors to His creatures has indeed closed the door to receiving them. Therefore, Sisters, let this never happen to you, but believe that God can do far more and don't turn your attention to whether the ones to whom He grants His favors are good or bad; for His Majesty knows this, as I have told you. There is no reason for us to meddle in the matter, but with humility and simplicity of heart we should serve and praise Him for His works and marvels.

8. Now then, to return to the sign that I say is the true one: you now see that God has made this soul a fool with regard to all so as better to impress upon it true wisdom. For during the time of this union it neither sees, nor hears, nor understands, because the union is always short and seems to the soul even much shorter than it probably is. God so places Himself in the interior of that soul that when it returns to itself it can in no way doubt that it was in God and God was in it. This truth remains with it so firmly that even though years go by without God's granting that favor again, the soul can neither forget nor doubt that it was in God and God was in it. This is what matters now, for I shall speak of the effects of this prayer afterward....

10. Don't be mistaken by thinking that this certitude has to do with a corporal form, as in the case of the bodily presence of our Lord Jesus Christ in the Most Blessed Sacrament even though we do not see Him. Here the matter isn't like that; it concerns only the divinity. How, then, is it that what we do not see leaves this certitude? I don't know; these are His works. But I do know I speak the truth. And I would say that whoever does not receive this certitude does not experience union of the whole soul with God, but union of some faculty, or that he experiences one of the many other kinds of favors God grants souls. In regard to all these

favors we have to give up looking for reasons to see how they've come about. Since our intellect cannot understand this union, why do we have to make this effort? It's enough for us to see that He who is the cause of it is almighty. Since we have no part at all to play in bringing it about no matter how much effort we put forth, but it is God who does so, let us not desire the capacity to understand this union.

The Sixth Dwelling Places

CHAPTER TWO

Deals with some of the ways in which our Lord awakens the soul. It seems that there is nothing in these awakenings to fear, even though the experience is sublime and the favors are great.

1. ...Let us begin, then, to discuss the manner in which the Spouse deals with it [the soul] and how before He belongs to it completely He makes it desire Him vehemently by certain delicate means the soul itself does not understand. (Nor do I believe I'll be successful in explaining them save to those who have experienced them.) These are impulses so delicate and refined, for they proceed from very deep within the interior part of the soul, that I don't know any comparison that will fit.

2. They are far different from all that we can acquire of ourselves here below and even from the spiritual delights that were mentioned. For often when a person is distracted and forgetful of God, His Majesty will awaken it. His action is as quick as a falling comet. And as with a thunderclap, even though no sound is heard, the soul understands very clearly that it was called by God. So well does it understand that sometimes, especially in the beginning, it is made to tremble and even complain without there being anything that causes it pain. It feels that it is wounded in the most delightful way, but it doesn't learn how or by whom it was wounded. It knows clearly that the wound is something precious, and it would never want to be cured. It complains to its Spouse with words of love, even outwardly, without being able to do

otherwise. It knows that He is present, but He doesn't want to reveal the manner in which He allows Himself to be enjoyed. And the pain is great, although delightful and sweet. And even if the soul does not want this wound, the wound cannot be avoided. But the soul, in fact, would never want to be deprived of this pain. The wound satisfies it much more than the delightful and painless absorption of the prayer of quiet.

3. I am struggling, Sisters, to explain for you this action of love, and I don't know how. For it seems a contradiction that the Beloved would give the soul clear understanding that He is with it and yet make it think that He is calling it by a sign so certain that no room is left for doubt and a whisper so penetrating that the soul cannot help but hear it. For it seems that when the Spouse, who is in the seventh dwelling place, communicates in this manner (for the words are not spoken), all the people in the other dwelling places keep still; neither the senses, nor the imagination, nor the faculties stir.

O my powerful God, how sublime are your secrets, and how different spiritual things are from all that is visible and understandable here below. There is nothing that serves to explain this favor, even though the favor is a very small one when compared with the very great ones You work in souls.

4. This action of love is so powerful that the soul dissolves with desire, and yet it doesn't know what to ask for since clearly it thinks that its God is with it.

You will ask me: Well, if it knows this, what does it desire or what pains it? What greater good does it want? I don't know. I do know that it seems this pain reaches to the soul's very depths and that when He who wounds it draws out the arrow, it indeed seems in accord with the deep love the soul feels that God is drawing these very depths after Him. I was thinking now that it's as though from this fire enkindled in the brazier that is my God a spark leapt forth and so struck the soul that the flaming fire was felt by it. And since the spark was not enough to set the soul on fire, and the fire is so delightful, the soul is left with that pain; but the spark merely by touching the soul produces that effect. It seems to me this is the best comparison I have come up with. This delightful pain—and it is not pain—is not continuous, although sometimes it lasts a long while; at other times it goes away quickly. This depends on the way the Lord wishes to communicate it, for it is not something that can be procured in any human way. But even though it sometimes lasts for a long while, it comes and goes. To sum up, it is never permanent. For this reason it doesn't set the soul on fire; but just as the fire is about to start, the spark goes out and the soul is left with the desire to suffer again that loving pain the spark causes.

5. Here there is no reason to wonder whether the experience is brought on naturally or caused by melancholy, or whether it is some trick of the devil or some illusion. It is something that leaves clear understanding of how this activity comes from the place where the Lord, who is unchanging, dwells. The activity is not like that found in other feelings of devotion, where the great absorption in delight can make us doubtful. Here all the senses and faculties remain free of any absorption, wondering what this could be, without hindering anything or being able, in my opinion, to increase or take away that delightful pain.

Anyone to whom our Lord may have granted this favor—for if He has, that fact will be recognized on reading this—should thank Him very much. Such a person doesn't have to fear deception. Let his great fear be that he might prove ungrateful for so generous a favor, and let him strive to better his entire life, and to serve, and he will see the results and how he receives more and more. In fact, I know a person[2] who received this favor for some years and was so pleased with it that had she served the Lord through severe trials for a great number of years she would have felt well repaid by it. May He be blessed forever, amen.

6. You may wonder why greater security is present in this favor than in other things. In my opinion, these are the reasons: First, the devil never gives delightful pain like this. He can give the savor and delight that seem to be spiritual, but he doesn't have the power to join pain—and so much of it—to the spiritual quiet and delight of the soul. For all of his powers are on the outside, and the

---

[2]She is alluding to herself. See her *Spir. Test.*, 59, no. 13.

pains he causes are never, in my opinion, delightful or peaceful, but disturbing and contentious. Second, this delightful tempest comes from a region other than those regions of which he can be lord. Third, the favor brings wonderful benefits to the soul, the more customary of which are the determination to suffer for God, the desire to have many trials, and the determination to withdraw from earthly satisfactions and conversations and other similar things.

CHAPTER EIGHT

Discusses how God communicates Himself to the soul through an intellectual vision; gives some counsels. Tells about the effects such a vision causes if it is genuine. Recommends secrecy concerning these favors.

1. For you to see, Sisters, that what I have told you is true and that the further a soul advances the more it is accompanied by the good Jesus, we will do well to discuss how, when His Majesty desires, we cannot do otherwise than walk always with Him. This is evident in the ways and modes by which His Majesty communicates Himself to us and shows us the love He bears us. He does this through some very wonderful apparitions and visions. That you might not be frightened if He grants you some of these, I want briefly to mention something about these visions—if the Lord be pleased that I succeed—so that we might praise Him very much even though He may not grant them to us. We would praise Him because being so filled with majesty and power He nonetheless desires to communicate thus with a creature.

2. It will happen while the soul is heedless of any thought about such a favor being granted to it, and though it never had a thought that it deserved this vision, that it will feel Jesus Christ, our Lord, beside it. Yet, it doesn't see Him, neither with the eyes of the body nor with those of the soul. This is called an intellectual vision; I don't know why. I saw the person[3] to whom God granted this favor, along with other favors I shall mention further on, quite worried in

---

[3]This person is Teresa herself. See *Life*, ch. 27, nos. 2–5.

the beginning because, since she didn't see anything, she couldn't understand the nature of this vision. However, she knew so certainly that it was Jesus Christ, our Lord, who showed Himself to her in that way that she couldn't doubt; I mean she couldn't doubt the vision was there. As to whether it was from God or not, even though she carried with her great effects to show that it was, she nonetheless was afraid. She had never heard of an intellectual vision, nor had she thought there was such a kind. But she understood very clearly that it was this same Lord who often spoke to her in the way mentioned. For until He granted her this favor I am referring to, she never knew who was speaking to her, although she understood the words.

3. I know that since she was afraid about this vision (for it isn't like the imaginative one that passes quickly, but lasts many days and sometimes even more than a year), she went very worried to her confessor. He asked her how, since she didn't see anything, she knew that it was our Lord—what kind of face He had. She told him she didn't know, that she didn't see any face, and that she couldn't say any more than what she had said, that what she did know was that He was the one who spoke to her and that the vision had not been fancied. And although some persons put many fears in her, she was still frequently unable to doubt, especially when the Lord said to her: "Do not be afraid, it is I."[4] These words had so much power that from then on she could not doubt the vision, and she was left very much strengthened and happy over such good company. She saw clearly that the vision was a great help toward walking with a habitual remembrance of God and a deep concern about avoiding anything displeasing to Him, for it seemed to her that He was always looking at her. And each time she wanted to speak with His Majesty in prayer, and even outside of it, she felt He was so near that He couldn't fail to hear her. But she didn't hear words spoken whenever she wanted; only unexpectedly when they were necessary. She felt He was walking at her right side, but she didn't experience this with those senses by which we can know that a person is beside us. This vision comes in another unexplainable, more delicate way. But it is so certain and leaves much certitude; even much more than the other

---

[4] See *Life*, ch. 25, no. 18.

visions do because in the visions that come through the senses one can be deceived, but not in the intellectual vision. For this latter brings great interior benefits and effects that couldn't be present if the experience were caused by melancholy; nor would the devil produce so much good; nor would the soul go about with such peace and continual desires to please God, and with so much contempt for everything that does not bring it to Him. Afterward she understood clearly that the vision was not caused by the devil, which became more and more clear as time went on.

4. Nonetheless, I know that at times she went about very much frightened; other times, with the most intense confusion, for she didn't know why so much good had come to her. We were so united, she and I, that nothing took place in her soul of which I was ignorant; so I can be a good witness, and believe me all I have said of this matter is the truth.

It is a favor from the Lord that she bears in herself the most intense confusion and humility. If the vision were from the devil, the effects would be contrary. And since the vision is something definitely understood to be a gift from God and human effort would not be sufficient to produce this experience, the one who receives it can in no way think it is his own good but a good given through the hand of God. And even though, in my opinion, some of those favors that were mentioned are greater, this favor bears with it a particular knowledge of God. This continual companionship gives rise to a most tender love for His Majesty, to some desires even greater than those mentioned to surrender oneself totally to His service, and to a great purity of conscience because the presence at its side makes the soul pay attention to everything. For even though we already know that God is present in all we do, our nature is such that we neglect to think of this. Here the truth cannot be forgotten, for the Lord awakens the soul to His presence beside it. And even the favors that were mentioned became much more common since the soul goes about almost continually with actual love for the One who it sees and understands is at its side.

5. In sum, with respect to the soul's gain, the vision is seen to be a most wonderful and highly valuable favor. The soul thanks the

Lord that He gives the vision without any merits on its part and would not exchange that blessing for any earthly treasure or delight. Thus, when the Lord is pleased to take the vision away, the soul feels very much alone. But all the efforts it could possibly make are of little avail in bringing back that companionship. The Lord gives it when He desires, and it cannot be acquired. Sometimes also the vision is of some saint, and this too is most beneficial.

6. You will ask how if nothing is seen one knows that it is Christ, or a saint, or His most glorious Mother. This, the soul will not know how to explain, nor can it understand how it knows, but it does know with the greatest certitude. It seems easier for the soul to know when the Lord speaks; but what is more amazing is that it knows the saint, who doesn't speak but seemingly is placed there by the Lord as a help to it and as its companion. Thus there are other spiritual things that one doesn't know how to explain, but through them one knows how lowly our nature is when there is question of understanding the sublime grandeurs of God, for we are incapable even of understanding these spiritual things. But let the one to whom His Majesty gives these favors receive them with admiration and praise for Him. Thus He grants the soul particular graces through these favors. For since the favors are not granted to all, they should be highly esteemed; and one should strive to perform greater services since God in so many ways helps the soul to perform these services. Hence the soul doesn't consider itself to be any greater because of this, and it thinks that it is the one who serves God the least among all who are in the world. This soul thinks that it is more obligated to Him than anyone, and any fault it commits pierces to the core of its being, and very rightly so.

The Seventh Dwelling Places

CHAPTER TWO

Explains the difference between spiritual union and spiritual marriage. Describes this difference through some delicate comparisons.

1. Now then let us deal with the divine and spiritual marriage, although this great favor does not come to its perfect fullness as long as we live; for if we were to withdraw from God, this remarkable blessing would be lost.

The first time the favor is granted, His Majesty desires to show Himself to the soul through an imaginative vision of His most sacred humanity so that the soul will understand and not be ignorant of receiving this sovereign gift; with other persons the favor will be received in another form. With regard to the one of whom we are speaking, the Lord represented Himself to her, just after she had received Communion, in the form of shining splendor, beauty, and majesty, as He was after His resurrection, and told her that now it was time that she consider as her own what belonged to Him and that He would take care of what was hers, and He spoke other words destined more to be heard than to be mentioned.

2. It may seem that this experience was nothing new since at other times the Lord had represented Himself to the soul in such a way. The experience was so different that it left her indeed stupefied and frightened: first, because this vision came with great force; second, because of the words the Lord spoke to her and also because in the interior of her soul, where He represented Himself to her, she had not seen other visions except the former one. You must understand that there is the greatest difference between all the previous visions and those of this dwelling place. Between the spiritual betrothal and the spiritual marriage the difference is as great as that which exists between two who are betrothed and between two who can no longer be separated.

3. I have already said that even though these comparisons are used, because there are no others better suited to our purpose, it should be understood that in this state there is no more thought of the body than if the soul were not in it, but one's thought is only of the spirit. In the spiritual marriage, there is still much less remembrance of the body because this secret union takes place in the very interior center of the soul, which must be where God Himself is, and in my opinion there is no need of any door for Him to enter. I say there is no need of any door because everything that has been

said up until now seems to take place by means of the senses and faculties, and this appearance of the humanity of the Lord must also. But that which comes to pass in the union of the spiritual marriage is very different. The Lord appears in this center of the soul, not in an imaginative vision but in an intellectual one, although more delicate than those mentioned, as He appeared to the apostles without entering through the door when He said to them *pax vobis.*[5] What God communicates here to the soul in an instant is a secret so great and a favor so sublime—and the delight the soul experiences so extreme—that I don't know what to compare it to. I can say only that the Lord wishes to reveal for that moment, in a more sublime manner than through any spiritual vision or taste, the glory of heaven. One can say no more—insofar as can be understood—than that the soul, I mean the spirit, is made one with God. For since His Majesty is also spirit, He has wished to show His love for us by giving some persons understanding of the point to which this love reaches so that we might praise His grandeur. For He has desired to be so joined with the creature that, just as those who are married cannot be separated, He doesn't want to be separated from the soul.

4. The spiritual betrothal is different, for the two often separate. And the union is also different because, even though it is the joining of two things into one, in the end the two can be separated and each remains by itself.[6] We observe this ordinarily, for the favor of union with the Lord passes quickly, and afterward the soul remains without that company; I mean, without awareness of it. In this other favor from the Lord, no. The soul always remains with its God in that center. Let us say that the union is like the joining of two wax candles to such an extent that the flame coming from them is but one, or that the wick, the flame, and the wax are all one. But

---

[5] Jn 20:19–21. The earlier-mentioned intellectual visions are those in VI, ch. 8.

[6] For the proper understanding of this paragraph, it should be noted that the word "union" is here used in two different senses. In the first three uses of the word, Teresa is referring to the "prayer of union" treated in the Fifth Dwelling Places—a form of contemplative prayer in which the faculties of memory, understanding, and will become completely silent for a time. Teresa then contrasts this temporary experience with what she calls the "union" that occurs "in the spiritual marriage," where there is no longer any division or separation.

afterward one candle can be easily separated from the other and there are two candles; the same holds for the wick. In the spiritual marriage the union is like what we have when rain falls from the sky into a river or fount; all is water, for the rain that fell from heaven cannot be divided or separated from the water of the river. Or it is like what we have when a little stream enters the sea; there is no means of separating the two. Or, like the bright light entering a room through two different windows; although the streams of light are separate when entering the room, they become one.

5. Perhaps this is what Saint Paul means in saying *He that is joined or united to the Lord becomes one spirit with him* (I Cor 6:17), and is referring to this sovereign marriage, presupposing that His Majesty has brought the soul to it through union. And he also says: *For me to live is Christ, and to die is gain* (Phil 1:21). The soul as well, I think, can say these words now because...its life is now Christ.

6. And that its life is Christ is understood better, with the passing of time, by the effects this life has. Through some secret aspirations the soul understands clearly that it is God who gives life to our soul. These aspirations come very, very often in such a living way that they can in no way be doubted. The soul feels them very clearly even though they are indescribable. But the feeling is so powerful that sometimes the soul cannot avoid the loving expressions they cause, such as: O Life of my life! Sustenance that sustains me! and things of this sort. For from those divine breasts where it seems God is always sustaining the soul there flow streams of milk bringing comfort to all the people of the castle. It seems the Lord desires that in some manner these others in the castle may enjoy the great deal the soul is enjoying and that from that full-flowing river, where this tiny fount is swallowed up, a spurt of that water will sometimes be directed toward the sustenance of those who in corporeal things must serve these two who are wed. Just as a distracted person would feel this water if he were suddenly bathed in it, and would be unable to avoid feeling it, so are these operations recognized, and even with greater certitude. For just as a great gush of water could not reach us if it didn't have a source,

as I have said, so it is understood clearly that there is Someone in the interior depths who shoots these arrows and gives life to this life, and that there is a Sun in the interior of the soul from which a brilliant light proceeds and is sent to the faculties. The soul, as I have said, does not move from that center nor is its peace lost, for the very One who gave peace to the apostles when they were together can give it to the soul....

10. ...This center of our soul, or this spirit, is something so difficult to explain, and even believe in, that I think, Sisters, I'll not give you the temptation to disbelieve what I say, for I do not know how to explain this center. That there are trials and sufferings and that at the same time the soul is in peace is a difficult thing to explain. I want to make one or more comparisons for you. Please God, I may be saying something through them; but if not, I know that I'm speaking the truth in what I say.

11. The King is in His palace and there are many wars in his kingdom and many painful things going on, but not on that account does he fail to be at his post. So here, even though in those other dwelling places there is much tumult and there are many poisonous creatures and the noise is heard, no one enters that center dwelling place and makes the soul leave. Nor do the things the soul hears make it leave; even though they cause it some pain, the suffering is not such as to disturb it and take away its peace. The passions are now conquered and have a fear of entering the center because they would go away from there more subdued.

Our entire body may ache; but if the head is sound, the head will not ache just because the body aches.

I am laughing to myself over these comparisons for they do not satisfy me, but I don't know any others. You may think what you want; what I have said is true.

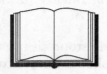

Selected Bibliography

TEXTS

Edition used:
The Collected Works of St. Teresa of Avila. Translated by Kieran Kavanagh and Otilio Rodriguez. 3 vols. Washington, D.C.: Institute of Carmelite Studies, 1976–85.

Other sources:
The Complete Works of St. Teresa of Jesus. Translated by E. Allison Peers. 3 vols. London and New York: Sheed and Ward, 1946.

The Interior Castle. Translated by Kieran Kavanaugh, O.C.D., and Otilio Rodriguez, O.C.D. The Classics of Western Spirituality. New York: Paulist Press; London: SPCK, 1979.

STUDIES

Ahlgren, Gillian T.W. *Teresa of Avila and the Politics of Sanctity.* Ithaca, N.Y.: Cornell University Press, 1996.

Ancilli, Ermanno. "At the Center of the Soul: A Commentary on the Sixth and Seventh Mansions of St. Teresa." *Word and Spirit: A Monastic Review* 4 (1983): 77–96.

Coelho, Mary C. "Saint Teresa of Avila's Transformation of the Symbol of the Interior Castle." *Teresianum* 38 (1987): 109–25.

De Groot, Jean. "Teresa of Avila and the Meaning of Mystical Theology." In *Hispanic Philosophy in the Age of Discovery*, ed. Kevin White, 145–59. Washington, D.C.: Catholic University of America Press, 1997.

Dicken, E. W. Trueman. *The Crucible of Love: A Study in the Mysticism of St. Teresa of Jesus and St. John of the Cross.* New York: Sheed and Ward, 1963.

Sullivan, John, O.C.D., ed. *The Centenary of St. Teresa.* Carmelite Studies, 3. Washington, D.C.: Institute of Carmelite Studies, 1984.

John of the Cross
(1542–91)

No one reading John of the Cross is likely to attribute the text to another author. Not only does he write in a distinctly personal style (as most great writers do), but his entire approach to the mystical life differs from that of others. Bossuet's saying that John's works enjoy the same authority in mystical theology as Thomas Aquinas's writings do in dogmatic theology both reveals and conceals his literary identity. Certainly no mystic wrote about spiritual life in a more scholastic way, doggedly pursuing the last Aristotelian distinction in a matter so reluctant to submit to such distinctions. Yet the reader never feels left with the dry bones of conceptualization long deserted by contemplative life. The poet's passion constantly reanimates the language of the School, allowing the living experience to radiate through the cold concepts. Nor does John ever sacrifice personal experience to theological *a priori*. He has been called the greatest psychologist in the history of mysticism.[1] Indeed, we may regard him as one of the first theologians to follow the modern "turn to the subject." Yet, he belongs to the small company of modern writers who succeeded in conveying a genuine content to that subject, rather than restricting it to its objective functions. The life of this withdrawn contemplative was

---

[1] E. Allison Peers, General Introduction to John of the Cross, *Ascent of Mount Carmel* (New York: Doubleday, Image Books, 1958), 42.

as filled with controversy and sensational developments as that of any statesman of his age.

Born Juan de Ypes at Fontiveros near Avila in 1542, he moved with his mother to Medina del Campo after the death of his father. A clerical benefactor took him in at the local hospital and allowed him to study at the town's Jesuit College. In 1562 he entered the Carmel in Medina. After his profession he studied three years in the Arts faculty at the University of Salamanca. At the end of this period he was ordained a priest, apparently with little formal training in theology. Desirous to devote himself to a life of total silence and solitude, he decided to join the Carthusian Order. When he revealed this plan to Teresa, who had founded a reformed convent in Medina, she replied that he could do exactly what he wanted to do within the reformed branch of the Carmel. The problem was that no reformed houses for men existed. So, with her characteristic mixture of cunning and boldness, Teresa suggested that John reform the male Carmel as she had done for the female branch. One may doubt whether the shy, unworldly Carmelite would have accepted this substitute for the peace of a Carthusian monastery if he had foreseen even part of the troubles that were awaiting him. Yet John proved as persistent as he was innocent. After one year of theology at Salamanca—the total extent of the formal education in theology of this *Doctor Ecclesiae*—he accompanied Teresa. In 1568 he started with two other priests the first "discalced" house in Duruelo. Soon Mother Teresa came to visit them. No stranger to evangelical poverty herself, she was nevertheless aghast when she saw the place—"a true stable of Bethlehem."

These were the happy years of the reformed Carmel's honeymoon. Teresa, perceiving the spiritual potential of the man she had so expeditiously hitched to her cause, was determined to use him for all he was worth. She succeeded in having him as confessor of the Convent of the Incarnation in Avila, where she had been appointed prioress by the general of the Order. From that period on he would become her theological and mystical guide, while she would provide him with practical counsel in the reform project.

The "calced" Carmelites, perceiving enough trouble in the Order with Teresa alone, decided to stop John in his attempts to extend the reform to the male branch. They abducted him from his Avila house and kept him imprisoned in Medina del Campo until the papal nuncio ordered his release. Two years later they repeated their assault and took him to a dark room in the Toledo convent. When Teresa heard about it, she wrote that she would have preferred him to have fallen "into the hands of the Moors." John spent over eighteen months in captivity and might have ended his days there had he not conceived an ingenious plot (of which few would have thought him capable) and escaped. He waited for the full moon, then carefully unscrewed the lock of the door with previously assembled and hidden tools, lowered himself from the city wall by means of his bed sheets, took one bold leap for the remaining distance, and ran to a nearby reformed convent. For posterity the Toledo captivity turned out to be an unmixed blessing. In his cell he started writing and—what he might never have done without the imposed leisure and scarcity of writing material—composing poetry. There he created the first part of his magnificent *Spiritual Canticle* as well as several other poems—among them, "The Dark Night." During the following period of relative quiet when he served as vicar at the reformed Convent of El Calvario, as rector of the college he founded in nearby Baeza, and as prior of Los Martires Convent in Granada, he wrote his two long mystical commentaries in prose on the Toledo poem: *Ascent of Mount Carmel* and *The Dark Night of the Soul*.

His trials might have seemed to be ending when the pope officially divided the Order into two autonomous branches. Such was far from being the case. John never gained the authority over the discalced friars to which his early initiative, numerous foundations, and constant inspiration would appear to have entitled him. Instead the General Chapter of 1591 deprived him of all offices and intended to send him to Mexico. John, fallen ill, spent his final months at the reformed Convent of Ubeda, where his hostile brothers refused him proper care. Covered with sores, he died a lonely death—as he had wished to do.

Commentary

It would be impossible to summarize his theology—for a veritable theology it is—in a few pages. Some of its spirit, however, may be captured in a letter he wrote to a Carmelite nun: "Our most important task consists in remaining silent before this great God, silent with our desires as well as with our tongue. He understands only one language, that of silent love." Spiritual life for John of the Cross aims at an ever-deeper negation—not only the negation of knowing, as for Dionysius, but also the abnegation of willing and feeling: "The road to Mount Carmel: the spirit of perfection, nothing, nothing, nothing, and even on the mountain nothing." Yet the ultimate motive in all of these negative endeavors is an eminently positive one: to attain the unconditioned, unqualified love that refuses to be distracted from its object, even for a moment.

Neither the absoluteness of that love ideal nor the negation of all relative values prevented John from being extremely methodical and meticulously concrete in his instructions for the spiritual life. *Ascent of Mount Carmel* and *The Dark Night of the Soul* together constitute the most systematic account of the mystical ascent in the spiritual literature of the modern age. To call it systematic, however, is not to say that the division between the various stages or even the coherence between the two works may be readily perceived. The poem "The Dark Night," featured at the beginning of each book, describes the mystical journey according to the traditional succession of purgation, illumination, and union. In *Ascent* John expresses his intention to follow the entire journey suggested in the stanzas "to the summit of the Mount, which is the high state of perfection which we here call union of the soul with God." Yet the following commentary discusses only the first two stanzas, which deal with purgation: illumination and union appear as modes of purifying the soul. The Prologue to *The Dark Night* states even more explicitly that all the stanzas of the poem will be expounded, not only the first two but also the six that treat "the wondrous effects of the spiritual illumination and union of love with God," yet no such treatment follows. Have those works remained incomplete or, as a few commentators have suggested, was part of them lost?

The relation between *Ascent* and *The Dark Night* appears even more complex. At first reading *Ascent* seems to treat the active purgation of the senses (Bk. I) and of the mind (Bks. II-III), while *The Dark Night* deals with the passive one. *The Dark Night* could then be considered the fourth part of *Ascent,* to which John alludes in *Ascent* I, 1, 2. But the first seven chapters of *The Dark Night* do not fit this scheme. Were they meant to recapitulate very briefly the subject matter of *Ascent* once the promised fourth part was made into an independent work? Possibly. But the later part of Book II of *Ascent* (especially chaps. 24–26) presents new problems, since it deals with what in John's scheme would have to be called *passive illumination.* Also, how do "the touches engendering sweetness and intimate delight" (II, 26) differ from what occurs in the *unitive* way? John himself informs us that "these lofty manifestations of knowledge can come only to the soul that attains to union with God, for they are themselves that union" (II, 26, 5). We may further wonder whether the term *purgation* still adequately defines the unitive love described in *The Dark Night* II, 11, 2: "Inasmuch as this love is informed, it is passive rather than active, and thus it begets in the soul a strong passion of love. This love has in it something of union with God." All this should caution us that, for John, *systematic* does not necessarily mean "consistent." Yet, more important, it shows how in the highest mystical stages the traditional division between cognitive and appetitive states of mind collapses altogether.

The excerpts taken from Book I of *Ascent* compactly describe the general attitude John considers indispensable to a contemplative life. Chapter 23 of Book II introduces the so-called intellectual visions, modes of passive illumination in which the senses and the imagination play no role or a purely subordinate one. To these total apprehensions none of the terms derived from the language of ordinary experience properly applies—not even that of vision. Nevertheless, John uses visionary terminology because, as he explains in the following chapter, they show a certain analogy with bodily visions: "Just as the eyes see bodily visions by means of natural light, so does the soul, by means of

334

supernaturally derived light, see those same things inwardly" (chap. 24). The difference between the two lies in the mode of perception. John cautions against all visions of the created world—even the spiritual ones. To stay with them is to encumber one's spiritual progress and to expose oneself to delusions. Still, among intellectual visions he excepts one kind from these reservations—the so-called knowledge of naked truths described in chapter 26. Among them we also find insights concerning the created world—not, however, of creatures as they exist in themselves, but as they derive from their divine source. Only the latter visions of creation are safe from illusions. (Similar distinctions appear in Ignatius of Loyola and Teresa of Avila, though both seem more readily inclined to ascribe the former directly to the devil.) Infused awareness of naked truths about God John equates with "touches" of substantial union. In that supreme state the distinction between illumination and union breaks down and this highest contemplation coincides with total darkness. The second book of *The Dark Night of the Soul* deals with this "dark contemplation" of the mind. Yet gradually John extends the subject beyond singular "visions" and "touches" to the entire mental state of the mystic who has attained that level of illumination.

The Living Flame of Love began as a short poem of four stanzas to which John later added a commentary at the request of a benefactress of the Order. He did so "somewhat unwillingly," as he writes in the prologue, because those stanzas speak of the most complete and perfect love in the soul that has become transformed in God. The state of union described in the poem lies beyond the one presented in *The Spiritual Canticle,* a pastoral poem of the love of the soul for her divine Bridegroom. In *The Living Flame of Love* the soul "is not only united with the divine Fire but has become one living flame with it." The text abruptly breaks off at the end of the passage here printed. The final three verses remain almost without comment. The same occurred in the second redaction of the text, which John wrote later. The stanzas refer "to things so interior and spiritual that words commonly fail to describe them" (prologue). The words "And in your sweet breathing" suggest the assumption of the soul within the divine Trinity, where the soul becomes one with the *spiratio* of the Holy Spirit. In this poem, then, and in its truncated commentary we learn what John considered the most intimate union of the soul with God—the deification of the Greek fathers, or the superessential unity of Ruusbroec.

Those who know John of the Cross best have been unanimous in ranking his poetry above his prose works as the decisive statement of his mystical theology. This judgment reflects John's own. He considered his commentaries quite inadequate compared to the poems. Patterned after the pastoral love songs of Garsilasos and Boscan, they suggest indirectly what lies beyond concepts and words. The one best known (here reprinted), "The Dark Night," which lay at the basis of the book of that name as well as of *The Ascent of Mount Carmel,* is a poetic masterpiece as well as a profound evocation of the mystical experience. Hans Urs von Balthasar compares its poet to "a Dante deprived of all images and concentrated in a single interior experience," and rightly so, for even though the poem is one long image, no "reality" corresponds to it. The poetic language both hides and discloses the nature of the experience. It is a refined expression of negative theology.

The negative quality of John's mystical poetry appears nowhere more clearly than in the poem that begins with the lines "I entered into unknowing" (also reprinted here). The poem itself, shorn of all imagery, assumes the stark language of Dionysius's *Mystical Theology* and Paul's letters. Yet it is a work of strong poetic power that makes the reader feel from within what the negative theology of the mystic means.

THE ASCENT OF MOUNT CARMEL

STANZAS

1. One dark night,
Fired by love's urgent longings
—Ah, the sheer grace!—
I went out unseen,
My house being now all stilled;

2. In darkness and secure,
By the secret ladder, disguised,
—Ah, the sheer grace!—
In darkness and concealment,
My house being now all stilled;

3. On that glad night,
In secret, for no one saw me,
Nor did I look at anything,
With no other light or guide
Than the one that burned in my heart;

4. This guided me
More surely than the light of noon
To where he waited for me

The selections from *The Ascent of Mount Carmel*, *The Dark Night*, and *The Living Flame of Love* are from *John of the Cross: Selected Writings*, ed. and trans. Kieran Kavanaugh, O.C.D., The Classics of Western Spirituality (New York: Paulist Press, 1987), 55–56, 61–62, 76–79, 81–82, 137–40, 293–94, 313–16. Reprinted with permission of the publisher.

—him I knew so well—
In a place where no one appeared.

5. O guiding night!
O night more lovely than the dawn!
O night that has united
The lover with his beloved,
Transforming the beloved in her lover.

6. Upon my flowering breast
Which I kept wholly for him alone,
There he lay sleeping,
And I caressing him
There in a breeze from the fanning cedars.

7. When the breeze blew from the turret
Parting his hair,
He wounded my neck
With his gentle hand,
Suspending all my senses.

8. I abandoned and forgot myself
Laying my face on my beloved;
All things ceased; I went out from myself,
Leaving my cares
Forgotten among the lilies.

BOOK ONE

Chapter One

Some remarks about the two different nights through which spiritual persons pass in both the lower and higher parts of their nature. A commentary on the first stanza....

1. The soul sings in this first stanza of its good luck and the grace it had in departing from its inordinate sensory appetites and imperfections. To understand this departure one should know that

a soul must ordinarily pass through two principal kinds of night—which spiritual persons call purgations or purifications of the soul—in order to reach the state of perfection. Here we will term these purgations "nights" because in both of them the soul journeys in darkness as though by night.

2. The first night or purgation, to which this stanza refers and which will be under discussion in the first section of this book, concerns the sensory part of the soul. The second night, to which the second stanza refers, concerns the spiritual part. We will deal with this second night, insofar as it is active, in the second and third sections of the book. In the fourth section we will discuss the night insofar as it is passive.

3. This first night is the lot of beginners, at the time God commences to introduce them into the state of contemplation. It is a night in which their spirit also participates, as we will explain in due time. The second night or purification takes place in those who are already proficients, at the time God desires to lead them into the state of divine union. This purgation, of course, is more obscure, dark, and dreadful, as we will subsequently point out....

Chapter Thirteen

The manner and method of entering this night of sense:

1. Some counsels are in order now that the individual may both know the way of entering this night and be able to do so. It should be understood, consequently, that a person ordinarily enters this night of sense in two ways: active and passive.

The active way, which will be the subject of the following counsels, comprises what one can do and does by oneself to enter this night. The passive way is that in which one does nothing, but God accomplishes the work in the soul, while the soul acts as the recipient. This will be the subject of the fourth book, where we will discuss beginners.[1] Since, with God's help, I will there give

---

[1] John never got to this fourth book as promised; however, he did deal in *The Dark Night* with what he mentions here.

counsels pertinent to the numerous imperfections beginners ordinarily possess on this road, I will not take the time to offer many here. Nor is this the proper place to give them, since presently we are dealing only with the reasons for calling this journey a night, and with the nature and divisions of this night.

Nevertheless, if we do not offer some immediate remedy or counsel, this part would seem very short and less helpful. Therefore I want to set down the following abridged method. And I will do the same at the end of my discussion of each of the next two parts (or reasons for the use of the term "night") which, with God's help, will follow.

2. Though these counsels for the conquering of the appetites are brief and few in number, I believe they are as profitable and efficacious as they are concise. A person who sincerely wants to practice them will need no others since all the others are included in these.

3. First, have a habitual desire to imitate Christ in all your deeds by bringing your life into conformity with His. You must then study His life in order to know how to imitate Him and behave in all events as He would.

4. Second, in order to be successful in this imitation, renounce and remain empty of any sensory satisfaction that is not purely for the honor and glory of God. Do this out of love for Jesus Christ. In His life He had no other gratification, nor desired any other, than the fulfillment of His Father's will, which He called His meat and food [Jn 4:34]....

5. Many blessings flow from the harmony and tranquility of the four natural passions: joy, hope, fear, and sorrow. The following maxims contain a complete remedy for mortifying and pacifying the passions. If put into practice these maxims will give rise to abundant merit and great virtues.

6. Endeavor to be inclined always:

not to the easiest, but to the most difficult;
not to the most delightful, but to the harshest;
not to the most gratifying, but to the less pleasant;
not to what means rest for you, but to hard work;

not to the consoling, but to the unconsoling;
not to the most, but to the least;
not to the highest and most precious, but to the lowest and
    most despised;
not to wanting something, but to wanting nothing;
do not go about looking for the best of temporal things, but
    for the worst, and desire to enter for Christ into complete
    nudity, emptiness, and poverty in everything in the world.

7. You should embrace these practices earnestly and try to overcome the repugnance of your will toward them. If you sincerely put them into practice with order and discretion, you will discover in them great delight and consolation....

10. As a conclusion to these counsels and rules it would be appropriate to repeat the verses in "The Ascent to Mount Carmel" (the drawing at the beginning of the book), which are instructions for climbing to the summit, the high state of union. Although in the drawing we admittedly refer to the spiritual and interior aspect, we also deal with the spirit of imperfection existent in the sensory and exterior part of the soul, as is evident by the two roads, one on each side of that path that leads to perfection. Consequently, these verses will here bear reference to the sensory part. Afterward, in the second division of this night, they may be interpreted in relationship to the spiritual part.

11. The verses are as follows:

To reach satisfaction in all
    desire its possession in nothing.
To come to possess all
    desire the possession of nothing.
To arrive at being all
    desire to be nothing.
To come to the knowledge of all
    desire the knowledge of nothing.
To come to the pleasure you have not
    you must go by a way in which you enjoy not.

To come to the knowledge you have not
　　you must go by a way in which you know not.
To come to the possession you have not
　　you must go by a way in which you possess not.
To come to be what you are not
　　you must go by a way in which you are not.
When you turn toward something
　　you cease to cast yourself upon the all.
For to go from all to the all
　　you must deny yourself of all in all.
And when you come to the possession of the all
　　you must possess it without wanting anything.
Because if you desire to have something in all
　　your treasure in God is not purely your all.

12. In this nakedness the spirit finds its quietude and rest. For in coveting nothing, nothing raises it up and nothing weighs it down, because it is in the center of its humility. When it covets something, in this very desire it is wearied....

BOOK TWO

This book is a treatise on faith, the proximate means to union with God. It consequently considers the second part of this night, the night of the spirit to which the following stanza refers.[2]

Chapter One

The Second Stanza

> In darkness and secure,
> By the secret ladder, disguised,
> —Ah, the sheer grace!—

---

[2]John gives an explanation of the second stanza in this chapter but then never returns to it until his work *The Dark Night*. There he interprets it from a different perspective and also explains the stanza verse by verse.

In darkness and concealment,
My house being now all stilled;

1. This second stanza tells in song of the sheer grace that was the soul's in divesting the spirit of all its imperfections and appetites for spiritual possessions. This grace is far greater here because of the greater hardship involved in quieting the house of one's spiritual nature and entering this interior darkness (the spiritual nudity of all sensory and immaterial things), leaning on pure faith alone, in an ascent by it to God.

The secret ladder represents faith, because all the rungs or articles of faith are secret to and hidden from both the senses and the intellect. Accordingly the soul lived in darkness, without the light of the senses and intellect, and went out beyond every natural and rational boundary to climb the divine ladder of faith that leads up to and penetrates the deep things of God [1 Cor 2:10].

The soul declares that it was disguised because in the ascent through faith its garments, apparel, and capacities were changed from natural to divine. On account of this disguise, neither the devil, nor temporal, nor rational things recognized or detained it. None of these can do harm to the one who walks in faith....

Chapter Twenty-Six

The two kinds of knowledge of naked truths. The proper conduct of the soul in their regard:

1. For an adequate exposition of this subject (the knowledge of naked truths), God would have to move my hand and pen. For you should know, beloved reader, that what they in themselves are for the soul is beyond words. Since, however, I intentionally speak of these only so as to impart instruction and guide the soul through them to the divine union, let me discuss them in a brief and restricted way, which will be sufficient for our purpose.

2. ...This intellectual vision is not like the vision of corporal objects, but rather consists in an intellectual understanding or vision of truths about God, or to a vision of present, past, or

future events, which bears great resemblance to the spirit of prophecy, as we shall perhaps explain later.

3. This type of knowledge is divided into two kinds: The object of the one kind is the Creator; and that of the other is the creature, as we said. Both kinds bring intense delight to the soul. Yet those of God produce an incomparable delight; there are no words or terms to describe them, for they are the knowledge and delight of God Himself. And as David says: *There is nothing like unto Him* [Ps 40:6]. God is the direct object of this knowledge in that one of His attributes (His omnipotence, fortitude, goodness, sweetness, and so on) is sublimely experienced. And as often as this experience occurs, it remains fixed in the soul. Since this communication is pure contemplation, the soul clearly understands that it is ineffable. People are capable of describing it only through general expressions—expressions caused by the abundance of the delight and good of these experiences. But they realize the impossibility of explaining with these expressions what they tasted and felt in this communication.

4. David, after having received a similar experience, spoke in these unprecise terms: *Judicia Domini vera, justificata in semetipsa. Desiderabilia super aurum et lapidem pretiosum multum, et dulciora super mel et favum* (God's judgments—the virtues and attributes we experience in God—are true, in themselves justified, more desirable than gold and extremely precious stone, and sweeter than the honey and the honeycomb) [Ps 19:11].

We read that Moses spoke only in general terms of the lofty knowledge that God, while passing by, gave him. And it happened that when the Lord passed before him in that knowledge, Moses quickly prostrated himself, crying: *Dominator Domine Deus, misericors and clemens, patiens, et multae miserationis, ac verax. Qui custodies misericordiam in millia,* and so on (Sovereign Lord God, merciful and clement, patient, and of great compassion, and true. You guard the mercy that you promise to thousands) [Ex 34:6–7]. Evidently, since Moses could not express with one concept what he knew in God, he did so through an overflow of words.

Although at times individuals use words in reference to this knowledge, they clearly realize that they have said nothing of what they experienced, for no term can give adequate expression to it. And thus when St. Paul experienced that lofty knowledge of God, he did not care to say anything else than that it was not licit for humans to speak of it [2 Cor 12:4].

5. This divine knowledge of God never deals with particular things, since its object is the Supreme Principle. Consequently one cannot express it in particular terms, unless a truth about something less than God is seen together with this knowledge of Him. But in no way can anything be said of that divine knowledge.

This sublime knowledge can be received only by a person who has arrived at union with God, for it is itself that very union. It consists in a certain touch of the divinity produced in the soul, and thus it is God Himself who is experienced and tasted there.[3] Although the touch of knowledge and delight that penetrates the substance of the soul is not manifest and clear, as in glory, it is so sublime and lofty that the devil is unable to meddle or produce anything similar (for there is no experience similar or comparable to it), or infuse a savor or delight like it. This knowledge savors of the divine essence and of eternal life, and the devil cannot counterfeit anything so lofty.

6. He could, nevertheless, ape that experience by presenting to the soul some very sensible feelings of grandeur and fulfillment, trying to persuade it that these are from God. But this attempt of the devil does not enter the substance of the soul and suddenly renew and fill it with love as does a divine touch. Some of these divine touches produced in the substance of the soul are so enriching that one of them would be sufficient not only to remove definitively all the imperfections that the soul would have been unable to eradicate throughout its entire life, but also to fill it with virtues and blessings from God.

7. These touches engender such sweetness and intimate delight in the soul that one of them would more than compensate

---

[3]Although the general topic in this book deals with the purification of the spiritual faculties, John speaks here of experiences of actual union, substantial touches, proper to the state of transformation in God and to one already purified.

for all the trials suffered in life, even though innumerable. Through these touches individuals become so courageous and so resolved to suffer many things for Christ that they find it a special suffering to observe that they do not suffer.

8. People are incapable of reaching this sublime knowledge through any comparison or imagining of their own, because it transcends what is naturally attainable. Thus God effects in the soul what it is incapable of acquiring. God usually grants these divine touches, which cause certain remembrances of Him, at times when the soul is least expecting or thinking of them. Sometimes they are produced suddenly through some remembrance, which may only concern some slight detail. They are so sensible that they sometimes cause not only the soul but also the body to tremble. Yet at other times with a sudden feeling of spiritual delight and refreshment, and without any trembling, they occur very tranquilly in the spirit.

9. Or again they may occur on uttering or hearing a word from Sacred Scripture or from some other source. These touches do not always have the same efficacy, nor are they always felt so forcefully, because they are often very weak. Yet no matter how weak they may be, one of these divine touches is worth more to the soul than numberless other thoughts and ideas about God's creatures and works.

Since this knowledge is imparted to the soul suddenly, without exercise of free will, individuals do not have to be concerned about desiring it or not. They should simply remain humble and resigned about it, for God will do His work at the time and in the manner He wishes.

10. I do not affirm that people should be negative about this knowledge as they should be with the other apprehensions, because this knowledge is an aspect of the union toward which we are directing the soul and which is the reason for our doctrine about the denudation and detachment from all other apprehensions. God's demands for granting such a grace are humility, suffering for love of Him, and resignation as to all recompense. God does not bestow these favors on a possessive soul, since He gives

them out of a very special love for the recipient. For the individual receiving them is one who loves with great detachment. The Son of God meant this when He stated: *Qui autem diligit me, diligetur a Patre meo, et ego diligam eum and manifestabo ei meipsum* (Those who love me will be loved by my Father, and I will love them and manifest Myself to them) [Jn 14:21]. This manifestation includes the knowledge and touches that God imparts to a person who has reached Him and truly loves Him....

THE DARK NIGHT

BOOK TWO

Chapter Five

[Begins to explain how this dark contemplation is not only night for the soul but also affliction and torment.]

1. This dark night is an inflow of God into the soul that purges it of its habitual ignorances and imperfections, natural and spiritual, and which contemplatives call infused contemplation or mystical theology. Through this contemplation, God teaches the soul secretly and instructs it in the perfection of love without its doing anything or understanding how this happens.

Insofar as infused contemplation is loving wisdom of God, it produces two principal effects in the soul: It prepares the soul for the union with God through love by both purging and illumining it. Hence the same loving wisdom that purges and illumines the blessed spirits purges and illumines the soul here on earth.

2. Yet a doubt arises: Why, if it is a divine light (for it illumines souls and purges them of their ignorances), does one call it a dark night? In answer to this, there are two reasons why this divine wisdom is not only night and darkness for the soul, but also affliction and torment. First, because of the height of the divine wisdom, which exceeds the capacity of the soul. Second, because of the soul's baseness and impurity; and on this account the wisdom is painful, afflictive, and also dark for the soul.

3. To prove the first reason, we must presuppose a certain principle of the Philosopher: that the clearer and more obvious divine things are in themselves, the darker and more hidden they are to the soul naturally. The brighter the light, the more the owl is blinded; and the more one looks at the brilliant sun, the more the sun darkens the faculty of sight, deprives it and overwhelms it in its weakness.[1]

Hence, when the divine light of contemplation strikes souls not yet entirely illumined, it causes spiritual darkness, for it not only surpasses them but also deprives and darkens their act of understanding. This is why St. Dionysius and other mystical theologians call this infused contemplation a ray of darkness; that is, for the soul not yet illumined and purged. For this great supernatural light overwhelms the intellect and deprives it of its natural vigor.

David also said that clouds and darkness are near God and surround Him [Ps 18:12], not because this is true in itself but because it appears thus to our weak intellects, which in being unable to attain so bright a light are blinded and darkened. Hence, he immediately added: *Clouds passed before the great splendor of His presence* [Ps 18:12], that is, between God and our intellect. As a result, when God communicates this bright ray of His secret wisdom to the soul not yet transformed, He causes thick darkness in its intellect....

Chapter Eleven

[The beginning of an explanation of verse 2 of the first stanza. Tells how the fruit of these dark straits is a vehement passion of divine love.]

1. In this second verse the soul refers to the fire of love that, like material fire acting on wood, penetrates it in this night of painful contemplation. Although this enkindling of love we are now discussing is in some way similar to that which occurs in the sensory part of the soul, it is as different from it in another way as is the soul from the body, or the spiritual part from the sensory part. For the enkindling of love occurs in the spirit and through it

---

[1]Aristotle, *Metaphysics,* 2,1.

the soul in the midst of these dark conflicts feels vividly and keenly that it is being wounded by a strong divine love, and it has a certain feeling and foretaste of God. Yet is understands nothing in particular, for as we said the intellect is in darkness.

2. The spirit herein experiences an impassioned and intense love because this spiritual inflaming engenders the passion of love. Since this love is infused, it is more passive than active and thus generates in the soul a strong passion of love. This love is now beginning to possess something of union with God and thereby shares to a certain extent in its properties. These properties are actions of God more than of the soul, and they reside in it passively, although the soul does give its consent. But only the love of God, which is being united to the soul, imparts the heat, strength, temper, and passion of love, or fire, as the soul terms it here. The more the soul is equipped to receive the wound and union the more this love finds that all the soul's appetites are brought into subjection, alienated, incapacitated, and unable to be satisfied by any heavenly or earthly thing.

3. This happens very particularly in this dark purgation, as we said, since God so weans and recollects the appetites that they cannot find satisfaction in any of their objects. God proceeds thus so that by withdrawing the appetites from other objects and recollecting them in Himself, He may strengthen the soul and give it the capacity for this strong union of love, which He begins to accord by means of this purgation. In this union the soul will love God intensely with all its strength and all its sensory and spiritual appetites. Such love is impossible if these appetites are scattered by their satisfaction in other things. In order to receive the strength of this union of love, David proclaimed to God: *I will keep my strength for You* [Ps 59:10], that is, all the ability, appetites, and strength of my faculties, by not desiring to make use of them or find satisfaction in anything outside of You....

THE LIVING FLAME OF LOVE

STANZAS

1. O living flame of love
That tenderly wounds my soul
In its deepest center! Since
Now you are not oppressive,
Now Consummate! if it be your will:
Tear through the veil of this sweet encounter!

2. O sweet cautery,
O delightful wound!
O gentle hand! O delicate touch
That tastes of eternal life
And pays every debt!
In killing you changed death to life.

3. O lamps of fire!
In whose splendors
The deep caverns of feeling,
Once obscure and blind,
Now give forth, so rarely, so exquisitely,
Both warmth and light to their beloved.

4. How gently and lovingly
You wake in my heart,
Where in secret you dwell alone;
And in your sweet breathing,
Filled with good and glory,
How tenderly you swell my heart with love.

COMMENTARY ON STANZA FOUR

3. ...How gentle and loving (that is, extremely loving and gentle) is your awakening, O Word, Spouse, in the center and depth of my soul, which is its pure and intimate substance, in which secretly and silently, as its only lord, you dwell alone, not only as in your house, nor only as in your bed, but also as in my own heart, intimately and closely united to it. And how delicately you captivate me and arouse my affections toward you in the sweet breathing you produce in this awakening, a breathing delightful to me and full of good and glory.

The soul uses this comparison because its experience here is similar to that of one who upon awakening breathes deeply.

The verse follows:

4.　　　　　　　How gently and lovingly
　　　　　　　　You wake in my heart

There are many kinds of awakening that God effects in the soul, so many that we would never finish explaining them all. Yet this awakening of the Son of God, which the soul wishes to refer to here, is one of the most elevated and most beneficial. For this awakening is a movement of the Word in the substance of the soul containing such grandeur, dominion, and glory, and intimate sweetness that it seems to the soul that all the balsams and fragrant spices and flowers of the world are commingled, stirred, and shaken so as to yield their sweet odor, and that all the kingdoms and dominions of the world and all the powers and virtues of heaven are moved; and not only this, but it also seems that all the virtues and substances and perfections and graces of every created thing glow and make the same movement all at once.

Since, as St. John says, *all things in Him are life* [Jn 1:3–4], and, as the Apostle declares, *in Him they live and are and move* [Acts 17:28], it follows that when, within the soul, this great Emperor moves (whose principality, as Isaiah says, He bears on His shoulders [Is 9:6]—which consists of the three spheres, celestial, terrestrial, and infernal, and the things contained in them—upholding them all, as St. Paul says [Heb 1:3], with the word of His power), all things seem to move in unison. This happens in the same manner as when at the movement of the earth all material things in it move as though they were nothing. So it is when this Prince moves, who Himself carries His court, instead of His court carrying Him.[1]

5. Even this comparison is most inadequate, for in this awakening they not only seem to move, but they all likewise disclose the beauties of their being, power, loveliness, and graces, and the root of their duration and life. For the soul is conscious of how all creatures, earthly and heavenly, have their life, duration, and strength in Him, and it clearly realizes what He says in the Book of Proverbs: *By me kings reign and princes rule and the mighty exercise justice and understand it* [Prv 8:15–16]. Although it is indeed aware that these things are distinct from God, insofar as they have created being, nonetheless that which it understands of God, by His being all these things with infinite eminence, is such that it knows these things better in God's being than in themselves.

And here lies the remarkable delight of this awakening: The soul knows creatures through God and not God through creatures. This amounts to knowing the effects through their cause and not the cause through its effects. The latter is knowledge *a posteriori*, and the former is essential knowledge....

14.   Where in secret you dwell alone

The soul says that He dwells in its heart in secret because this sweet embrace is wrought in the depths of its substance.

It should be known that God dwells secretly in all souls and is hidden in their substance, for otherwise they would not last. Yet there is a difference, a great difference, in His dwelling in them. In some souls He dwells alone, and in others He does not dwell alone. Abiding in some, He is pleased; and in others, He is displeased. He lives in some as though in His own house, commanding and ruling

---

[1] It would seem that John accepted the Copernican theory, which was disputed in his time but taught at the University of Salamanca, the first to accept the theory. When the first edition of John's works was published, this text was altered because Copernicus's work was by then on the Index.

everything; and in others as though a stranger in a strange house, where they do not permit Him to give orders or do anything.

It is in that soul in which less of its own appetites and pleasures dwell that He dwells more alone, more pleased, and more as though in His own house, ruling and governing it. And He dwells more in secret, the more He dwells alone. Thus in this soul, in which neither any appetite nor any other images or forms nor any affections for created things dwell, the beloved dwells secretly with an embrace so much the closer, more intimate, and interior, the purer and more alone the soul is to everything other than God. His dwelling is in secret, then, because the devil cannot reach the area of this embrace, nor can one's intellect understand how it occurs.

Yet it is not secret to the soul itself that has attained this perfection, for within itself it has the experience of this intimate embrace. It does not, however, always experience these awakenings, for when the beloved produces them, it seems to the soul that he is awakening in its heart, where before he remained as though asleep. Although it was experiencing and enjoying him, this took place as though with a loved one who is asleep, for knowledge and love are not communicated mutually while one is still asleep.

15. Oh, how happy is this soul that ever experiences God resting and reposing within it! Oh, how fitting it is for it to withdraw from things, flee from business matters, and live in immense tranquility, so that it may not even with the slightest mote or noise disturb or trouble its heart where the beloved dwells.

He is usually there, in this embrace with his bride, as though asleep in the substance of the soul. And it is very well aware of him and ordinarily enjoys him. Were he always awake within it, communicating knowledge and love, it would already be in glory. For if, when he does waken, scarcely opening his eyes, he has such an effect on the soul, what would it be like were he ordinarily in it fully awake?

16. Although he is not displeased with other souls that have not reached this union, for after all they are in the state of grace, yet insofar as they are not well disposed, his dwelling is secret to them, even though he does dwell in them. They do not experience

him ordinarily, except when he grants them some delightful awakening. But such an awakening is not of this kind and high quality, nor is it comparable to these, nor as secret to the intellect and the devil, which are still able to understand something through the movements of the senses. For the senses are not fully annihilated until the soul reaches this union, and they still have some activity and movements concerning the spiritual, since they are not yet totally spiritual.

But in this awakening of the bridegroom in the perfect soul, everything that occurs and is caused is perfect, for he is the cause of it all. And in that awakening, which is as though one were to awaken and breathe, the soul feels a strange delight in the breathing of the Holy Spirit in God, in which it is sovereignly glorified and taken with love. Hence it says in the subsequent verses:

17.   And in your sweet breathing,
        Filled with good and glory,
        How tenderly you swell my heart with love!

I do not desire to speak of this spiration, filled for the soul with good and glory and delicate love of God, for I am aware of being incapable of so doing; and were I to try, it might seem less than it is.[2] It is a spiration that God produces in the soul, in which, by that awakening of lofty knowledge of the Godhead, He breathes the Holy Spirit in it in the same proportion as was its knowledge and understanding of Him, absorbing it most profoundly in the Holy Spirit, rousing its love with divine excellence and delicacy according to what it beheld in Him. Since the breathing is filled with good and glory, the Holy Spirit, through this breathing, filled the soul with good and glory, in which He enkindled it in love of Himself, indescribably and incomprehensibly, in the depths of God, to whom be honor and glory forever and ever. Amen.

---

[2]Actually John does not finish his work but abandons it, giving as his excuse, now at the end of his writings, the ineffable character of the mystical experience of God.

STANZAS CONCERNING AN ECSTASY EXPERIENCED IN HIGH CONTEMPLATION

I entered into unknowing,
and there I remained unknowing,
transcending all knowledge.

1. I entered into unknowing
yet when I saw myself there
without knowing where I was
I understood great things;
I will not say what I felt
for I remained in unknowing
transcending all knowledge.

2. That perfect knowledge
was of peace and holiness
held at no remove
in profound solitude;
it was something so secret
that I was left stammering,
transcending all knowledge.

This poem is taken from *The Collected Works of St. John of the Cross,* trans. Kieran Kavanaugh, O.C.D., and Otilio Rodriguez, O.C.D., rev. ed. (Washington, D.C.: Institute of Carmelite Studies, 1991), 53–54. Reprinted with permission of the publisher.

356

3. I was so 'whelmed,
so absorbed and withdrawn,
that my senses were left
deprived of all their sensing,
and my spirit was given
an understanding while not understanding,
transcending all knowledge.

4. He who truly arrives there
cuts free from himself;
all that he knew before
now seems worthless,
and his knowledge so soars
that he is left in unknowing
transcending all knowledge.

5. The higher he ascends
the less he understands,
because the cloud is dark
which lit up the night;
whoever knows this
remains always in unknowing
transcending all knowledge.

6. This knowledge in unknowing
is so overwhelming
that wise men disputing
can never overthrow it,
for their knowledge does not reach
to the understanding of not-understanding,
transcending all knowledge.

7. And this supreme knowledge
is so exalted
that no power of man or learning
can grasp it;
he who masters himself

will, with knowledge in unknowing,
always be transcending.

8. And if you should want to hear:
this highest knowledge lies
in the loftiest sense
of the essence of God;
this is a work of his mercy,
to leave one without understanding,
transcending all knowledge.

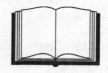

Selected Bibliography

TEXTS

Editions used:
John of the Cross: Selected Writings. Translated by Kieran Kavanaugh, O.C.D. The Classics of Western Spirituality. New York: Paulist Press; London: SPCK, 1987.

The Collected Works of St. John of the Cross. Translated by Kieran Kavanaugh, O.C.D., and Otilio Rodriguez, O.C.D. Washington, D.C.: Institute of Carmelite Studies, 1991.

Another source:
The Complete Works of Saint John of the Cross. Translated by E. Allison Peers. 3 vols. London: Burns, Oates and Washbourne, 1934–35; Westminster, Md.: Newman, 1945.

STUDIES

Dombrowski, Daniel A. *St. John of the Cross: An Appreciation.* Albany, N.Y.: SUNY Press, 1992.

Grennan, John, ed. *Toward Greater Heights: Aspects of the Spirituality of St. John of the Cross.* Dublin: Carmelite Centre of Spirituality, 1991.

Orcibal, Jean. *Saint Jean de la Croix et les mystiques rhéno-flamands.* Bruges, 1966.

Sanderlin, David. "Faith and Ethical Reasoning in the Mystical Theology of St. John of the Cross." *Religious Studies* 25 (1989): 317–33.

Stein, Edith. *The Science of the Cross*, Translated by Hilda Graef. Chicago: Henry Regnery, 1960.

Volker, Joseph A. "The Spirituality of Dialogue." *Journal of Ecumenical Studies* 24 (1987): 285–95.

Francis de Sales (1567–1622) and Jeanne de Chantal (1572–1641)

Spiritual writers rarely distinguish themselves as stylists. Francis de Sales may well represent the most outstanding exception. The very name of the movement he initiated, devout humanism, suggests the friendly relation in which his spirituality stands to the aesthetic ideals of the Renaissance. The recent Council of Trent had solemnly declared that the two are not incompatible: nature, though wounded by sin, was not intrinsically corrupt. The *idea* of a Christian humanism had existed before. Erasmus had supported it and so had, less elegantly but more effectively, Ignatius of Loyola. But not until the final chapters of Baldassare Castiglione's *Courtier (Il Cortegiano)* had it become an ideal of style and courtly conduct.

Francis himself was born in an aristocratic family in Savoy at the time when the rustic customs of the French nobility were giving way to refinement in manners and education. His tactful behavior was to be a major asset in accomplishing the delicate task that his appointment, first as provost, later as bishop of Geneva had imposed upon him: to try to regain the diocese for the Catholic faith. When he was consecrated, Geneva was the theocratic center of the Calvinist reformation. Catholics were banned from Geneva, and the episcopal see had been moved to the small city of Annecy.

Francis's own spiritual experience had well prepared him for his pastoral work in a predominantly Calvinist area. During his student days in Paris and in Padua he had suffered a severe crisis concerning the predestinationist theory of salvation that he read in the Thomistic theologians of his day. It made him sensitive to the Calvinist position and ready for dialogue. While still provost of the diocese he engaged in secret conversations with Theodore Beza, the chief reformed theologian of the day. His own manner of bringing separated Christians back to the church consisted not in engaging in polemics but in giving an example of virtue and kindness and in enforcing the education and good behavior of his clergy. But, more than anything, his conferences and spiritual writings were the effective tools of his apostolate. The extremely popular *Introduction to the Devout Life,* still a favorite today, written in the elegant, somewhat precious style of the time, was intended for lay men and, even more, for lay women, composed as it was from letters to several spiritual daughters. Francis attempted to show that gracious living culminates in living in God's grace. Without adding much theological justification, the young bishop gave spiritual guidance to civilized young people who, though heavily involved in mundane matters, nevertheless aspired to lead a religious life.

The *Introduction* prepared the terrain, but it was the *Treatise on the Love of God* that earned Francis a place among the great spiritual writers of the Christian faith. Here he showed why an uninterrupted continuity can exist between grace and nature. Nature, for Francis, is dynamically oriented toward the love of God:

> We have been created to the image and likeness of God. What does this mean but that we stand in a relation of extreme correspondence with his divine majesty? Even as the person cannot become perfect except through God's goodness, that

goodness itself can nowhere better activate its eternal perfection than in our humanity.

Grace transforms nature from within, resulting in a single reality that is both human and divine. Charity, the sanctifying agent, is "infused," but since charity is a virtue, it requires active cooperation.

Grace rules spiritual life by attraction. As he writes in book two of the *Treatise,* "When the will follows the attraction and consents to the divine motion, it follows freely, just as it freely resists when it resists, even though our consent to grace depends much more on grace than on the will." Francis leans toward the (questionable) doctrine of Molina in his attempt to clarify the relation between nature and grace, but without being committed to that doctrine, he merely insists that grace corresponds to nature's inclination. Despite his religious naturalism, Francis's doctrine in the *Treatise* is very demanding; in fact, he favors a withdrawal from the world. Later movements that were influenced by him, in particular the early Jansenism of the nuns of Port Royal, absorbed more of this ascetic unworldliness than of his theological humanism.

This devout humanism nonetheless penetrated Francis's own way of dealing with others. In particular, it inspired his intimate friendship with Jeanne Frances de Chantal. He had spiritually assisted her during the difficult days of her widowhood, and together they founded the women's religious congregation of the Visitation of the Blessed Mary. Their relationship was as intense as that between Clare and Francis of Assisi; indeed, some have suggested that it might more appropriately be called love than friendship. If so, it was love at first sight. In 1604, while preaching Lenten sermons in Dijon, Francis noticed her in the congregation and was immediately drawn to her. He hesitated, however, when she requested his spiritual guidance, but in the end he judged that it was his duty to accept. Already on the way back to Annecy he wrote to her: "God, so it seems to me, has given me to you; of that I am convinced every hour." A few weeks later: "The greater the physical distance between us, the closer I feel is our interior bond." And yet a few days later: "Our souls should give birth, not outside themselves, but within, to the dearest, most charming and handsome male child that one could wish for. It is Jesus whom we must form and bring to birth in ourselves....I never say holy Mass without you and all those closest to you; I never receive communion without you, and finally I am as much yours as you could ever wish me to be."

It would be hard to deny the presence of an erotic element in this agapic love. But it is a testimony to the sanctity of these two people that they were fully aware of it and succeeded in keeping their love religiously pure. They perceived their affection for each other as continuous with God's love and, in fact, as instrumental to it. This required submitting themselves to severe conditions of abnegation and sacrifice. After their foundation was well on its way Francis suggested that they should "let each other go." In a letter of 1611 he wrote to Jeanne: "May that sacred fire that changes everything into itself also transform our heart, so that it may not be anything but love, and then that we may not be lovers, but love; not two, but one single dual self *[un seul nous-même]*, since love unites all things in its sovereign unity." The passionate tone of this letter ought not mislead us about its intention: it was a call to total physical separation rather than union. When in 1616 he, despite a continuing deep attachment, decided that they had to make the sacrifice of their friendship, Jeanne's response shows how painful was the sacrifice to which she consented:

> I now remember, my only Father, that one day you ordered me to deprive myself of everything. I said: "I would not know of what!" You responded: "Did I not tell you that I would deprive you of everything?" O my God, how easy it is to abandon all that is around us! But to give up one's skin, one's flesh, one's bones, and to penetrate into the inner marrow, it seems that this is what we have done; it is great, difficult, impossible except by God's grace.

They remained faithful to their pact. During the three years before his death, they saw each other only once.

The reader may wonder: Was Francis, this great writer and perceptive spiritual director, also a mystic? The question is not whether he knew "supernatural experiences"—this was never the standard for inclusion in this collection—but whether his theories aimed at, were conducive to, and revealed something of the highest forms of spiritual life. There appears to linger some doubt about this. Francis was never more categorical than in his rejection of extraordinary forms of piety and even of a concern about one's progress in the ways of prayer. To live in God's presence is the goal, a goal that does not depend on our works but on God's grace. When Jeanne considered inviting to Annecy a religious woman who was said to have received extraordinary spiritual gifts, Francis promptly replied: "Please don't!" He even suspects any form of severe corporal asceticism. Sanctity consists in total submission to God's will. When during his final visit to the Visitation the nuns asked him for a short synthesis of spiritual life, he said: "Desire nothing, refuse nothing. With these two principles I have said it all." These principles, in fact, prepare an attitude, articulated by Madame Guyon, Bishop Fénelon, and Father de Caussade, of total abandonment to God's will. For Francis, however, it had none of the passivity that the Quietists put in it. His idea of spiritual life is essentially active and comes closer to that of Ignatius of Loyola than that of Fénelon.

Jeanne de Chantal's writings consist mainly of her letters. She too is an excellent writer. Though she possesses none of her spiritual father's originality, she makes up for it by the warm, natural tone of her correspondence. Her letters often take a very practical turn, as when she tries to persuade her somewhat mundane daughter Françoise to accept the prospective husband she has chosen for her, even though he is fifteen years older: "You will be much happier with him than with rash, dissolute young fools like the young men of today." The letters to her daughter are a delight—gentle, witty, yet persuasive. In the end she always succeeds in winning the recalcitrant young lady over to her view, especially in the case of her prearranged marriage. Obviously Jeanne was as well acquainted with the ways of her aristocratic society as with the ways of God. Her spiritual qualifications are more visible in her correspondence with her brother, Archbishop André Frémyot of Bourges, or with Commandeur de Sillery, ambassador to Spain and to Rome, both of whom had come to her for spiritual guidance. Here her tone is deferential, and she supports her advice consistently by the authority of Francis de Sales. Quite naturally, the bulk of her letters were addressed to the members of her congregation—at first to all her companions, later to the local superiors, assistants, and novice mistresses. What is so striking here is the warm, genuine affection she had for each of these women. Some read like love letters. Even the sisters who cause trouble in the community she continues to love. She tries to change their ways by gently suggesting alternatives rather than by direct criticism. She is never harsh and rarely stern. She leaves full responsibility to the superiors of the houses, however young and inexperienced they may be, and shows an endless patience for all. As she reveals herself in her letters, Jeanne is one of those persons one regrets not having met. In fact, she and Francis totally reformed the spirit of women's religious congregations toward openness, kindness, and charity and away from physical severity, introspection, and harshness.

FRANCIS DE SALES:
TREATISE ON THE LOVE OF GOD

BOOK SIX, CHAPTER ONE
A Description of Mystical Theology

...If prayer be a colloquy, a discourse or a conversation of the soul with God, by it then we speak to God, and he again speaks to us; we aspire to him and breathe in him, and he reciprocally inspires us and breathes upon us.

But of what do we discourse in prayer? What is the subject of our conference? Theotimus, in it we speak of God only, for of what can love discourse and talk but of the well-beloved? And therefore prayer, and mystical theology, are one same thing. It is called theology, because, as speculative theology has God for its object, so this also treats only of God, yet with three differences: (1) The former treats of God as God, but the latter treats of him as sovereignly amiable; that is, the former regards the Divinity of the supreme goodness, and the latter the supreme goodness of the Divinity. (2) The speculative treats of God with men and amongst men, the mystical speaks of God with God, and in God himself. (3) The speculative tends to the knowledge of God, and the mystical to the love of God; that, therefore, makes its scholars wise and learned theologians, but this makes its scholars fervent and affectionate lovers of God, a *Philotheus* or a *Theophilus*.

From *Treatise on the Love of God*, trans. Henry Benedict Mackey, O.S.B. (London: Burns Oates & Washbourne Ltd., n.d.), 232–40, 244–50. Reprinted with permission of the publisher.

Now it is called mystical because its conversation is altogether secret, and there is nothing said in it between God and the soul save only from heart to heart, by a communication incommunicable to all but those who make it. Lovers' language is so peculiar to themselves that none but themselves understand it. *I sleep,* said the holy spouse, *and my heart watcheth.* Ah, hark! *The voice of my beloved knocking* [Sg 3:6]. Who would have guessed that this spouse, being asleep, could yet talk with her beloved? But where love reigns, the sound of exterior words is not necessary, nor the help of sense to entertain and to hear one another. In fine, prayer and mystical theology is nothing else but a conversation in which the soul amorously entertains herself with God concerning his most amiable goodness, to unite and join herself thereto....

Love speaks not only by the tongue but by the eyes, by sighs, and by the play of features; yea, silence and dumbness are words for it. *My heart hath said to thee, my face sought thee: thy face, O Lord, will I still seek* [Ps 36:8]....

BOOK SIX, CHAPTER TWO
Of Meditation—The First Degree of Prayer or Mystical Theology

This word [meditation] is much used in the holy Scriptures and means simply an attentive and reiterated thought, proper to produce good or evil affections. In the first Psalm, the man is said to be blessed *whose will is in the way of the Lord, and who in his law shall meditate day and night.* But in the second Psalm: *Why did the Gentiles rage, and the people meditate vain things?* Meditation therefore is made as well for evil as for good. Yet whereas in the holy Scripture, the word meditation is ordinarily applied to the attention which we have to divine things to stir us up to love them, it has, as one might say, been canonized by the common consent of theologians, like the name angel....

Every meditation is a thought, but every thought is not a meditation. For we have thoughts to which our mind is carried without any design or aim, by way of simple musing, as we see common flies flying from one flower to another, without drawing anything from them. And be this kind of thought as attentive as it may, it can never bear the name of meditation, but should simply be called thought. Sometimes we consider a thing attentively to learn its causes, its effects, its qualities, and this thought is named study, in which the mind acts as locusts do, which promiscuously fly upon flowers and leaves to eat them and nourish themselves therewith. But when we think of divine things not to learn but to make ourselves love them, this is called meditating, and this exercise, meditation; in it our spirit, not as a fly for simple amusement, nor as a locust to eat and be filled, but as a sacred bee, moves over the flowers of holy mysteries, to extract from them the honey of divine love....

...Thus in the Canticle of Canticles the heavenly spouse, as a mystical bee, settles now on the eyes, now on the lips, on the cheeks, on the hair of her beloved, to draw thence the sweetness of a thousand passions of love, noting in particular whatever she finds best for this. So that, inflamed with holy love, she speaks with him, she questions him, she listens to him, sighs, aspires, admires him, as he on his part fills her with delight, inspiring her, touching and opening her heart, and pouring into it brightness, lights, and sweetnesses without end, but in so secret a manner that one may rightly say of this holy conversation of the soul with God, what the holy text says of God's with Moses: that Moses being alone upon the top of the mountain *spoke* to God, *and God answered him* [Exod 19:19].

BOOK SIX, CHAPTER THREE
A Description of Contemplation, and of the First Difference That There Is Between It and Meditation

Theotimus, contemplation is no other thing than a loving, simple, and permanent attention of the spirit to divine things, which you may easily understand by comparing meditation with it.

Little bees are called nymphs or *schadons* until they make honey, and then they are called bees; so prayer is named meditation until it has produced the honey of devotion, and then it is converted into contemplation. For as the bees fly though their meadows, settling here and there and gathering honey, which having heaped together, they work in it for the pleasure they take in its sweetness, so we meditate to gather the love of God, but having gathered it we contemplate God, and are attentive to his goodness, by reason of the sweetness which love makes us find in it. The desire we have to obtain divine love makes us meditate, but love obtained makes us contemplate, for by love we find so agreeable a sweetness in the thing beloved that we can never satiate our spirits in seeing and considering it.

Behold, Theotimus, how the queen of Saba—regarding the proofs of Solomon's wisdom in his answers, in the beauty of his house, in the magnificence of his table, in his servants' lodgings, in the order that his courtiers kept while executing their charges, in their apparel and behaviour, in the multitude of holocausts which were offered in the Temple—was taken with an ardent love, which changed her meditation into contemplation, in which, being rapt out of herself, she uttered divers words of extreme satisfaction. The sight of so many wonders begot in her heart an exceeding love, and that love enkindled a new desire, to see still more and enjoy the presence of him whose they were, whence she cried: *Blessed are thy servants who stand before thee always and hear thy wisdom* [1 Kgs 10:8]. In like manner we sometimes begin to eat to get an appetite, but our appetite being excited, we continue eating to content it. And in the beginning we consider the goodness of God to excite our will to love him, but love being formed in our hearts, we consider the same goodness to content our love, which cannot be satiated in seeing continually what it loves. In conclusion, meditation is the mother and contemplation is the daughter of love, and for this reason I called contemplation a loving attention, for children are named after their fathers, and not fathers after their children....

BOOK SIX, CHAPTER FIVE
The Second Difference Between Meditation and Contemplation

Meditation considers in detail, and as it were piece by piece, the objects calculated to move us, but contemplation takes a very

370

simple and collected view of the object which it loves, and the consideration thus brought to a point causes a more lively and strong movement. One may behold the beauty of a rich crown two ways: either by looking upon all its ornaments, and all the precious stones of which it is composed, one after the other; or again, having considered all the particular parts, by beholding all the work of it together in one single and simple view. The first kind resembles meditation, in which, for example, we consider the effects of God's mercy to excite us to his love; but the second is like to contemplation, in which we consider with one single steady regard of our mind all the variety of the same effects as a single beauty, composed of all these pieces, making up a single splendid brilliance. In meditating we, as it were, count the divine perfections which we find in a mystery, but in contemplating we sum up their total....

Meditation reminds [us] of one who smells a pink, a rose, rosemary, thyme, jessamine, orange-flower, separately one after the other; but contemplation is like to one smelling the perfumed water distilled from all those flowers: for the latter, in one smell, receives all the scents together, which the other had smelt divided and separated. There is no doubt that this one scent alone, arising from the mingling together of all these scents, is more sweet and precious by itself than the scents of which it is composed, smelt separated one after another. Hence it is that the heavenly lover so prizes being seen by his well-beloved with one of her eyes, and that her hair is so well plaited that it seems to be but one hair, for what is this beholding the spouse with one eye only, except beholding him with a single attentive view without multiplying looks? And what is it to have her hair thus plaited together, except the not scattering of her thoughts in the multiplicity of considerations. Oh! How happy are they who, having run over the multitude of motives which they have to love God, reducing all their looks to only one look and all their thoughts to one conclusion, stay their mind in the unity of contemplation, after the example of St. Augustine or St. Bruno pronouncing secretly in their soul in a permanent admiration: "O Goodness! Goodness! Goodness ever old and ever new!" Or after the example of the great St. Francis, who kneeling in prayer passed the whole night in these words: "O God, thou art my God and my All!" repeating the same continually, as the Blessed Brother Bernard of Quintaval relates, who had heard it with his own ears....

BOOK SIX, CHAPTER SIX
That Contemplation Is Made Without Labour, Which Is the Third Difference Between It and Meditation

Now the simple view of contemplation is performed in one of these three ways. Sometimes we regard only some of God's perfections, as for example his infinite goodness, not thinking of his other attributes or virtues, like a bridegroom who simply stays his eye upon the beautiful complexion of his bride and by this means truly sees all her countenance, inasmuch as her colour is spread over almost all the parts of it....Sometimes also we attentively behold in God several of his infinite perfections, yet with a simple view and without distinction, as he who with one glance, passing his eyes from the head to the feet of his richly dressed spouse, would attentively have seen all in general and nothing in particular, not well discerning what neck-jewels or gown she wore, nor what countenance she bore, nor what expression she had, nor what her eyes were saying, but only that all was fair and agreeable. Just so in contemplation, we often cast one single regard of simple contemplation over several divine greatnesses and perfections together, and we could not describe anything in particular but only say that all is perfectly good and lovely. And finally we at other times consider neither many nor only one of the divine perfections, but only some divine action or work, to which we are attentive, as for example the act of mercy by which God pardons sins, or the act of creation, or the resurrection of Lazarus, or the conversion of St. Paul, just as a bridegroom who might not regard the eyes but only the sweetness of the looks which his spouse casts upon him, nor take notice of her mouth but only of the sweetness of the words uttered by it....

But take which of the three ways you will, contemplation has still this excellency that it is made with delight, for it supposes that we have found God and his holy love, that we enjoy it and delight in it, saying: *I have found him whom my soul loveth: I held him and I will not let him go* [Sg 3:4]. In this it differs from meditation, which almost always is performed with difficulty, labour and reasoning, our mind passing in it from consideration to consideration, searching in many places either the well-beloved of her love or the love of her well-beloved. Jacob labours in meditation to obtain Rachel, but in contemplation he rejoices with her, forgetting all his labour. The divine lover, like a shepherd, and indeed he is one, prepared a sumptuous banquet according to the country fashion for his sacred spouse, which he so described that mystically it represented all the mysteries of man's redemption. *I am come into my garden,* said he. *O my sister, my spouse, I have gathered my myrrh, with aromatical spices; I have eaten the honey-comb with my honey, I have drunk my wine with my milk. Eat, O friends, and drink, and be inebriated, my dearly beloved* [Sg. 5:1]....

...Now to eat is to meditate, for in meditating a man doth chew, turning his spiritual meat hither and thither between the teeth of consideration, to bruise, break and digest it, which is not done without some labour. To drink is to contemplate, which we do without labour or difficulty, yes, with pleasure and tranquillity. But to be inebriated is to contemplate so frequently and so ardently as to be quite out of self to be wholly in God. O holy and sacred inebriation, which, contrarily to corporal inebriation, does not alienate us from the spiritual sense, but from the corporal senses; does not dull or besot us, but *angelicizes* and in a sort deifies us, putting us out of ourselves not to abase us and rank us with beasts, as terrestrial drunkenness does, but to raise us above ourselves and range us with angels, so that we may live more in God than in ourselves, being attentive to and occupied in seeing his beauty and being united to his goodness by love!

JEANNE DE CHANTAL:
LETTERS OF SPIRITUAL DIRECTION

TO NOEL BRULART, THE COMMANDEUR DE SILLERY
[Annecy] 14 August [1634]

My very honored and most dear Father,

Well, my dear Father, I see you have fallen into the condition where I've always feared your great fervor would bring you. And even so, you tell me that you're afraid of flattering yourself, yet do not fear enough your own fears. Oh, for the love of God, dearest Father, do not make such reflections. Take my word for it, our Lord is more pleased with our accepting the relief our body and spirit require, than by all these apprehensions of not doing enough and wanting to do more. All God wants is our heart. And He is more pleased when we value our uselessness and weakness out of love and reverence for His holy will, than when we do violence to ourselves and perform great works of penance. Now, you know that the peak of perfection lies in our wanting to be what God wishes us to be: so, having given you a delicate constitution, He expects you to take care of it and not demand of it what He himself, in his gentleness, does not ask for. Accept this fact. What God, in His goodness, asks of you is not this excessive zeal which has reduced you to your present condition, but a calm, peaceful uselessness, a resting near Him with no special attention or action

From *Francis de Sales, Jane de Chantal: Letters of Spiritual Direction*, trans. Péronne Marie Thibert, V.H.M., The Classics of Western Spirituality (New York: Paulist Press, 1988), 194, 201–3, 249–50. Reprinted with permission of the publisher.

374

of the understanding or will except a few words of love, or of faithful, simple surrender, spoken softly, effortlessly, without the least desire to find consolation or satisfaction in them. If you put that into practice, my dear Father, in peace and tranquility of mind, I promise you, it will please God more than anything else you might do.

TO HER BROTHER, ANDRÉ FRÉMYOT, ARCHBISHOP OF BOURGES
[Chambery, 1625]

My very dear Lord,

Since God, in His eternal goodness, has moved you to consecrate all your love, your actions, your works, and your whole self to Him utterly without any self-interest but only for His greater glory and His satisfaction, remain firm in this resolve. With the confidence of a son, rest in the care and love which divine Providence has for you in all your needs. Look upon Providence as a child does its mother who loves him tenderly. You can be sure that God loves you incomparably more. We can't imagine how great is the love which God, in His goodness, has for souls who thus abandon themselves to His mercy, and who have no other wish than to do what they think pleases Him, leaving everything that concerns them to His care in time and in eternity.

After this, every day in your morning exercise, or at the end of it, confirm your resolutions and unite your will with God's in all that you will do that day in whatever he sends you. Use words like these: "O most holy Will of God, I give You infinite thanks for the mercy with which You have surrounded me; with all my strength and love, I adore You from the depths of my soul and unite my will to Yours now and forever, especially in all that I shall do and all that You will be pleased to send me this day, consecrating to Your glory my soul, my mind, my body, all my thoughts, words and actions, and my whole being. I beg You, with all the humility of my heart, accomplish in me Your eternal designs, and do not allow me to present any obstacle to this. Your eyes, which can see the most intimate recesses of my heart, know the intensity of my desire to live out Your holy will, but they can also see my weakness and limitations. That is why, prostrate before Your infinite mercy, I implore You, my Savior, through the gentleness and justice of this same will of Yours, to grant me the grace of accomplishing it perfectly, so that, consumed in the fire of Your love, I may be an acceptable holocaust which, with the glorious Virgin and all the saints, will praise and bless You forever. Amen."

During the activities of the day, spiritual as well as temporal, as often as you can, my dear Lord, unite your will to God's by confirming your morning resolution. Do this either by a simple, loving glance at God, or by a few words spoken quietly and cast into His heart, by assenting in words like: "Yes, Lord, I want to do this action because You want it," or simply, "Yes, Father," or, "O Holy Will, live and rule in me," or in other words that the Holy Spirit will suggest to you. You may also make a simple sign of the cross over your heart, or kiss the cross you are wearing. All this will show that above everything, you want to do the holy will of God and seek nothing but His glory in all that you do.

As for the will of God's good pleasure, which we know only through events as they occur, if these events benefit us, we must bless God and unite ourselves to this divine will which sends them. If something occurs which is disagreeable, physically or mentally, let us lovingly unite our will in obedience to the divine good pleasure, despite our natural aversion. We must pay no attention to these feelings, so long as at the fine point of our will we acquiesce very simply to God's will, saying, "O my God, I want this because it is Your good pleasure." Chapter 6 of Book IX of the *Love of God* throws a clear light on this practice and invites us to be courageous and simple in performing it. Whatever good or evil befalls you, be confident that God will convert it all to your good.

As for prayer, don't burden yourself with making considerations; neither your mind nor mine is good at that. Follow your own way of speaking to our Lord sincerely, lovingly, confidently, and simply, as your heart dictates. Sometimes be content to stay ever so short a while in His divine presence, faithfully and humbly, like a child before his father, waiting to be told what to do, totally dependent on the paternal will in which he has placed all his love and trust. You may, if you wish, say a few words on this subject, but very quietly: "You are my Father and my God from whom I expect all my happiness." A few moments later (for you must always wait a little to hear what God will say to your heart): "I am Your child, all Yours; good children think only of pleasing their father; I don't want to have any worries and I leave in Your care everything that concerns me, for You love me, my God. Father, You are my good. My soul rests and trusts in Your love and eternal providence." Try to let yourself be penetrated by words like these.

When you have committed some fault, go to God humbly, saying to Him, "I have sinned, my God, and I am sorry." Then, with loving confidence, add: "Father, pour the oil of Your bountiful mercy on my wounds, for You are my only hope; heal me." A little later: "By the help of your grace, I shall be more on my guard and will bless you eternally," and speak like this according to the different movements and feelings of your soul. Sometimes put yourself very simply before God, certain of His presence everywhere, and without any effort, whisper very softly to His sacred heart whatever your own heart prompts you to say.

When you are experiencing some physical pain or a sorrowful heart, try to endure it before God, recalling as much as you can that He is watching you at this time of affliction, especially in physical illness when very often the heart is weary and unable to pray, for a simple adherence to God's will, expressed from time to time, is enough. Moreover, suffering borne in the will quietly and patiently is a continual, very powerful prayer before God, regardless of the complaints and anxieties that come from the inferior part of the soul.

Finally, my dear Lord, try to perform all your actions calmly and gently, and keep your mind ever joyful, peaceful and content. Do not worry about your perfection, or about your soul. God to whom it belongs, and to whom you have completely entrusted it, will take care of it and fill it with all the graces, consolations and blessings of His holy love in the measure that they will be useful in this life. In the next life He will grant you eternal bliss. Such is the wish of her to whom your soul is as precious as her own; pray for her, for she never prays without you, my Lord.

TO SISTER ANNE-CATHERINE DE SAUTEREAU, NOVICE MISTRESS AT GRENOBLE
Annecy, c. 12 December 1626

My dearest daughter,

As you wished, and in God's presence, I shall tell you what His goodness will inspire me to say to you, for I ask Him to help me. First of all, it seems to me, my dear sister, that you should try to make your own devotion, and that of your novices, generous, noble, straightforward, and sincere. Try to foster that spirit in all those whom God will ever commit to your care—a spirit founded on that deep humility which results in sincere obedience, sweet charity which supports and excuses all, and an innocent, guileless simplicity which makes us even-tempered and friendly toward everyone.

From there, my dearest daughter, move on to a total surrender of yourself into the hands of our good God, so that, insofar as you can, you may help your own dear soul and those you are guiding, to be free of all that is not God. May these souls have such a pure, upright intention that they do not waste time worrying about created things—their friends, their appearance, their speech. Without stopping at such considerations or at any other obstacle they may meet along the way, may they go forward on the road to perfection by the exact observances of the Institute, seeing in all things only the sacred face of God, that is, His good pleasure. This way is very narrow, my dear Sister, but it is solid, short, simple and sure, and soon leads the soul to its goal: total union with God. Let us follow this way faithfully. It certainly precludes multiplicity and leads us to that unity which alone is necessary. I know you are drawn to this happiness, so pursue it, and rest quietly on the breast of divine Providence. Those souls who have put aside all ambition except that of pleasing God alone should remain peaceful in this holy tabernacle.

My dearest Sister, Abraham (how I love this patriarch!) left his country and his family in order to obey God; but the only Son of God accomplished the will of His heavenly Father by working in the country of his birth. So be content, dear, to imitate the Lord, for nothing can equal His perfection. Don't look elsewhere, but carefully try to accomplish lovingly and with good heart all the tasks that Providence and obedience place in your hands. The principal exercises of the novitiate are mortification and prayer.

This is enough—and perhaps too much—for me to be telling a soul who is already enlightened and led by God. I beg Him in His goodness to guide you to perfection in His most pure love. My soul cherishes yours more than I can say; be absolutely assured of this, and pray for her who is yours unreservedly.

God be praised! Amen.

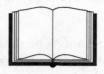

Selected Bibliography

TEXTS

Editions used:

Treatise on the Love of God. Translated by Henry Benedict Mackey, O.S.B. 6th ed. London: Burns, Oates and Washbourne Ltd., n.d.

Francis de Sales, Jane de Chantal: Letters of Spiritual Direction. Translated by Péronne Marie Thibert, V.H.M. The Classics of Western Spirituality. New York: Paulist Press; London: SPCK, 1988.

Other sources:

Treatise on the Love of God. 2 vols. Translated by John K. Ryan. Rockford, Ill.: TAN Books, 1974.

St. Francis de Sales: A Testimony by St. Chantal. Translated by Elisabeth Stopp. Hyattsville, Md.: Institute of Salesian Studies, 1967.

STUDIES

Bremond, Henri. *Devout Humanism.* Translated by K. L. Montgomery. London: SPCK, 1928.

Camus, Jean-Pierre (Bishop of Belley). *The Spirit of St. François de Sales.* Translated by C. F. Kelley. New York: Harper and Brothers, 1952.

Charmot, François. *Ignatius Loyola and François de Sales: Two Masters, One Spirituality.* St. Louis: Herder, 1966.

Liuima, Antanas. "St. François de Sales et les mystiques." *Revue d'Ascétique et de Mystique* 24 (1948): 220–39 and 376–85.

Wright, Wendy M. *Bond of Perfection: Jeanne de Chantal and François de Sales.* New York: Paulist Press, 1985.

————. "This Is What It Is Made For: The Image of the Heart in the Spirituality of Francis de Sales and Jane de Chantal." In *Spiritualities of the Heart,* ed. Annice Callahan, 143–58. New York: Paulist Press, 1990.

Jonathan Edwards
(1703–58)

Nothing has damaged Jonathan Edwards's spiritual reputation more than the sermon by which he earned his greatest fame among his contemporaries, "Sinners in the Hands of an Angry God." The tone of that and a few similar sermons has obscured the far more fundamental insight that inspired them, namely, that religion consists so much in affection "that without affection there is no true religion." Edwards's theology of affective knowledge in religion, complete with rules for discerning genuine religious affection from "natural" *enthusiasm,* ranks him among the leading masters of spiritual life in Christianity. But there is more than theory. The personal narrative of his own "awakening" to a life in God's presence provides us with one of the most convincing documents of mystical experience in our entire tradition. It alone would suffice to refute the preposterous claim once made by W. T. Stace that there are no Protestant mystics.

Jonathan Edwards was born on October 5, 1703, at East Windsor, Connecticut. His father, for sixty-four years pastor of the local Congregational church, provided Jonathan with enough instruction in languages to allow him to enter Yale College before his thirteenth birthday. Probably during his final year of college he read John Locke's *An Essay Concerning Human Understanding* (1690). This interpretation of all knowledge on the basis of sensation would in due time exert a strong influence upon the development of Edwards's own theory of religious emotions.[1]

Eighteenth-century intellectual life in New England still centered entirely around the Puritan faith. Most of the writing occurred in parsonages, and oratory consisted mainly of sermons. Colleges had as their primary function the training of future clergy: Harvard, Yale, the College of New Jersey (now Princeton) all developed out of what were basically divinity schools. It was quite natural, then, that the young Edwards, after graduation and some private study of theology, would become a preacher. Still too young to hold a permanent pastoral position at age nineteen, Edwards briefly served as temporary minister of a small Presbyterian congregation in New York and then returned as tutor to his alma mater. The direct exposure to rowdy Yale undergraduates had a sobering effect upon his early views of human nature. Reflecting upon the experience of his first year he writes: "I have now abundant reason to be convinced of the troublesomeness and vexation of the world, and that it never will be another kind of world." Those laboring in the same vineyard can testify that this conclusion still stands today. In 1726 the young tutor was called to a less profane environment as pastor at the same Northampton (Massachusetts) parish where his famous maternal grandfather, Solomon Stoddard, had served for over half a century. During Edwards's tenure here that sudden, intense religious revival known as the Great Awakening profoundly stirred the New England churches. He himself played a leading role in the movement, and it was in the course of it (1741) that he delivered the notorious sermon at the end of which the congregation's crying and weeping drowned out the preacher's voice. But before becoming such a powerful voice in the Great Awakening, Edwards had to go through his own "conversion."

The narrative from which our first selection is taken forms part of a report on this spiritual process that stretches from the

---

[1]Recent studies by Leon Howard and Norman Fiering have shown, however, that this reading was far from being the "decisive" event in Edwards's intellectual life that it appeared to earlier commentators (especially Perry Miller) to be.

time when Edwards was an eighteen-year-old student at Yale in 1721 until the year 1739, when he was serving as a minister in Northampton. The conversion consisted in a transference of a concern with his own salvation to an exclusive concentration on God's sovereign glory in this world, regardless of his own fate. It resolved the profound crisis that the idea of predestination had caused in the young man. How could he trust a God who might, despite his pious, virtuous life, still reject him? The transforming experience that resolved the crisis began with his reading the words of 1 Timothy 1:17: "Now unto the King eternal, immortal, invisible, the one wise God, be honor and glory forever and ever. Amen." In this theocentric view the fearsome doctrine of predestination slowly assumed a positive meaning in Edwards's mind. It invited him to a total surrender to God's will, which, in the order of things, was alone important. The change in his attitude occurred through an awareness of the mystery of Christ in which the distant God had come near to him. The sense of God's glorious sovereignty thereby became revealed to him as a mystery of majesty and meekness combined.

Still, he felt, the longing for God's presence and for holiness had at first depended greatly on his own efforts and constant self-examination. Suffering, sickness, and disappointment as a tutor at Yale gradually purified his attitude and transformed it into one of attentive waiting. Then in 1737 came the first revelation, the vision of "the glory of the Son of God as Mediator between God and man." This was followed by revelations of the Holy Spirit, the source of divine glory and the sweet guest of the soul. Edwards's experience of the *theologia gloriae* brings him into close proximity with the man from whom church and dogma divided him so profoundly—Ignatius of Loyola.

The experience also helped equip him to compose his *Treatise Concerning Religious Affections* (1746), so different from his fire-and-brimstone sermons. Written to defend the need for affection in faith, the treatise turned out to be an outstanding contribution to the theory of Christian mysticism. For support of his position, Edwards somewhat surprisingly turned to the theories of the sober-minded and staunchly anti-enthusiastic John Locke. In his *Essay* Locke had argued that all ideas in the mind originate in, or are derived from, *passively* received sensations and reflections. Edwards regarded affections, which he defines as "the more vigorous and sensible exercises of the inclination and will of the soul," as belonging to that primary layer of simple, underived ideas on which our entire mental life is based. They function as "the springs of motion and action" that determine our moral life. Indeed, for Edwards, who rejects a theory of free will, the affections *are* the will and inclination.

Now, if the empiricist foundation of Edwards's theory of affections may be traced to Locke, the emphasis upon affection in moral and religious life connects it with Shaftesbury and Hutcheson. They denied that moral perception may be derived as the conclusion from a process of reasoning. It rather consists in a quasi-aesthetic, direct feeling or intuition of what is good and evil. Early on, Edwards had drawn a parallel between this moral sense and the religious one. In *Divine and Supernatural Light* (1734) we read:

> As with God, so with the *good*. There is a twofold understanding or knowledge of God that God has made the mind capable of. The first...is merely *speculative* or *notional*.... And the *other* is that which consists in a sense of the heart. As when there is a sense of the beauty, amiableness, or sweetness of a thing.

Thus Edwards distinguishes a purely theoretical knowledge of God from the "sense of the heart." The distinction reminds us of Pascal's *raison du coeur* and anticipates Newman's *real* knowledge.

At first Edwards appears to have considered religious affections part of the natural, God-given structure of the mind itself. Even as a person is capable, without "supernatural" assistance, of some sense of good and evil, so are a person's natural affections capable of ascending to that supreme Object in which they find their ultimate fulfillment. Later he reversed his position. Even when directed toward a divine object, natural affections remain "unsanctified" and, as part of a human being's cognitive and volitive natural apparel, inadequate for establishing a true relation with God. Though there exists a natural "fitness" in the human heart for entering into such a relation, its disposition can provide no more than a foundation. The "true" religious affections, absent from fallen nature, exclusively result from God's special grace. Hence that aesthetic attraction which Shaftesbury had posited as the core of moral perceptiveness, and which Edwards had transferred to religious life, served merely as the soil into which God could plant religious affections. The process was to be reversed. Instead of an aesthetic *eros* propelling the soul to God, a divine sense of holiness had first to be infused if a person was to attain a genuine sense of God's beauty. Only "a supernatural sense" conveyed by God's special grace would enable a person to perceive those divine realities that "the natural man discerns nothing of." God's Spirit may influence one's natural disposition in "common grace," but such grace does not communicate God's proper nature as a new, indwelling principle of action.

Despite the insurmountable separation between the two kinds of affections, they display a genuine parallelism. In the religion of the Spirit also, the springs of action are the affections. "Religion in the hearts of the truly godly, is ever in exact proportion to the degree of affection."

> For although to true religion there must indeed be something else besides affection; yet true religion consists so much in the affections, that there can be no true religion without them. He who has no religious affection is in a state of spiritual death, and is wholly destitute of the powerful, quickening, saving influences of the Spirit of God upon his heart.

How can Edwards exclude from fallen nature any "godly" activity and yet consider *affections* (the mainsprings of *nature's* activity) the basis of a genuinely spiritual life? By defining the religious affections themselves as a new, infused sense, "entirely different in its nature and kind from anything that ever their minds were the subjects of before they were sanctified," Edwards adds a principle of consciousness conceived after Locke's *passively* formed sensations and affections but proceeding from a different, supernatural source. He calls it "a new foundation laid in the nature of the soul for a new kind of exercise of the same faculty of understanding." Epistemologically he justifies these religious affections as merely another, passively communicated *idea,* equal to such underived, simple ideas as sensations and reflections. Yet theologically the new *sense* is of an entirely different nature. For Edwards, the nature and quality of a thing is determined by its origin. Precisely their supernatural origin essentially distinguishes divine affections from others, even though the same "faculty of understanding" elicits them:

> Edwards is irredeemably "supernaturalist" if we take this...term to mean that whatever human nature is and does from itself is qualitatively different from what it is and does from beyond itself or from the Spirit of God. And the difference is owing to the difference between natural and supernatural origins.[2]

Theologically Edwards identifies the infused spiritual sense with the spirit of *agapē* poured out in our hearts. This identification with supernatural love forced him to take a stand on the theories of love that had come to dominate the moral discussion of his time. Two positions divided the philosophical camp. The first, as Edwards saw it, held that all love arises from self-love, and hence "that it is impossible in the nature of things, for any man to have any love to God, or any other being, but that love to himself must be the foundation of it." Such a love could clearly not serve as the basis of the divine *agapē* that introduces into the soul an ability to love God for God's own sake. Yet the opposite, "benevolist" position appeared equally inadequate. Hutcheson, Hume, and other contemporaries had argued that benevolent, disinterested love, far from being a self-deception, stands on a par with self-love. Such an altruistic moral sense, however, fell far short of a divine love whereby the regenerate Christian loves God *for what God is in God's self*. This remains entirely hidden as

---

[2]Conrad Cherry, *The Theology of Jonathan Edwards* (New York: Doubleday, Anchor Books, 1966), 230.

much to altruistic love as to self-love and becomes accessible only to the person whose heart God has changed so as to apprehend "a beauty, glory, and supreme good, in God's nature as it is in itself." Agapic love transcends altruism as well as self-love: while the latter loves another being because it *appears lovely to me,* the former loves only because of "some gift bestowed" that both renders God lovable and compels the regenerate to love God independently of any pleasure he or she may derive from it. The taste for the beauty and loveliness of things divine originates in God's "special grace," and only after having been regenerated does the soul perceive the divine beauty. Despite its similarities, Edwards's position on divine love did not agree with that of the "pure love" theory of his contemporaries, the French Quietists. According to them, truly divine love *excludes* self-love to a point where a person becomes wholly indifferent to his or her personal salvation. Edwards deemed self-love as well as "benevolent" love to be supported, on the natural level, by common grace. But it played no decisive part in the functioning of the supernatural, infused love of the elect.[3] On this issue the Calvinist Edwards may have come closer to the traditional Catholic doctrine than Bishop Fénelon. Edwards continued to maintain, whether consistently or not, that the totally selfless infused love of God is built upon the foundation of natural love that becomes inevitably mixed with self-love.

What distinguishes Edwards from the extreme forms of Calvinism as well as from Quietism is his determination to maintain a divine operation on two levels of reality—one, supernatural and thus granted only by special grace; the other, belonging to a human nature that despite the separation caused by original sin continues to undergo the divine impact and in its basic structure deserves to be called good insofar as it serves as a natural foundation for the supernatural. God, Edwards writes in his final work, *The Great Christian Doctrine of Original Sin Defended* (1758), originally implanted two kinds of principles: those that belong to

---

[3] On this entire question we have followed the excellent analysis of "The Permutations of Self-Love" in Norman Fiering, *Jonathan Edwards's Moral Thought in British Context* (Chapel Hill, N.C.: University of North Carolina Press, 1981), 150–99.

human nature as such, and "those that were spiritual, holy, and divine." When Adam sinned the superior principles left him "as light ceases when the candle is withdrawn," and the interior principles, left to themselves, became "absolute masters of the heart." Thus the good servant became the bad master. But the basic structure, however distorted by sin, remains when by special grace the higher principles are restored.

Some readers may object to the austere predestination theory expressed in the theology of special grace reserved to the elect. Others may find the emphasis on sin and punishment hard to take. But Edwards's wonderful theory of religious affections is not bound up with spiritual elitism or pessimism. To deny oneself its riches because of either of these Puritan characteristics would be to miss some of the finest spiritual literature written on this side of the Atlantic.

PERSONAL NARRATIVE

The first instance that I remember of that sort of inward, sweet delight in God and divine things that I have lived much in since, was on reading those words, 1 Tim. i.17. *Now unto the King eternal, immortal, invisible, the only wise God, be honor and glory for ever and ever, Amen.* As I read the words, there came into my soul, and was as it were diffused through it, a sense of the glory of the Divine Being; a new sense, quite different from any thing I ever experienced before. Never any words of scripture seemed to me as these words did. I thought with myself, how excellent a Being that was, and how happy I should be, if I might enjoy that God, and be rapt up to him in heaven, and be as it were swallowed up in him for ever! I kept saying, and as it were singing over these words of scripture to myself; and went to pray to God that I might enjoy him, and prayed in a manner quite different from what I used to do; with a new sort of affection. But it never came into my thought, that there was any thing spiritual, or of a saving nature in this.

From about that time, I began to have a new kind of apprehensions and ideas of Christ, and the work of redemption, and the glorious way of salvation by him. An inward, sweet sense of these things, at times, came into my heart; and my soul was led away in pleasant views and contemplations of them. And my mind was greatly engaged to spend my time in reading and meditating on Christ, on the beauty and excellency of his person, and the lovely

From *The Works of President Edwards,* ed. Samuel Austin, 8 vols. (Worcester, Mass., 1808–9), 1:34–44.

way of salvation by free grace in him. I found no books so delightful to me, as those that treated of these subjects. Those words Cant. ii.1, used to be abundantly with me, *I am the Rose of Sharon, and the Lilly of the valleys.* The words seemed to me, sweetly to represent the loveliness and beauty of Jesus Christ. The whole book of Canticles used to be pleasant to me, and I used to be much in reading it, about that time; and found, from time to time, an inward sweetness, that would carry me away, in my contemplations. This I know not how to express otherwise, than by a calm, sweet abstraction of soul from all the concerns of this world; and sometimes a kind of vision, or fixed ideas and imaginations, of being alone in the mountains, or some solitary wilderness, far from all mankind, sweetly conversing with Christ, and wrapt and swallowed up in God. The sense I had of divine things, would often of a sudden kindle up, as it were, a sweet burning in my heart; an ardor of soul, that I know not how to express.

Not long after I first began to experience these things, I gave an account to my father of some things that had passed in my mind. I was pretty much affected by the discourse we had together; and when the discourse was ended, I walked abroad alone, in a solitary place in my father's pasture, for contemplation. And as I was walking there, and looking up on the sky and clouds, there came into my mind so sweet a sense of the glorious *majesty* and *grace* of God, that I know not how to express. I seemed to see them both in a sweet conjunction; majesty and meekness joined together; it was a sweet, and gentle, and holy majesty; and also a majestic meekness; an awful sweetness; a high, and great, and holy gentleness.

After this my sense of divine things gradually increased, and became more and more lively, and had more of that inward sweetness. The appearance of every thing was altered; there seemed to be, as it were, a calm, sweet cast, or appearance of divine glory, in almost every thing. God's excellency, his wisdom, his purity and love, seemed to appear in every thing; in the sun, moon, and stars; in the clouds, and blue sky; in the grass, flowers, trees; in the water, and all nature; which used greatly to fix my mind. I often used to sit and view the moon for continuance; and in the day, spent much time in viewing the clouds and sky, to behold the sweet glory of God in these things; in the mean time, singing forth, with a low voice my contemplations of the Creator and Redeemer. And scarce any thing, among all the works of nature, was so sweet to me as thunder and lightning; formerly, nothing had been so terrible to me. Before, I used to be uncommonly terrified with thunder, and to be struck with terror when I saw a thunder storm rising; but now, on the contrary, it rejoiced me. I felt God, so to speak, at the first appearance of a thunder storm; and used to take the opportunity, at such times, to fix myself in order to view the clouds, and see the lightnings play, and hear the majestic and awful voice of God's thunder, which oftentimes was exceedingly entertaining, leading me to sweet contemplations of my great and glorious God. While thus engaged, it always seemed natural to me to sing, or chant for my meditations; or, to speak my thoughts in soliloquies with a singing voice.

I felt then great satisfaction, as to my good state; but that did not content me. I had vehement longings of soul after God and Christ, and after more holiness, wherewith my heart seemed to be full, and ready to break; which often brought to my mind the words of the Psalmist, Psal. cxix.28. *My soul breaketh for the longing it hath.* I often felt a mourning and lamenting in my heart, that I had not turned to God sooner, that I might have had more time to grow in grace. My mind was greatly fixed on divine things; almost perpetually in the contemplation of them. I spent most of my time in thinking of divine things, year after year; often walking alone in the woods, and solitary places, for meditation, soliloquy, and prayer, and converse with God; and it was always my manner, at such times, to sing forth my contemplations. I was almost constantly in ejaculatory prayer, wherever I was. Prayer seemed to be natural to me, as the breath by which the inward burnings of my heart had vent. The delights which I now felt in the things of religion, were of an exceeding different kind from those before mentioned, that I had when a boy; and what I then had no more notion of, than one born blind has of pleasant and beautiful colors. They were of a more inward, pure, soul animating and refreshing nature. Those former delights never reached the heart; and did not arise from any sight of the divine excellency of the things of God; or any taste of the soul satisfying and lifegiving good there is in them.

My sense of divine things seemed gradually to increase, until I went to preach at Newyork, which was about a year and a half after they began; and while I was there, I felt them, very sensibly, in a much higher degree than I had done before. My longings after God and holiness, were much increased. Pure and humble, holy and heavenly Christianity, appeared exceeding amiable to me. I felt a burning desire to be in every thing a complete Christian; and conformed to the blessed image of Christ; and that I might live, in all things, according to the pure, sweet and blessed rules of the gospel. I had an eager thirsting after progress in these things; which put me upon pursuing and pressing after them. It was my continual strife day and night, and constant inquiry, how I should *be* more holy, and *live* more holily, and more becoming a child of God, and a disciple of Christ. I now sought an increase of grace and holiness, and a holy life, with much more earnestness, than ever I sought grace before I had it. I used to be continually examining myself, and studying and contriving for likely ways and means, how I should live holily, with far greater diligence and earnestness, than ever I pursued any thing in my life; but yet with too great a dependence on my own strength; which afterwards proved a great damage to me. My experience had not then taught me, as it has done since, my extreme feebleness and impotence, every manner of way; and the bottomless depths of secret corruption and deceit there was in my heart. However, I went on with my eager pursuit after more holiness, and conformity to Christ.

The heaven I desired was a heaven of holiness; to be with God, and to spend my eternity in divine love, and holy communion with Christ. My mind was very much taken up with contemplations on heaven, and the enjoyments there; and living there in perfect holiness, humility and love: And it used at that time to appear a great part of the happiness of heaven, that there the saints could express their love to Christ. It appeared to me a great clog and burden, that what I felt within, I could not express as I desired. The inward ardor of my soul, seemed to be hindered and pent up, and could not freely flame out as it would. I used often to think, how in heaven this principle should freely and fully vent and express itself. Heaven appeared exceedingly delightful, as a world of love; and that all happiness consisted in living in pure, humble, heavenly, divine love.

I remember the thoughts I used then to have of holiness; and said sometimes to myself, "I do certainly know that I love holiness, such as the gospel prescribes." It appeared to me, that there was nothing in it but what was ravishingly lovely; the highest beauty and amiableness...a *divine* beauty; far purer than any thing here upon earth; and that every thing else was like mire and defilement, in comparison of it.

Holiness, as I then wrote down some of my contemplations on it, appeared to me to be of a sweet, pleasant, charming, serene, calm nature; which brought an inexpressible purity, brightness, peacefulness and ravishment to the soul. In other words, that it made the soul like a field or garden of God, with all manner of pleasant flowers; all pleasant, delightful, and undisturbed; enjoying a sweet calm, and the gently vivifying beams of the sun. The soul of a true Christian, as I then wrote my meditations, appeared like such a little white flower as we see in the spring of the year; low and humble on the ground, opening its bosom to receive the pleasant beams of the sun's glory; rejoicing as it were in a calm rapture; diffusing around a sweet fragrancy; standing peacefully and lovingly, in the midst of other flowers round about; all in like manner opening their bosoms, to drink in the light of the sun. There was no part of creature holiness, that I had so great a sense of its loveliness, as humility, brokenness of heart and poverty of spirit; and there was nothing that I so earnestly longed for. My heart panted after this, to lie low before God, as in the dust; that I might be nothing, and that God might be ALL, that I might become as a little child.

While at Newyork, I was sometimes much affected with reflections of my past life, considering how late it was before I began to be truly religious; and how wickedly I had lived till then; and once so as to weep abundantly, and for a considerable time together.

On January 12, 1723, I made a solemn dedication of myself to God, and wrote it down; giving up myself, and all that I had to God; to be for the future, in no respect, my own; to act as one that had no right to himself, in any respect. And solemnly vowed, to take God for my whole portion and felicity; looking on nothing else, as any part of my happiness, nor acting as if it were; and his law for the constant rule of my obedience: engaging to fight, with all my might, against the world, the flesh, and the devil, to the end of my life. But I have reason to be infinitely humbled, when I consider, how much I have failed, of answering my obligation.

I had, then, abundance of sweet, religious conversation, in the family where I lived, with Mr. John Smith, and his pious mother. My heart was knit in affection, to those, in whom were appearances of true piety; and I could bear the thoughts of no other companions, but such as were holy, and the disciples of the blessed Jesus. I had great longings, for the advancement of Christ's kingdom in the world; and my secret prayer used to be, in great part, taken up in praying for it. If I heard the least hint, of any thing that happened, in any part of the world, that appeared, in some respect or other, to have a favourable aspect, on the interests of Christ's kingdom, my soul eagerly catched at it; and it would much animate and refresh me. I used to be eager to read public news-letters, mainly for that end; to see if I could not find some news, favourable to the interest of religion in the world.

I very frequently used to retire into a solitary place, on the banks of Hudson's River, at some distance from the city, for contemplation on divine things and secret converse with God; and had many sweet hours there. Sometimes Mr. Smith and I walked there together, to converse on the things of God; and our conversation used, to turn much on the advancement of Christ's kingdom in the world, and the glorious things that God would accomplish for his church in the latter days. I had then, and at other times, the greatest delight in the holy scriptures, of any book whatsoever. Oftentimes in reading it, every word seemed to touch my heart. I felt a harmony between something in my heart, and those sweet and powerful words. I seemed often to see so much light exhibited by every sentence, and such a refreshing food communicated, that I could not get along in reading; often dwelling long on one sentence, to see the wonders contained in it; and yet almost every sentence seemed to be full of wonders.

I came away from Newyork in the month of April, 1723, and had a most bitter parting with Madam Smith and her son. My heart seemed to sink within me, at leaving the family and city, where I had enjoyed so many sweet and pleasant days. I went from New York to Wethersfield, by water; and as I sailed away, I kept sight of the city as long as I could. However, that night after this sorrowful parting, I was greatly comforted in God at Westchester, where we went ashore to lodge: and had a pleasant time of it all the voyage to Saybrook. It was sweet to me to think of meeting dear christians in heaven, where we should never part more. At Saybrook we went ashore to lodge on Saturday, and there kept the Sabbath; where I had a sweet and refreshing season, walking alone in the fields.

After I came home to Windsor, I remained much in a like frame of mind, as when at Newyork; only sometimes I felt my heart ready to sink, with the thoughts of my friends at Newyork. My support was in contemplations on the heavenly state; as I find in my Diary of May 1, 1723. It was a comfort to think of that state, where there is fulness of joy; where reigns heavenly, calm, and delightful love, without alloy; where there are continually the dearest expressions of this love; where is the enjoyment of the persons loved, without ever parting; where those persons who appear so lovely in this world, will really be inexpressibly more lovely, and full of love to us. And how sweetly will the mutual lovers join together, to sing the praises of God and the Lamb! How will it fill us with joy to think, that this enjoyment, these sweet exercises, will never cease, but will last to all eternity....I continued much in the same frame, in the general, as when at Newyork, till I went to Newhaven, as Tutor of the College; particularly, once at Bolton, on a journey from Boston, while walking out alone in the fields. After I went to Newhaven, I sunk in religion; my mind being diverted from my eager pursuits after holiness, by some affairs, that greatly perplexed and distracted my thoughts.

In September, 1725, 1 was taken ill at Newhaven, and while endeavouring to go home to Windsor, was so ill at the North Village, that I could go no farther; where I lay sick, for about a quarter of a year. In this sickness, God was pleased to visit me again, with the sweet influences of his Spirit. My mind was greatly engaged there, on divine and pleasant contemplations, and longings of soul. I observed, that those who watched with me, would often be looking out wishfully for the morning; which brought to my mind those words of the Psalmist, and which my soul with delight made its own language, *My soul waiteth for the Lord, more than they that watch for the morning;* I say, more than they that watch for the morning; and when the light of day came in at the window, it refreshed my soul, from one morning to another. It seemed to be some image of the light of God's glory.

I remember, about that time, I used greatly to long for the conversion of some, that I was concerned with; I could gladly honour them, and with delight be a servant to them, and lie at their feet, if they were but truly holy. But some time after this, I was again greatly diverted with some temporal concerns, that exceedingly took up my thoughts, greatly to the wounding of my soul; and went on, through various exercises, that it would be tedious to relate, which gave me much more experience of my own heart, than I ever had before.

Since I came to this town [Northampton, Massachusetts], I have often had sweet complacency in God, in views of his glorious perfections and the excellency of Jesus Christ. God has appeared to me a glorious and lovely Being, chiefly on account of his holiness. The holiness of God has always appeared to me the most lovely of all his attributes. The doctrines of God's absolute sovereignty, and free grace, in shewing mercy to whom he would shew mercy; and man's absolute dependence on the operations of God's Holy Spirit, have very often appeared to me as sweet and glorious doctrines. These doctrines have been much my delight. God's sovereignty has ever appeared to me, great part of his glory. It has often been my delight to approach God, and adore him as a sovereign God, and ask sovereign mercy of him.

I have loved the doctrines of the gospel; they have been to my soul like green pastures. The gospel has seemed to me the richest treasure; the treasure that I have most desired, and longed that it might dwell richly in me. The way of salvation by Christ has appeared, in a general way, glorious and excellent, most pleasant and most beautiful. It has often seemed to me, that it would in a great measure spoil heaven, to receive it in any other way. That text has often been affecting and delightful to me, Isa. xxxii. 2. *A man shall be an hiding place from the wind, and a covert from the tempest, &c.*

It has often appeared to me delightful, to be united to Christ; to have him for my head, and to be a member of his body; also to have Christ for my teacher and prophet. I very often think with sweetness, and longings, and pantings of soul, of being a little child, taking hold of Christ, to be led by him through the wilderness of this world. That text, Matth. xviii.3, has often been sweet to me, *except ye be converted and become as little children, &c.* I love to think of coming to Christ, to receive salvation of him, poor in spirit, and quite empty of self, humbly exalting him alone; cut off entirely from my own root, in order to grow into, and out of Christ; to have God in Christ to be all in all; and to live by faith in the son of God, a life of humble, unfeigned confidence in him. That scripture has often been sweet to me, Psal. cxv.1. *Not unto us, O Lord, not unto us, but unto thy name give glory, for thy mercy, and for thy truth's sake.* And those words of Christ, Luke x.21. *In that hour Jesus rejoiced in spirit, and said, I thank thee, O Father, Lord of heaven and earth, that thou hast hid these things from the wise and prudent, and hast revealed them unto babes: Even so, Father, for so it seemed good in thy sight.* That sovereignty of God which Christ rejoiced in, seemed to me worthy of such joy; and that rejoicing seemed to shew the excellency of Christ, and of what spirit he was.

Sometimes, only mentioning a single word caused my heart to burn within me; or only seeing the name of Christ, or the name of some attribute of God. And God has appeared glorious to me, on account of the Trinity. It has made me have exalting thoughts of God, that he subsists in three persons; Father, Son and Holy Ghost. The sweetest joys and delights I have experienced, have not been those that have arisen from a hope of my own good estate; but in a direct view of the glorious things of the gospel. When I enjoy this sweetness, it seems to carry me above the thoughts of my own estate; it seems at such times a loss that I cannot bear, to take off my eye from the glorious, pleasant object I behold without me, to turn my eye in upon myself, and my own good estate.

My heart has been much on the advancement of Christ's kingdom in the world. The histories of the past advancement of Christ's kingdom have been sweet to me. When I have read histories of past ages, the pleasantest thing in all my reading has been, to read of the kingdom of Christ being promoted. And when I have expected, in my reading, to come to any such thing, I have rejoiced in the prospect, all the way as I read. And my mind has been much entertained and delighted with the scripture promises and prophecies, which relate to the future glorious advancement of Christ's kingdom upon earth.

I have sometimes had a sense of the excellent fulness of Christ, and his meetness and suitableness as a Saviour; whereby he has appeared to me, far above all, the chief of ten thousands. His blood and atonement have appeared sweet, and his righteousness sweet; which was always accompanied with ardency of spirit; and inward strugglings and breathings, and groanings that cannot be uttered, to be emptied of myself, and swallowed up in Christ.

Once, as I rode out into the woods for my health, in 1737, having alighted from my horse in a retired place, as my manner commonly has been, to walk for divine contemplation and prayer, I had a view that for me was extraordinary, of the glory of the Son of God, as Mediator between God and man, and his wonderful, great, full, pure and sweet grace and love, and meek and gentle condescension. This grace that appeared so calm and sweet, appeared also great above the heavens. The person of Christ appeared ineffably excellent with an excellency great enough to swallow up all thought and conception...which continued as near as I can judge, about an hour; which kept me the greater part of the time in a flood of tears, and weeping aloud. I felt an ardency of soul to be, what I know not otherwise how to express, emptied and annihilated; to lie in the dust, and to be full of Christ alone; to love him with a holy and pure love; to trust in him; to live upon him; to serve and follow him; and to be perfectly sanctified and made pure, with a divine and heavenly purity. I have, several other times, had views very much of the same nature, and which have had the same effects.

I have many times had a sense of the glory of the third person in the Trinity, in his office of Sanctifier; in his holy operations, communicating divine light and life to the soul. God, in the communications of his Holy Spirit, has appeared as an infinite fountain of divine glory and sweetness; being full, and sufficient to fill and satisfy the soul; pouring forth itself in sweet communications; like the sun in its glory, sweetly and pleasantly diffusing light and life. And I have sometimes had an affecting sense of the excellency of the word of God, as a word of life; as the light of life; a sweet, excellent lifegiving word; accompanied with a thirsting after that word, that it might dwell richly in my heart.

A Treatise Concerning Religious Affections

PART THREE: THE DISTINGUISHING SIGNS

The First Sign

1. On the one hand it must be observed, that not everything which in any respect appertains to spiritual affections, is new and entirely different from what natural men can conceive of, and do experience; some things are common to gracious affections with other affections; many circumstances, appendages and effects are common. Thus a saint's love to God has a great many things appertaining to it, which are common with a man's natural love to a near relation: love to God makes a man have desires of the honor of God, and a desire to please him; so does a natural man's love to his friend make him desire his honor, and desire to please him: love to God causes a man to delight in the thoughts of God, and to delight in the presence of God, and to desire conformity to God, and the enjoyment of God; and so it is with a man's love to his friend; and many other things might be mentioned which are common to both. But yet that idea which the saint has of the loveliness of God, and that sensation, and that kind of delight he has in that view, which is as it were the marrow and quintessence of

From *Religious Affections*, ed. John E. Smith, vol. 2 of *The Works of Jonathan Edwards* (New Haven, Conn.: Yale University Press, 1959), 208–10, 392–97. Reprinted with permission of the publisher.

his love, is peculiar, and entirely diverse from anything that a natural man has, or can have any notion of. And even in those things that seem to be common, there is something peculiar: both spiritual love and natural, cause desires after the object beloved; but they be not the same sort of desires; there is a sensation of soul in the spiritual desires of one that loves God, which is entirely different from all natural desires: both spiritual love and natural love are attended with delight in the object beloved; but the sensations of delight are not the same, but entirely and exceedingly diverse. Natural men may have conceptions of many things about spiritual affections; but there is something in them which is as it were the nucleus, or kernel of them, that they have no more conceptions of, than one born blind has of colors.

It may be clearly illustrated by this: we will suppose two men; one is born without the sense of tasting, the other has it; the latter loves honey and is greatly delighted in it because he knows the sweet taste of it; the other loves certain sounds and colors: the love of each has many things that appertain to it, which is common; it causes both to desire and delight in the object beloved, and causes grief when it is absent, etc.: but yet, that idea or sensation which he who knows the taste of honey, has of its excellency and sweetness, that is the foundation of his love, is entirely different from anything the other has or can have; and that delight which he has in honey, is wholly diverse from anything that the other can conceive of; though they both delight in their beloved objects. So both these persons may in some respects love the same object: the one may love a delicious kind of fruit, which is beautiful to the eye, and of a delicious taste; not only because he has seen its pleasant colors, but knows its sweet taste; the other, perfectly ignorant of this, loves it only for its beautiful colors: there are many things seen, in some respect, to be common to both; both love, both desire, and both delight; but the love, and desire, and delight of the one, is altogether diverse from that of the other. The difference between the love of a natural man and spiritual man is like to this; but only it must be observed, that in one respect it is vastly greater, viz. that the kinds of excellency which are perceived in spiritual objects, by these different kinds of persons, are in themselves vastly more diverse, than the different kinds of excellency perceived in delicious fruit, by a tasting and a tasteless man; and in another respect it may not be so great, viz. as the spiritual man may have a spiritual sense or taste, to perceive that divine and most peculiar excellency, but in small beginnings, and in a very imperfect degree.

2. On the other hand, it must be observed, that a natural man may have those religious apprehensions and affections, which may be in many respects very new and surprising to him, and what before he did not conceive of; and yet what he experiences be nothing like the exercises of a principle of new nature, or the sensations of a new spiritual sense: his affections may be very new, by extraordinarily moving natural principles, in a very new degree, and with a great many new circumstances, and a new cooperation of natural affections, and a new composition of ideas; this may be from some extraordinary powerful influence of Satan and some great delusion; but there is nothing but nature extraordinarily acted. As if a poor man, that had always dwelt in a cottage, and had never looked beyond the obscure village where he was born, should in a jest, be taken to a magnificent city and prince's court, and there arrayed in princely robes, and set in the throne, with the crown royal on his head, peers and nobles bowing before him, and should be made to believe that he was now a glorious monarch; the ideas he would have, and the affections he would experience, would in many respects be very new, and such as he had no imagination of before; but all is no more, than only extraordinarily raising and exciting natural principles, and newly exalting, varying and compounding such sort of ideas, as he has by nature; here is nothing like giving him a new sense.

Upon the whole, I think it is clearly manifest, that all truly gracious affections do arise from special and peculiar influences of the Spirit, working that sensible effect or sensation in the souls of the saints, which are entirely different from all that it is possible a natural man should experience, not only different in degree and circumstances, but different in its whole nature: so that a natural man not only cannot experience that which is individually the same, but can't experience anything but what is exceeding diverse, and immensely below it, in its kind; and that which the power of men or devils is not sufficient to produce the like of, or anything of the same nature....

The Twelfth Sign

The reason why gracious affections have such a tendency and effect [to bear fruit in Christian practice], appears from many things that have already been observed, in the preceding parts of this discourse.

The reason of it appears from this, that gracious affections do arise from those operations and influences which are spiritual, and that the inward principle from whence they flow, is something divine, a communication of God, a participation of the divine nature, Christ living in the heart, the Holy Spirit dwelling there, in union with the faculties of the soul, as an internal vital principle, exerting his own proper nature, in the exercise of those faculties. This is sufficient to show us why true grace should have such activity, power and efficacy. No wonder that which is divine, is powerful and effectual; for it has omnipotence on its side. If God dwells in the heart, and be vitally united to it, he will shew that he is a God, by the efficacy of his operation. Christ is not in the heart of a saint, as in a sepulcher, or as a dead Saviour, that does nothing; but as in his temple, and as one that is alive from the dead. For in the heart where Christ savingly is, there he lives, and exerts himself after the power of that endless life, that he received at his resurrection. Thus every saint that is the subject of the benefit of Christ's sufferings, is made to know and experience the power of his resurrection. The spirit of Christ, which is the immediate spring of grace in the heart, is all life, all power, all act; "In demonstration of the Spirit, and of power" (2 Cor 2:4). "Our gospel came not unto you in word only, but also in power, and in the Holy Ghost" (1 Thess 1:5). "The kingdom of God is not in word, but in power" (1 Cor 4:20). Hence saving affections, though oftentimes they don't make so great a noise and show as others; yet have in them a secret solidity, life and strength, whereby they take hold of, and carry away the heart, leading it into a kind of captivity (2 Cor 10:5), gaining a full and steadfast determination of the will for God and holiness; "Thy people shall be willing in the day of thy power" (Ps 110:3). And thus it is that holy affections have a governing power in the course of a man's life. A statue may look very much like a real man, and a beautiful man; yea it may have, in its appearance to the eye, the resemblance of a very lively, strong and active man; but yet an inward principle of life and strength is wanting; and therefore it does nothing, it brings nothing to pass, there is no action or operation to answer the shew. False discoveries and affections don't go deep enough, to reach and govern the spring of men's actions and practice. The seed in stony ground had not deepness of earth, and the root did not go deep enough to bring forth fruit. But gracious affections go to the very bottom of the heart, and take hold of the very inmost springs of life and activity. Herein chiefly appears the power of true godliness, viz. in its being effectual in practice. And the efficacy of godliness in this respect, is what the Apostle has respect to, when he speaks of the power of godliness (2 Tim 3:5), as is very plain; for he there is particularly declaring, how some professors of religion would notoriously fail in the practice of it; and then in the fifth verse observes, that in being thus of an unholy practice, they deny the power of godliness, though they have the form of it. Indeed the power of godliness is exerted in the first place within the soul, in the sensible, lively exercise of gracious affections there. Yet the principal evidence of this power of godliness, is in those exercises of holy affections that are practical, and in their being practical; in conquering the will, and conquering the lusts and corruptions of men, and carrying men on in the way of holiness, through all temptation, difficulty and opposition.

Again, the reason why gracious affections have their exercise and effect in Christian practice, appears from this (which has also been before observed) that the first objective ground of gracious affections, is the transcendently excellent and amiable nature of divine things, as they are in themselves, and not any conceived relation they bear to self, or self-interest. This shews why holy affections will cause men to be holy in their practice universally. What makes men partial in religion is, that they seek themselves, and not God, in their religion, and close with religion, not for its own excellent nature, but only to serve a turn. He that closes with religion only to serve a turn, will close with no more of it than he imagines serves that turn: but he that closes with religion for its own excellent and lovely nature closes with all that has that nature: he that embraces religion for its own sake, embraces the whole of religion. This also shows why gracious affections will cause men to practice religion perseveringly, and at all times. Religion may alter greatly in process of time, as to its consistence with men's private interest, in many respects; and therefore he that complies with it only from selfish views, is liable, in change of times, to forsake it: but the excellent nature of religion, as it is in itself, is invariable; it is always the same, at all times, and through all changes; it never alters in any respect.

The reason why gracious affections issue in holy practice, also further appears from the kind of excellency of divine things, that it has been observed is the foundation of all holy affection, viz. their moral excellency, or the beauty of their holiness. No wonder that a love to holiness, for holiness' sake, inclines persons to practice holiness, and to practice everything that is holy. Seeing holiness is the main thing that excites, draws and governs all gracious affections, no wonder that all such affections tend to holiness. That which men love, they desire to have and to be united to, and possessed of. That beauty which men delight in, they desire to be adorned with. Those acts which men delight in, they necessarily include to do.

And what has been observed of that divine teaching and leading of the Spirit of God, which there is in gracious affections, shews the reason of this tendency of such affections to an universally holy practice. For as has been observed, the Spirit of God in this his divine teaching and leading, gives the soul a natural relish of the sweetness of that which is holy, and of everything that is holy, so far as it comes in view, and excites a disrelish and disgust of everything that is unholy.

The same also appears from what has been observed of the nature of that spiritual knowledge, which is the foundation of all holy affection, as consisting in a sense and view of that excellency in divine things, which is supreme and transcendent. For hereby these things appear above all others, worthy to be chosen and adhered to. By the sight of the transcendent glory of Christ, true Christians see him worthy to be followed; and so are powerfully drawn after him: they see him worthy that they should forsake all for him: by the sight of that superlative amiableness, they are thoroughly disposed to be subject to him, and engaged to labor with earnestness and activity in his service, and made willing to go through all difficulties for his sake. And 'tis the discovery of this divine excellency of Christ, that makes 'em constant to him: for it makes a deep impression upon their minds, that they cannot forget him; and they will follow him whithersoever he goes, and it is in vain for any to endeavor to draw them away from him.

The reason of this practical tendency and issue of gracious affections, further appears, from what has been observed of such affections being attended with a thorough conviction of the judgment, of the reality and certainty of divine things. No wonder that they who were never thoroughly convinced that there is any reality in the things of religion, will never be at the labor and trouble of such an earnest, universal and persevering practice of religion, through all difficulties, self-denials and sufferings, in a dependence on that, which they are not convinced of. But on the other hand, they who are thoroughly convinced of the certain truth of those things, must needs be governed by them in their practice; for the things revealed in the Word of God are so great, and so infinitely more important, than all other things, that it is inconsistent with the human nature, that a man should fully believe the truth of them, and not be influenced by them above all things, in his practice.

Again, the reason of this expression and effect of holy affections in the practice, appears from what has been observed of a change of nature, accompanying such affections. Without a change of nature, men's practice will not be thoroughly changed. Till the tree be made good, the fruit will not be good. Men don't gather grapes of thorns, nor figs of thistles. The swine may be washed, and appear clean for a little while, but yet, without a change of nature, he will still wallow in the mire. Nature is a more powerful principle of action, than anything that opposes it: though it may be violently restrained for a while, it will finally overcome that which restrains it: 'tis like the stream of a river, it may be stopped a while with a dam, but if nothing be done to dry the fountain, it won't be stopped always; it will have a course, either in its old channel, or a new one. Nature is a thing more constant and permanent, than any of those things that are the foundation of carnal men's reformation and righteousness. When a natural man denies his lust, and lives a strict, religious life, and seems humble, painful and earnest in religion, 'tis not natural, 'tis all a force against nature; as when a stone is violently thrown upwards; but that force will be gradually spent; yet nature will remain in its full strength, and so prevails again, and the stone returns downwards. As long as corrupt nature is not mortified, but the principle left whole in a man, 'tis a vain thing to expect that it should not govern. But if the old nature be indeed mortified, and a new and heavenly nature infused; then may it well be expected, that men will walk in newness of life, and continue to do so to the end of their days.

The reason of this practical exercise and effect of holy affections, may also be partly seen, from what has been said of that spirit of humility which attends them. Humility is that wherein a spirit of obedience does much consist. A proud spirit is a rebellious spirit, but a humble spirit is a yieldable, subject, obediential spirit. We see among men, that the servant who is of a haughty spirit, is not apt in everything to be submissive and obedient to the will of his master; but it is otherwise with that servant who is of a lowly spirit.

And that lamblike, dovelike spirit, that has been spoken of, which accompanies all gracious affections, fulfills (as the Apostle observes, Rom 13:8–10 and Gal 5:14) all the duties of the second table of the law; wherein Christian practice does very much consist, and wherein the external practice of Christianity chiefly consists.

And the reason why gracious affections are attended with that strict, universal and constant obedience which has been spoken of, further appears, from what has been observed of that tenderness of spirit, which accompanies the affections of true saints, causing in them so quick and lively a sense of pain, through the presence of moral evil, and such a dread of the appearance of evil.

And one great reason why the Christian practice which flows from gracious affections, is universal, and constant, and persevering, appears from what has been observed of those affections themselves, from whence this practice flows, being universal and constant, in all kinds of holy exercises, and towards all objects, and in all circumstances, and at all seasons, in a beautiful symmetry and proportion.

And much of the reason why holy affections are expressed and manifested in such an earnestness, activity, and engagedness and perseverance in holy practice, as has been spoken of, appears from what has been observed, of the spiritual appetite and longing after further attainments in religion, which evermore attends true affection, and don't decay, but increases, as those affections increase.

Thus we see how the tendency of holy affections to such a Christian practice as has been explained, appears from each of those characteristics of holy affection, that have been before spoken of.

And this point may be further illustrated and confirmed, if it be considered, that the Holy Scriptures do abundantly place sincerity and soundness in religion, in making a full choice of God as our only Lord and portion, forsaking all for him, and in a full determination of the will for God and Christ, on counting the cost; in our hearts closing and complying with the religion of Jesus Christ, with all that belongs to it, embracing it with all its difficulties, as it were hating our dearest earthly enjoyments, and even our own lives, for Christ; giving up ourselves, with all that we have, wholly and forever, unto Christ, without keeping back anything or making any reserve; or in one word, in the great duty of self-denial for Christ; or in denying, i.e. as it were disowning and renouncing ourselves for him, making ourselves nothing that he may be all. See the texts to this purpose referred to in the margin.[1] Now surely having an heart to forsake all for Christ, tends to actually forsaking all for him, so far as there is occasion, and we have the trial. And having an heart to deny ourselves for Christ, tends to a denying ourselves in deed, when Christ and self-interest stand in competition. A giving up ourselves, with all that we have in our hearts, without making any reserve there, tends to our behaving ourselves universally as his, as subject to his will, and devoted to his ends. Our hearts entirely closing with the religion of Jesus, with all that belongs to it, and as attended with all its difficulties, upon a deliberate counting the cost, tends to an universal closing with the same in act and deed, and actually going through all the difficulties that we meet with in the way of religion, and so holding out with patience and perseverance.

---

[1]Edwards here refers to forty passages from Scripture, including Matt 5:29–30; Lk 5:27–28; Acts 4:34–35; Rom 6:3–8; Phil 3:7–10; Ruth 1:6–16; Ps 16:5–6; and Jer 10:16.

Selected Bibliography

TEXTS

Edition used:
The Works of President Edwards, vol. 1. Edited by Samuel Austin. Worcester, Mass., 1808.

Other sources:
The Works of Jonathan Edwards. Edited by Perry Miller, John E. Smith, et al. 17 vols. to date. New Haven, Conn.: Yale University Press, 1957–.

Jonathan Edwards: Representative Selections. Edited by Clarence H. Faust and Thomas H. Johnson. Rev. ed. New York: Hill and Wang, 1962.

STUDIES

Cherry, Conrad. *The Theology of Jonathan Edwards: A Reappraisal.* Garden City, N.Y.: Doubleday, Anchor Books, 1966.

Fiering, Norman. *Jonathan Edwards's Moral Thought and Its British Context.* Chapel Hill, N.C.: University of North Carolina Press, 1981.

Hatch, Nathan O., Harry S. Stout, eds. *Jonathan Edwards and the American Experience.* New York: Oxford University Press, 1987.

Jenson, Robert W. *America's Theologian: A Recommendation of Jonathan Edwards.* New York: Oxford University Press, 1987.

Stein, Stephen J. ed. *Jonathan Edwards's Writings: Text, Context, Interpretation.* Bloomington, Ind.: Indiana University Press, 1996.

Wainwright, William. "Jonathan Edwards and the Sense of the Heart." *Faith and Philosophy* 7 (1990): 43–62.

Thérèse of Lisieux (1873–97)

The short life of Thérèse of Lisieux was outwardly so uneventful that some of the nuns with whom she lived during the final nine years of her life were not aware of any particular virtue in her and wondered aloud what could possibly be said in praise of her on the obituary notices that were to be sent to other Carmelite houses after her death. If today no one doubts her genuine sanctity, many would nevertheless deny that she should be counted among the mystics. In explaining our choice of Thérèse for inclusion in this anthology, we will at the same time be making some fundamental points about the nature and compass of Christian mysticism.

Thérèse was born at Alençon in Normandy on January 2, 1873, the ninth and youngest child of Louis Martin and Zélie Guérin. Of the five children who lived beyond childhood, four became Carmelite nuns in the convent at Lisieux, the city to which the family moved after Zélie's death in August 1877. Years later, Thérèse wrote of her mother's death as ushering in a particularly sad and trying period of her life, one that lasted more than nine years and was marked by bouts of depression, scrupulosity, and what we would call a nervous breakdown, which occurred when she was only ten years old. Already during these years she had a strong desire to enter Carmel, perhaps at first largely in order to follow the path of her elder sister and "second mother," Pauline, but later out of a firm conviction that this was God's will for her.

With dogged persistence she finally obtained special permission to join the community at Lisieux only three months beyond her fifteenth birthday. During her early years in the convent she was regularly assigned only the menial employments common to postulants, novices, and the newly professed, but at the age of twenty she was named to the important position of assistant to the novice mistress. The first signs of tuberculosis appeared in the summer of the following year, 1894. After this she became progressively weaker, although she continued her regular duties without any relaxation for nearly two years. By early July 1897, Thérèse had become so ill that she was moved to the convent infirmary, where she died on the evening of September 30. She was beatified by Pope Pius XI in 1923 and canonized only two years later, May 17, 1925.

If there is any "secret" to the holiness of this young saint, it lies in her complete conviction that it is not so much what we do that counts in God's eyes but rather the love with which we do it—or more exactly, the love with which we allow God to love in and through ourselves.[1] From John of the Cross she took the verse that she used on her own Carmelite coat of arms, "Love is repaid by love alone," and from the New Testament she absorbed and lived out the teaching that this love must be extended in utterly practical ways to everyone, starting with those whom we find naturally least attractive: one must render them "all possible services," search out their virtues rather than their faults, and answer with a kind word when tempted to respond in a disagreeable manner. The simple, even naive way in which she describes all this in the three manuscripts that together compose her autobiographical *Story of a Soul* has inspired countless readers throughout the world and once led Pope Pius X to call her "the greatest saint of

---

[1] Thérèse once wrote: "Ah! Lord, I know you don't command the impossible. You know better than I do my weakness and imperfection; You know very well that never would I be able to love my Sisters as You love them, unless *You*, O my Jesus, *loved them in me*" (*Story of a Soul: The Autobiography of St. Thérèse of Lisieux*, trans. John Clarke, O.C.D., 2d ed. [Washington, D.C.: Institute of Carmelite Studies, 1976], 221).

modern times." Something more must be said, however, to explain why she is also rightly to be considered a mystic.

To begin, it is worth examining why some would deny her this title. The eminent Swiss theologian Hans Urs von Balthasar, in his long and generally positive study of her spirituality, states categorically that she never "crossed the threshold into what is known as mysticism."[2] He justifies this claim on the basis that her life was free of the presence of or even the longing for extraordinary "mystical phenomena"; after all, he notes, Thérèse repeatedly said or wrote such things as "I have never longed for visions"; "I have no wish...to have ecstasies"; "I have never wished for extraordinary graces. That does not fit in with my little way."[3]

In this line of argumentation, we have a particularly clear instance of what we referred to in our General Introduction as the increasing subjectivization of the understanding of mysticism in recent centuries. For many writers today, mysticism has come to mean simply an extraordinary grace given to those who directly experience the divine presence. If this understanding is accepted, then one might have to agree with von Balthasar that Thérèse of Lisieux was no mystic. But one should also recall that in its original Christian usage, the word *mystical* referred to the objective but "hidden" *(mystikos)* reality of Christ in scripture, in the sacraments, and in all of history.[4] An immediate, vivid, and at times overwhelmingly ecstatic consciousness of this real presence has indeed often been found in those who have dedicated themselves in a particularly single-hearted way to the following of the gospel. But this kind of experience did not belong to the essence of the mystical as this was originally understood by writers like Origen, Gregory of Nyssa, and Maximus the Confessor. According to that more objective understanding, as Louis Bouyer observes in the concluding chapter of his long and excellent study *Mysterion,*

---

[2]Hans Urs von Balthasar, *Thérèse of Lisieux: The Story of a Mission,* trans. Donald Nicholl (New York: Sheed and Ward, 1954), 252.
[3]Ibid., 254.
[4]Louis Bouyer, Cong. Orat., "Mysticism: An Essay on the History of the Word," in *Understanding Mysticism,* ed. Richard Woods, O.P. (Garden City, N.Y.: Doubleday, Image Books, 1980), 42–55.

"the main thing is to be fully convinced that Christ is living in us, and especially to act accordingly, not to experience more or less directly the feeling that this is indeed so."[5]

That Thérèse had this conviction to a preeminent degree seems evident from almost every page of her writings. Looking back over her life, she once said that she did not believe she had ever gone more than a few minutes without thinking about God. For her, unlike Teresa of Avila or Marie of the Incarnation, this conviction of God's reality was not accompanied by personal experiences of ecstasy, nor did her conviction inspire Augustinian or Eckhartian reflections on the trinity of the mind as an image of God or on that "spark in the soul" which entirely transcends the world of space and time. In these respects Thérèse actually differs from all the other authors included in this anthology, for she offers neither personal descriptions of ecstatic experience nor theological articulation about the nature of God's presence to the soul. What she does offer is a detailed, unembarrassed account of her growing abandonment to God's love in pure faith and of the ways this manifested itself both in her prayer and in her relations with other persons, especially with those whose companionship she would otherwise have avoided: "Jesus is telling me that it is this Sister who must be loved, she must be prayed for even though her conduct would lead me to believe that she doesn't love me....And it isn't enough to love; we must prove it."[6] Her own awareness of the heroically faithful if unspectacular ways in which she did prove her love allowed her to say less than a month before she died: "Ah! It is incredible how all my hopes have been fulfilled. When I used to read St. John of the Cross, I begged God to work out in me what he wrote...to consume me rapidly in Love, and I have been answered."[7] The frequent, loving invocations of the Father and Jesus in her writings, her willingness to suffer tormenting temptations against faith in the conviction that there is no greater joy

[5]Louis Bouyer, *Mysterion: Du mystère à la mystique* (Paris, 1986), 348.
[6]*Story of a Soul*, 225.
[7]*St. Thérèse of Lisieux: Her Last Conversations*, trans. John Clarke, O.C.D. (Washington, D.C.: Institute of Carmelite Studies, 1977), 177.

"than that of suffering out of love for You," her fervent desire to take up all of humanity in her offering of herself to God, and her constant attempts to show her love for all, especially for the most contrary and neglected of the nuns with whom she lived: all of this allows us to see in her—in the original, objective sense of the term—a preeminent example of the "mysticism of love."

STORY OF A SOUL

CHAPTER TEN:
THE TRIAL OF FAITH

June, 1897

You have told me, my dear Mother,[1] of your desire that I finish *singing* with you *the Mercies of the Lord* (Ps 88:2). I began this sweet song with your dear daughter, Agnes of Jesus, who was the mother entrusted by God with guiding me in the days of my childhood. It was with her that I had to sing of the graces granted to the Blessed Virgin's *little flower* when she was in the springtime of her life. And it is with you that I am to sing of the happiness of this little flower now that the timid glimmerings of the dawn have given way to the burning heat of noon. Yes, dear Mother, I shall try to express, in answer to your wishes, the sentiments of my soul, my gratitude to God and to you, who represent Him visibly to me, for was it not into your maternal hands that I delivered myself entirely to Him? O Mother, do you not remember the day?[2] Yes, I know your heart could not forget it. As for me, I must await heaven because I cannot find here on earth words capable of expressing what took place in my heart on that beautiful day....

From *Story of a Soul The* Autobiography *of St. Thérèse of Lisieux,* trans. John Clarke, O.C.D., 2d ed. (Washington, D.C.: Institute of Carmelite Studies, 1976), 205, 207–8, 210–14, 219–20, 224–26. Reprinted with permission of the publisher. Copyright © 1975, 1976, 1996, by Washington Province of Discalced Carmelites, ICS Publications, 2131 Lincoln Rd., N.E., Washington, D.C. 20002-1199.
[1]Thérèse is writing at the request of Mother Marie de Gonzague, elected prioress March 21, 1896, to succeed Thérèse's sister Pauline (Mother Agnes of Jesus).
[2]The day of her profession, September 8, 1890.

O Mother, how different are the ways through which the Lord leads souls! In the life of the saints, we find many of them who didn't want to leave anything of themselves behind after their death, not the smallest souvenir, not the least bit of writing. On the contrary, there are others, like our holy Mother St. Teresa, who have enriched the Church with their lofty revelations, having no fears of revealing the secrets of the King in order to make Him more loved and known by souls. Which of these two types of saints is more pleasing to God? It seems to me, Mother, they are equally pleasing to Him, since all of them followed the inspiration of the Holy Spirit and since the Lord has said: *"Tell the just man ALL is well"* (Is 3:10). Yes, all is well when one seeks only the will of Jesus, and it is because of this that I, a poor little flower, obey Jesus when trying to please my beloved Mother.

You know, Mother, I have always wanted to be a saint. Alas! I have always noticed that when I compared myself to the saints, there is between them and me the same difference that exists between a mountain whose summit is lost in the clouds and the obscure grain of sand trampled underfoot by the passers-by. Instead of becoming discouraged, I said to myself: God cannot inspire unrealizable desires. I can, then, in spite of my littleness, aspire to holiness. It is impossible for me to grow up, and so I must bear with myself such as I am with all my imperfections. But I want to seek out a means of going to heaven by a little way, a way that is very straight, very short, and totally new.

We are living now in an age of inventions, and we no longer have to take the trouble of climbing stairs, for, in the homes of the rich, an elevator has replaced these very successfully. I wanted to find an elevator which would raise me to Jesus, for I am too small to climb the rough stairway of perfection. I searched, then, in the Scriptures for some sign of this elevator, the object of my desires, and I read these words coming from the mouth of Eternal Wisdom: *"Whoever is a LITTLE ONE, let him come to me"* (Prov 9:4). And so I succeeded. I felt I had found what I was looking for. But wanting to know, O my God, what You would do to *the very little one* who answered Your call, I continued my search and this is what I discovered: *"As one whom a mother caresses, so will I comfort you; you shall be carried at the breasts, and upon the knees they shall caress you"* (Is 66:13, 12). Ah! never did words more tender and more melodious come to give joy to my soul. The elevator which must raise me to heaven is Your arms, O Jesus! And for this I had no need to grow up, but rather I had to remain *little* and become this more and more.

O my God, You surpassed all my expectation. I want only to sing of Your Mercies. "You have taught me from my youth, O God, and until now I will declare Your wonderful works. And until old age and grey hairs, O God, forsake me not" (Ps 70:17–18). What will this old age be for me? It seems this could be right now, for two thousand years are not more in the Lord's eyes than are twenty years, than even a single day (Ps 89:4).

Ah! don't think, dear Mother, that your child wants to leave you; don't think she feels it is a greater grace to die at the dawn of the day rather than at its close. What she esteems and what she desires only is *to please* Jesus. Now that He seems to be approaching her in order to draw her into the place of His glory, your child is filled with joy. For a long time she has understood that God needs no one (much less her) to do good on earth. Pardon me, Mother, if I make you sad because I really want only to give you joy. Do you believe that though your prayers are really not heard on earth, though Jesus separates the child from its mother for a *few days,* that these prayers will be answered in heaven?...

Dear Mother, you know well that God has deigned to make me pass through many types of trials. I have suffered very much since I was on earth, but, if in my childhood I suffered with sadness, it is no longer in this way that I suffer. O Mother, you must know all the secrets of my soul in order not to smile when you read these lines, for is there a soul less tried than my own if one judges by appearances? Ah! if the trial I am suffering for a year now appeared to the eyes of anyone, what astonishment would be felt![3]

---

[3]Her temptation against faith, which lasted from Easter, 1896.

Dear Mother, you know about this trial; I am going to speak to you about it, however, for I consider it a great grace I received during your office as Prioress.

God granted me, last year, the consolation of observing the fast during Lent in all its rigor. Never had I felt so strong, and this strength remained with me until Easter. On Good Friday, however, Jesus wished to give me the hope of going to see Him soon in heaven. Oh! how sweet this memory really is! After remaining at the Tomb until midnight,[4] I returned to our cell, but I had scarcely laid my head upon the pillow when I felt something like a bubbling stream mounting to my lips. I didn't know what it was, but I thought that perhaps I was going to die and my soul was flooded with joy. However, as our lamp was extinguished, I told myself I would have to wait until the morning to be certain of my good fortune, for it seemed to me that it was blood I had coughed up. The morning was not long in coming; upon awakening, I thought immediately of the joyful thing that I had to learn, and so I went over to the window. I was able to see that I was not mistaken. Ah! my soul was filled with a great consolation; I was interiorly persuaded that Jesus, on the anniversary of His own death, wanted to have me hear His first call. *It was like a sweet and distant murmur which announced the Bridegroom's arrival.*[5]

It was with great fervor that I assisted at Prime and the Chapter of Pardons.[6] I was in a rush to see my turn come in order to be able, when asking pardon from you, to confide my hope and my happiness to you, dear Mother; however, I added that I was not suffering in the least (which was true) and I begged you, Mother, to give me nothing special. In fact, I had the consolation of spending Good Friday just as I desired. Never did Carmel's austerities appear so delightful to me; the hope of going to heaven soon transported me with joy. When the evening of that blessed day arrived, I had to go to my rest; but just as on the preceding night,

[4]The Altar of Reposition. The Carmelite nuns remained all night in prayer before the Blessed Sacrament.
[5]*The Imitation of Christ*, 3, 47.
[6]On Good Friday, the prioress customarily gave the community an exhortation to greater charity; then each begged pardon from her Sisters.

good Jesus gave me the same sign that my entrance into eternal life was not far off.

At this time I was enjoying such a living faith, such a clear faith, that the thought of heaven made up all my happiness, and I was unable to believe there were really impious people who had no faith. I believed they were actually speaking against their own inner convictions when they denied the existence of heaven, that beautiful heaven where God Himself wanted to be their Eternal Reward. During those very joyful days of the Easter season, Jesus made me feel that there were really souls who have no faith, and who, through the abuse of grace, lost this precious treasure, the source of the only real and pure joys. He permitted my soul to be invaded by the thickest darkness, and that the thought of heaven, up until then so sweet to me, be no longer anything but the cause of struggle and torment. This trial was to last not a few days or a few weeks, it was not to be extinguished until the hour set by God Himself, and this hour has not yet come. I would like to be able to express what I feel, but alas! I believe this is impossible. One would have to travel through this dark tunnel to understand its darkness. I will try to explain it by a comparison.

I imagine I was born in a country which is covered in thick fog. I never had the experience of contemplating the joyful appearance of nature flooded and transformed by the brilliance of the sun. It is true that from childhood I have heard people speak of these marvels, and I know the country in which I am living is not really my true fatherland, and there is another I must long for without ceasing. This is not simply a story invented by someone living in the sad country where I am, but it is a reality, for the King of the Fatherland of the bright sun actually came and lived for thirty-three years in the land of darkness. Alas! the darkness did not understand that this Divine King was the Light of the world (Jn 1:5, 9).

Your child, however, O Lord, has understood Your divine light, and she begs pardon for her brothers. She is resigned to eat the bread of sorrow as long as You desire it; she does not wish to rise up from this table filled with bitterness at which poor sinners are eating until the day set by You. Can she not say in her name and in the name of her brothers, *"Have pity on us, O Lord, for we are poor sinners!"* (Lk 18:13). Oh! Lord, send us away justified. May all those who were not enlightened by the bright flame of faith one day see it shine. O Jesus! if it is needful that the table soiled by them be purified by a soul who loves You, then I desire to eat this bread of trial at this table until it pleases You to bring me into Your bright Kingdom. The only grace I ask of You is that I never offend You!

What I am writing, dear Mother, has no continuity; my little story which resembled a fairy-tale is all of a sudden changed into a prayer, and I don't know what interest you could possibly have in reading all these confused and poorly expressed ideas. Well, dear Mother, I am not writing to produce a literary work, but only through obedience, and if I cause you any boredom, then at least you will see that your little child has given proof of her good will. I am going to continue my little comparison where I left off.

I was saying that the certainty of going away one day far from the sad and dark country had been given me from the day of my childhood. I did not believe this only because I heard it from persons much more knowledgeable than I, but I felt in the bottom of my heart real longings for this most beautiful country. Just as the genius of Christopher Columbus gave him a presentiment of a new world when nobody had even thought of such a thing; so also I felt that another land would one day serve me as a permanent dwelling place. Then suddenly the fog which surrounds me becomes more dense; it penetrates my soul and envelops it in such a way that it is impossible to discover within it the sweet image of my Fatherland; everything has disappeared! When I want to rest my heart fatigued by the darkness which surrounds it by the memory of the luminous country after which I aspire, my torment redoubles; it seems to me that the darkness, borrowing the voice of sinners, says mockingly to me: "You are dreaming about the light, about a fatherland embalmed in the sweetest perfumes; you are dreaming about the *eternal* possession of the Creator of all these marvels; you believe that one day you will walk out of this fog which surrounds you! Advance, advance; rejoice in death which will give you not what you hope for but a night still more profound, the night of nothingness."

Dear Mother, the image I wanted to give you of the darkness that obscures my soul is as imperfect as a sketch is to the model; however, I don't want to write any longer about it; I fear I might blaspheme; I fear even that I have already said too much.

Ah! may Jesus pardon me if I have caused Him any pain, but He knows very well that while I do not have *the joy of faith,* I am trying to carry out its works at least. I believe I have made more acts of faith in this past year than all through my whole life. At each new occasion of combat, when my enemy provokes me, I conduct myself bravely. Knowing it is cowardly to enter into a duel, I turn my back on my adversary without deigning to look him in the face; but I run towards my Jesus. I tell Him I am ready to shed my blood to the last drop to profess my faith in the existence of *heaven.* I tell Him, too, I am happy not to enjoy this beautiful heaven on this earth so that He will open it for all eternity to poor unbelievers. Also, in spite of this trial which has taken away all *my joy,* I can nevertheless cry out: *"You have given me DELIGHT, O Lord, in ALL your doings"* (Ps 91:5). For is there a *joy* greater than that of suffering out of love for You? The more interior the suffering is and the less apparent to the eyes of creatures, the more it rejoices You, O my God! But if my suffering was really unknown to You, which is impossible, I would still be happy to have it, if through it I could prevent or make reparation for one single sin against *faith.*

My dear Mother, I may perhaps appear to you to be exaggerating my trial. In fact, if you are judging according to the sentiments I express in my little poems composed this year, I must appear to you as a soul filled with consolations and one for whom the veil of faith is almost torn aside; and yet it is no longer a veil for me, it is a wall which reaches right up to the heavens and covers the starry firmament. When I sing of the happiness of heaven and of the eternal possession of God, I feel no joy in this, for I sing simply what I WANT TO BELIEVE. It is true that at times a very small ray of the sun comes to illumine my darkness, and then the trial ceases for *an instant,* but afterwards the memory of this ray, instead of causing me joy, makes my darkness even more dense.

Never have I felt before this, dear Mother, how sweet and merciful the Lord really is, for He did not send me this trial until the moment I was capable of bearing it. A little earlier I believe it would have plunged me into a state of discouragement. Now it is taking away everything that could be a natural satisfaction in my desire for heaven. Dear Mother, it seems to me now that nothing could prevent me from flying away, for I no longer have any great desires, except that of loving to the point of dying of love....

This year, dear Mother, God has given me the grace to understand what charity is; I understood it before, it is true, but in an imperfect way. I had never fathomed the meaning of these words of Jesus: *"The second commandment is LIKE the first: You shall love your neighbor as yourself"* (Mt 22:39). I applied myself especially to loving God, and it is in loving Him that I understood my love was not to be expressed only in words, for: *"It is not those who say: 'Lord, Lord!' who will enter the kingdom of heaven, but those who do the will of my Father in heaven"* (Mt 7:21). Jesus has revealed this will several times or I should say on almost every page of His Gospel. But at the Last Supper, when He knew the hearts of His disciples were burning with a more ardent love for Him who had just given Himself to them in the unspeakable mystery of His Eucharist, this sweet Savior wished to give them *a new commandment.* He said to them with inexpressible tenderness: *"A new commandment I give you, that you love one another: THAT AS I HAVE LOVED YOU, YOU ALSO LOVE ONE ANOTHER. By this will all men know that you are my disciples,* if you have love for one another" (Jn 13:34–35).

How did Jesus love His disciples and why did He love them? Ah! it was not their natural qualities which could have attracted Him since there was between Him and them an infinite distance. He was knowledge, Eternal Wisdom, while they were poor ignorant fishermen filled with earthly thoughts. And still Jesus called them his *friends, His brothers* (Jn 15:15). He desires to see them reign with Him in the kingdom of His Father, and to open that kingdom to them He wills to die on the cross, for He said: *"Greater love than this no man has than that he lay down his life for his friends"* (Jn 15:13).

Dear Mother, when meditating upon these words of Jesus, I understood how imperfect was my love for my Sisters. I saw I didn't love them as God loves them. Ah! I understand now that charity consists in bearing with the faults of others, in not being surprised at their weakness, in being edified by the smallest acts of virtue we see them practice. But I understood above all that charity must not remain hidden in the bottom of the heart. Jesus has said: *"No one lights a lamp and puts it under a bushel basket, but upon the lamp-stand, so as to give light to ALL in the house"* (Mt 5:15). It seems to me that this lamp represents charity, which must enlighten and rejoice not only those who are dearest to us but *"All who are in the house"* without distinction.

When the Lord commanded His people to love their neighbor as themselves (Lev 19:18), He had not as yet come upon the earth. Knowing the extent to which each one loved himself, He was not able to ask of His creatures a greater love than this for one's neighbor. But when Jesus gave His Apostles a new commandment, HIS OWN COMMANDMENT (Jn 15:12), as He calls it later on, it is no longer a question of loving one's neighbor as oneself but of loving him as *He, Jesus, has loved him,* and will love him to the consummation of the ages....

The Lord, in the Gospel, explains in what *His new commandment* consists. He says in St. Matthew: *"You have heard that it was said, 'You shall love your neighbor and hate your enemy.' But I say to you, love your enemies...pray for those who persecute you"* (Mt 5:43–44). No doubt, we don't have any enemies in Carmel, but there are feelings. One feels attracted to this Sister, whereas with regard to another one would make a long detour in order to avoid meeting her. And so, without even knowing it, she becomes the subject of persecution. Well, Jesus is telling me that it is this Sister who must be loved, she must be prayed for even though her conduct would lead me to believe that she doesn't love me: *"If you love those who love you, what reward will you have?*

For even sinners love those who love them" (Lk 6:32)....And it isn't enough to love; we must prove it. We are naturally happy to offer a gift to a friend; we love especially to give surprises; however, this is not charity, for sinners do this too. Here is what Jesus teaches me also: *"Give to EVERYONE who asks of you, and from HIM WHO TAKES AWAY your goods, ask no return"* (Lk 6:30). Giving to all those who *ask* is less sweet than offering oneself by the movement of one's own heart; again, when they ask for something politely, it doesn't cost so much to give, but if, unfortunately, they don't use very delicate words, the soul is immediately up in arms if she is not well founded in charity. She finds a thousand reasons to refuse what is asked of her, and it is only after having convinced the asker of her tactlessness that she will finally give what is asked, and then only *as a favor;* or else she will render a light service which could have been done in one-twentieth of the time that was spent in setting forth her imaginary rights.

Although it is difficult to give to one who asks, it is even more so to allow one *to take what belongs to you, without asking it back.* O Mother, I say it is difficult; I should have said that this *seems* difficult, for *the yoke of the Lord is sweet and light* (Mt 11:30). When one accepts it, one feels its sweetness immediately, and cries out with the Psalmist: *"I have run the way of your commandments when you enlarged my heart"* (Ps 118:32). It is only charity which can expand my heart. O Jesus, since this sweet flame consumes it, I run with joy in the way of *Your NEW commandment.* I want to run in it until that blessed day when, joining the virginal procession, I shall be able to follow You in the heavenly courts, singing Your *NEW canticle* (Rev 14:3) which must be *Love.*

Selected Bibliography

TEXTS

Edition used:
Story of a Soul: The Autobiography of St. Thérèse of Lisieux.
Translated by John Clarke, O.C.D. 2d ed. Washington, D.C.:
Institute of Carmelite Studies, 1976.

Other sources:
St. Thérèse of Lisieux: General Correspondence. Translated by
John Clarke, O.C.D. 2 vols. Washington, D.C.: Institute of
Carmelite Studies, 1982 and 1988.

St. Thérèse of Lisieux: Her Last Conversations. Translated by
John Clarke, O.C.D. Washington, D.C.: Institute of Carmelite
Studies, 1977.

STUDIES

Balthasar, Hans Urs von. *Thérèse of Lisieux: The Story of a Mission.* Translated by Donald Nicholl. London and New York:
Sheed and Ward, 1954.

Combes, André. *The Spirituality of St. Thérèse: An Introduction.*
Translated by Philip E. Hallett. New York: P. J. Kenedy, 1950.

Gaucher, Guy. *The Story of a Life: St. Thérèse of Lisieux.* Translated by Sister Anne Marie Brennan, O.C.D. San Francisco:
Harper & Row, 1987.

Miller, Frederick L. *The Trial of Faith of St. Thérèse of Lisieux.*
New York: Alba House, 1998.

Sullivan, John, O.C.D., ed. *Experiencing St. Thérèse Today.* Carmelite Studies, 5. Washington, D.C.: Institute of Carmelite Studies, 1990.

Ulanov, Barry. *The Making of a Modern Saint: A Biographical Study of St. Thérèse of Lisieux.* Garden City, N.Y.: Doubleday, 1966.

Evelyn Underhill
(1875–1941)

Few spiritual writers were more influential in the twentieth century than the Anglo-Catholic poet, novelist, and scholar of mysticism Evelyn Underhill. Indeed, former Archbishop of Canterbury Michael Ramsey once claimed that it was primarily Underhill who kept the spiritual life alive in the Anglican Church between the two world wars. Her achievements are all the more remarkable inasmuch as she had no formal theological training and was similarly self-taught in other disciplines, such as philosophy and psychology, that comprise the background of her work.

Raised in London by a barrister father and philanthropist mother, Underhill was baptized and confirmed in the Church of England, but by her teens she had become disenchanted with institutional religion. She acquired a liberal arts education at King's College, London; afterward spent some time as a member of an occult society dedicated to Christian mysticism and ritual; and then, around the age of thirty, began regularly attending Catholic Mass and considered joining the church. This did not happen, in part because Pope Pius X's condemnation of the Modernist movement led her to conclude that becoming a Catholic would jeopardize her intellectual freedom.

Underhill turned to the study of mysticism instead, beginning work on her *magnum opus* in 1907 and having it published four years later under the title *Mysticism: A Study of the Nature and*

Development of Man's Spiritual Consciousness. The book was generally well received. In rather quick succession followed *The Mystic Way* (1913), *Practical Mysticism* (1914), *The Life of the Spirit and the Life of Today* (1922), from which the selection in this anthology was taken, and *The Mystics of the Church* (1925). A careful study of these works will reveal a shift in Underhill's own life from being a solitary believer to being a member of a church, for the last-named book clearly emphasizes mystics as integral members of organized religion, whereas *Mysticism* had been criticized by her eventual spiritual director, the Roman Catholic lay man Friedrich von Hügel, for teaching "the supposed non-necessity of institutional, historical religion for many or for some." By the early 1920s Underhill's spiritual journey had led her back to the church of her baptism, and for the rest of her life she made major contributions to the Church of England. Giving retreats and spiritual direction to both clergy and laity became the central focus of her later years, while her frequent lectures and radio broadcasts were generally intended for persons from various religious backgrounds. In 1935 she took a pause from her retreat work to start work on her last major book, *Worship,* which, like *Mysticism,* has remained in print continuously.

Underhill's approach to mysticism reopened a longstanding medieval dispute: Does mystical union consist in a cognitive experience conditioned by the love of God, as Gerson had maintained in the fifteenth century, or is it a "dark" experience of the will and the inner affections, as the more extreme followers of Pseudo-Dionysius claimed? Though Underhill sided with neither position, she took a rather polemical stance against the former in her confrontation with William James's four characteristics of the mystical experience in his *Varieties of Religious Experience.* James had insisted on the cognitive quality of the mystical consciousness, whereas Underhill instead emphasizes the practical (as opposed to the theoretical) character of mystical writings. She holds that it is this character that distinguishes such writings from theological tracts, which do no more than *inspire* what is properly mystical. Similarly, the so-called mystical philosophers (mostly Neoplatonists) are but stepping stones to the practical, mystical life. Plotinus, Dionysius, and Eckhart may have speculated profoundly on the relation between God and the soul, but without an actual *experience* of this relation they would be thinkers rather than mystics. To be sure, Underhill does not conceive of the mystical as irrational, but neither does she want it to coincide with a cognitive experience, however much the spiritual person may have been inspired by theory. She admits that mysticism contains a cognitive element that renders it *specific,* but she places more emphasis on love—a love that consists not so much in feelings of affection as in a movement of the will. In *The Mystics of the Church* she writes: "Mysticism has been defined as 'the science of the love of God' and certainly these words describe its essence. But, looking at it as it appears in the Christian Church in all its degrees and forms, I would prefer to call it 'the life which aims at union with God.' These terms—life, aim, union—suggest its active and purposive character."

The active impulse of love, then, plays as important a part as the passive givenness of the experience. Mysticism consists, indeed, of grace, but this is the dynamic grace of a growth that requires active cooperation. It fulfills the fundamental aspirations of life as a dynamic process. In *Mysticism* Underhill had sought philosophical support for her theory in such vitalist thinkers as Eucken and Bergson. Later she realized the danger of possible misunderstanding inherent in such an association. In her preface to the twelfth edition of *Mysticism* Underhill regrets not having sufficiently stressed the essential "givenness" of the mystical "against all merely revolutionary or emergent theories of spiritual transcendence." For the same reason, she had second thoughts about the support she had sought in the vitalist philosophers.

At no time, however, did Underhill consider mysticism a result obtained by human effort. Nor did she consider all forms of mysticism to be grounded in an identical experience, *subsequently* articulated in different theological languages. The theological tradition that nurtured the mystic was also the very source of the mystic's experience. Her work was essentially Christian from the beginning: the texts on which she drew were mostly Christian; and

431

the model of development she adopted consisted of the conventional stages of awakening or conversion, purification, illumination, and union. As she grew older, however, the Christian character of her work became more pronounced. Increasingly she insisted on situating the spiritual life within the whole of Christian worship: the experience must be integrated with the objective symbols of scripture and liturgy. Not only are the symbols themselves revealed but also the spiritual impulse that drives the mind to accept them and to perceive their mysterious meaning. Thus, she writes in *Worship:* "That awareness of the absolute, that sense of God, which in one form or another is the beginning of all worship, whether it seems to break in from without or to arrive within the soul, does not and cannot originate in man. It comes to him where he is, as a message from another order." Worship, born in the awareness of God's presence, intensifies that religious sense. From the start it contains in it "the seed of contemplation." Particularly in her later years Underhill cautioned against a mysticism of pure experience. Spiritual life consists of an objective pole as well as a subjective pole, and the two must remain attached to each other.

Underhill was more than a writer *about* the mystical life or a psychologist, as she sometimes referred to herself. Her descriptions reveal a thoroughly spiritual person, personally acquainted with what she describes. The reader senses the presence of the same spirit she so perceptively detects in others. For her, spiritual life meant more than an object of psychological or phenomenological observation; it was the life she lived and actively attempted to communicate to others in days of recollection and retreats. This surely justifies her place among the major spiritual writers of the Christian faith. In the words of her biographer, Dana Greene, Underhill's "broadest contribution is in redefining religion and what it means to be a religious person. Although religion may be connected to dogma, doctrine, institution, and moral code, she believed its essential element was the mystical, that is, the personal experience of the love of God that gives authenticity and authority to religion."[1]

---

[1]Dana Greene, *Evelyn Underhill: Artist of the Infinite Life* (New York: Crossroad, 1990), 148.

THE LIFE OF THE SPIRIT
AND THE LIFE OF TO-DAY

CHAPTER SIX
THE LIFE OF THE SPIRIT IN THE INDIVIDUAL

What are we to regard as the heart of spirituality? When we have eliminated the accidental characters with which varying traditions have endowed it, what is it that still so definitely distinguishes its possessor from the best, most moral citizen or devoted altruist? Why do the Christian saint, Indian *rishi*, Buddhist *arhat*, Moslem *sufi*, all seem to us at bottom men of one race, living under differing sanctions one life, witnessing to one fact? This life, which they show in its various perfections, includes, it is true, the ethical life, but cannot be equated with it. Wherein do its differentia consist? We are dealing with the most subtle of realities and have only the help of crude words, developed for other purposes than this. But surely we come near to the truth, as history and experience show it to us, when we say again that the spiritual life in all its manifestations from smallest beginnings to unearthly triumph is simply the life that means God in all His richness, immanent and transcendent: the whole response to the Eternal and Abiding of which any one man is capable, expressed in and through his this-world life. It requires then an objective vision or certitude, something to aim at; and also a total integration of the

From Evelyn Underhill, *The Life of the Spirit and the Life of To-day* (London: Methuen & Co., 1922), 148–60. Reprinted with permission of the publisher.

self, its dedication to that aim. Both terms, vision and response, are essential to it.

This definition may seem at first sight rather dull. It suggests little of that poignant and unearthly beauty, that heroism, that immense attraction, which really belong to the spiritual life. Here indeed we are dealing with poetry in action: and we need not words but music to describe it as it really is. Yet all the forms, all the various beauties and achievements of this life of the Spirit, can be resumed as the reactions of different temperaments to the one abiding and inexhaustibly satisfying Object of their love. It is the answer made by the whole supple, plastic self, rational and instinctive, active and contemplative, to any or all of those objective experiences of religion which we considered in the first chapter; whether of an encompassing and transcendent Reality, of a Divine Companionship or of Immanent Spirit. Such a response we must believe to be itself divinely actuated. Fully made, it is found on the one hand to call forth the most heroic, most beautiful, most tender qualities in human nature; all that we call holiness, the transfiguration of mere ethics by a supernatural loveliness, breathing another air, satisfying another standard, than those of the temporal world. And on the other hand, this response of the self is repaid by a new sensitiveness and receptivity, a new influx of power. To use theological language, will is answered by grace: and as the will's dedication rises towards completeness the more fully does new life flow in. Therefore it is plain that the smallest and humblest beginning of such a life in ourselves—and this inquiry is useless unless it be made to speak to our own condition—will entail not merely an addition to life, but for us too a change in our whole scale of values, a self-dedication. For that which we are here shown as a possible human achievement is not a life of comfortable piety, or the enjoyment of the delicious sensations of the armchair mystic. We are offered, it is true, a new dower of life; access to the full possibilities of human nature. But only upon terms, and these terms include new obligations in respect of that life; compelling us, as it appears, to perpetual hard and difficult choices, a perpetual refusal to sink back into the next-best, to slide along a gentle incline. The spiritual life is not lived upon the heavenly hearth-rug, within safe distance from the Fire of Love. It demands, indeed, very often things so hard that seen from the hearth-rug they seem to us superhuman: immensely generous compassion, forbearance, forgiveness, gentleness, radiant purity, self-forgetting zeal. It means a complete conquest of life's perennial tendency to lag behind the best possible; willing acceptance of hardship and pain. And if we ask how this can be what it is that makes possible such enhancement of human will and of human courage, the only answer seems to be that of the Johannine Christ: that it does consist in a more abundant life....

The greatest and most real of living writers on this subject, Baron von Hügel, has given us another definition of the personal spiritual life which may fruitfully be compared with this. It must and shall, he says, exhibit rightful contact with and renunciation of the Particular and Fleeting; and with this ever seeks and finds the Eternal—deepening and incarnating within its own experience this "transcendent Otherness." Nothing which we are likely to achieve can go beyond this profound saying. We see how many rich elements are contained in it: effort and growth, a temper both social and ascetic, a demand for and a receiving of power....Let us then begin by examining its chief characters one by one.

If we do this, we find that it demands of us:—

(1) Rightful contact with the Particular and Fleeting. That is, a willing acceptance of all this-world tasks, obligations, relations, and joys; in fact, the Active Life of Becoming in its completeness.

(2) But also, a certain renunciation of that Particular and Fleeting. A refusal to get everything out of it that we can for ourselves, to be possessive, or attribute to it absolute worth. This involves a sense of detachment or asceticism; of further destiny and obligation for the soul than complete earthly happiness or here-and-now success.

(3) And with this ever—not merely in hours of devotion—to seek and find the Eternal; penetrating our wholesome this-world action through and through with the very spirit of contemplation.

435

(4) Thus deepening and incarnating—bringing in, giving body to, and in some sense exhibiting by means of our own growing and changing experience—that transcendent Otherness, the fact of the Life of the Spirit in the here-and-now.

The full life of the Spirit, then, is once more declared to be active, contemplative, ascetic and apostolic; though nowadays we express these abiding human dispositions in other and less formidable terms. If we translate them as work, prayer, self-discipline and social service they do not look quite so bad. But even so, what a tremendous programme to put before the ordinary human creature, and how difficult it looks when thus arranged! That balance to be discovered and held between due contact with this present living world of time, and due renunciation of it. That continual penetration of the time-world with the Spirit of Eternity.

But now, in accordance with the ruling idea which has occupied us in this book, let us arrange these four demands in different order. Let us put number three first: "ever seeking and finding the Eternal." Conceive, at least, that we do this really, and in a practical way. Then we discover that, placed as we certainly are in a world of succession, most of the seeking and finding has got to be done there; that the times of pure abstraction in which we touch the non-successive and supersensual must be few. Hence it follows that the first and second demands are at once fully met; for, if we are indeed faithfully seeking and finding the Eternal whilst living—as all sane men and women must do—in closest contact with the Particular and Fleeting, our acceptances and renunciations will be governed by this higher term of experience. And further, the transcendent Otherness, perpetually envisaged by us as alone giving the world of sense its beauty, reality, and value, will be incarnated and expressed by us in this sense-life, and thus ever more completely tasted and known. It will be drawn by us, as best we can, and often at the cost of bitter struggle, into the limitations of humanity; entincturing our attitude and our actions. And in the degree in which we thus appropriate it, it will be given out by us again to other men.

All this, of course, says again that which men have many times been told by those who sought to redeem them from their confusions, and show them the way to fullness of life. "Seek first the Kingdom of God," said Jesus, "and all the rest shall be added to you." "Love," said St. Augustine, "and *do* what you like." "Let nothing," says Thomas à Kempis, "be great or high or acceptable to thee but purely God;" and Kabir, "Open your eyes of love, and see Him who pervades this world! Consider it well, and know that this is your own country." "Our whole teaching," says Boehme, "is nothing else than how man should kindle in himself God's light-world." I do not say that such a presentation of it makes the personal spiritual life any easier: nothing does that. But it does make its central implicit rather clearer, shows us at once its difficulty and its simplicity; since it depends on the consistent subordination of every impulse and every action to one regnant aim and interest—in other words, the unification of the whole self round one centre, the highest conceivable by man. Each of man's behaviour-cycles is always directed towards some end, of which he may or may not be vividly conscious. But in that perfect unification of the self which is characteristic of the life of the Spirit, all his behaviour is brought into one stream of purpose, and directed towards one, transcendent end. And this simplification alone means for him a release from conflicting wishes, and so a tremendous increase of power.

If then we admit this formula, "ever seeking and finding the Eternal"—which is of course another rendering of Ruysbroeck's "aiming at God"—as the prime character of a spiritual life, the secret of human transcendence; what are the agents by which it is done?

Here, men and women of all times and all religions, who have achieved this fullness of life, agree in their answer: and by this answer we are at once taken away from dry philosophic conceptions and introduced into the very heart of human experience. It is done, they say, on man's part by Love and Prayer: and these, properly understood in their inexhaustible richness, joy, pain, dedication and noble simplicity, cover the whole field of the spiritual life. Without them, that life is impossible; with them, if the self be true to their implications, some measure of it cannot be escaped. I said, Love and Prayer properly understood: not as two

moments of emotional piety, but as fundamental human dispositions, as the typical attitude and action which control man's
growth into greater reality. Since then they are of such primary
importance to us, it will be worth while at this stage to look into
them a little more closely.

First, Love: that over-worked and ill-used word, often confused on the one hand with passion and on the other with amiabil-
ity. If we ask the most fashionable sort of psychologist what love
is, he says that it is the impulse urging us towards that end which
is the fulfillment of any series of deeds or "behaviour-cycle;" the
psychic threat, on which all the apparently separate actions making up that cycle are strung and united. In this sense love need not
be fully conscious, reach the level of feeling; but it must be an
imperative, inward urge. And if we ask those who have known
and taught the life of the Spirit, they too say that love is a passionate tendency, an inward vital urge of the soul towards its Source;
which impels every living thing to pursue the most profound trend
of its being, reaches consciousness in the form of self-giving and of
desire, and its only satisfying goal in God. Love is for them much
more than its emotional manifestations. It is "the ultimate cause
of the true activities of all active things"—no less. This definition,
which I take as a matter of fact from St. Thomas Aquinas, would
be agreeable to the most modern psychologist; though he might
give the hidden steersman of the psyche in its perpetual movement
towards novelty a less beautiful and significant name. "This
indwelling Love," says Plotinus, "is no other than the Spirit
which, as we are told, walks with every being, the affection dominant in each several nature. It implants the characteristic desire;
the particular soul, strained towards its own natural objects,
brings forth its own Love, the guiding spirit realizing its worth
and the quality of its being."

Does not all this suggest to us once more, that at whatever
level it be experienced, the psychic craving, the urgent spirit within
us pressing out to life, is always *one;* and that the sublimation of this
vital craving, its direction to God, is the essence of regeneration?
There, in our instinctive nature—which, as we know, makes us the

438

kind of animal we are—abides that power of loving which is, really, the power of living; the cause of our actions, the controlling factor in our perceptions, the force pressing us into any given type of experience, turning aside for no obstacles but stimulated by them to a greater vigour. Each level of the universe makes solicitations to this power: the worlds of sense, of thought, of beauty, and of action. According to the degree of our development, the trend of the conscious will, is our response; and according to that response will be our life. "The world to which a man turns himself," says Boehme, "and in which he produces fruit, the same is lord in him, and this world becomes manifest in him."

From all this it becomes clear what the love of God is; and what Augustine meant when he said that all virtue—and virtue after all means power, not goodness—lay in the right ordering of love, the conscious orientation of desire. Christians, on the authority of their Master, declare that such love of God requires all that they have, not only of feeling, but also of intellect and of power; since He is to be loved with heart and mind and strength. Thought and action on highest levels are involved in it, for it means, not religious emotionalism, but the unflickering orientation of the whole self towards Him, ever seeking and finding the Eternal; the linking up of all behaviour on that string, so that the apparently hard and always heroic choices which are demanded, are made at last because they are inevitable. It is true that this dominant interest will give to our lives a special emotional colour and a special kind of happiness; but in this, as in the best, deepest, richest human love, such feeling-tone and such happiness— though in some natures of great beauty and intensity—are only to be looked upon as secondary characters, and never to be aimed at.

When St. Teresa said that the real object of the spiritual marriage was "the incessant production of work, work," I have no doubt that many of her nuns were disconcerted; especially the type of ease-loving conservatives whom she and her intimates were accustomed to refer to as the pussy-cats. But in this direct application to religious experience of St. Thomas' doctrine of love, she set up an ideal of the spiritual life which is as valid at the present day in the entanglements of our social order, as it was in the enclosed convents of sixteenth-century Spain. Love, we said, is the cause of action. It urges and directs our behaviour, conscious and involuntary, towards an end. The mother is irresistibly impelled to act towards her child's welfare, the ambitious man towards success, the artist towards expression of his vision. All these are examples of behaviour, love-driven towards ends. And religious experience discloses to us a greater, more inclusive end, and this vital power of love as capable of being used on the highest levels, regenerated, directed to eternal interests; subordinating behaviour, inspiring suffering, unifying the whole self and its activities, mobilizing them for this transcendental achievement. This generous love, to go back to the quotation from Baron von Hügel which opened our inquiry, will indeed cause the behaviour it controls to exhibit both rightful contact with and renunciation of the particular and fleeting; because in and through this series of linked deeds it is uniting with itself all human activities, and in and through them is seeking and finding its eternal end. So, in that rightful bringing-in of novelty which is the business of the fully living soul, the most powerful agent is love, understood as the controlling factor of behaviour, the sublimation and union of will and desire. "Let love," says Boehme, "be the life of thy nature. It killeth thee not, but quickeneth thee according to its life, and then thou livest, yet not to thy own will but to its will: for thy will becometh its will, and then thou art dead to thyself but alive to God." There is the true, solid and for us most fruitful doctrine of divine union, unconnected with any rapture, trance, ecstasy or abnormal state of mind: a union organic, conscious, and dynamic with the Creative Spirit of Life.

If we now go on to ask how, specially, we shall achieve this union in such degree as is possible to each one of us; the answer must be, that it will be done by Prayer. If the seeking of the Eternal is actuated by love, the finding of it is achieved through prayer. Prayer, in fact—understood as a life or state, not an act or an asking—is the beginning, middle and end of all that we are now considering. As the social self can only be developed by contact with society, so the spiritual self can only be developed by contact with the spiritual world. And such humble yet ardent contact with the spiritual world—opening up to its suggestions our impulses, our reveries, our feelings, our most secret dispositions as well as our mere thoughts—is the essence of prayer, understood in its widest sense. No more than surrender or love can such prayer be reduced to "one act." Those who seek to sublimate it into "pure" contemplation are as limited at one end of the scale, as those who reduce it to articulate petition are at the other. It contains in itself a rich variety of human reactions and experiences. It opens the door upon an unwalled world, in which the self truly lives and therefore makes widely various responses to its infinitely varying stimuli. Into that world the self takes, or should take, its special needs, aptitudes and longings, and matches them against its apprehension of Eternal Truth. In this meeting of the human heart with all that it can apprehend of Reality, not adoration alone but unbounded contrition, not humble dependence alone but joy, peace and power, not rapture alone but mysterious darkness, must be woven into the fabric of love. In this world the soul may sometimes wander as if in pastures, sometimes is poised breathless and intent. Sometimes it is fed by beauty, sometimes by most difficult truth, and experiences the extremes of riches and destitution, darkness and light. "It is not," says Plotinus, "by crushing the Divine into a unity but by displaying its exuberance, as the Supreme Himself has displayed it, that we show knowledge of the might of God."

Thus, by that instinctive and warmly devoted direction of its behaviour which is love, and that willed attention to and communion with the spiritual world which is prayer, all the powers of the self are united and turned towards the seeking and finding of the Eternal. It is by complete obedience to this exacting love, doing difficult and unselfish things, giving up easy and comfortable things— in fact by living, living hard on the highest levels—that men more and more deeply feel, experience, and enter into their spiritual life. This is a fact which must seem rather awkward to those who put forward pathological explanations of it. And on the other hand it is only by constant contacts with and recourse to the energizing life of

Spirit, that this hard vocation can be fulfilled. Such a power of reference to reality, of transcending the world of succession and its values, can be cultivated by us; and this education of our inborn aptitude is a chief function of the discipline of prayer. True, it is only in times of recollection or of great emotion that this profound contact is fully present to consciousness. Yet, once fully achieved and its obligations accepted by us, it continues as a grave melody within our busy outward acts: and we must by right direction of our deepest instincts so find and feel the Eternal all the time, if indeed we are to actualize and incarnate it all the time. From this truth of experience, religion has deduced the doctrine of grace, and the general conception of man as able to do nothing of himself. This need hardly surprise us. For equally on the physical plane man can do nothing of himself, if he be cut off from his physical sources of power; from food to eat, and air to breathe. Therefore the fact that his spiritual life too is dependent upon the life-giving atmosphere that penetrates him, and the heavenly food which he receives, makes no fracture in his experience. Thus we are brought back by another path to the fundamental need for him, in some form, of the balanced active and contemplative life.

In spite of this, many people seem to take it for granted that if a man believes in and desires to live a spiritual life, he can live it in utter independence of spiritual food. He believes in God, loves his neighbour, wants to do good, and just goes ahead. The result of this is that the life of the God-fearing citizen or the Social Christian, as now conceived and practised, is generally the starved life. It leaves no time for silence, the withdrawal, the quiet attention to the spiritual, which is essential if it is to develop all its powers. Yet the literature of the Spirit is full of warnings on this subject. *Taste* and see that the Lord sweet. They that wait upon the Lord shall renew their *strength*. In quietness and confidence shall be your *strength*. These are practical statements; addressed, not to specialists but to ordinary men and women, with a normal psycho-physical make-up. They are literally true now, or can be if we choose. They do not involve any peculiar training, or unnatural effort. A sliding scale goes from the simplest prayer-experience of the ordinary man to that complete self-loss and complete self-finding, which is called the transforming union of the saint; and somewhere in this series, every human soul can find a place.

If this balanced life is to be ours, if we are to receive what St. Augustine called the food of the full-grown, to find and feel the Eternal, we must give time and place to it in our lives. I emphasize this, because its realization seems to me to be a desperate modern need; a need exhibited supremely in our languid and ineffectual spirituality, but also felt in the too busy, too entirely active and hurried lives of the artist, the reformer and the teacher. St. John of the Cross says in one of his letters: "What is wanting is not writing or talking—there is more than enough of that—but, silence and action. For silence joined to action produces recollection, and gives the spirit a marvelous strength." Such recollection, such a gathering up of our interior forces and retreat of consciousness to its "ground," is the preparation of all great endeavour, whatever its apparent object may be. Until we realize that it is better, more useful, more productive of strength, to spend, let us say, that odd ten minutes in the morning in feeling and finding the Eternal than in flicking the newspaper—that this will send us off to the day's work properly orientated, gathered together, recollected, and really endowed with new power of dealing with circumstance—we have not begun to live the life of the Spirit, or grasped the practical connection between such a daily discipline and the power of doing our best work, whatever it may be.

Selected Bibliography

TEXTS

Edition used:
The Life of the Spirit and the Life of To-Day. London: Methuen & Co., 1922.

Other sources:
Mysticism: The Study of the Nature and Development of Man's Spiritual Consciousness. 12th ed. Oxford: One World, 1993.

Fragments from an Inner Life. Edited by Dana Greene. Harrisburg, Pa.: Morehouse, 1993.

STUDIES

Callahan, Annice. *Evelyn Underhill: Spirituality for Daily Living.* Lanham, Md.: University Press of America, 1997.

Cropper, Margaret. *Life of Evelyn Underhill.* New York: Harper, 1958.

Greene, Dana. *Evelyn Underhill: Artist of the Infinite Life.* New York: Crossroad, 1990.

Jantzen, Grace. "The Legacy of Evelyn Underhill." *Feminist Theology* 4 (Sept. 1993): 79–100.

Tastard, Terry. "Divine Presence and Human Freedom: The Spirituality of Evelyn Underhill Reconsidered." *Theology* 94 (1991): 426–32.

Thomas Merton
(1915–68)

"On the last day of January 1915, under the sign of the Water Bearer, in a year of a great war, and down in the shadow of some French mountains on the borders of Spain, I came into the world." Thus begins *The Seven Storey Mountain,* the autobiographical work that set Thomas Merton on the way to becoming the most widely read monk in the history of Christianity. Published only four years after Merton's first monastic profession, this book recounts his journey to religious and Christian conversion over the first three decades of his life. The continual rearrangement of his early life as he traveled about with his artist father after his mother's early death; the unhappiness of his years at a boarding school in France and the frank secularity of his life as a student at Cambridge University; the wholesome effect of his transfer to Columbia University and the lifelong friendships he formed there with professors and students alike; the profound influence of works by Christian authors, both ancient and modern; the impact of the simple, unaffected piety of worshipers at Corpus Christi Church in Manhattan; his reception into the Roman Catholic Church on November 16, 1938; and the retreat he made at the Trappist Abbey of Gethsemani during Holy Week of 1941—these were among the most important episodes and turning points in Merton's life up to the time of his acceptance into that monastic community eight months after his first visit.

In the monastery, and quite to Merton's surprise, the abbot encouraged him to cultivate his gift for writing. As a result, over the years he published numerous books and articles, including collections of his poetry, reflections on contemplative prayer and the mysteries of the Christian faith, studies of Christian mystics and Zen masters, essays of protest against social injustices, and entries from the journals that he kept with meticulous care throughout his life. Important responsibilities within the monastery were also entrusted to him: in 1951 he was placed in charge of the young monks studying for priestly ordination, and four years later he was given the still more responsible position of master of choir novices, an office he held for ten years until, in 1965, he became the first American Trappist monk ever to obtain permission to live as a hermit. It was while living in his hermitage on the monastic property in the late 1960s that he received and was allowed to accept an invitation to address a meeting of Catholic religious in Bangkok, and it was while attending that conference that he suffered accidental death by electrocution on December 10, 1968, twenty-seven years to the day after his entrance into the monastery.

Those who knew Merton best often remarked on his multifaceted personality and the coruscating, dialectical nature of his intellect, which eluded facile pigeonholing. In his later years he even sharply distanced himself from the world-renouncing, rather narrow-minded young man who, in his early thirties, had published the account of his conversion to Catholicism and his eventual embracing of monastic life. But however much Merton may have changed during the years he lived as a monk, there were also some definite constants in his monastic life. One of these was his commitment to a contemplative way of life, as is evident in the titles of some of his best-known books and essays: *Seeds of Contemplation; New Seeds of Contemplation;* "Contemplation in a World of Action."

Our first selection presents some of Merton's mature reflections on the subject of contemplation. As is evident in this passage, Merton was instinctively drawn to the tradition of apophatic mysticism. Like Gregory of Nyssa, he singles out the sixth Beatitude—

"Blessed are the pure of heart, for they shall see God"—as pointing the way to a vision of God in "clear darkness," apart from all the concepts and images with which we usually try to apprehend God. And like Eckhart, he insists that God will grant this gift only if we properly dispose ourselves to receive it "by resting in the heart of our own poverty, keeping our soul as far as possible empty of desires for all the things that please or preoccupy our nature, no matter how pure or sublime they may be in themselves."

The somewhat general description of contemplation found in that opening selection is counterbalanced by the following piece, the very personal reflections on his own prayer life that Merton included in a letter written in 1966 to the Pakistani sufi scholar Abdul Aziz. That Merton, who in his earliest writings had said some very harsh things about non-Christian ways of prayer and meditation, should have written in so open and trusting a manner to a Muslim is an indication of how much he now differed from the bigoted young man who had entered the monastery twenty-five years earlier. At that time, as he once wrote with vivid imagery, he had "spurned New York, spat on Chicago, and tromped on Louisville, heading for the woods with Thoreau in one pocket, John of the Cross in another, and holding the Bible open to the Apocalypse." His conversion from a rather extreme attitude of *fuga mundi* was quite complete by the late 1950s, for by then he had actually come to rejoice in his connectedness with people living outside the cloister.

Merton's rejection of a "spurious self-isolation in a special world" did not, however, mean a rejection of the monastic life. Instead, he now embarked upon a period marked by intense engagement with the world from within the monastery and eventually from within his hermitage. It was, indeed, in the hermitage that he co-authored our final selection, a message sent to the synod of bishops meeting in Rome in October 1967. Collaborating with two European monks, Dom J.-B. Porion and Dom André Louf, Merton wrote "Contemplatives and the Crisis of Faith." One finds here not only the apophatic emphases already prominent in some of his earliest work (Christian mysticism as "an obscure knowledge of the invisible God") but also a forthright assertion of the experience of God as "a personal, loving encounter" with the self-revealing Trinity, allowing us to become "sharers in the dialogue of the Father and the Son in the Holy Spirit."

In a talk once given to the novices under his care, Merton said that if it had been up to him he would have chosen to be born in the fourteenth century, the era of Eckhart, Tauler, Julian, and Ruusbroec. None of these medieval mystics are named in our Merton selections, but one senses their influence on almost every page: hints of the dark abyss of the Godhead, of the Trinity of Persons shining out of that darkness in inexhaustible light, and of a desire not merely to return to the divine Source of life but to bring others along with oneself through that exercise of loving concern that Ruusbroec called "the common life." Commentators have regularly noted that Merton did not so much inaugurate new ways as revivify ways already present in his chosen tradition. For having done this in so genial and engaging a way, Merton may fittingly conclude this anthology of two millennia of Christian mysticism.

NEW SEEDS OF CONTEMPLATION

CHAPTER THIRTY-ONE

The Gift of Understanding

Contemplation, by which we know and love God as He is in Himself, apprehending Him in a deep and vital experience which is beyond the reach of any natural understanding, is the reason for our creation by God. And although it is absolutely above our nature, St. Thomas teaches that it is our proper element because it is the fulfillment of deep capacities in us that God has willed should never be fulfilled in any other way. All those who reach the end for which they were created will therefore be contemplatives in heaven: but many are also destined to enter this supernatural element and breathe this new atmosphere while they are still on earth.

Since contemplation has been planned for us by God as our true and proper element, the first taste of it strikes us at once as utterly new and yet strangely familiar.

Although you had an entirely different notion of what it would be like (since no book can give an adequate idea of contemplation except to those who have experienced it), it turns out to be just what you seem to have known all along that it ought to be.

The utter simplicity and obviousness of the infused light which contemplation pours into our soul suddenly awakens us to a new level of awareness. We enter a region which we had never even suspected, and yet it is this new world which seems familiar and obvious. The old world of our senses is now the one that seems to us strange, remote and unbelievable—until the intense light of contemplation leaves us and we fall back to our own level.

Compared with the pure and peaceful comprehension of love in which the contemplative is permitted to see the truth not so much by seeing it as being absorbed into it, ordinary ways of seeing and knowing are full of blindness and labor and uncertainty.

The sharpest of natural experiences is like sleep, compared with the awakening which is contemplation. The keenest and surest natural certitude is a dream compared to this serene comprehension.

Our souls rise up from our earth like Jacob waking from his dream and exclaiming: "Truly God is in this place and I knew it not"! God Himself becomes the only reality, in Whom all other reality takes its proper place—and falls into insignificance.

Although this light is absolutely above our nature, it now seems to us "normal" and "natural" to see, as we now see, without seeing, to possess clarity in darkness, to have pure certitude without any shred of discursive evidence, to be filled with an experience that transcends experience and to enter with serene confidence into depths that leave us utterly inarticulate.

"O the depth of the riches of the wisdom and knowledge of God!"

A door opens in the center of our being and we seem to fall through it into immense depths which, although they are infinite, are all accessible to us; all eternity seems to have become ours in this one placid and breathless contact.

God touches us with a touch that is emptiness and empties us. He moves us with a simplicity that simplifies us. All variety, all complexity, all paradox, all multiplicity cease. Our mind swims in the air of an understanding, a reality that is dark and serene and includes in itself everything. Nothing more is desired. Nothing more is wanting. Our only sorrow, if sorrow be possible at all, is the awareness that we ourselves still live outside of God.

For already a supernatural instinct teaches us that the function of this abyss of freedom that has opened out within our own midst, is to draw us utterly out of our own selfhood and into its own immensity of liberty and joy.

You seem to be the same person and you are the same person that you have always been: in fact you are more yourself than you have ever been before. You have only just begun to exist. You feel as if you were at last fully born. All that went before was a mistake, a fumbling preparation for birth. Now you have come out into your element. And yet now you have become nothing. You have sunk to the center of your own poverty, and there you have felt the doors fly open into infinite freedom, into a wealth which is perfect because none of it is yours and yet it all belongs to you.

And now you are free to go in and out of infinity.

It is useless to think of fathoming the depths of wide-open darkness that have yawned inside you, full of liberty and exultation.

They are not a place, not an extent, they are a huge, smooth activity. These depths, they are Love. And in the midst of you they form a wide, impregnable country.

There is nothing that can penetrate into the heart of that peace. Nothing from the outside can get in. There is even a whole sphere of your own activity that is excluded from that beautiful airy night. The five senses, the imagination, the discoursing mind, the hunger of desire do not belong in that starless sky.

And you, while you are free to come and go, yet as soon as you attempt to make words or thoughts about it you are excluded—you go back into your exterior in order to talk.

Yet you find that you can rest in this darkness and this unfathomable peace without trouble and without anxiety, even when the imagination and the mind remain in some way active outside the doors of it.

They may stand and chatter in the porch, as long as they are idle, waiting for the will their queen to return, upon whose orders they depend.

But it is better for them to be silent. However, you now know that this does not depend on you. It is a gift that comes to you from the bosom of that serene darkness and depends entirely on the decision of Love.

Within the simplicity of this armed and walled and undivided interior peace is an infinite unction which, as soon as it is grasped, loses its savor. You must not try to reach out and possess it altogether. You must not touch it, or try to seize it. You must not try to make it sweeter or try to keep it from wasting away....

The situation of the soul in contemplation is something like the situation of Adam and Eve in Paradise. Everything is yours, but on one infinitely important condition: that it is all *given*.

There is nothing that you can claim, nothing that you can demand, nothing that you can *take*. And as soon as you try to take something as if it were your own—you lose your Eden. The angel with the flaming sword stands armed against all selfhood that is small and particular, against the "I" that can say "I want..." "I need..." "I demand...." No individual enters Paradise, only the integrity of the *Person*.

Only the greatest humility can give us the instinctive delicacy and caution that will prevent us from reaching out for pleasures and satisfactions that we can understand and savor in this darkness. The moment we demand anything for ourselves or even trust in any action of our own to procure a deeper intensification of this pure and serene rest in God, we defile and dissipate the perfect gift that He desires to communicate to us in the silence and repose of our own powers.

If there is one thing we must do it is this: we must realize to the very depths of our being that this is a pure gift of God which no desire, no effort and no heroism of ours can do anything to deserve or obtain. There is nothing we can do directly either to procure it or to preserve it or to increase it. Our own activity is for the most part an obstacle to the infusion of this peaceful and pacifying light, with the exception that God may demand certain acts and works of us by charity or obedience, and maintain us in deep experimental union with Him through them all, by His own good pleasure, not by any fidelity of ours.

At best we can dispose ourselves for the reception of this great gift by resting in the heart of our own poverty, keeping our soul as far as possible empty of desires for all the things that please and preoccupy our nature, no matter how pure or sublime they may be in themselves.

And when God reveals Himself to us in contemplation we must accept Him as He comes to us, in His own obscurity, in His own silence, not interrupting Him with arguments or words, conceptions or activities that belong to the level of our own tedious and labored existence.

We must respond to God's gifts gladly and freely with thanksgiving, happiness and joy: but in contemplation we thank Him less by words than by the serene happiness of silent acceptance. "Be empty and see that I am God." It is our emptiness in the presence of the abyss of His reality, our silence in the presence of His infinitely rich silence, our joy in the bosom of the serene darkness in which His light holds us absorbed, it is all this that praises Him. It is this that causes love of God and wonder and adoration to swim up into us like tidal waves out of the depths of that peace, and break upon the shores of our consciousness in a vast, hushed surf of inarticulate praise, praise and glory!

This clear darkness of God is the purity of heart Christ spoke of in the sixth Beatitude, *Beati mundo corde, quoniam ipsi Deum videbunt.* And this purity of heart brings at least a momentary deliverance from images and concepts, from the forms and shadows of all the things men desire with their human appetites. It brings deliverance even from the feeble and delusive analogies we ordinarily use to arrive at God—not that it denies them, for they are true as far as they go, but it makes them temporarily useless by fulfilling them all in the sure grasp of a deep and penetrating experience.

In the vivid darkness of God within us there sometimes come deep movements of love that deliver us entirely, for a moment, from our old burden of selfishness, and number us among those little children of whom is the Kingdom of Heaven.

And when God allows us to fall back into our own confusion of desires and judgments and temptations, we carry a scar over the place where that joy exulted for a moment in our hearts.

The scar burns us. The sore wound aches within us, and we remember that we have fallen back into what we are not, and are not yet allowed to remain where God would have us belong. We long for the place He has destined for us and weep with desire for the time when this pure poverty will catch us and hold us in its liberty and never let us go, when we will never fall back from the Paradise of the simple and the little children into the forum of prudence where the wise of this world go up and down in sorrow and set their traps for a happiness that cannot exist.

This is the gift of understanding: we pass out of ourselves into the joy of emptiness, of nothingness, in which there are no longer any particular objects of knowledge but only God's truth without limit, without defect, without stain. This clean light, which tastes of Paradise, is beyond all pride, beyond comment, beyond proprietorship, beyond solitude. It is in all, and for all. It is the true light that shines in everyone, in "every man coming into this world." It is the light of Christ, "Who stands in the midst of us and we know Him not."

FROM A LETTER TO ABDUL AZIZ

...Now you ask about my method of meditation. Strictly speaking I have a very simple way of prayer. It is centered entirely on attention to the presence of God and to His will and His love. That is to say that it is centered on *faith* by which alone we can know the presence of God. One might say this gives my meditation the character described by the Prophet as "being before God as if you saw Him." Yet it does not mean imagining anything or conceiving a precise image of God, for to my mind this would be a kind of idolatry. On the contrary, it is a matter of adoring Him as invisible and infinitely beyond our comprehension, and realizing Him as all. My prayer tends very much to what you call *fana*. There is in my heart this great thirst to recognize totally the nothingness of all that is not God. My prayer is then a kind of praise rising up out of the center of Nothing and Silence. If I am still present "myself" this I recognize as an obstacle. If He wills He can then make the Nothingness into a total clarity. If He does not will, then the Nothingness actually seems to itself to be an object and remains an obstacle. Such is my ordinary way of prayer, or meditation. It is not "thinking about" anything, but a direct seeking of the Face of the Invisible. Which cannot be found unless we become lost in Him who is Invisible.

I do not ordinarily write about such things and ask you therefore to be discreet about it. But I write this as a testimony of

From *The Hidden Ground of Love: The Letters of Thomas Merton on Religious Experience and Social Concerns,* sel. and ed. William H. Shannon (New York: Farrar Straus Giroux, 1985), 63–64. Reprinted with permission of the publisher. Copyright 1985 by the Merton Legacy Trust.

confidence and friendship. It will show you how much I appreciate the tradition of Sufism. Let us therefore adore and praise God and pray to Him for the world which is in great trouble and confusion. I am united with you in prayer during this month of Ramadan and will remember you on the Night of Destiny. I appreciate your prayers for me. May the Most High God send His blessing upon you and give you peace.

CONTEMPLATIVES
AND THE CRISIS OF FAITH

While the Synod of Bishops is meeting in Rome, we, a group of contemplative monks, feel ourselves closely united with our bishops in their pastoral cares. We are thinking especially of the difficulties which many Christians are experiencing at the present time concerning their faith—difficulties which even go so far as to lead them to call into question the possibility of attaining to knowledge of the transcendent God who has revealed himself to men.

In this situation, it seems to us that our way of life puts us in a position where we can address a few simple words to all. Since we do not want to make our silence and solitude an excuse for failing to render what may be a service to our brothers, especially to those who are struggling to keep or to find faith in Jesus Christ, we are addressing ourselves in a spirit of sonship to you who are the witnesses to that faith, and the guides and masters of souls, so that you can judge in what measure our message might be useful to the people of God in the world of today.

Our personal qualifications for offering such a testimony are poor indeed. But it is more in the name of the way of life that we lead, rather than in our own names, that we dare to speak.

On the one hand, the cloistered contemplative life is simply the Christian life, but the Christian life lived in conditions which favor the "experience" of God. It could be described as a sort of specialization in relationship with God which puts us in a position to offer a testimony to this aspect of things.

On the other hand, while the contemplative withdraws from the world, this does not mean that he deserts either it or his fellow-men. He remains wholly rooted in the earth on which he is born, whose riches he has inherited, whose cares and aspirations he has tried to make his own. He withdraws from it in order to place himself more intensely at the divine source from which the forces that drive the world onwards originate, and to understand in this light the great designs of mankind. For it is in the desert that the soul most often receives its deepest inspirations. It was in the desert that God fashioned his people. It was in the desert he brought his people back after their sin, in order to "allure her, and speak to her tenderly" (Hos 2.14). It was in the desert, too, that the Lord Jesus, after he had overcome the devil, displayed all his power and foreshadowed the victory of his Passover.

And in every generation, surely, the people of God has to pass through a similar experience in order to renew itself and to be "born again." The contemplative, whose vocation leads him to withdraw into this spiritual desert, feels that he is living at the very heart of the Church. His experience does not seem to him to be esoteric, but, on the contrary, typical of all Christian experience. He can recognize his own situation in the trials and temptations which many of his fellow-Christians are undergoing. He can understand their sufferings and discern the meaning of them. He knows all the bitterness and anguish of the dark night of the soul: *My God, my God, why have you forsaken me?* (Ps 21.1; cf. Matt 27.46). But he knows, too, from the story of Christ, that God is the conqueror of sin and death.

The world of today is sorely tempted to fall into atheism—into the denial of this God who cannot be grasped on its own level, and is not accessible to its instruments and calculations. Some Christians, even, moved by the desire to share the condition of their fellow-men in the fullest possible way, are yielding to this outlook when they proclaim the need for a certain measure of unbelief as a necessary basis for any fully human sincerity.

According to some of them, it is just not possible to reach a God who is, by definition, transcendent—"wholly other." To be a Christian, it is enough, they say, to devote oneself generously to the service of mankind.

We are not insensitive to everything that is attractive in such a standpoint, although it leads to absurd results. The contemplative Christian, too, is aware of that fundamental datum, so firmly anchored in mystical tradition, that God who has revealed himself to us in his word, has revealed himself as "unknown," inasmuch as he is inaccessible to our concepts in this life (Exod 33.20). He lies infinitely beyond our grasp, for he is beyond all being. Familiar with a God who is "absent," and, as it were, "non-existent" as far as the natural world is concerned, the contemplative is, perhaps, better placed than most to understand the attitude of those who are no longer satisfied by a mystery whose presentation is reduced to the level of *things*. But he knows very well, nevertheless, that God does allow the attentive and purified soul to reach him beyond the realm of words and ideas.

In the same way, the contemplative can more readily understand how the temptation to atheism which is confronting many Christians at the present time can affect their faith in a way which may, in the long run, be salutary. For this is a trial which bears a certain analogy with the "nights" of the mystics. The desert strips us, too, of our imperfect images of God. It reduces us to what is essential and forces us to see the truth about ourselves. Grace, that extraordinary power from God, works at the very heart of our dullness and inertia, for "his power is made perfect in weakness" (2 Cor 12.9).

It is precisely here that the sympathy and understanding of the contemplative make him want to offer a word of comfort and hope. For his experience is not a negative thing, even though it leads him along the paths of the desert with which the temptation to atheism may well have something in common. The absence of the transcendent God is also, paradoxically, his immanent presence, though it may well be that recollection, silence and a certain measure of withdrawal from the agitation of life are necessary for perceiving this. But all Christians are called to taste God, and we want to proclaim this fact in order to put them on their guard against a certain lassitude and pessimism which might tend to create for them conditions which, from this point of view, are less favorable than our own.

Our Lord was tempted in the desert; but he overcame the tempter. Our faith constantly needs to be purified and disentangled from the false images and ideas which we tend to mix with it. But the night of faith emerges into the unshakable assurance placed in our hearts by God whose will it has been to test us.

The cloistered life in itself bears witness to the reality of this victory. It still attracts hundreds of men and women in our own day. But what meaning would it have if grace did not provide the remedy for our blindness, and if it were not true that the Father, "after having spoken many times and in many ways to our fathers through the prophets, has spoken to us in these latter days through the Son"? (Heb 1.1–2). For "if it is only for this life that we have set our hope in Christ, then we are of all men the most to be pitied" (1 Cor 15.19).

The truth is that this experience is indescribable. But, fundamentally, it is that which Paul, John and the other Apostles proclaimed as being the experience of every Christian; and it is by using the same expressions as they used that we can best speak about it. We are dealing here with a gift of the Spirit which is, as it were, a guarantee of our inheritance (Eph 1.14). We are dealing here with a gift of that Spirit through whom love has been poured into our hearts (Rom 5.5), the Spirit who knows what is of God, because he searches everything, even the depths of God (1 Cor 2.10), the Spirit whose anointing teaches us all things, so that we have no need for anyone else to teach us (1 John 2.27), the Spirit who unceasingly bears witness to our spirit that we are truly sons of God (Rom 8.16).

It is in this same Spirit that we have come to understand how true it is that Christ died for our sins and rose again for our justification (Rom 4.25), and that in him we have access through faith to the Father and are restored to our dignity as sons of God (cf. Rom 5.2; Heb 10.19).

The mystical knowledge of the Christian is not only an obscure knowledge of the invisible God. It is also an experience of God—a personal, loving encounter with the one who has revealed himself to us and saved us, in order to make us sharers in the dialogue of the Father and the Son in the Holy Spirit. For it is surely in the Trinity of Persons that God appears to us most clearly as the "wholly other," and, at the same time, as closer to us than any being.

This, then, is the good fortune which we have felt it our duty to declare to our Shepherds upon whom the trials of faith bear most heavily at the present time. We ask them for their blessing, and we remain constantly united with them in prayer. In communion with the whole Church, we unite ourselves to the sufferings of the world, carrying on before God a silent dialogue even with those of our brothers who keep themselves apart from us.

Our message can only end on a note of thanksgiving. For that is the feeling which will always predominate in the hearts of those who have experienced the loving-kindness of God. The Christian, that pardoned sinner whom God's mercy has qualified beyond all expectation to share in the inheritance of the saints in light (Col 1.12), can only stand before God endlessly proclaiming a hymn of thanksgiving: "He is good, for his love is eternal" (Ps 135).

It is our wish to offer our own testimony to this sense of wonder and thankfulness, while inviting our brothers everywhere to share them with us in hope, and in this way to develop the precious seeds of contemplation implanted in their hearts.

Selected Bibliography

TEXTS

Editions used:

The Hidden Ground of Love: The Letters of Thomas Merton on Religious Experience and Social Concerns. Edited by William H. Shannon. New York: Farrar Straus Giroux, 1985.

Conjectures of a Guilty Bystander. Garden City, N.Y.: Doubleday, Image Books, 1968.

The Monastic Journey. Edited by Brother Patrick Hart. Garden City, N.Y.: Doubleday, Image Books, 1978.

Other sources:

The Seven Storey Mountain. New York: Harcourt Brace and Co., 1948. Often reprinted.

A Thomas Merton Reader. Rev. ed. Edited by Thomas P. McDonnell. Garden City, N.Y.: Doubleday, Image Books, 1974.

Thomas Merton: Spiritual Master. The Essential Writings. Edited by Lawrence S. Cunningham. New York: Paulist Press, 1992.

STUDIES

Carr, Anne. *A Search for Wisdom and Spirit: Thomas Merton's Theology of the Self.* Notre Dame, Ind.: University of Notre Dame Press, 1988.

Hart, Patrick, ed. *Thomas Merton, Monk: A Monastic Tribute.* New York: Sheed and Ward, 1974.

Mott, Michael. *The Seven Mountains of Thomas Merton.* Boston: Houghton Mifflin, 1984.

Shannon, William H. *The Silent Lamp: The Thomas Merton Story.* New York: Crossroad, 1992.

Teahan, John F. "A Dark and Empty Way: Thomas Merton and the Apophatic Tradition." *Journal of Religion* 58 (1978): 263–87.